T0113479

CRIME, LAW, AND SOCIETY

Crime, Law,

READINGS
Selected by Abraham S. Goldstein

and Society

and Joseph Goldstein

 THE FREE PRESS
A Division of Macmillan Publishing Co., Inc.
New York

Collier Macmillan Publishers
London

Copyright © 1971 by The Free Press
A DIVISION OF MACMILLAN PUBLISHING CO., INC.
Printed in the United States of America
All rights reserved. No part of this book may be
reproduced or transmitted in any form or by any means,
electronic or mechanical, including photocopying, recording,
or by any information storage and retrieval system,
without permission in writing from the Publisher.

The Free Press
A Division of Macmillan Publishing Co., Inc.
866 Third Avenue, New York, New York 10022

Collier Macmillan Canada Ltd.

Library of Congress Catalog Card Number: 77–136009

printing number
      3   4   5   6   7   8   9   10

ISBN 978-0-02-912260-0

For Sonja and Ruth

Preface

Not long ago we were discussing reading lists that we had prepared for our separate courses in criminal law and regretting the extent to which law students have come to rely entirely on casebooks, and the bits and pieces of articles and books contained therein. We concluded that a reader made up of selections of article and chapter length would be a useful addition to the literature and agreed to put one together, but only if it did not become a chore. From the beginning it has been good and instructive fun. We found several new pieces and discovered that some of our early favorites did not survive the many readings we gave to the articles considered for inclusion.

The pleasure of collaboration was enhanced by the thought that we might further confound the confusion that has sometimes led readers in criminal law to attribute the work of each of us to the other. Because we have for so long shared under a common surname membership on the Yale Law faculty, a field of scholarly interest, a clerkship with Judge Bazelon and a Yale legal education, each of us has on occasion enjoyed credit, and blame, for a bibliography that has not been entirely his own. We are pleased then to assume responsibility for this reader in which we have an equal share.

This is a volume which could not have been produced but for the cooperation of the authors and publishers who have granted us permission to reprint their work. We appreciate greatly their willingness to participate in this venture. We wish also to acknowledge with thanks the able and generous research assistance of Jose de Lasa and the cheerful and competent secretarial assistance of Mrs. Helen Minor and Mrs. Gertrude Facciuto.

Contents

Part Three:
PURPOSE AND PROCESS   *269*

ILLUSTRATIONS

I would like to express my thanks to Judge Lyle Quick and to Presiding Judge John R. King of the Town of Poughkeepsie Justice Court, and to the Police Department of the City of Poughkeepsie, whose invaluable cooperation helped make the illustrations in this book both accurate and (hopefully) interesting.

With gratitude
Jacqueline Kahane

An Introductory Note

Since the turn of the century, criminal law scholars have become increasingly concerned with questions of purpose, function, and process. Influenced principally by the legal realists, they have moved beyond a narrowly conceived preoccupation with criminal liability—beyond law as a set of logical relations among received propositions—to a broad emphasis on the goals and consequences of legal decisions.

At first the legal realists assumed that they had only to reveal how open-textured the law was in order for all manner of insights to be poured into the legal categories. This hope for instant clarification proved to be an illusion. Law and behavioral science would have to probe more deeply—less to find answers than to formulate the questions which must be answered. The result was an effort to appraise law in functional terms. Searching questions were asked about those who made important decisions at each stage of the legal process: what moved them; whence came their value-systems; what was the impact upon those value-systems of the variety of roles the actors were called upon to play.

Increasingly, the judicial process was seen as only one among several legal processes. The legislative process, the administrative process, and even less formal processes of decision also demanded consideration. More significantly, the limits and the limitations of law began to be identified. Criminal law came to be seen as a last-resort process that had to be studied and understood as a single piece in the mosaic of public and private, external and internal, controls over human behavior.

As law came to be regarded as a process of decision in which men use institutions to shape norms, to interpret them and to enforce them, it became obvious that many gaps in our knowledge had to be filled. In criminal law we had to know more about the

1

work of: (1) the legislators who decide what conduct under what circumstances constitutes an offense, what official conduct may be authorized to determine whether such an offense has occurred, and what official responses by way of sanctions may be imposed; (2) the police and the prosecutor who, with varying degrees of discretion, may invoke the process and in effect seek review by judge and jury of their decisions; (3) the appellate courts who review the decisions of all those who have participated in the process to this point, including the legislature; (4) the administrators, e.g., the warden, probation officer, prison official, executioner, parole or pardoning agencies, who, following an affirmance of conviction, have to decide how to implement it in accord with its purposes. Unfortunately little of this information was available. It could be obtained only if the scope of legal teaching and research were changed drastically.

In expanding this perspective, legal scholars have had to take into account two major developments. The first is the influence of the United States Supreme Court. Over the past generation the Court has set out to narrow the gap between ideal and reality in the administration of criminal law. It has pressed especially hard, because it has been mindful of the ease with which illegality at the initial stages can be swallowed up in the great mass of guilty pleas that characterize the process. More and more the court has viewed criminal law and procedure in instrumental terms, treating legal doctrine as only one of a variety of devices for shaping institutions and the manner in which men use them.

The second of these developments is the codification movement. We are witnessing sustained efforts to rationalize the body of criminal law and procedure in accordance with norms that are often being made explicit for the first time. Brought to their most advanced, though inevitably compromised, form in the American Law Institute's Model Penal Code, these codes recite the central propositions of the criminal law and then try to apply the propositions consistently in a variety of substantive and procedural settings. Though these efforts cannot be said to qualify as models in the truest sense, they have gone a long way toward refining existing thought about criminal law and clarifying the extent to which such thought remains clouded by ambiguity and ambivalence.

An Introductory Note

The impact of these developments upon teaching materials has been quite direct. Until recently we have relied almost entirely upon casebooks made up of the opinions of appellate courts and arranged to show development of judicial doctrine in response to new fact situations. The objective has been to teach the student how to work within a common law system that changes relatively slowly and draws imaginatively from precedent and counter-precedent. Casebooks, being problem-oriented, have lent themselves almost as well to the new requirements as to the old. As the scope of the lawyer's concern has expanded to include the full range of the legal process—the trial, the legislative process, the administrative process—samples of such processes have been included. As materials from the behavioral sciences were seen to be relevant to the understanding or solution of legal problems (or, more accurately, worth evaluating for their relevance), they too were included. Appellate opinions remain, of course, but only as one part of an ongoing process that must determine which persons or agencies should be assigned the role of promulgating, invoking, implementing, and appraising decisions to grant or restrict the state's control over its citizens and its official agents.

The objective has been to prepare lawyers to use as wide a variety of materials as a constantly changing social situation will require: to teach them not only to use behavioral scientists as expert witnesses, but also to frame legal problems in ways which permit them both to draw upon existing scholarship and to bend theoretical and empirical inquiries to the needs of law. An inevitable consequence of the use of so wide a variety of materials has been pressure on casebook editors, and on those who use the books, to present the materials in ways which frame hypotheses about the legal system and the relations among its parts. The result is the beginning of a style of thought which should prove congenial to behavioral scientists. In time, it should become possible to evaluate the adequacy of law as a multifunctional process designed to meet man's need for stability in the external world and, at the same time, to meet his internal need for flexibility and growth.

Ultimately, of course, we need a fuller body of scholarship on deterrence, rehabilitation, and retribution; on the inevitability and meaning of discretion in decision-making; and on the methods of measuring the impact of decisions in terms of the functions they, and the legal system, are designed to serve. When it becomes apparent that the judicial process is only a small part of the administration of criminal justice, the symbolic role of law will take on greater significance, as an instrument for shaping public opinion and for affecting the behavior of those who administer processes where rules of law seem now to bind hardly at all, e.g., police, bail bondsmen, and prosecutors. We shall also find ourselves considering far more than in the past the special function of the criminal sanction as an instrument of control; the extent to which problems of a quite similar sort may be dealt with through a criminal or medical or welfare process, or one as yet unlabeled; the criteria for choosing among them; and the strategies of enforcement policy in obtaining compliance with legal norms from both the governors and the governed.

THE SELECTIONS

The selections in this volume are made up for the most part of articles and chapters at nearly original length. They are intended to take the reader into a body of literature that explores the purposes of criminal law, its processes, and the interrelation of purpose and process. In the summaries that follow, we have emphasized that which attracted our attention, knowing full well you may find them worthwhile or insignificant for other reasons. Similarly, in dividing the selections into categories, we have sought to highlight our emphasis; we recognize, however, that many of the pieces could as easily have been placed elsewhere. Our hope is that these essays will provoke serious consideration of the theory and research needed to appraise the criminal law and its administration.

We begin our exploration of the purposes of the criminal law with *Of Crimes in General and of Punishments*, taken from Sir James Fitzjames Stephen's classic, "A History of the Criminal Law of England" (1883). Stephen opens the question of the role the criminal law can and should play as a vehicle for the enforcement of morals. He argues that, where morality and law support each other, punishment should express the hatred of the community toward the criminal, thereby channeling society's anger and feelings of vengeance in an orderly and relatively humane fashion. The argument anticipates Durkheim's theory of the function of deviance, developed by Erikson later in this volume, and remains a continuing challenge to those who would deemphasize retribution in the movement toward the rehabilitative ideal.

In *Theories of Punishment and the External Standard*, from "The Common Law" (1881), Oliver Wendell Holmes, Jr. challenges the widely held assumption that punishment in criminal law is based on individual blameworthiness as reflected in an offender's evil intent, *mens rea*. In a disarmingly simple style,

5

The Selections

Holmes submits that there is no mystic bond between wrong and punishment; infliction of pain is only a means to an end. Though in theory *mens rea* remains an underlying assumption of criminal liability, the criminal law is not administered or enacted on that theory. The law, he argues, exceeds the limits of individual retribution and subordinates consideration of the individual to that of the public well-being, to general deterrence and a shaping of general standards of conduct.

We turn next to *Moral Aspects of the Criminal Law* (1940) by one of our great philosophers, Morris Raphael Cohen. Cohen analyzes the idea of justice in punishment and the shortcomings of the retributive, rehabilitative, and preventive aims of the law. He examines the criteria which legislators should use as they, and the law, oscillate between moral principles and facts in deciding what acts should be classified as "crimes." Cohen suggests that, since "civilized" peoples vary in their moral sense, law and morality coincide only in fundamental assumptions as to the proper procedure; their common ideal is a system that corrects itself by the process of testing principles by consequences (the facts), and conversely, judging actual consequences in the light of principles.

Henry Hart's *The Aims of the Criminal Law* (1958) sees the criminal law as a means of identifying the relationship, and of establishing priorities, among the several purposes which the criminal process should serve. Recognizing the importance of examining a problem systematically, from the vantage point of each of the major agencies of criminal justice, he stresses multi-valued appraisals that take into account the interplay between substance and procedure. Hart also presents the case, much in the spirit of Stephen, against a primarily curative-rehabilitative theory of criminal law. He believes that such a theory cannot be applied consistently in defining and grading crimes, and that the effort to do so poses too great a risk that punishment will be inflicted for what the individual is or is believed to be, rather than for what he has done.

William E. Nelson, in his *Emerging Notions of Modern Criminal Law in the Revolutionary Era—An Historical Perspective* (1967), illustrates Cohen's "oscillation" thesis—here between religious or moral principles and the economic facts of life. Taking colonial Massachusetts as an example, Nelson demonstrates the shift in criminal law from primary emphasis on the enforcement of religious morality to protection of property. In colonial times religion was a way of life; crime was equated to sin, and the criminal law was meant to be the earthly arm of God. Most cases were within the category of offenses against God and religion; these offenses were widespread among all segments of the community, and the penalties imposed usually did not sever the offender's tie with society. Following periods of economic distress, there was a rise in economically motivated crimes, and prosecutions for offenses against God and religion declined accordingly. Hard labor was used as punishment in order to pay the cost of imprisoning those punished, usually those economically deprived. There emerged a new concern with political and economic order, followed by the rejection of the previously unquestioned assumption that government should enforce morality.

Kai Erikson, in his chapter *On the Sociology of Deviance,* from "The Wayward Puritans" (1966) turns from a jurisprudential analysis of the purposes of criminal law to the societal function of a concept of crime as a means of defining the boundaries of the social group. Deviant forms of behavior, by marking the outer edges of group life, give the inner structure of society its special character and thus supply the framework within which the total community develops an orderly sense of its own cultural identity. To that extent, deviance supplies a focus and an outlet for group feeling, enhancing social cohesion by drawing attention to those values which constitute the collective conscience of the community. Deviance, it would seem, also derives a measure of nourishment from the very agencies designed to inhibit it. Erikson, following Durkheim, casts doubt on the assumption that any well structured society can eliminate deviant behavior through criminal law.

Part Two deals with "process" in criminal law. It opens with an essay on *Criminal Justice in the American City* (1922) by Roscoe Pound, a major force in the American school of sociological jurisprudence. Pound's essay seeks to identify the bounds within which criminal law may function "effectively" as a practical system. He examines the legal order as a means of social engineering through which men attempt to conserve shared values by adjusting and ordering human relations with a minimum of friction or waste. Pointing to the tension between a strict application of rules and magisterial discretion, to the dissatisfactions developing from the common lag between law and public opinion, and to the conflicts inevitably arising among the various goals of the criminal law, he alerts us to the failure of the process to provide an adequate means of self-appraisal and to the political setting in which the administration of criminal law takes place.

In *Facts Are Guesses*, taken from his book "Courts on Trial" (1950), we sample the work of Jerome Frank, who as teacher, scholar, and judge, was always a legal realist. His essay demonstrates how much legal rules are at the mercy of the "fact" finding process at every point in the administration of law, particularly at trial. In describing the wide gap between objective and perceived fact, Frank shows how error-prone the process is and therefore how essential it is to devise procedural safeguards for the accused. The vivid blending of the actual and the theoretical in Frank and Pound finds application in many of the selections which follow.

Criminal Statistics: A Reformulation of the Problem (1967) by Stanton Wheeler introduces a method of gathering and presenting data for an appraisal of the criminal process. Wheeler identifies some of the weakness in the statistical design for determining crime rates. Rather than rely exclusively on a simple count of "reported" criminal offenses to establish the rate, he proposes a statistical model which accounts for three crucial variables: the offender, the citizen (either victim or observer), and the law enforcement agent. For example, to the extent that the data of criminal statistics are records of community response to different offenses and different offenders, we should study both the reporters and the victims—alert to the extent to which "facts are guesses." Wheeler's proposal should make it possible to focus on areas of currently low visibility and to facilitate evaluations of the broad discretion exercised by police and prosecutor.

In *Police Discretion Not To Invoke the Criminal Process: Low-Visibility Decisions in the Administration of Justice* (1960), Joseph Goldstein identifies the multiple purposes of the criminal law and, after describing the interrelated points of decision in the process, develops a model for appraising the work of each agency of decision in terms of purpose and function. He places special emphasis on the discretion exercised by the police and the impact of their decisions on all other agencies of decision. Three case studies are presented and analyzed: police decisions not to enforce the narcotics laws against certain violators who serve as informers; the nonenforcement of felonious assault laws against an assailant whose victim does not sign a complaint; and decisions to harass persons involved in the numbers rackets rather than to enforce gambling laws. In focusing on areas of nonenforcement, Goldstein identifies a gap in the procedures of review and in the normal course of data-gathering—a gap which must be filled before any appraisal can provide a basis for developing and implementing a process in practice which approximates the process in theory.

Abraham S. Goldstein, in *The State and the Accused: Balance of Advantage in Criminal Procedure* (1960), appraises the oft-quoted assertion by Learned Hand that our system gives the accused "every advantage." He examines the relation between the pretrial screening agencies (police, prosecutor, magistrate, grand jury) and the trial process and concludes that concepts used at trial, such as "proof beyond reasonable doubt," are essential to compensate for the inevitable inadequacy of the earlier screens. Turning to the problems of notice and disclosure which are central to a fair trial in an adversary system, he finds an unequal distribution of resources and procedural options which favor the state. His perspective is that of the entire process; he demonstrates that the question of "advantage" and "disadvantage" can be answered only in the context of a species of systems analysis and that changes at one point may be negated at another unless the process is seen whole.

Two Models of the Criminal Process (1968) by Herbert L. Packer emphasizes the importance of building normative models that would facilitate the identification of available value choices. He develops two models—the "crime control" and the "due process" models. The first is based on the proposition that repression of criminal conduct is the most important function of criminal law. The definition of "efficiency" under that model requires a relatively large number of convictions with a minimum expenditure of effort. The plea of guilty is preeminently "efficient," since it represents a crime "solved" without the many costs of trial and appeal or the risk of a conviction overturned. Procedural guarantees, such as free access to counsel, are of very little use. On the other hand, the "due process" model, which seems to be assumed or preferred in the earlier selections, particularly the essays by the Goldsteins, insists on the avoidance of error; it is interested in quality control rather than in quantitative output. The demand for finality is very low; the appeal stage is thus very important—to ferret out procedural error and to insure that due process norms prevail. Packer suggests that the crime control model is more characteristic of the real world than is the due process one.

The Packer article forces us to the question whether there is, in fact, a conflict between the due process and crime control models. If the goal of crime control is not just the creation of a facade of "law and order," is not due process an essential part of either model? Jerome Hall examines this question in *The Basic Dilemma of Criminal Procedure* (1942). He describes the conflicting ends of any civilized criminal procedure and deftly exposes the fallacies of many arguments which fail to take that conflict into account. More importantly, he develops the thesis that criminal procedure serves nonrational functions that cannot be ignored by those who employ "scientific" methods in the administration of criminal law and by those who design statistical measures for evaluating their work.

In *The Characteristics of Total Institutions* (1960) by Erving Goffman, a sociologist takes the vantage point of an observer rather than statistician and gives the empirical a descriptive–theoretical dimension. He explores the nature of total institutions, of which the prison is an example, and finds them arranging all phases of "inmate" life under a single authority in which staff and inmate develop very special cultures and characteristics. Upon becoming an inmate, a stripping process takes place in which personal identity and equipment is removed; the new inmate may come to share the guilty feelings of his fellows as well as a deep sense of injustice and bitterness. Goffman submits that the rehabilitative aim of the decision to incarcerate is seldom achieved. When permanent alteration occurs, it is often not the kind intended by the staff or by the process. To the extent that hospitals share many of the features of prisons and other total institutions, Goffman's conclusions raise questions that must be confronted by those who urge a medical model as an alternative to the criminal process.

Part Three, on *Purpose and Process*, contains a group of essays that, despite the focus of each on a specific problem, deals with the total system of criminal administration. Francis A. Allen, in *Criminal Justice, Legal Values and the Rehabilitative Ideal* (1959), argues that the euphemistic language of therapy has led to an unjustified complacency about the system and institutions of "correction." He shows how individual liberty and justice are being subordinated to the therapeutic ideal, how indeterminate sentences begin to seem appropriate and procedural laxness becomes tolerable, since the criminal law wants only to "help" not "punish" the criminal. The importation of preventive detention under the banner of the rehabilitative ideal makes urgent the need to determine what behavior justifies commitment, for how long, in what kinds of institutions, and with what authority to impose what kinds of "therapy."

In *The Use and Abuse of the Criminal Law* (1965), H. L. A. Hart reopens the ancient question of whether criminal law should enforce morality, specifically sexual morality. Drawing on philosophical propositions as well as empirical findings, he gives a negative answer, arguing the impracticality of general control because of the difficulty of obtaining evidence; the inequality of treatment since detection is totally fortuitous; and the element of judicial economy since society can only afford a given degree of law enforcement. Finally, he introduces the notion of law-created misery, using as his example the suppression of sexual instincts and its effect on the emotional life and development of the personality. He seeks to find out, but cannot, a value which may outweigh the "misery" caused by legally enforced morality. He submits that there is no evidence that a failure of the law to enforce society's sexual morality is likely to lead to the destruction of all morality or to jeopardize the very existence of society.

In *The Overreach of the Criminal Law* (1970), Norval Morris and Gordon Hawkins pursue Hart's inquiry into the practical as well as moral limits of a system of criminal justice. Their search for a way of increasing the effectiveness of available law enforcement resources, and of reducing crime, leads to their asking "what constitutes and what ought to constitute a crime" or "when should we use the criminal law to regulate human conduct.?" In exploring these questions in relation to drunkenness, drug abuse, gambling, vagrancy, abortion and sexual behavior, they argue for removing the criminal law from these areas of private morality so that it might more effectively serve the "essential" function of safeguarding persons and property.

In Alan M. Dershowitz's *On Preventive Detention* (1969) we introduce the difficulties of predicting human behavior when sanctions are involved. Taking as his starting point the proposals for detention before trial of persons charged with crime, Dershowitz examines the law of inchoate crimes and civil commitment. He concludes that we are a long distance away from being able to predict crime (in terms of which individuals will do what and when) with very much accuracy. He counsels, therefore, as did Henry Hart in *The Aims of the Criminal Law*, against preventive detention until carefully designed experiments provide evidence of prediction that will permit the risk of error to be weighed against the cost of violating the right to liberty.

The next three essays are also concerned with prevention. Johannes Andenaes, in *The General Preventive Effects of Punishment* (1966), draws the essential distinction between the impact of the existence and the imposition of a sanction on the actual offender (individual prevention) and its impact upon society at large (general prevention). He argues for a total system of criminal justice that gives priority to general prevention rather than one that expends substantial resources on preventing a particular offender from further criminal acts. General prevention, he suggests, takes place through a series of "messages," resulting from an interplay between the provisions of the law and its enforcement in specific cases. Punishment has a moral or socio-pedagogical influence: the message not only conveys the "threat" of punishment for disobedience to the law, but also that it is "wrong" to disobey, thus exerting a "moral" influence. Andenaes notes that there is little significant research in this area. He points to socio-statistical and psychological studies which might help unravel the connection, if any, between changes in the function of the legal apparatus and changes in the extent and nature of criminality. Throughout the essay, we are being asked, much in the spirit of Holmes: how much general deterrence do we want and at what cost?

In his essay, *On the Function of Criminal Law in Riot Control* (1969), Joseph Goldstein discusses the potential of increased penalties as a means of reducing criminal offenses by members of a mob. Using psychoanalytic theory, and more specifically knowledge about the psychology of groups, he raises questions about the meaning of individual choice and its relation to the concept of deterrence. Through a description of the dehumanization and loss of control that comes from mob action, he presents the criminal law's dilemma when it tries to respond to the psychology of the individual caught up in a riot situation: the effort to control riotous conduct through authorizing greater force by the police may produce a net increase in the quantum of damage done; the effort to treat loss of control in a mob as a mitigating factor may invite an increase in violence. Confronting the dilemma, the author concludes that the criminal process has limited utility not only in dealing with the underlying causes of riots but also in affecting the individual choices on which ideas of deterrence ultimately rest.

Sanford H. Kadish explores a specific area of general prevention in *Some Observations on the Use of Criminal Sanctions in Enforcing Economic Regulations* (1963). He attributes special problems in this area of criminal law enforcement to the fact that alternate civil routes to enforcement are usually available and that restraint of private choice in economic matters is basically in conflict with the preference for *laissez faire;* the proscribed conduct does not, therefore, generally carry with it a moral stigma. His analysis illustrates the singular relationship between the criminal law and the "moral sense of the community" and opens to view the possible aggressive use of the criminal sanction as a "moralizing weapon" rather than as a reflection of prevailing value preferences.

We close the volume with two essays on a subject which has dominated the literature of criminal law. That problem is criminal responsibility, more specifically the extent to which "insanity" should relieve an offender of "punishment." Abraham S. Goldstein, in *M'Naghten: The Stereotype Challenged* from his book "The Insanity Defense" (1967), demonstrates how history, psychiatric convention, public attitudes, and the evidentiary rules have combined to narrow the application of the M'Naghten rule to but a few of those accused who suffer from serious mental illness. He argues that courts, without altering the M'Naghten formulation, could provide a construction and guidelines for its application which would meet the major challenges contained in the vast body of critical literature. In the course of his argument, he makes the larger point that a rule of law is less a function of its text than of the manner in which it is understood and administered inside and outside the legal process.

This analysis is juxtaposed with *Abolish the "Insanity Defense"—Why Not?* (1963) by Joseph Goldstein and Jay Katz. They come to the problem from a different vantage point, asking not what the insanity test should be but rather: Why an "insanity defense" in a system of criminal justice? Goldstein and Katz, recalling to mind Allen's essay, argue that the insanity defense in practice is not a defense, but rather a device for triggering indeterminate restraints. Their analysis suggests the need for reexamining the function of restraint as a consequence of conviction in terms of several factors; the fear of dangerousness, the need for care, the need for destigmatization, the kinds of institutions involved, the duration of detention—for what conduct and at whose initiative. This paper brings into the open the conflict between the need to restrain those feared to be dangerous, and society's own moral justification for punishment, thus compelling us to define the status of those who are not to "blame" but who should nevertheless be deprived of their liberty.

PART ONE

Purposes

SIR JAMES FITZJAMES STEPHEN

Of Crimes in General and of Punishments

The substantive criminal law . . . relates to actions which, if there were no criminal law at all, would be judged of by the public at large much as they are judged of at present. If murder, theft, and rape were not punished by law, the words would still be in use, and would be applied to the same or nearly the same actions. The same or nearly the same distinctions would be recognized between murder and manslaughter, robbery and theft, rape and seduction. In short, there is a moral as well as a legal classification of crimes, and the merits and defects of legal definitions cannot be understood unless the moral view of the subject is understood. Law and morals are not and cannot be made co-extensive, or even completely harmonious. Law may be intended to supplement or to correct morality. There may in some cases be an inevitable conflict between them, but whatever may be their relation, it is essential to a just criticism of the law to understand what may be called the natural distribution of the class of actions to which it applies.

From his *History of the Criminal Law of England*, Vol. II, pp. 75–93 (Macmillan, 1883).

Stephen was a Judge of the Queen's Bench and author, inter alia, *of* General View of the Criminal Law of England (1863).

Sir James Fitzjames Stephen

For this purpose it will be necessary to say a few words of law in general, and of morals in general. By law, I mean what Austin meant by the word, namely, a system of commands addressed by the sovereign of the state to his subjects, imposing duties and enforced by punishments. By morals I mean a system of rules of conduct imposed in part by the opinion of others and in part by each man's own opinion of his own actions, which is what I understand by the word conscience. The sanction of morality as such is the approbation or disapprobation of others and of ourselves. Moral rules are not so determinate as legal rules, but the sanction by which they are enforced is more certain, as men cannot escape from their own opinion of themselves, nor from their desire of the approbation or fear of the disapprobation of others, nor can they flatter themselves that they are mistaken in the facts from which their estimate of themselves and their own conduct proceeds.

. . .

The great difference between the legal and the popular or moral meaning of the word crime is that whereas the only perfectly definite meaning which a lawyer can attach to the word is that of an act or omission punished by law, the popular or moral conception adds to this the notion of moral guilt of a specially deep and degrading kind. By a criminal, people in general understand not only a person who is liable to be punished, but a person who ought to be punished because he has done something at once wicked and obviously injurious in a high degree to the commonest interests of society. Perhaps the most interesting question connected with the whole subject is how far these views respectively ought to regulate legislation on the subject of crimes, "ought" meaning in this instance how far it is for the good of those whose good is considered in legislation that the view in question should be adopted, and "good" meaning the end which the legislator has in view in his legislation. In other words, the question is, what ought to be the relation between criminal law and moral good and evil as understood by the person who imposes the law?

The answer to this question will vary according to circumstances. The first circumstance affecting it is the relation between the legislator and the persons for whom the laws are made. There is a great difference between a small number of Englishmen legislating for India and a comparatively large number of Englishmen legislating for England. There is also a great difference between a dictator like Napoleon, placed in such circumstances that he can practically impose his own will on a great nation, or at least interpret to that nation their own permanent wishes in a way which will continue for ages to be accepted as a practically final interpretation of them, and an English minister who thinks that it would add to the popularity and stability of his government to pass a penal code through Parliament.

When the legislator is a ruler, properly so called, when the word denotes a single person or a small body of persons, enabled by circumstances to impose his or their will on others, the ruler will, of course, be guided in doing so by his own conceptions of the effect which he wishes to produce upon his subjects, and of the extent to which circumstances enable him to produce that effect by legislation. The problem for him, therefore, is, What ought to be the relation of his conception of right and wrong to the laws which he proposes to enact? How far ought he to aim at sanctioning, and how far ought he to aim at correcting, the moral conceptions of those for whom he legislates?

. . .

Where the legislature tends to represent directly the will of a large proportion of the community, it is unnecessary to distinguish between the morality of the legislature and that of the persons legislated for, for the two may be considered as practically identical, so that the question in this case will be the comparatively simple one, In what relation ought criminal law to stand to morality when the effective majority of a great nation legislates for the whole of it, and when there are no other differences of moral standard or sentiment than those which inevitably result from individual differences of opinion and unrestricted discussion on religion and morals?

The answer to this question is not quite simple. In the first place criminal law must, from the nature of the case, be far narrower than morality. In no age or nation, at all events, in no age or nation which has any similarity to our own, has the attempt been made to treat every moral defect as a crime. In different ages of the world injuries to individuals, to God, to the gods, or to the community, have been treated as crimes, but I think that in all cases the idea of crime has involved the idea of some definite, gross, undeniable injury to some one. In our own country this is now, and has been from the earliest times, perfectly well-established. No temper of mind, no habit of life, however pernicious, has ever been treated as a crime, unless it displayed itself in some definite overt act. It never entered into the head of any English legislator to enact, or of any English court, to hold, that a man could be indicted and punished for ingratitude, for hard-heartedness, for the absence of natural affection, for habitual idleness, for avarice, sensuality, pride, or, in a word, for any vice whatever as such. Even for purposes of ecclesiastical censure some definite act of immorality was required. Sinful thoughts and dispositions of mind might be the subject of confession and of penance, but they were never punished in this country by ecclesiastical criminal proceedings.

The reasons for imposing this great leading restriction upon the sphere of criminal law are obvious. If it were not so restricted it would be utterly intolerable; all mankind would be criminals, and most of their lives would be passed in trying and punishing each other for offences which could never be proved.

Criminal law, then, must be confined within narrow limits, and can be applied only to definite overt acts or omissions capable of being distinctly proved, which acts or omissions inflict definite evils, either on specific persons or on the community at large. It is within these limits only that there can be any relation at all between criminal law and morality.

Some modern writers of eminence on this subject have been in the habit of regarding criminal law as being entirely independent of morality. According to this view the one object of criminal law in each case to which it applies is to deter people by threats from doing certain acts. If murder is to be prevented the threat is death. If the cultivation of tobacco is to be prevented, the threat is fine and forfeiture; but in every case the only question is as to the deterrent effect of the punishment, which is regarded as profit; and the pain caused by the infliction of the punishment, which is regarded as loss or expense. Bentham (if I am not mistaken) says that if a fine of a shilling was as efficient in preventing murder as the punishment of death, a fine of one shilling would be the proper punishment for murder, and anything further would be unjustifiable cruelty.

It is possible that by giving an unnaturally wide meaning to common words this statement might be so explained that most people would agree with it. If, for instance, a fine of a shilling were, for some reason, generally recognised as embodying the common feeling of hatred against assassins, and moral indignation at assassination, as fully as the infliction of a shameful death, Bentham's statement might be true; but to discuss so unnatural a supposition would be waste of time. Probably, however, Bentham's meaning was that if murderers in general feared a fine as much as death, they ought, upon conviction, to be fined instead of being put to death, although putting them to death would be more in accordance with the moral sentiments of the community at large than fining them.

If this was his meaning I dissent from it, being of opinion that if in all cases criminal law were regarded only as a direct appeal to the fears of persons likely to commit crimes, it would be deprived of a large part of its efficiency, for it operates not only on the fears of criminals, but upon the habitual sentiments of those who are not criminals. Great part of the general detestation of crime which happily prevails amongst the decent part of the community in all civilized countries arises from the fact that the commission of offences is associated in all such communities with the solemn and deliberate infliction of punishment wherever crime is proved.

The relation between criminal law and morality is not in all cases the same. The two may harmonize, there may be a conflict between them, or they may be independent. In all common cases they do, and, in my opinion, wherever and so far as it is possible, they ought, to harmonize with, and support one another.

In some uncommon but highly important cases there is a possibility that they may to a certain extent come into conflict, inasmuch as a minority of the nation more or less influential and extensive may disapprove morally of the objects which the criminal law is intended to promote, and may regard as virtuous actions what it treats as crimes. There is a third class of cases in which the criminal law is supported by moral sentiment, in so far as moral sentiment recognises obedience to the law as a duty, but no further. This is where it enjoins or forbids acts, which if no law existed in relation to them would be regarded as matters of indifference. The laws which forbid the cultivation of tobacco, and which require marriages to be celebrated at certain times and places only, are instances of legislation of this kind.

. . .

I will consider the normal case, that in which law and morals are in harmony, and ought to and usually do support each other. This is true of all the gross offences which consist of instances of turbulence, force, or fraud. Whatever may be the nature or extent of the differences which exist as to the nature of morals, no one in this country regards murder, rape, arson, robbery, theft, or the like, with any feeling but detestation. I do not think it admits of any doubt that law and morals powerfully support and greatly intensify each other in this matter. Everything which is regarded as enhancing the moral guilt of a particular offence is recognised as a reason for increasing the severity of the punishment awarded to it. On the other hand, the sentence of the law is to the moral sentiment of the public in relation to any offence what a seal is to hot wax. It converts into a permanent final judgment what might otherwise be a transient sentiment. The mere general suspicion or knowledge that a man has done something dishonest may never be brought to a point, and the disapprobation excited by it may in time pass away, but the fact that he has been convicted and punished as a thief stamps a mark upon him for life. In short, the infliction of punishment by law gives definite expression and a solemn ratification and justification to the hatred which is excited by the commission of the offence, and which constitutes the moral or popular as distinguished from the conscientious sanction of that part of morality which is also sanctioned by the criminal law. The criminal law thus proceeds upon the principle that it is morally right to hate criminals, and it confirms and justifies that sentiment by inflicting upon criminals punishments which express it.

I think that whatever effect the administration of criminal justice has in preventing the commission of crimes is due as much to this circumstance as to any definite fear entertained by offenders of undergoing specific punishment. If this is doubted, let any one ask himself to what extent a man would be deterred from theft by the knowledge that by committing it he was exposed, say, to one chance in fifty of catching an illness which would inflict upon him the same amount of confinement, inconvenience, and money loss as six months' imprisonment and hard labour. In other words, how many people would be deterred from stealing by the chance of catching a bad fever? I am also of opinion that this close alliance between criminal law and moral sentiment is in all ways healthy and advantageous to the community. I think it highly desirable that criminals should be hated, that the punishments inflicted upon them should be so contrived as to give expression to that hatred, and to justify it so far as the public provision of means for expressing and gratifying a healthy natural sentiment can justify and encourage it.

These views are regarded by many persons as being wicked, because it is supposed that we never ought to hate, or wish to be revenged upon, any one. The doctrine that hatred and vengeance are wicked in themselves appears to me to contradict plain facts, and to be unsupported by any argument deserving of attention. Love and hatred, gratitude for benefits, and the desire of vengeance for injuries, imply each other as much as convex and concave. Butler vindicated resentment which cannot be distinguished from revenge and hatred except by name, and Bentham included the pleasures of malevolence amongst the fifteen which, as he said, constitute all our motives of action. The unqualified manner in which they have been denounced is in itself a proof that they are deeply rooted in human nature. No doubt they are peculiarly liable to abuse, and in some states of society are commonly in excess of what is desirable, and so require restraint rather than excitement, but unqualified denunciations of them are as ill-judged as unqualified denunciations of sexual passion. The forms in which deliberate anger and righteous disapprobation are expressed, and the execution of criminal justice is the most emphatic of such forms, stand to the one set of passions in the same relation in which marriage stands to the other. I also think that in the present state of public feeling, at all events amongst the classes which principally influence legislation, there is more ground to fear defect than excess in these passions. Whatever may have been the case in periods of greater energy, less knowledge, and less sensibility than ours, it is now far more likely that people should witness acts of grievous cruelty, deliberate fraud, and lawless turbulence, with too little hatred and too little desire for deliberate measured revenge than that they should feel too much.

The expression and gratification of these feelings is however only one of the objects for which legal punishments are inflicted. Another object is the direct prevention of crime, either by fear, or by disabling or even destroying the offender, and this which is I think commonly put forward as the only proper object of legal punishments is beyond all question distinct from the one just mentioned and of coordinate importance with it. The two objects are in no degree inconsistent with each other, on the contrary they go hand in hand, and may be regarded respectively as the secondary and the primary effects of the administration of criminal justice. The only practical result in the actual administration of justice of admitting each as a separate ground for punishment is that when a discretion as to the punishment of an offence is placed in the judge's hands, as it is in almost all cases by our law, the judge in the exercise of that discretion ought to have regard to the moral guilt of the offence which he is to punish as well as to its specific public danger. In criminal legislation the distinction is of greater importance, as one of the arguments in favour of exemplary punishments (death, flogging, and the like) is that they emphatically justify and gratify the public desire for vengeance upon such offenders.

The views expressed above are exposed to an objection which may be regarded as the converse of the one which I have just tried to answer. Many persons, who would not say that hatred and punishments founded on it are wicked, would say that both the feeling itself and the conduct which it suggests are irrational, because men and human conduct are as much the creatures of circumstance as things, and that it is therefore as irrational to desire to be revenged upon a man for committing murder with a pistol as to desire to be revenged on the pistol with which the man commits murder. The truth of the premiss of this argument I neither assert nor deny. It is certainly true that human conduct may be predicted to a great extent. It is natural to believe that an omniscient observer of it might predict not only every act, but every modification of every thought and feeling, of every human being born or to be born; but this is not inconsistent with the belief that each individual man is an unknown something—that as such he is other and more than a combination of the parts which we can see and touch,—and that his conduct depends upon the quality of the unknown something which he is.

However this may be, the conclusion drawn from the premiss of the argument just stated does not appear to follow from it. There is nothing to show that if all conduct could be predicted praise and blame would cease to exist. If, notwithstanding the doctrine of philosophical necessity, love and hatred are as powerful as ever, and not less powerful in those who are most firmly convinced of that doctrine than in other persons, it follows that there is no real inconsistency between that doctrine and those passions, however the apparent inconsistency, if any, is to be explained. If the doctrine in question should ever be so completely established as to account for the whole of human life (and no one will assert that this has as yet been done), it will account for love and hatred as well as for other things, and will no more disturb them than other things are disturbed by being accounted for.

. . .

In my opinion, the importance of the moral side of punishment, the importance that is of the expression which it gives to a proper hostility to criminals, has of late years been much underestimated. The extreme severity of the old law has been succeeded by a sentiment which appears to me to be based upon the notion that the passions of hatred and revenge are in themselves wrong; and that therefore revenge should be eliminated from law as being simply bad.

It is useless to argue upon questions of sentiment. All that any one can do is to avow the sentiments which he holds, and de-

Sir James Fitzjames Stephen

nounce those which he dislikes. I have explained my own views. Those which commonly prevail upon the subject appear to me to be based on a conception of human life which refuses to believe that there are in the world many bad men who are the natural enemies of inoffensive men, just as beasts of prey are the enemies of all men.

. . .

Great and indiscriminate severity in the law no doubt defeats itself, but temperate, discriminating, calculated severity is, within limits, effective, and I am not without hopes that in time the public may be brought to understand and to act upon this sentiment; though at present a tenderness prevails upon the subject which seems to me misplaced and exaggerated. It cannot, however, be denied that it springs from very deep roots, and that no considerable change in it can be expected unless the views current on several matters of deep importance should be greatly modified in what must at present be called an unpopular direction.

OLIVER WENDELL HOLMES, JR.

Theories of Punishment
and the External Standard

The first requirement of a sound body of law is, that it should correspond with the actual feelings and demands of the community, whether right or wrong. If people would gratify the passion of revenge outside of the law, if the law did not help them, the law has no choice but to satisfy the craving itself, and thus avoid the greater evil of private retribution. At the same time, this passion is not one which we encourage, either as private individuals or as law-makers. Moreover, it does not cover the whole ground. There are crimes which do not excite it, and we should naturally expect that the most important purposes of punishment would be coextensive with the whole field of its application. It remains to be discovered whether such a general purpose exists, and if so what it is. Different theories still divide opinion upon the subject.

It has been thought that the purpose of punishment is to reform the criminal; that it is to deter the criminal and others from

From his *The Common Law*, pp. 41–51 (Little, Brown, 1881).

Holmes taught at the Harvard Law School before his appointment to the Supreme Court of Massachusetts in 1883. He served on the United States Supreme Court from 1902 to 1932.

27

Oliver Wendell Holmes, Jr.

committing similar crimes; and that it is retribution. Few would now maintain that the first of these purposes was the only one. If it were, every prisoner should be released as soon as it appears clear that he will never repeat his offence, and if he is incurable he should not be punished at all. Of course it would be hard to reconcile the punishment of death with this doctrine.

The main struggle lies between the other two. On the one side is the notion that there is a mystic bond between wrong and punishment; on the other, that the infliction of pain is only a means to an end. Hegel, one of the great expounders of the former view, puts it, in his quasi mathematical form, that, wrong being the negation of right, punishment is the negation of that negation, or retribution. Thus the punishment must be equal, in the sense of proportionate to the crime, because its only function is to destroy it. Others, without this logical apparatus, are content to rely upon a felt necessity that suffering should follow wrong-doing.

It is objected that the preventive theory is immoral, because it overlooks the ill-desert of wrong-doing, and furnishes no measure of the amount of punishment, except the lawgiver's subjective opinion in regard to the sufficiency of the amount of preventive suffering. In the language of Kant, it treats man as a thing, not as a person; as a means, not as an end in himself. It is said to conflict with the sense of justice, and to violate the fundamental principle of all free communities, that the members of such communities have equal rights to life, liberty, and personal security.

In spite of all this, probably most English-speaking lawyers would accept the preventive theory without hesitation. As to the violation of equal rights which is charged, it may be replied that the dogma of equality makes an equation between individuals only, not between an individual and the community. No society has ever admitted that it could not sacrifice individual welfare to its own existence. If conscripts are necessary for its army, it seizes them, and marches them, with bayonets in their rear, to death. It runs highways and railroads through old family places in spite of the owner's protest, paying in this instance the market value, to be sure, because no civilized government sacrifices the citizen more than it can help, but still sacrificing his will and his welfare to that of the rest.

If it were necessary to trench further upon the field of morals, it might be suggested that the dogma of equality applied even to individuals only within the limits of ordinary dealings in the common run of affairs. You cannot argue with your neighbor, except on the admission for the moment that he is as wise as you, although you may by no means believe it. In the same way, you cannot deal with him, where both are free to choose, except on the footing of equal treatment, and the same rules for both. The ever-growing value set upon peace and the social relations tends to give the law of social being the appearance of the law of all being. But it seems to me clear that the *ultima ratio*, not only *regum*, but of private persons, is force, and that at the bottom of all private relations, however tempered by sympathy and all the social feelings, is a justifiable self-preference. If a man is on a plank in the deep sea which will only float one, and a stranger lays hold of it, he will thrust him off if he can. When the state finds itself in a similar position, it does the same thing.

The considerations which answer the argument of equal rights also answer the objections to treating man as a thing, and the like. If a man lives in society, he is liable to find himself so treated. The degree of civilization which a people has reached, no doubt, is marked by their anxiety to do as they would be done by. It may be the destiny of man that the social instincts shall grow to control his actions absolutely, even in anti-social situations. But they have not yet done so, and as the rules of law are or should be based upon a morality which is generally accepted, no rule founded on a theory of absolute unselfishness can be laid down without a breach between law and working beliefs.

If it be true, as I shall presently try to show, that the general principles of criminal and civil liability are the same, it will follow from that alone that theory and fact agree in frequently punishing those who have been guilty of no moral wrong, and who could not be condemned by any standard that did not avowedly disregard the personal peculiarities of the individuals concerned. If punishment stood on the moral grounds which are proposed for it, the first thing to be considered would be those limitations in the capacity for choosing rightly which arise from abnormal instincts, want of education, lack of intelligence, and all the other defects which are most marked in the criminal classes. I do not

Oliver Wendell Holmes, Jr.

say that they should not be, or at least I do not need to for my argument. I do not say that the criminal law does more good than harm. I only say that it is not enacted or administered on that theory.

There remains to be mentioned the affirmative argument in favor of the theory of retribution, to the effect that the fitness of punishment following wrong-doing is axiomatic, and is instinctively recognized by unperverted minds. I think that it will be seen, on self-inspection, that this feeling of fitness is absolute and unconditional only in the case of our neighbors. It does not seem to me that any one who has satisfied himself that an act of his was wrong, and that he will never do it again, would feel the least need or propriety, as between himself and an earthly punishing power alone, of his being made to suffer for what he had done, although, when third persons were introduced, he might, as a philosopher, admit the necessity of hurting him to frighten others. But when our neighbors do wrong, we sometimes feel the fitness of making them smart for it, whether they have repented or not. The feeling of fitness seems to me to be only vengeance in disguise, and I have already admitted that vengeance was an element, though not the chief element, of punishment.

But, again, the supposed intuition of fitness does not seem to me to be coextensive with the thing to be accounted for. The lesser punishments are just as fit for the lesser crimes as the greater for the greater. The demand that crime should be followed by its punishment should therefore be equal and absolute in both. Again, a *malum prohibitum* is just as much a crime as a *malum in se*. If there is any general ground for punishment, it must apply to one case as much as to the other. But it will hardly be said that, if the wrong in the case just supposed consisted of a breach of the revenue laws, and the government had been indemnified for the loss, we should feel any internal necessity that a man who had thoroughly repented of his wrong should be punished for it, except on the ground that his act was known to others. If it was known, the law would have to verify its threats in order that others might believe and tremble. But if the fact was a secret between the sovereign and the subject, the sovereign, if wholly free from passion, would undoubtedly see that punishment in such a case was wholly without justification.

On the other hand, there can be no case in which the law-maker makes certain conduct criminal without his thereby showing a wish and purpose to prevent that conduct. Prevention would accordingly seem to be the chief and only universal purpose of punishment. The law threatens certain pains if you do certain things, intending thereby to give you a new motive for not doing them. If you persist in doing them, it has to inflict the pains in order that its threats may continue to be believed.

If this is a true account of the law as it stands, the law does undoubtedly treat the individual as a means to an end, and uses him as a tool to increase the general welfare at his own expense. It has been suggested above, that this course is perfectly proper; but even if it is wrong, our criminal law follows it, and the theory of our criminal law must be shaped accordingly.

Further evidence that our law exceeds the limits of retribution, and subordinates consideration of the individual to that of the public well-being, will be found in some doctrines which cannot be satisfactorily explained on any other ground.

The first of these is, that even the deliberate taking of life will not be punished when it is the only way of saving one's own. This principle is not so clearly established as that next to be mentioned; but it has the support of very great authority. If that is the law, it must go on one of two grounds, either that self-preference is proper in the case supposed, or that, even if it is improper, the law cannot prevent it by punishment, because a threat of death at some future time can never be a sufficiently powerful motive to make a man choose death now in order to avoid the threat. If the former ground is adopted, it admits that a single person may sacrifice another to himself, and *a fortiori* that a people may. If the latter view is taken, by abandoning punishment when it can no longer be expected to prevent an act, the law abandons the retributive and adopts the preventive theory.

The next doctrine leads to still clearer conclusions. Ignorance of the law is no excuse for breaking it. This substantive principle is sometimes put in the form of a rule of evidence, that every one is presumed to know the law. It has accordingly been defended by Austin and others, on the ground of difficulty of proof. If justice requires the fact to be ascertained, the difficulty of doing so is no ground for refusing to try. But every one must feel that

Oliver Wendell Holmes, Jr.

ignorance of the law could never be admitted as an excuse, even if the fact could be proved by sight and hearing in every case. Furthermore, now that parties can testify, it may be doubted whether a man's knowledge of the law is any harder to investigate than many questions which are gone into. The difficulty, such as it is, would be met by throwing the burden of proving ignorance on the law-breaker.

The principle cannot be explained by saying that we are not only commanded to abstain from certain acts, but also to find out that we are commanded. For if there were such a second command, it is very clear that the guilt of failing to obey it would bear no proportion to that of disobeying the principal command if known, yet the failure to know would receive the same punishment as the failure to obey the principal law.

The true explanation of the rule is the same as that which accounts for the law's indifference to a man's particular temperament, faculties, and so forth. Public policy sacrifices the individual to the general good. It is desirable that the burden of all should be equal, but it is still more desirable to put an end to robbery and murder. It is no doubt true that there are many cases in which the criminal could not have known that he was breaking the law, but to admit the excuse at all would be to encourage ignorance where the law-maker has determined to make men know and obey, and justice to the individual is rightly outweighed by the larger interests on the other side of the scales.

If the foregoing arguments are sound, it is already manifest that liability to punishment cannot be finally and absolutely determined by considering the actual personal unworthiness of the criminal alone. That consideration will govern only so far as the public welfare permits or demands. And if we take into account the general result which the criminal law is intended to bring about, we shall see that the actual state of mind accompanying a criminal act plays a different part from what is commonly supposed.

For the most part, the purpose of the criminal law is only to induce external conformity to rule. All law is directed to conditions of things manifest to the senses. And whether it brings those conditions to pass immediately by the use of force, as when it protects a house from a mob by soldiers, or appropriates private property to public use, or hangs a man in pursuance of a judicial sentence, or whether it brings them about mediately through men's fears, its object is equally an external result. In directing itself against robbery or murder, for instance, its purpose is to put a stop to the actual physical taking and keeping of other men's goods, or the actual poisoning, shooting, stabbing, and otherwise putting to death of other men. If those things are not done, the law forbidding them is equally satisfied, whatever the motive.

Considering this purely external purpose of the law together with the fact that it is ready to sacrifice the individual so far as necessary in order to accomplish that purpose, we can see more readily than before that the actual degree of personal guilt involved in any particular transgression cannot be the only element, if it is an element at all, in the liability incurred. So far from its being true, as is often assumed, that the condition of a man's heart or conscience ought to be more considered in determining criminal than civil liability, it might almost be said that it is the very opposite of truth. For civil liability, in its immediate working, is simply a redistribution of an existing loss between two individuals; and . . . sound policy lets losses lie where they fall, except where a special reason can be shown for interference. The most frequent of such reasons is, that the party who is charged has been to blame.

It is not intended to deny that criminal liability, as well as civil, is founded on blameworthiness. Such a denial would shock the moral sense of any civilized community; or, to put it another way, a law which punished conduct which would not be blameworthy in the average member of the community would be too severe for that community to bear. It is only intended to point out that, when we are dealing with that part of the law which aims more directly than any other at establishing standards of conduct, we should expect there more than elsewhere to find that the tests of liability are external, and independent of the degree of evil in the particular person's motives or intentions. The conclusion follows directly from the nature of the standards to which conformity is required. These are not only external, as was shown above, but they are of general application. They do not merely require that every man should get as near as he can to the best conduct possible for him. They require him at his own peril to come up to a certain height. They take no account of incapacities,

Oliver Wendell Holmes, Jr.

unless the weakness is so marked as to fall into well known exceptions, such as infancy or madness. They assume that every man is as able as every other to behave as they command. If they fall on any one class harder than on another, it is on the weakest. For it is precisely to those who are most likely to err by temperament, ignorance, or folly, that the threats of the law are the most dangerous.

The reconciliation of the doctrine that liability is founded on blameworthiness with the existence of liability where the party is not to blame . . . is found in the conception of the average man, the man of ordinary intelligence and reasonable prudence. Liability is said to arise out of such conduct as would be blameworthy in him. But he is an ideal being, represented by the jury when they are appealed to, and his conduct is an external or objective standard when applied to any given individual. That individual may be morally without stain, because he has less than ordinary intelligence or prudence. But he is required to have those qualities at his peril. If he has them, he will not, as a general rule, incur liability without blameworthiness.

MORRIS RAPHAEL COHEN

Moral Aspects of the Criminal Law

I n passing moral judgments, as we all sooner or later inevitably do, in regard to legal and other human arrangements, we generally oscillate between the appeal to self-evident principles and the appeal to the obvious demands of the specific situation before us. This seems a highly unsatisfactory procedure to those who feel that certainty must be found in one or other terminus, else all our moral judgments fail for lack of an assured support. This Article is based on the view that such oscillation is under certain logical precautions and scientific systematization the only proper procedure, that to trust rigid principles regardless of specific consequences makes for inhuman absolutism, while to rely on nothing but the feeling of the moment leads to brutal anarchy. Consider the ethical atomists who think that life breaks itself up into a number of separate autonomous situations, each immediately revealing its own good or proper solution to our conscience, intuition, or intuitive reason, intelligence or common sense. When these moralists are confronted by a challenge to any of their par-

Reprinted by permission of The Yale Law Journal Company and Fred B. Rothman & Company from the *Yale Law Journal*, Vol. 49, pp. 987–1026 (1940).

Notes to this Selection will be found on page 423.

Cohen was Professor of Philosophy at City College of New York and the University of Chicago. He was the author, inter alia, *of* Law and the Social Order (1933) *and* Reason and Nature (1931).

Morris Raphael Cohen

ticular judgments, they generally adduce some reason or at least cite an analogous case, thus involving explicitly or implicitly an appeal to some determining principle more abstract and wider than the specific case before them. On the other hand, those who rely on principles to decide specific cases do, and have to, defend these principles by showing that they lead to the proper consequences. By a consideration of some of the ethical problems of the criminal law, I wish to illustrate the truth that the procedure from principles to facts and from facts to principles, without assuming either to be absolute or unquestionable, does not at all lead to complete moral nihilism, but rather clarifies the process of building a systematic view of what the law should do, even though it tolerates a certain amount of probabilism and pluralism in taking into account the wide variations of social conditions and sentiments. . . .

What Is a Crime?

With this question, we are at once plunged into an ancient and persistent controversy. On one hand, we have the legalists who urge that any act or omission is a crime when, and only when, it is declared to be such by the legislative power or by those who speak with the authority of the law; an act may be sinful, immoral or contrary to the public good, but it is not a crime unless it is legally so declared. On the other hand, we have those who claim this view to be superficial, and who insist that no legislature can or should treat anything as a crime unless it is so in fact or in the nature of things. This issue dates back to the old Greek controversy of the fifth century B.C. between those who saw everything determined by nature and those who pressed the claims of convention or human legislation. To Aristotle may be traced the classical compromise of distinguishing between those acts which are crimes by nature (*mala per se*) and are prohibited among all peoples, and those others (*mala prohibita*) which are prohibited only in certain places by special legislation. This view has been largely influential in molding the classical doctrine of natural rights in the criminal as well as in other branches of the law. In point of fact, however, no one has ever made a critical catalogue of the acts which have actually been prohibited by all peoples at all times. Almost all those who insist that there are *mala per se* put into that class those acts which in an undefined way seem to them to be shocking. But they do not give any clear criterion by which to judge what acts should thus be included and what acts should be excluded from the category of crime.

The Traditional Moralistic Views of Crime

The oldest traditions view crime as a violation of some eternal law set by the gods, nature or reason. These find expression in two forms, the theologic and the rationalist (more properly intuitive). Both have the advantage over the positivist that they do not have to use empirical evidence to establish absolute distinctions between what is and what is not properly a crime.

I. THE THEOLOGIC POINT OF VIEW.

. . .

It regards the criminal law, and indeed all law, as divinely ordained for all time by Manu or by Zeus, given by Jahweh to Moses or to Mohammed by Allah. Without entering into any theologic controversy, it may be granted as an historic fact that communities as a rule do not allow any one who pleases to decide what acts the divine will has ordained as criminal. That is a function left in fact to some recognized authorities, *e.g.*, priests, religiously trained judges, scribes who interpret certain texts, or the like. When the judgment of these authorities can in any way be questioned, there is some attempt to justify it on the basis of reason and human history. Thus great moralists of the Catholic church, such as St. Thomas, are willing to rest the distinction between what are and what are not crimes on mere authority. The divine Will is not despotically arbitrary, but is viewed as essentially rational and just. Hence in practice, theologic moralists appeal also to a rationalist view of human nature and experience.

Of course, there are theologians who insist that the essence of crime is the violation of the divine will, and that our frail human

Morris Raphael Cohen

reason cannot determine what is just or unjust for the Perfect Whole.

. . .

[However,] not all sins or violations of God's law are treated by theologians as crimes. Many evil acts are left to the direct punishment of the divine power here or hereafter, *e.g.*, covetousness, sex relations that are prohibited by the divine but not by human law, uncharitable attitudes to others, or failure to honor our parents.

. . .

2. THE POINT OF VIEW OF MORAL INTUITION.

Of those who have attempted to give us an absolute moral basis for a penal code, Kant is the foremost. He rejects the claims of all authority, secular or sacred, as inconsistent with the autonomy of the free will in ethical relations. The universal principle of all moral conduct, the categorical imperative to live so that the maxim of our action can become a principle of universal legislation, is not the source but rather a formula for what conscience, moral faith or "practical reason" immediately dictates as our duty in any specific case. In the end Kant falls back on the assumption that just as our moral conscience tells us that "Thou shalt not kill" is an absolute duty for the individual, so is "You shall kill the murderer" an equally absolute duty for the community. If a society is to be dissolved, the last murderer must be executed, else the blood of the victim will be on the heads of those who fail to do so.

While the Kantian theory is fairly close to the popular conscience, which often regard the prevailing *mores* as eternal laws of nature and reason, it fails as a guide in the determination of what specific acts are or ought to be treated as criminal.

. . .

We all agree that murder should be a crime. But such agreement is purely verbal unless we are agreed as to what is murder. Surely, not all instances of killing can be regarded as criminal, even on Kantian grounds. What distinction does he offer between excusable or even commendable homicide, and murder? No one today regards it as criminal to kill a man in self-defense. But the line between justifiable and unjustifiable fear of attack varies and is somewhat arbitrarily fixed by law.

.   .   .

I am not arguing that there is no such thing as morally revolting criminal murder, simply because in the nature of things there is not any sharp line to define it. That would be like arguing that there is no difference between day and night because there is no sharp line but rather a twilight zone between them. But I am calling attention to the inadequacy of the intuitionists' account which supposes that the common conscience has a clear and universally acknowledged answer as to when an act is or is not criminal.

Similar considerations hold in regard to theft. Apart from existing law, it is hard to say what does and what does not morally belong to another. Especially is this true in modern society when no man can point to anything and say, "This is exclusively the product of my own work in which I received no help from others." For, in fact, the author of a book, or the farmer who raises crops, has been supported by others during his work, and the relative value of his services is largely determined by the conditions created by the legal system. The notion of theft is relatively clear if it denotes taking something in a way that the law prohibits. But on purely moral grounds, apart from the law, it is by no means clear. Is it immoral for a manufacturer to copy the brilliant ideas that his rival has developed? If the design of a dress should be made property by law on the analogy of copyright, then imitating it will become theft. Among many primitive people there is no sense of private property in food. But it is a grave theft for one man to sing the personal song of another. Before the copyright laws, there was no conception of property in the literary composition itself. But when the legal rules in regard to property change, our moral duties in respect to it change.

Even if there were an absolute duty to obey the law always (which is dubious), legislation in a modern state would still have to go beyond traditional morality precisely because the latter does not offer sufficiently definite rules to regulate the life of people

Morris Raphael Cohen

that in fact have conflicting notions of right and wrong. We see this in the conflicting claims of different classes of society, *e.g.*, employer and employee. The truth is that our specific moral rules are not, as is often assumed, fixed for all time, but vary with changing conditions; and to maintain the order necessary for the good life, we must have the power to terminate controversies definitively. This involves rules that generally are not free from all elements of arbitrariness. Moral duties thus become more definite and clear after the law is enacted.

. . .

The Positivistic View

The positivists who wish to develop a science of criminology, and who believe that a science can deal only with facts of existence, find it difficult to admit that what is a crime is determined by legislation. They are thus forced to maintain that certain acts are criminal by nature. . . . The most thoroughgoing attempt to define natural crime is that of Garofalo who identifies it with those harmful actions which shock the moral sense of pity and probity of all civilized people. This moral sense, he holds, is not only unaffected by legislation which makes acts criminal that were not so before, but it is independent also of the circumstances and exigencies of any given epoch.[1] But how can positivists who identify science with determinism hold that social changes can occur without having any effect on what is deemed criminal? Garofalo admits the obvious and well authenticated fact that laws as to what constitutes crime do vary, but he thinks that the sentiments of pity and probity are the same among all civilized peoples. But who are civilized people? The naive answer is: those whose views are like our own,[2] from which it follows that our ancestors were not, and that other people with different conceptions of the requisites of pity and probity are not, civilized. This use of the term *civilized* seems amazingly naive but it is supported by the fashionable assumption that there is a cosmic law according to which all people must, regardless of diverse circumstances in their environment, evolve along the same uniform line of which we today represent the highest point. There is, however, no scientific evidence, logical or empirical, for any such law. As a matter of historic fact, not only do different "civilized'" peoples vary in their moral sense or sentiment as to what pity and probity require, but within any community there is a large variation in this respect. And which view, or way of feeling, will prevail depends on temporal changes that do not follow any one line, but are dependent on so many circumstances or factors that the future is unpredictable.

It is hardly necessary to show that hatred, pugnacity and brutality have not only been human traits at all times, but have been glorified in religion and literature. . . . Civilized Italians and Germans at the time that Garofalo wrote might have been shocked at the suggestion that their people would ever be capable of perpetrating the cruelties which Fascists and Nazis have exercisd on their opponents or even on innocent children who happened to live in Ethiopian villages or to be of Jewish ancestry. Yet . . . those responsible for these acts [were] national heroes and their cruelty [had] become the virtue of fortitude and patriotic devotion to the national state.

Within American society . . . there is a violent difference of feeling or sentiment in regard to birth control. There are those who consider it an abominable crime against nature, so that spreading information about it or abetting it should remain a penal offense. On the other hand, there are those who feel strongly that the best interests of society demand that such information be more widely diffused. The question as to which party will prevail cannot be answered by any law of evolution. . . . It depends upon such factors as legislation for improved and more ample housing.

In the end, Garofalo admits that besides natural crime there are many offenses which even civilized peoples do and should punish. The latter category will be found to include most of the offenses of our criminal law. Garofalo himself mentions not only political crimes, such as meetings to conspire against the government, seditious utterances, prohibited political demonstrations, refusal to perform required military or other services to the state, irregularities in the conduct of elections, etc., but also clandestine prostitution, smuggling, helping prisoners to escape, and the like. Now if all these are not natural crimes, our prisons contain very

Morris Raphael Cohen

many who have not committed any natural crime, while many who practice gross cruelty and improbity in business or elsewhere are not in prison at all. There is therefore no ground for the basic assumption of the "anthropologic" school of criminology, that the physical or mental traits common to prisoners are distinctive of natural criminals.

Positivistic sociologists and jurists as well as moralists often identify crime with acts which are contrary to the social interests or endanger social existence. But the most obvious reflection shows that this begs the question. Acts are criminal not because they *are* harmful, but because they are *deemed* harmful by those who make or interpret the law. The most serious crimes are sometimes those acts that in the judgment of enlightened and heroically unselfish people will best promote the common good, for example, criticism of the errors of established governments or churches. The history of the martyrs of religion and science amply indicates that acts deemed criminal at a given time in a given community often turn out to be of the greatest value for human life.

. . .

The Legal and the Moral

The foregoing discussion has indicated not only the impossibility of identifying the contents of the penal code with eternal morality or with any invariant nature of things, but also the difficulty of regarding legislation as purely arbitrary. Laws must often be changed if our rules of conduct are to facilitate the good life under changing conditions. How this is to be brought about in any given determinate social situation is not something known in advance, but must be determined in the processes of adjustment of our economic and political life. To be effective, the law must have back of it the organized force of the state against those who refuse to conform to it. This force, to be sure, can not be exercised for any long time unless the law itself is felt by a large part of the community to be in harmony with their prevailing customs and moral views. But we cannot escape legal penalties by trying to show in court that the law is unjust—for example, that the Fugitive Slave Law is inconsistent with the natural rights of man, with the Declaration of Independence, or with judicial dicta to the effect that our constitutional government rests on the principles of freedom and equality. . . . Those who are convinced of the existence of injustices in the established law and who struggle for their abolition are more often defeated by general inertia and unreasoning fear of change than by any rational counter argument. Even a convinced and determined majority may for a considerable time be unable to effect the legal change it desires. Hence while the criminal law, like other branches, is largely influenced by various moral views and sentiments, it cannot be identified with the latter—certainly not so long as we admit the possibility of unjust laws, so often used for purposes of oppression.

We hear a good deal of complaint about too many statutory crimes. These complaints are rather superficial, if not entirely thoughtless. We need new penal laws in cases where new conditions cannot be adequately dealt with by reliance on customary ways. This is obviously the case where, having introduced, *e.g.*, the secret ballot, we need to protect its secrecy, or having introduced telephony, we need to protect the privacy of communications. . . . Of course, legislative enactments as to crime may soon become obsolescent. But that is not an inherent evil if legislatures are as quick to repeal old laws as to enact new ones.

It is of the utmost importance that the law be just. But it is also important that our conception of justice and the nature of things be not so rigid as to prevent experiments in legislation to attain optimum conditions. For since we lack omniscience as to all the possible forms of social adjustment, experimentation, or the process of learning from experience, is indispensible. Law and morality can coincide only in the fundamental assumptions as to the proper procedure to enable us to correct our mistakes. Their common ideal is thus like that of science, to wit, a system that corrects itself by the process of testing principles by their consequences, and conversely, judging actual consequences in the light of principles.

Judges and jurists are tempted to take the position that they have to deal only with the existing law and need not be concerned with what the law should be. And this is, because of the principle of strict interpretation, easier to maintain in the criminal than in

Morris Raphael Cohen

any other branch of the law. Nevertheless, in the end it is impossible for any thoughtful and sensitive person dealing with the criminal law consistently to refrain from passing moral judgment. And such judgment exerts a powerful influence on the actual administration of the civil law. Yet, the legislative question of what acts should be made criminal and which should no longer be so treated cannot be settled by ethical principles alone. To apply the latter we need to have factual knowledge as to what are going to be the various consequences of the enactment or repeal to the different individuals that will be effected thereby. As the complexity and uncertainty of future social events generally make it next to impossible to obtain complete knowledge on this point, and as even the acquisition of some approximate knowledge open to our various social sciences involves enormous difficulties, moralists have tended to ignore this factual side altogether and have asserted that right is right regardless of all consequences.

. . .

It is easy enough to dismiss this as a lazy evasion or even as inherently absurd. It is more difficult to determine the amount of truth back of it which has made this act appeal to so many noble spirits. We can begin the latter task if we realize the inadequacy of the maxim that the good or ill of any act is to be judged by its consequences only. For this does not determine which consequences are to be deemed good and which are to be regarded as bad. And any discriminating test which applies to consequences should be applicable as well to the original act. If nothing has any inherent or intrinsic goodness in itself, neither can the consequences have it. The insistence on taking the consequences of an act into consideration is valid only if we realize that the problem is one of balancing immediate or present goods or ills against future ones. This is not a solution of the problem of ethical evaluation, but it calls our attention to our fundamental difficulty, which is that of determining the relative weights of the different interests that are often in conflict. The principle of the greatest good to the greatest number not only fails to give us a common denominator or common unit for the different kinds of value, but it is not possible to take all men and women equally into account.

Moral Aspects of Criminal Law

The obligation to those of our own family or community, state or nation generally seems to outweigh the interests of any equal number of others, and it does not seem that our obligation to remotely future generations is as great as to our more immediate ones. In the absence of any accurate determination of the relative weights of different obligations, all sorts of variations of opinion in this respect are possible.

When we consider any course of harmful conduct, our first impulse is to urge the enactment of a law to prohibit it; but on reflection we become aware of the enormous cost of bringing the criminal law into play. This includes not only the direct cost of policing and detection of crime, of judicial procedure and penal institutions, but also the indirect costs of social fear, spying, and the often unsavory effects of criminal proceedings, as for example, in the case of adultery.

Justice in Punishment

When we raise the question of punishment, we are met at the outset with the challenge, what right has the state to punish at all? This challenge sometimes comes from determinists who hold that the criminal could not help doing what he did, and sometimes it comes from those who maintain that society itself, through the conditions and institutions which it tolerates, is ultimately the cause and therefore responsible for the offensive acts.

Though it is customary for writers on ethics or penology to discuss in this connection the question of determinism versus free will, that is really not necessary for our purpose. When we are considering whether we should or should not punish certain individuals, it is irrelevant to argue that no one can help doing what he does. For against such an argument it is fair to reply as the irate father did to the wayward son who used it: "If no one can help doing what he does, then I can't help punishing you." The truth is that the ethical question is not the metaphysical one, whether the human will as such is or is not absolutely uncaused, but rather how to discriminate properly between those who should and those who should not be held accountable for legally prohibited acts. And here the prevailing ethical conscience . . .

Morris Raphael Cohen

seems to recognize a common sense distinction between voluntary and involuntary acts and generally holds that no one should be punished for any act in which his will did not enter.

. . .

The Principle of Individual Responsibility for Voluntary Acts

The main principle of just criminal punishment, one that is generally regarded as self-evident, is that one shall never be answerable for the crime of anyone else, and for his own only to the extent that it is voluntary. Before the advent of the . . . [Nazi] regime in Germany, it would have been easier to argue that these principles have been established as the result of the long process of human evolution. But . . . experience, if not critical reflection, should make us hesitate to ignore the past experience of the human race which has by no means always accepted the principle of no punishment except for individual voluntary action. . . . As a result of [World War I,] Germany was made to pay reparations, and the burden fell upon the innocent children who had no part and could in no way prevent the invasion of Belgium and the destruction which it involved. Was this unjust? By no means, if we recognize collective responsibility. It is obvious that in many relations the family or the nation rather than the individual is regarded as the moral unit. This does not deny the individual's responsibility for his own acts. But what acts are his own alone? It is not always possible to reduce social action to that of a number of independent atomic units each responsible for his own deeds, since in fact we are parts of each other's fate; and punishment or reward of any one individual naturally affects others.

. . .

Just as the history of religious literature impresses one with the fact that the most dangerous sins have been involuntary ones, so does the history of the criminal law reveal the fact that unintentional acts have been and to some extent still are punished. Even in Biblical law the man who unintentionally caused the death of another was subject to the same penalties as if he had done it intentionally. . . . In general the conditions of modern life and the emphasis on the subjective elements in our thought, have stressed the voluntary phase of conduct in the criminal law as elsewhere. We no longer punish animals or inanimate objects for injuries that result from them. The law no longer holds me responsible when I am deprived of the usual freedom of action by purely external physical forces, *e.g.*, when I am pushed or thrown. Similarly, I am not a free agent in the legal sense if purely physiologic factors prevent normally conscious action, *e.g.*, if I faint and fall or if my arm gets paralyzed and I cannot do the things that the law requires me to do. In more recent times the law is beginning to give more recognition to psychic hindrances to normally voluntary action. It is now considered useless cruelty to punish those who are so insane that they do not know what they are doing, or cannot distinguish between right and wrong. The deterrent value of such punishment would be almost nil. I say *almost*, for it may be argued that the deterrent effect of punishment depends upon the certainty of its being applied and that this is somewhat diminished when there is the ability to hire experts to convince a jury that the one who committed a criminal act was not sane at the time he did it.

.   .   .

The Retributive, Expiatory or Retaliatory Theory

Against the doubt as to whether the state has any right to punish at all, this theory maintains it to be a positive moral duty. It regards crime as a violation or disturbance of the divine or moral order. When Cain kills Abel, the very earth cries for vengeance. The moral order can be restored, or the violation atoned for only by inflicting evil (generally pain) upon the one guilty.

It is easy, far too easy, to dismiss this theory with the remark that it is a remnant of the barbaric conception of vengeance as an absolute duty. The sentiment of just vengeance or retribution is too deeply grounded in human nature, and embodied in too many moral and religious codes, to be thus lightly dismissed. It is profoundly foolish to suppose that anyone can by the free use of ugly epithets eradicate the desire to return a blow or to give active

Morris Raphael Cohen

expression to the resentment against injury. . . . In religion, this sentiment expresses itself in the orthodox theory that heaven would be less fair or that God's justice would be tarnished if there were no hell for the sinners, even when the sins are not the result of free will. Kant, who went to extremes in putting duty for duty's sake foremost, expressed an undoubtedly wide sentiment when he urged that we could not regard a world as moral if in it virtue went unrewarded or sin unpunished.

But does this retributive theory offer us a criterion whereby to discriminate between just and unjust punishment? Kant offers us the *jus talionis*, the principle of equality between the crime and the penalty. This sounds simple in the case of murder, a life for a life. But it is obviously not capable of being extended. Crime and punishment are different things. Can they really be equated? What penalty equals the crime of forgery, perjury or kidnapping? For the state to exercise the same amount of fraud or brutality on the criminal that the criminal exercised on his victim would be demoralizing to any community. . . . Moreover, if we accept the *jus talionis* as absolute, we make it immoral to pardon a criminal. Yet, the moral and religious conscience of mankind has always regarded charity or mercy as of supreme value and forgiveness has been preached as a divine virtue.

But if the old form of the *lex talionis*, an eye for an eye or a tooth for a tooth, sounds too barbaric today, may we not reformulate the retributive theory and put it thus: everyone is to be punished alike in proportion to the gravity of his offense or to the extent to which he has made others suffer? As Mittermeier, the leading criminalist of the early nineteenth century once put it, "The penalty which transgresses by even one atom the seriousness of the crime is unjust." But by what yardstick or measure can we determine the precise degree of offensiveness, or the exact amount of suffering that the criminal has imposed on the victim or on all those who depend on the latter? And how can we measure the severity of the punishment? Historically the plea for equality has meant a reaction or revulsion against the ignoring of it in previous criminal laws: let us have no more favorites, no more tariff of offenses with different rates according to the social standing of the offenders as in Anglo-Saxon England or in the France of the ancient regime. But what is the same punishment?

Is the same fine, for example, productive of the same effect on rich and poor? Or does the same number of years in prison have the same effect on different individuals regardless of their diverse temperaments or physique? If we took the principle of equality literally as absolute, we should not have any right to make any distinction in the punishment of a first offender and a hardened criminal, between a man acting under natural passion, for example an outraged father or husband, and a shrewdly calculating villain.

Despite the foregoing and other limitations of the retributive theory, it contains an element of truth which only sentimental foolishness can ignore. The sentiment that injuries should be avenged still prevails in the relations between nations and cannot be ignored within the life of any community. The problem of enlightened social morality is not to suppress the natural desires of human beings. Such suppression may itself be vain or cruel. Morality should aim to eliminate or minimize the brutality of natural vengeance or such results as would breed more general evil than the suffering of any particular injury. If the natural desire for vengeance is not met and satisfied by the orderly procedure of the criminal law we shall revert to the more bloody private vengeance of the feud and of the vendetta.

.   .   .

The Reform Theory

The most popular theory is that the proper aim of criminal procedure is to reform the criminal so that he may become adjusted to the social order. . . . The growing belief in education and in the healing powers of medicine encourages people to suppose that the delinquent may be re-educated to become a useful members of society. Even from the strictest economic point of view, individual men and women are the most valuable assets of any society. Is it not better to save them for a life of usefulness rather than punish them by imprisonment which generally makes them worse after they leave than before they entered?

There are, however, a number of highly questionable assump-

Morris Raphael Cohen

tions back of this theory which need to be critically examined. . . . Human beings are not putty that can be remolded at will by benevolent intentions. The overwhelming majority of our criminals have been exposed to the influence of our school system which we have at great cost tried to make as efficient as possible. Most criminals are also religious, as prison chaplains can testify. Yet with all our efforts school education and religion do not eliminate crime. It has not even been demonstrated that they are progressively minimizing it. Let us abandon the light-hearted pretension that any of us know how all cases of criminality can be readily cured, and ask the more modest and serious question: to what extent *can* criminals be re-educated or re-conditioned so that they can live useful lives? . . . And here we must not neglect the question of cost. When we refer to any measure as impracticable, we generally mean that the cost is too great. There is doubtless a tremendous expense in maintaining our present system of punishment. But this expense is not unlimited. Suppose that fiendish perpetrators of horrible crimes on children could be reformed by being sent first for several years to a special hospital. Will people vote large funds for such purposes when honest law-abiding citizens so often cannot get adequate hospital facilities? Suppose that we find that a certain social environment or that an elaborate college course will reform a burglar or gunman, would our community stand for the expense when so many worthy young people cannot afford to go to college because they have to go to work? We certainly should not give even the appearance of reward for criminality. Let us not forget that there is always a natural resentment in any society against those who have attacked it. Will people be satisfied to see one who is guilty of horrible crimes simply reformed, and not give vent to the social horror and resentment against the miscreant? It is difficult to believe that any such course would not result in a return to personal vengeance on the part of the relatives or friends of the victim.

A crucial instance of the inadequacy of the reform theory is the case of a man who we are fairly certain will not commit the given offense again. A burglar, for instance, in trying to enter a house breaks his leg so that he can never again engage in that enterprise. A man in desperation kills one who has ruined his family life and it becomes obvious that he will never again have a chance to be in a similar situation. Or take the case of one who can for any reason convince us that the criminal act itself has sobered him so that never again will he commit such an act. What more can reform achieve in these cases? Shall we then close the account and let the guilty one off? That would arouse not only general resentment but would open the gates to all sorts of abuses and would certainly so encourage crime that the suffering of innocent people would increase.

It has been argued that on the theory of protection to society there should be no punishment for one who is no longer capable of doing harm. But this ignores the fact that the law contemplates not only the individual at the bar but all others who might be tempted to commit similar offenses even under conditions not quite the same.

Punishment as a Means of Preventing Crime

If we look at the criminal as one who assails or endangers the proper life of the community, it is not only our right but our duty to defend, if not ourselves, at least our dependents. Primitive communities effect this by getting rid of the unruly member through death or outlawry. In the course of time, this is largely replaced by fine or imprisonment. Societies, however, never abandon the effort to minimize crime by punishing the offenders. We do this by incapacitating the criminal either through death or detention, and by deterring him and others through the example of the painful consequences of crime to the criminal.

Few have ever argued against the right of society to protect itself and prevent crime by detaining the criminal at least so long as there is some reason to suppose that it would be dangerous to set him free. But the right to punish anyone to deter him or others from future acts, has been widely challenged on grounds of (1) justice and (2) utility.

1. Kant and others have urged that it cannot be just to punish anyone except for a wrong actually committed; and much less can it be just to punish Peter in order to prevent Paul from attempting any crime. This is an appeal to a principle so seemingly self-evident that most writers on the criminal law have preferred

Morris Raphael Cohen

to ignore the objection rather than to meet it. But modern science has made enormous progress by learning to distrust self-evident principles. We need not, therefore, hesitate to challenge Kant's assumption in this case. Why should we not inflict pain on A if that is the only way of securing the safety of the society of which he is a part, or preserving the general conditions of desirable life on which he depends for all his goods? We tax an old bachelor for the support of the education of other men's children and we conscript our youth and put them in positions where they will be killed in order that others shall be able to live. Consider the case of the typhoid carrier Mary who spreads the germs of that dreadful disease wherever she goes. Do we not by detaining her and limiting her freedom in effect punish her for her misfortune rather than for her fault? We are at all times inflicting pains on innocent people in order to promote the common good, in time of peace, as well as in war.

. . .

This does not mean the complete abandonment of the principle that one should be responsible only for his own voluntary act. That would be opening the floodgates to the most extreme and outrageous injustice. But our principle may be viewed not as an isolated independent absolute, but as the statement of a general condition of the social order necessary for the good life. Certainly nothing would be so detrimental to the effective enforcement of the law than the feeling in any community that some may commit crimes and others will be punished. . . . A state has as much right to reform a criminal, even against his will, as to educate a child or to compel one with a contagious disease to be quarantined or to undergo curative treatment. And while it would destroy the basis of all that we hold dear in civilized life to make one man suffer merely that another be advantaged thereby, no society under present conditions can achieve the good of the whole without causing more suffering to some than to others. . . . Unfortunately, however, the actual choice that life presents to any society is seldom a clear issue between absolute good and absolute evil but generally a choice between alternatives, all of which are imperfect embodiments of justice or of the highest good. Wisdom consists in such a balancing of rival considerations, that the total amount of evil is minimized.

2. We come now to the much more common objection that punishment does not in fact deter either the one punished, or others. . . . There are more dangerous occupations than crime; yet people are not deterred from taking the risk.

Those who urge this objection illustrate the abuse of absolutism in the discussion of practical issues. To prove the utility of medicine it is not necessary to prove that it always prevents death and cures all instances of disease. It is enough if life is often prolonged and suffering sometimes diminished by its wise use. And to justify punishment it is not necessary to prove that it *always* prevents crime by its deterrent quality. It is enough to indicate that there would be more crime if all punishment were abolished. Now we may ignore the positivistic dogma that punishment cannot possibly have any deterrent effect, that criminals are bound to commit crimes. That kind of fatalism is not only opposed by human experience but it is not even consistent with scientific determinism which it professes to follow. All experiments on animals as well as the historic observations of human experience indicate that fear of painful consequences is as effective a force in life as is the prospect of pleasant rewards. We are living at a time when terror on a large scale has succeeded in removing the effective temptation to rebellion. When in 1920 the police of Boston struck and left their posts, a lot of young men broke store windows and possessed themselves of goods which they tried to sell at prices which no trained or professional criminal would demand. Sir James F. Stephen has suggested the following query. Suppose a burglar feels that he might catch a cold that would incapacitate him for as long a period as the usual prison term for burglary. Would that not deter him? Of course that largely depends on the exercise of the imagination. And the law, if wisely administered, should dramatize its punishment. It is the fact that all men live more or less in their imagination and any imaginative realization that one will be hissed off the social stage or suffer pain is bound to act as a strong deterrent. In this connection, it is well to repeat the frequently-made, but still just observation that not only the severity but the certainty of punishment is a factor in the case. Men will risk their lives if they

Morris Raphael Cohen

think that there is some chance of winning something. And while many will take very "long" chances, as in lotteries, it is a fact that professional crime, like any other business, ceases to grow in extent when the chances of failure rise. That is why bandits do not try to rob the United States Treasury, or the Mint.

In general we know that just as certain factors will tend to increase crime, so certain factors will tend to diminish the amount of it; and that the penalties of the law, if enforced, constitute one of these minimizing causes. There is no doubt that the abolition of the police force, or the lessening of their vigilance or competence to detect the crime and to apprehend the criminal will tend to increase the amount of crime. Thus not only the specific penalty but the question of the procedure or mechanism of its enforcement, the ease of its proof, and the likelihood of finding proper witnesses are all determinants.

It is true that men follow the *mores* apart from any fear of punishment, because normally that seems the only way in which one can act. But in a heterogeneous society, where diverse moral standards prevail and where conditions are rapidly changing, the temptation to depart from the hitherto accepted ways rises rapidly; and the fear of social disapproval decreases even more rapidly when we associate only with those who have the same inclinations that we have.

Punishment as Reprobation

We may look upon punishment as a form of communal expression. An organized group, like an individual, needs to give vent to its feeling of horror, revulsion or disapproval. We turn away in disgust at certain uncleanly or unaesthetic traits of an individual and exclude him from our company without inquiring as to whether it is within his power to prevent being repulsive. It is only personal love like that of a mother that can train itself to overlook repellent features or devote time and energy to eliminate them. It is *one* of the functions of the criminal law to give expression to the collective feeling of revulsion toward certain acts, even when they are not very dangerous—for example, buggery. There are, of course, various forms and degrees of social disapproval and it is not always necessary to bring the legal machinery into operation. But at some point or other the collective feeling must be embodied in some objective communal act. By and large such expression of disapproval is a deterrent. But deterrence here is secondary. Expression is primary. Such disapproval need not be cruel or take extreme forms. An enlightened society will recognize the futility of severely punishing unavoidable retrogression in human dignity. But it is vain to preach to any society that it must suppress its feelings. In all our various social relations, in business, in public life, in our academic institutions and even in a church, people are rewarded for being attractive and therefore penalized for not being so.

The reprobative theory will explain why it is difficult to repeal penal statutes where no one believes that the punishment will have any reformatory effect on the offender or any deterrent effect on others and consequent diminution of the number of offenses. An example of this is the law against suicide. There are also statutes such as those making adultery a crime which the community does not want to see enforced. For the publicity in the matter would do more harm than good. Yet people will not vote to repeal it; for such repeal would look like removing the social disapproval.

. . .

If civilization means rationality in the elimination of needless cruelty, then our methods of punishment must certainly undergo profound changes even though they cannot cease to be punishments. Thus it is progress if we stop branding criminals, even though we keep their records; and it would be retrogression if we went back to the whipping post, the stocks, the practice of breaking men's bones on the wheel and the other old forms of torture. While the sterilization of certain kinds of criminals may be indicated, it may also open the gates for unlimited cruelty.

. . .

The punishment provided by the criminal law is a sad necessity. But even if it is bitter medicine, there is no wisdom in unlimited doses of it. It is well to realize that the mere conviction

Morris Raphael Cohen

of a crime brings social dishonor, and that may in some, though not in all cases, be sufficient. Thus, impeachment and removal from office does not necessarily demand subsequent imprisonment. But above all it is needlessly cruel to add to human temptation, or to make it more difficult for unfortunates to overcome the temptation, and then to punish them for it. Of course, every progress in civilization may add to the difficulties of adapting ourselves to the new social standards; and it may be argued that it is of the very essence of civilization that we should increase the temptation and with it the power of self-control. That might be claimed as the superiority of the West over the East in regard to sex relations. But after all civilization may be purchased at too great a price. Of what value is a civilization if it leads to physical and moral misery? May not one reverse the argument and say that only those social arrangements represent true progress which make life more serene and less tortured? So judged, many of the improvements of civilization might well be condemned. And the criminal law would offer a great deal of evidence along this line.

The Individualization of Punishment

Dominated by the reaction against the abstractness of the classical emphasis on equality and influenced by the prevailing tendency to think of crime as a disease, the idea has recently spread that in punishment we should pay more attention to the individual criminal rather than to the abstract crime. Just as medicine is turning from specific remedies, the same for everybody, to greater emphasis on individual diagnosis and treatment, so penologists are urging that since no given punishment has the same effect on different individuals, it would be more humane as well as realistic to make the punishment fit the criminal rather than the crime.

While this theory has elements of novelty in its formulation and application, it is not altogether new in principle. Theoretically it is but a re-assertion of the old idea of equity as the correction of the undue rigor of the law, a corrective to the injustice which results from the fact that the abstract rule cannot take into account all the specific circumstances that are relevant to the case. It assumes its simplest and oldest form in the pardoning power.

Strictly speaking, the pardoning power is inconsistent with the view that punishment is an absolute duty prescribed by the moral law for all those found guilty by the proper tribunal.

. . .

Let us look at the matter a little more closely. Let us distinguish the pardoning power from the corrective justice exercised by a court when it frees a man because of a flaw in the evidence or procedure by which he has been condemned. When the technicalities of legal administration prevent courts from correcting such legal errors, the Chief Executive exercises the same judicial power when, after a hearing, he pardons the person convicted.

There are cases of undoubted technical guilt, where the results of the strict application of abstract law are felt to be shocking to our moral sense. The abstract law cannot take difficulties and temptations into account, but a humane administration of it must if it is to keep the respect of the people. Theft is always a crime but few of us would be shocked at the pardoning of a mother who stole food to prevent her children from starving. Nor would we feel that justice suffered if an escaped convict, like Jean Valjean, were pardoned after he had for so long shown the qualities of a good citizen as mayor of his town. On the contrary, we think the administration of justice inept if he is returned to the galleys. The pardoning power is also generally regarded as necessary or desirable in mass phenomena, as in the case of a general pardon for rebels, rioters, or whole classes of prisoners. It is generally issued in the form of a favor but it is actuated by a desire to promote good will to the government by placating discontented elements or diminishing the current amount of resentment. In the main, amnesty is like making peace with an army with which one has fought. If we have to live with people, it is well to have their good will. But if we allow such acts of wholesale pardon, we have abandoned absolute theories of punishment.

. . .

When all this is said, it remains true that the pardoning power can be, and has been, a prolific source of injustice. We need not refer to the Texas governor who pardoned hundreds of criminals for his political advantage. There are other and subtler forms of

Morris Raphael Cohen

injustice in the exercise of the pardoning power. A young man of good family is convicted. Then all sorts of good people intervene with testimonials which a less advantageously situated individual cannot get. When the rich or those who have political influence can thus "get away with murder," the general expectation of justice through law tends to disintegrate. . . . If the mitigation of the rigor of the law is to be done intelligently and justly on the basis of thorough knowledge, should it not also be given to the judge who has heard all the evidence in the case and has had the guilty one before him? The recognition of this has led [to increasing] the discretionary power of the judge in imposing sentence. Instead of fixing the penalties for diverse crimes, legislatures now tend to fix upper and lower limits between which the judge can determine by himself the proper sentence. He may even suspend sentence altogether in some cases, or put the guilty one on probation.

Any sentence, however, that the judge imposes, involves more or less a guess as to its effect on the character of the convict. But a board of prison officials who have had an opportunity to study the actual conduct of the prisoner ought to be in a better position as to when he is ready to leave prison fit to reenter the "free" world and engage in its lawful activities. On this theory are based the various forms of our parole system.

Any plausible attempt to reform something that has worked as horribly as our prison system should have its frailties viewed with benevolent patience. Given time and experience, the new movement may overcome many of the evils which it has already manifested, such as the abuse of discretion by judges and parole boards, and the number of paroled prisoners who commit new crimes. But it is always helpful to clarify the issue by critically examining fundamental ideas.

1. The advocates of individualization of punishment should beware of overworking the analogy between crime and disease. Crime is not the direct result of physiologic factors but depends directly on social institutions. It is foolish to talk glibly of treating the criminal according to his individual nature when in fact we have no means of adequately knowing it. The physician does not need to know all about a man's individual character. In his diagnosis he looks for very definite facts of a recurrent

character and once that is determined, the treatment moves along a limited number of alternatives. But can any judge be honestly said to know the character of a person convicted sufficiently to determine what precise treatment is needed? Similarly with parole boards. A man's conduct in prison is not always the best indication of what he will do when released. And in point of fact prison officials can be and have been influenced by political and social pressure.

2. The ideology of individualization tends to an extremely nominalistic position. That is, it tends to forget the logical fact that we are apt to have more reliable knowledge about classes than about individuals and that for certain purposes classes rather than individuals are relevant. If our country is invaded, we try to take measures against the invading army or armies. The treatment of individual soldiers is determined by these general policies. Of course, we may avoid the false ideology criticized here by admitting all this and saying that the law needs more individualization of treatment than exists at present. But it is of the utmost importance not to forget that the abuse of discretion was one of the principal causes which led to the revolt expressed in the classical views on penology—a revolt that has undoubtedly done much for the humanization of the criminal law and its administration. And it would be a great calamity if this gain were frittered away by hastily conceived novelties.

. . .

The criminal law represents the pathology of civilization. But just as the study of animal pathology has illumined normal physiology, and has been helpful in physical hygiene, or just as the study of insanity has thrown light on mental processes and has been at times somewhat helpful in mental hygiene, so the study of criminality may illumine normal human motives and be helpful in bringing about just humane social relations. The necessary conditions for this study, however, is the most rigorous, intellectual integrity, the concentration on seeing the facts as they are, regardless of natural sentimental predilections. We must learn to live in an imperfect world, though we dare not relax the effort to make it better.

HENRY M. HART, JR.

The Aims of the Criminal Law

The statement has been made, as if in complaint, that "there is hardly a penal code that can be said to have a single basic principle running through it." But it needs to be clearly seen that this is simply a fact, and not a misfortune. A penal code that reflected only a single basic principle would be a very bad one. Social purposes can never be single or simple, or held unqualifiedly to the exclusion of all other social purposes, and an effort to make them so can result only in the sacrifice of other values which also are important. Thus, to take only one example, the purpose of preventing any particular kind of crime, or crimes generally, is qualified always by the purposes of avoiding the conviction of the innocent and of enhancing that sense of security throughout the society which is one of the prime functions of the manifold safeguards of American criminal procedure. And the same thing would be true even if the dominant purpose of the criminal law were thought to be the rehabilitation of offenders rather than the prevention of offenses.

Reprinted with permission from a symposium, "Sentencing," appearing in *Law and Contemporary Problems*, Vol. 23, pp. 401–11 (1958), published by the Duke University School of Law, Durham.

Hart was Professor of Law at Harvard University. He was coauthor (with Herbert Wechsler) of The Federal Courts and the Federal System (1953).

Henry M. Hart, Jr.

Examination of the purposes commonly suggested for the criminal law will show that each of them is complex and that none may be thought of as wholly excluding the others. Suppose, for example, that the deterrence of offenses is taken to be the chief end. It will still be necessary to recognize that the rehabilitation of offenders, the disablement of offenders, the sharpening of the community's sense of right and wrong, and the satisfaction of the community's sense of just retribution may all serve this end by contributing to an ultimate reduction in the number of crimes. Even socialized vengeance may be accorded a marginal role, if it is understood as the provision of an orderly alternative to mob violence.

The problem, accordingly, is one of the priority and relationship of purposes as well as of their legitimacy—of multivalued rather than of single-valued thinking.

There is still another range of complications which are ignored if an effort is made to formulate any single "theory" or set of "principles" of criminal law. The purpose of having principles and theories is to help in organizing thought. In the law, the ultimate purpose of thought is to help in deciding upon a course of action. In the criminal law, as in all law, questions about the action to be taken do not present themselves for decision in an institutional vacuum. They arise rather in the context of some established and specific procedure of decision: in a constitutional convention; in a legislature; in a prosecuting attorney's office; in a court charged with the determination of guilt or innocence; in a sentencing court; before a parole board; and so on. This means that each agency of decision must take account always of its own place in the institutional system and of what is necessary to maintain the integrity and workability of the system as a whole. A complex of institutional ends must be served, in other words, as well as a complex of substantive social ends.

We can get our broadest view of the aims of the criminal law if we look at them from the point of view of the makers of a constitution—of those who are seeking to establish sound foundations for a tolerable and durable social order. From this point of view, these aims can be most readily seen, as they need to be seen, in their relation to the aims of the good society generally.

In this setting, the basic question emerges: Why should the good society make use of the method of the criminal law at all?

The question posed raises preliminarily an even more fundamental inquiry: What do we mean by "crime" and "criminal"? Or, put more accurately, what should we understand to be "the method of the criminal law," the use of which is in question? This latter way of formulating the preliminary inquiry is more accurate, because it pictures the criminal law as a process, a way of doing something, which is what it is. A great deal of intellectual energy has been misspent in an effort to develop a concept of crime as "a natural and social phenomenon" abstracted from the functioning system of institutions which make use of the concept and give it impact and meaning. But the criminal law, like all law, is concerned with the pursuit of human purposes through the forms and modes of social organization, and it needs always to be thought about in that context as a method or process of doing something.

What then are the characteristics of this method?

1. The method operates by means of a series of directions, or commands, formulated in general terms, telling people what they must or must not do. Mostly, the commands of the criminal law are "must-nots," or prohibitions, which can be satisfied by inaction. "Do not murder, rape, or rob." But some of them are "musts," or affirmative requirements, which can be satisfied only by taking a specifically, or relatively specifically, described kind of action. "Support your wife and children," and "File your income tax return."

2. The commands are taken as valid and binding upon all those who fall within their terms when the time comes for complying with them, whether or not they have been formulated in advance in a single authoritative set of words. They speak to members of the community, in other words, in the community's behalf, with all the power and prestige of the community behind them.

3. The commands are subject to one or more sanctions for disobedience which the community is prepared to enforce.

Thus far, it will be noticed, nothing has been said about the criminal law which is not true also of a large part of the non-

Henry M. Hart, Jr.

criminal, or civil, law. The law of torts, the law of contracts, and almost every other branch of private law that can be mentioned operate, too, with general directions prohibiting or requiring described types of conduct, and the community's tribunals enforce these commands. What, then, is distinctive about the method of the criminal law?

Can crimes be distinguished from civil wrongs on the ground that they constitute injuries to society generally which society is interested in preventing? The difficulty is that society is interested also in the due fulfillment of contracts and the avoidance of traffic accidents and most of the other stuff of civil litigation. The civil law is framed and interpreted and enforced with a constant eye to these social interests. Does the distinction lie in the fact that proceedings to enforce the criminal law are instituted by public officials rather than private complainants? The difficulty is that public officers may also bring many kinds of "civil" enforcement actions—for an injunction, for the recovery of a "civil" penalty, or even for the detention of the defendant by public authority. Is the distinction, then, in the peculiar character of what is done to people who are adjudged to be criminals? The difficulty is that, with the possible exception of death, exactly the same kinds of unpleasant consequences, objectively considered, can be and are visited upon unsuccessful defendants in civil proceedings.

If one were to judge from the notions apparently underlying many judicial opinions, and the overt language even of some of them, the solution of the puzzle is simply that a crime is anything which is *called* a crime, and a criminal penalty is simply the penalty provided for doing anything which has been given that name. So vacant a concept is a betrayal of intellectual bankruptcy. Certainly, it poses no intelligible issue for a constitution-maker concerned to decide whether to make use of "the method of the criminal law." Moreover, it is false to popular understanding, and false also to the understanding embodied in existing constitutions. By implicit assumptions that are more impressive than any explicit assertions, these constitutions proclaim that a conviction for crime is a distinctive and serious matter—a something, and not a nothing. What is that something?

4. What distinguishes a criminal from a civil sanction and all

that distinguishes it, it is ventured, is the judgment of community condemnation which accompanies and justifies its imposition.

. . .

If this is what a "criminal" penalty is, then we can say readily enough what a "crime" is. It is not simply anything which a legislature chooses to call a "crime." It is not simply antisocial conduct which public officers are given a responsibility to suppress. It is not simply any conduct to which a legislature chooses to attach a "criminal" penalty. It is conduct which, if duly shown to have taken place, will incur a formal and solemn pronouncement of the moral condemnation of the community.

5. The method of the criminal law, of course, involves something more than the threat (and, on due occasion, the expression) of community condemnation of antisocial conduct. It involves, in addition, the threat (and, on due occasion, the imposition) of unpleasant physical consequences, commonly called punishment. But . . . these added consequences take their character as punishment from the condemnation which precedes them and serves as the warrant for their infliction. Indeed, the condemnation plus the added consequences may well be considered, compendiously, as constituting the punishment. Otherwise, it would be necessary to think of a convicted criminal as going unpunished if the imposition or execution of his sentence is suspended.

In traditional thought and speech, the ideas of crime and punishment have been inseparable; the consequences of conviction for crime have been described as a matter of course as "punishment." The Constitution of the United States and its amendments, for example, use this word or its verb form in relation to criminal offenses no less than six times. Today, "treatment" has become a fashionable euphemism for the older, ugly word. This bowdlerizing of the Constitution and of conventional speech may serve a useful purpose in discouraging unduly harsh sentences and emphasizing that punishment is not an end in itself. But to the extent that it dissociates the treatment of criminals from the social condemnation of their conduct which is implicit in their conviction, there is danger that it will confuse thought and do a disservice.

Henry M. Hart, Jr.

At least under existing law, there is a vital difference between the situation of a patient who has been committed to a mental hospital and the situation of an inmate of a state penitentiary. The core of the difference is precisely that the patient has not incurred the moral condemnation of his community, whereas the convict has.

We are in a position now to restate the basic question confronting our hypothetical constitution-makers. The question is whether to make use, in the projected social order, of the method of discouraging undesired conduct and encouraging desired conduct by means of the threat—and, when necessary, the fulfillment of the threat—of the community's condemnation of an actor's violation of law and of punishment, or treatment, of the actor as blameworthy for having committed the violation.

The question, like most legal questions, is one of alternatives. Perhaps the leading alternative, to judge from contemporary criticism of the penal law, would be to provide that people who behave badly should simply be treated as sick people to be cured, rather than as bad people to be condemned and punished. A constitutional guarantee to accomplish this could be readily drafted: "No person shall be subjected to condemnation or punishment for violation of law, but only to curative-rehabilitative treatment." Would the establishment of this new constitutional liberty be well-advised?

Paradoxically, this suggested guarantee, put forward here as an abandonment of the method of the criminal law, is not far removed from a point of view that has been widely urged in recent years as a proper rationale of existing law.

. . .

This suggests the possibility of a modified version of the constitutional guarantee in question, directing that "The corrective theory of crime and criminal justice, based upon a conception of multiple causation and curative-rehabilitative treatment, shall predominate in legislation and in judicial and administrative practices." Would such a provision be workable? Would it be wise?

Any theory of criminal justice which emphasizes the criminal rather than the crime encounters an initial and crucial difficulty when it is sought to be applied at the stage of legislative enactment, where the problem in the first instance is to define and grade the crime. How *can* a conception of multiple causation and curative-rehabilitative treatment predominate in the definition and grading of crimes, let alone serve as the sole guide? But even if it were possible to gauge in advance the types of conduct to be forbidden by the expected need for reformation of those who will thereafter engage in them, would it be sensible to try to do so? Can the content of the law's commands be rationally determined with an eye singly or chiefly to the expected deficiencies of character of those who will violate them? Obviously not. The interests of society in having certain things not done or done are also involved.

Precisely because of the difficulties of relating the content of the law's commands to the need for reformation of those who violate them, a curative-rehabilitative theory of criminal justice tends always to depreciate, if not to deny, the significance of these general formulations and to focus attention instead on the individual defendant at the time of his apprehension, trial, and sentence. This has in it always a double danger—to the individual and to society. The danger to the individual is that he will be punished, or treated, for what he is or is believed to be, rather than for what he has done. If his offense is minor but the possibility of his reformation is thought to be slight, the other side of the coin of mercy can become cruelty. The danger to society is that the effectiveness of the general commands of the criminal law as instruments for influencing behavior so as to avoid the necessity for enforcement proceedings will be weakened.

This brings us to the crux of the issue confronting our supposed constitution-makers. The commands of the criminal law are commands which the public interest requires people to comply with. This being so, will the public interest be adequately protected if the legislature is allowed only to say to people, "If you do not comply with any of these commands, you will merely be considered to be sick and subjected to officially-imposed rehabilitative treatment in an effort to cure you"? Can it be adequately protected if the legislature is required to say, "If you do not comply, your own personal need for cure and rehabilitation will be the predominating factor in determining what happens to you"? Or should the legislature be enabled to say, "If you violate any of these laws and the violation is culpable, your conduct will receive the formal and solemn condemnation of the community as morally blameworthy, and you will be subjected to whatever punishment, or treatment, is appropriate to vindicate the law and to further its various purposes"?

On the sheerly pragmatic ground of the need for equipping the proposed social order with adequate tools to discourage undesired conduct, a responsible constitution-maker assuredly would hesitate long before rejecting the third of these possibilities in favor of either of the first two. To be sure, the efficacy of criminal punishment as a deterrent has often been doubted. But it is to be observed that the doubts are usually expressed by those who are thinking from the restrospective, sanction-imposing point of view. From this point of view, it is natural to be impressed by the undoubted fact that many people do become criminals, and will continue to do so, in spite of all the threats of condemnation and of treatment-in-consequence-of-condemnation that society can offer. But the people who do *not* commit crimes need to be taken into account, too. A constitution-maker, thinking from the prospective point of view of the primary, as distinguished from the remedial, law has especially to think of them, if he is to see his problem whole. So doing, he will be likely to regard the desire of the ordinary man to avoid the moral condemnation of his community, as well as the physical pains and inconveniences of punishment, as a powerful factor in influencing human behavior which can scarcely with safety be dispensed with. Whether he is right or wrong in this conclusion, he will align himself, in reaching it, with the all but universal judgment, past and present, of mankind.

Moreover, there are other and larger considerations to be weighed in the balance. The case against a primarily rehabilitative theory of criminal justice is understated if it is rested solely on the need for the threat of criminal conviction as an instrument of deterrence of antisocial conduct. Deterrence, it is ventured, ought not to be thought of as the overriding and ultimate purpose of the criminal law, important though it is. For deterrence is negative, whereas the purposes of law are positive. And the practical fact must be faced that many crimes, as just recognized, are undeterrable. The grim negativism and the frequent seeming futility of the criminal law when it is considered simply as a means of preventing undesired behavior no doubt help to explain why sensitive people, working at close hand with criminals, tend so often to embrace the more hopeful and positive tenets of a curative-rehabilitative philosophy.

However, a different view is possible if an effort is made to fit the theory of criminal justice into a theory of social justice—to see the purposes of the criminal law in their relation to the purposes of law as a whole. Man is a social animal, and the function of law is to enable him to realize his potentialities as a human being through the forms and modes of social organization. It is important to consider how the criminal law serves this ultimate end.

Human beings, of course, realize their potentialities in part through enjoyment of the various satisfactions of human life, both tangible and intangible, which existing social resources and their own individual capacities make available to them. Yet, the social resources of the moment are always limited, and human capacities for enjoyment are limited also. Social resources for providing the satisfactions of life and human capacities for enjoying them, however, are always susceptible of enlargement, so far as we know, without eventual limit. Man realizes his potentialities most significantly in the very process of developing these resources and capacities—by making himself a functioning and participating member of his community, contributing to it as well as drawing from it.

What is crucial in this process is the enlargement of each individual's capacity for effectual and responsible decision. For it is only through personal, self-reliant participation, by trial and error, in the problems of existence, both personal and social, that the capacity to participate effectively can grow. Man learns wisdom in choosing by being confronted with choices and by being made aware that he must abide the consequences of his choice. In the training of a child in the small circle of the family, this principle is familiar enough. It has the same validity in the training of an adult in the larger circle of the community.

Seen in this light, the criminal law has an obviously significant and, indeed, a fundamental role to play in the effort to create the good society. For it is the criminal law which defines the minimum conditions of man's responsibility to his fellows and holds him to that responsibility. The assertion of social responsibility has value in the treatment even of those who have become criminals. It has far greater value as a stimulus to the great bulk of mankind to abide by the law and to take pride in so abiding.

This, then, is the critical weakness of the two alternative constitutional provisions that have been discussed—more serious by far than losing or damaging a useful, even if imperfect, instrument of deterrence. The provisions would undermine the foundation of a free society's effort to build up each individual's sense of responsibility as a guide and a stimulus to the constructive development of his capacity for effectual and fruitful decision.

If the argument which has been made is accepted and it is concluded that explicit abandonment of the concept of moral condemnation of criminal conduct would be unsound, what then is to be said of the soundness of an interpretation of existing law which tries to achieve a similar result by indirection—treating the purpose of cure and rehabilitation as predominating, while sweeping under the rug the hard facts of the social need and the moral rightness of condemnation and of treatment which does not dilute the fact of condemnation?

It is evident that the view which the constitution-maker takes of the function of criminal law will be important in shaping his attitude on inclusion in the document of many of the traditional guarantees of fair procedure in criminal trials. Most of these, such, for example, as indictment by a grand jury or even trial by a petit jury, are largely or wholly irrelevant to the offender's need for, or his susceptibility to, curative-rehabilitative treatment. Indeed, as already suggested, even the basic concept that criminality must rest upon criminal conduct, duly proved to have taken place, would come into question under a purely rehabilitative theory. Present laws for the confinement and care of mentally-ill persons do not insist upon this requirement, and, if criminality were to be equated with sickness of personality generally, its rationale would not be readily apparent. But if what is in issue is the community's solemn condemnation of the accused as a defaulter in his obligations to the community, then the default to be condemned ought plainly to consist of overt conduct, and not simply of a condition of mind; and the fact of default should be proved with scrupulous care. The safeguards which now surround the procedure of proof of criminality or the essentials of them, in other words, will appear to be appropriate.

Should the constitution-makers go further and prescribe not only procedural safeguards, but substantive limitations on the kinds of conduct that can be declared criminal? For the most part, American constitution-makers have not done this. They have relied, instead, primarily on the legislature's sense of justice. Secondarily, they have relied on the courts to understand what a crime is and, so, by appropriate invocation of the broad constitutional injunction of due process, to prevent an arbitrary application of the criminal sanction when the legislature's sense of justice has failed.

WILLIAM E. NELSON

Emerging Notions of Modern Criminal Law in the Revolutionary Era

Historians have devoted a great deal of attention to studying the law of the early American colonies, especially the criminal law,[1] and no jurisdiction has commanded as much attention as the Puritan colony of Massachusetts Bay.[2] One reason for this interest, perhaps, is that Puritan criminal law was vastly different from the criminal law of today. Religion "was a way of life"[3] for the early settlers of Massachusetts, and all of the Bay Colony's institutions reflected its religious values. Thus, the early settlers "adopt[ed] the Judicial Laws of Moses which were given to the Israelites of Old . . . [and] punished Adultery . . . [and] Blasphemy, with Death. . . ."[4] They equated crime with sin and thought of the state as the arm of God on earth. Modern law, on the other hand, rarely seeks to enforce morality and has thrown up a "wall of separation"[5] between religion and the state. Only incidently is today's criminal considered a sinner; first and foremost, he is regarded as a threat to the peace and order of society.

Reprinted with permission from *New York University Law Review*, vol. 42, pp. 450–66 (1967).

Notes to this Selection will be found on pages 423–425.

Nelson is a member of the New York bar and a graduate student in History at Harvard University.

William E. Nelson

The purpose of this article is to study the forces which have altered criminal law since early colonial times—a subject much neglected in our legal history. Such a study requires close attention to trial court records, and the large number of these records necessitates limitation to one locality. Middlesex County, Massachusetts, was chosen largely for convenience, but also because it seems to have been more typical of Massachusetts and perhaps of the United States during the period under study than, for example, urban Boston or frontier Berkshire.

The court records indicate that most of the developments which transformed Puritan criminal law into the criminal law of today occurred during the three decades following the American Revolution. This article will concentrate upon that period. Of course changes, sometimes important ones, had occurred earlier, but nonetheless, the criminal law of pre-Revolutionary Massachusetts was remarkably similar to that of the Puritan era. The old Puritan ethic remained strong enough in the 1750s so that crime was still looked upon as sin; the criminal, as a sinner; and criminal law, as the earthly arm of God. Criminal law surely was not the tool of the royal government in Boston, which was unconcerned with the outcome of most cases and, in any event, had little real power to influence that outcome. As a result, the chief function of the courts, the primary law-enforcement agencies, remained, as in the early colonial era, the identification and punishment of sinners.

By 1810, some thirty years after the Revolution, a system of law enforcement similar to today's had emerged. This article will trace the development of the new system . . . [and] the shift in the law's basic function between 1760 and 1810, from the preservation of morality to the protection of property.

.   .   .

A. Criminal Law at the Close of the
Colonial Period: 1760–1774

Describing the criminal law of pre-Revolutionary Massachusetts in terms that will have meaning for the reader and that also

would have been meaningful to the Revolutionary generation is a matter of some difficulty. A scheme for the classification of crimes must be adopted for today's reader; but, unfortunately, no such scheme was ever developed in colonial Massachusetts. Blackstone did develop a classification scheme in England, however, and, by the Revolution, lawyers in Massachusetts knew of it. It included offenses against God and religion, offenses against government, offenses against public justice, offenses against public trade and health, homicide, offenses against the person, and offenses against habitations and other private property.

Most cases were within the category of offenses against God and religion. Between 1760 and 1774 there were 370 prosecutions in Middlesex in the Superior and General Sessions Courts. Of these, 210 were for fornication. Since only mothers of illegitimate children were brought into court, one might think that fornication was punished not because it offended God but because it burdened towns with the support of the children. Such a conclusion would be premature. Although the economic interests of the towns cannot be denied, the fact is that prosecutions were brought even when no economic interests were at stake, and the same penalties were imposed in those prosecutions as in cases where economic interests may have played a part. That the offense, when committed by a woman who did not marry, happened to burden her town was of little import; her offense against God was the essential evil for which she, like the woman who did marry, was punished.

Also within Blackstone's category of offenses against God and religion were 27 prosecutions for violation of the Sabbath, 2 for cohabitation, and 1 for adultery. These 240 cases accounted for 65 percent of all prosecutions.

Statistically the next most significant category was that of offenses against habitations and other private property. Between 1760 and 1775, there were 32 larceny prosecutions and 15 prosecutions for burglary and breaking and entering—which, together with 6 miscellaneous cases within this category, amounted to 53 prosecutions, or 14 percent of the total. The fact that Blackstone placed offenses against property in a separate category should not be taken to mean, however, that in pre-Revolutionary Massachusetts, these crimes were prosecuted solely because their commission interfered with the enjoyment of property. Blackstone's classification scheme is useful primarily as an analytical tool for giving the modern reader a statistical picture of pre-Revolutionary law. While lawyers were aware of the scheme, it does not represent the mainstream of thought in mid-eighteenth century Massachusetts, which still adhered to the traditional view of crime as synonymous with sin. For example, grand jurors were urged by a judge to present wrongdoers so "that they may Receive the Just Demerit of their Crimes [and so that] all vice prophaness & Imorality may be Suppressed & man-kind Reformed and Brought to act with a Due Regard to God. . . ."[6] Several years later the same judge, disturbed that despite efforts made by the government to create "a Civil and Christian State," the people "remain[ed] a Savage & Barba[ric] People, Lead by their Lusts, Gove[rned] by their Passions . . . ," charged another grand jury to make "Inquiry into all Capital Offenses . . . , More Especially as to ye Sin of Murder."[7] Theft, like fornication and murder, was a sin against God, which government was obligated to suppress.

Related to men's view of crime was their view of the criminal. The typical criminal was not, as today, an outcast from society, but only an ordinary member who had sinned. Like sin, crime could strike in any man's family or among any man's neighbors. As Sir Michael Foster, with whose work Massachusetts lawyers of 1760 were especially familiar, observed:

> "For no Rank, no Elevation in Life, and let me add, no Conduct how circumspect soever, ought to tempt a reasonable Man to conclude that these Inquiries [into criminal law] do not, nor possibly can, concern Him. A Moment's cool Reflection on the utter Instability of Human Affairs, and the numberless unforeseen Events which a Day may bring forth, will be sufficient to guard any Man conscious of his own Infirmities against a Delusion of this Kind."[8]

Blacksone concurred, and contemporaries in Massachusetts, aware of no contrary authority and constantly reminded by their clergymen of the omnipresence of sin, probably would have too.

The court records of the 1760s and 1770s indicate that all elements of society committed crimes. Of 47 men accused between 1770 and 1774 of being fathers of illegitimate children, 18 were laborers, 15 were farmers, 12 were artisans, and 2 were gentlemen. Moreover, unlike today, a convicted criminal was not placed in a prison and segregated from the rest of society; in the fifteen-year period before the Revolution, there was only one instance of a person being imprisoned for more than one year. Colonial penalties usually did not sever a criminal's ties with society; fines and mild corporal punishments which left no permanent mark were the usual chastisements. Nor did the only punishment that was commonly of a long duration—the sale into servitude of a convicted thief unable to pay treble damages—result in the thief's segregation from society; rather, its probable effect was to integrate him more fully into society by reorienting him toward normal social contacts.

The years after the Revolution brought forth vast changes in attitudes toward crime and the criminal. Prosecutions for various sorts of immorality nearly ceased, while economically motivated crimes and prosecutions therefor greatly increased. During the same period, old punishments were being discarded and new sanctions imposed.

B. The Decline in Prosecutions for Offenses Against God and Religion

During the last fifteen years before the Revolution, there had been an average of fourteen prosecutions for fornication each year. The first ten years after the Revolution produced no change. However, in 1786, the General Court enacted a new statute for the punishment of fornication, permitting a woman guilty of the crime to confess her guilt before a justice of the peace, pay an appropriate fine, and thereby avoid prosecution by way of indictment in the Court of General Sessions. Although the new law did not immediately produce any significant decline in prosecutions, by 1789 only five convictions were recorded. The last indictment was returned in 1790, and, after 1791, women stopped confessing their guilt, apparently aware that even though they did not confess, they would not be indicted.

William E. Nelson

Prosecutions for Sabbath breaking also continued at the prewar rate of about two per year until the mid-1780s, after which, except for a brief interval in 1800–1802, only three cases appear. As a publication issued in 1816 stated, "[F]or many years previous to 1814, the Laws of this State against profanations of the Sabbath, had fallen into general neglect . . . [T]housands of violations occurred every year, with scarcely a single instance of punishment."[9]

The law's attitude toward adultery was also changing, although the number of prosecutions remained relatively constant. In 1793, three divorces were granted by the Supreme Judicial Court for the commission of adultery, but the guilty spouses were never criminally punished. After 1793, divorces for adultery were regular occurrences, yet only one prosecution was commenced. This increase in divorce indicates not a rise in the incidence of adultery, but rather, the development of an attitude of legal hypocrisy which made it possible, at least in divorce proceedings, for a court to acknowledge publicly the existence of sin without prosecuting it.

A parallel development occurred in paternity litigation. As prosecutions for fornication ceased, it appears that a question arose whether an unwed mother not convicted of the crime could bring a paternity action against the putative father. One woman instituted such a suit in 1790 and gave bond to appear at the next term of court to prosecute it. At that term, however, a new condition was added to her bond—namely, that she also appear to answer a criminal charge of fornication. Thus, the first attempt by a woman to sue without first suffering the consequences of her own misdeed failed. Yet, within five years, a new attempt had succeeded, and thereafter paternity suits by women not punished for their own sin succeeded regularly. Allowing such suits was a step even more radical than granting divorce for adultery without prosecuting the adulterer. In the divorce cases, the courts took merely a neutral attitude toward the sinner. In paternity cases, on the other hand, the courts not only ignored the plaintiff's "sinner" status, but also rendered the sinner affirmative help in obtaining relief from the consequences of her sin.

The de-emphasis of prosecution for sin appears to have been related to what the Congregational ministry condemned as "a declension in morals."[10] President Timothy Dwight of Yale traced the decline to the French and Indian War, and especially to the Revolution, which, he said, added "to the depravation still remaining [from the French War] . . . a long train of immoral doctrines and practices, which spread into every corner of the country. The profanation of the Sabbath, before unusual, profaneness of language, drunkenness, gambling, and lewdness were exceedingly increased. . . ."[11] Others also alluded to habits of card playing and gambling, and to instances of social vice and illegitimacy. Chief Justice William Cushing, for example, feared that "some men have been so liberal in thinking as to religion as to shake off all religion, & while they have labored to set up heathen above Christian morals, have shown themselves destitute of all morality. . . ."[12]

Notwithstanding these complaints, a modern author has concluded that there was no "deep-seated coarseness or general immorality"[13] during the closing years of the eighteenth century. What seems to have occurred after the Revolution was a relaxation not of private, personal morality but of what contemporaries referred to as public morality. What occurred was "a general relaxing of social customs"[14]—an emergence not of significantly more immorality but of a new social and legal attitude toward the immorality that had always existed.

C. The Increase in Prosecutions for Offenses Against Habitations and Private Property

In the late eighteenth and early nineteenth centuries, prosecutions for offenses against habitations and private property greatly increased; but the increase did not commence immediately after the Revolution. From 1776 to 1783, there was an average of 3 cases per year, the same as before the Revolution. But in 1784 the number of prosecutions quadrupled, and then averaged 11 per year for the remainder of the decade, a period of economic difficulty.[15] With the return of prosperity in the 1790s, the average dropped to 7 per year, and, apart from an unexplained rise in 1800–1801, remained constant until 1806. Then came the embargo of 1807, depression, and an increase in

William E. Nelson

the average of theft prosecutions during the remainder of the decade to 21 per year.

Apart from the correspondence in time of the periods of economic distress and two of the periods of increasing prosecutions, there are other reasons for believing that the increases were results of the distress. As indicated by Josiah Quincy, Jr., in a speech on the relationship of "Poverty, Vice and Crime," larceny was a crime committed almost entirely by the urban poor.[16] Court records support this view. Of the 38 theft prosecutions in the Supreme Judicial Court between 1807 and 1809, 27 were against the urban poor, and urban poor were defendants in 53 of 71 cases in all courts between 1784 and 1790. It is also significant that many thought of crime as a product of idleness. Governor Strong, for example, told the legislature in 1802 that "a great proportion of crimes are the effects of idleness. . . ."[17] Such a view indicates that crime was often committed by the unemployed, such as poor laborers unable to find work during periods of economic dislocation.

Both the statistical and the impressionistic evidence suggests, then, that most theft was to some extent a consequence of poverty. Economic distress was apparently causing increasing numbers of the poor to turn to crimes against property during the post-Revolutionary years.

D. The Use of Hard Labor as a Punishment

The third development occurring during the years between 1776 and 1810 was the gradual emergence of hard labor as a punishment in place of the wide variety of penalties used before the Revolution. Hard labor was first imposed with frequency in theft cases. Although there is no direct evidence of why the punishment was first used, the reason can be surmised by tracing the gradual evolution in the penalties imposed for theft during the Revolutionary era.

The basic penalty for theft in pre-Revolutionary Massachusetts was twofold: first, a fine or some sort of mild corporal punishment was imposed on behalf of the government; second, the convicted thief was required to pay treble damages to the owner of the stolen goods. Enforcement of the second part of the penalty was apparently difficult, for many thieves simply could not pay. In such circumstances, the owner of the stolen goods was usually authorized to sell the defendant in service for a specified period varying according to the amount of the treble damages. The market for convict-servants must have been depressed, however, for judgments as early as 1772 contain provisions that, if an owner could not sell a defendant within thirty days of his conviction, the defendant was to be released, unless the owner compensated the government for the costs of keeping the defendant in jail. The government, it seems, did not want to be charged with the burden of supporting thieves. Its dilemma, though, was that setting convicted thieves free excused them from "that grievous . . . [penalty] of being sold in servitude"[18] —the most severe of the penalties imposed upon them.

The dilemma was resolved in 1785, when the legislature provided for the imprisonment of thieves at hard labor, for the state expected that the proceeds of such labor would pay the costs of imprisoning those so punished. Originally hard labor was to be imposed only in cases where the old penalty of treble damages was not workable, but the Supreme Judicial Court soon began to impose it even in cases where the old punishments could be used, apparently because the judges thought it a more efficacious penalty. At the same time, though, they continued to impose the old penalties in some cases. As a result, a defendant convicted of larceny could, by the early 1800s, look forward to almost any penalty.

Meanwhile, a movement for general penology reform had begun. Having had its origin in Philadelphia in 1776, this movement may have been partly responsible for the legislation of 1785. Any influence it may have had in 1785, however, was slight, for the legislature in that year explicitly decided to retain the old punishments for certain crimes. This was directly contrary to the reform movement's aims, which are best stated in a message from Governor Hancock to the General Court in 1793:

"It may well be worthy of your attention to investigate the question whether the infamous punishments of cropping [ears] and branding, as well as that of the public whipping

William E. Nelson

post, so frequently administered in this Government, are the best means to prevent the commission of crimes, or absolutely necessary to the good order of Government or to the security of the people. It is an indignity to human nature, and can have but little tendency to reclaim the sufferer. Crimes have generally idleness for their source, and where offences are not prevented by education, a sentence to hard labor will perhaps have a more salutary effect than mutilating or lacerating the human body. . . ."[19]

The movement reached fruition in 1805, when the state prison was reopened, and corporal punishment and treble damages were imposed for the last time in a Middlesex case.

E. The New Attitude Toward Crime and the Criminal

Each of the three developments discussed thus far was, of course, important in itself. Moreover, in combination with an ideological outgrowth of the Revolution, they transformed the legal and social attitudes toward crime and the criminal. Before the Revolution, two-thirds of all prosecutions were for immorality, and crime was pictured as sin. By 1810, on the other hand, crime was prosecuted to "insure the peace and safety of society"[20] and to relieve the public from the "depradations" of "notorious offenders"[21] and the "tax levied on the community by . . . privateering"[22] of thieves. More than fifty percent of all prosecutions were for theft, and only one-half of one percent for conduct offensive to morality. The criminal in 1810 was no longer envisioned as a sinner against God, but rather as one who preyed upon his fellow citizens.

The transition from the attitude of 1760 to that of 1810 seems to have occurred largely during the decade following the conclusion of peace with Britain in 1783. But the first step in the change began earlier, in the 1760s. During that decade and the first half of the following one, Massachusetts Tories carefully cultivated a fear that rebellion against British authority would lead ultimately to the destruction of all authority. The consequence of rebellion, they maintained, would be that "the bands of society would be dissolved, the harmony of the world confounded and the order of nature subverted. . . ."[23] In a series of grand jury charges given during the 1760s, Chief Justice Thomas Hutchinson suggested how law should be used to prevent the destruction of authority. Expressing his concern that "Disorders are seldom confined to one Point" and that "people who begin with one Vice seldom end there,"[24] Hutchinson urged the jurors "to point out and bring forward all Crimes and Offenses against the Tranquillity and Order of the Society. . . ."[25] Hutchinson's argument essentially was that in order for society to protect itself, its better elements had to be watchful of attacks by mean, lawless, and ignorant men upon order—that is, upon authority and wealth. Proper watchfulness included reliance upon law to punish and hence deter such attacks.

Many Whigs had similar apprehensions. John Adams was as concerned as Hutchinson when, in 1765, a mob of rioters broke into a royal official's home. "[T]o have his Garden torn in Pieces, his House broken open, his furniture destroyed and his whole family thrown into Confusion and Terror, is a very atrocious Violation of the Peace and of dangerous Tendency and Consequence."[26] By the outbreak of hostilities between the British and Americans in 1774–1775, apprehension of the danger of possible lawlessness and mob rule had grown into an obsession common to all. An example is the conduct of the people of Groton in sending supplies in 1774 for the relief of residents of Boston. With the supplies, the town clerk of Groton sent a letter: "The inhabitants of this Town have . . . this day sent forty bushels of grain . . . and we earnestly desire you will use your utmost endeavor to prevent and avoid all mobs, riots, and tumults, and the insulting of private persons and property."[27]

This emerging fear of the mob seems to have been primarily of a political nature. Adams and Hutchinson were not worried that *sinners* would break into their homes and take away their property; nor did they fear an individual thief motivated by a longing for personal material gain. Rather, they feared organized groups of malcontents bent upon the reconstruction of society. Yet they feared such political activity because they expected that it would be economically motivated. They were concerned that debtors would grow insolvent and that mobs would "invade

William E. Nelson

private rights."[28] In short, their fear was that the economically underprivileged would seek material gain by banding together to deprive more privileged persons of their wealth and standing.

Despite these new concerns, however, the old conception of the purpose of criminal law still persisted at the outset of the Revolution. Thus, the General Court in 1776 urged the people to

> "lead sober, Religious and peaceable Lives, avoiding all Blasphemies, contempt of the holy Scriptures, and of the Lord's day and all other Crimes and Misdemeanors, all Debauchery, Prophaneness, Corruption, Venality, all riotous and tumultuous Proceedings, and all Immoralities whatsoever. . . ."[29]

In this statement, though, one can also see the emergence of a new concern with political and economic disorder. Although the new concern was at first peripheral, by the early 1780s it was becoming a central one, as men came to view criminal law as having a dual function, "to discourage [both] vice . . . and disorders in society. . . ."[30]

Although quite real, the new concern had little support in the events of the time. During the 1760s and early 1770s, Middlesex experienced relatively few violent attacks on property; indeed, during the two decades, only four instances of such violence were prosecuted. Although there were undoubtedly additional cases, historians of the Revolution are nonetheless agreed that very little violence of the sort Adams and Hutchinson feared did take place during the course of struggle with Britain.

In the 1780s, however, fears previously ungrounded were confirmed by a number of attacks upon authority and property. Between 1781 and 1786, there were four prosecutions for rioting and five for assaults on tax collectors, in one of which eighteen codefendants had participated. Then a most noteworthy attack occurred when, on September 12, 1786, the Court of General Sessions was scheduled by law to meet at Concord. "But a large armed Force, under the Command of one Job Shattuck of Groton (as it was said) being previously collected had taken Possession of the Court House to prevent their sitting. The Justices of the said Court did not attempt to open the Court."[31] Thus did Shays' Rebellion, which sought to close the courts to prevent the collection of debts, extend eastward into Middlesex. It led to several prosecutions.

Culminating in open rebellion, these five years of violence undoubtedly strengthened the fear which society's well-to-do had of the designs of the lower classes upon their wealth and standing. The simultaneous increase in the incidence of theft appears to have contributed to both a strengthening and a modification of the fear. Adams and Hutchinson, it will be recalled, did not worry about individual thieves. A man living in 1786, however, must have viewed all attacks upon property, on the one hand by poverty-stricken mobs and, on the other, by poverty-stricken individuals, as part of a single phenomenon. What was at stake, ultimately, was his security of person and property, which members of the lower classes were seeking to disrupt. They used a variety of techniques: they rioted; they attacked courts and tax collectors; they refused to pay debts; they entered men's homes and carried away their possessions. Logically, though, their various techniques could be reduced to two. Some men—the thieves and recalcitrant debtors—broke the law and infringed property rights directly; others—the rioters and those who attacked the courts and tax collectors—worked indirectly by destroying the institutions of government upon which enforcement of law, and thus security of property rights, rested. Thus, when Governor Hancock, in an address to the legislature in 1793, suggested that the primary function of criminal law was to insure "the good order of Government . . . [and] the security of the people,"[32] he was saying in effect that it must perform two functions: first, it must punish and deter direct attacks on property, and second, it must preserve the power of government to perform that first function.

Hancock's address, which said nothing about the preservation of religion and morality, further shows that the old theocratic view of crime was rapidly dying. A "liberalizing of the older New England religious tradition" was occurring, especially among the upper classes of eastern Massachusetts. As Chief Justice Cushing explained, when men rejected the old religious traditions, they also rejected many of the old moral ones, among them the theretofore unquestioned assumption that government should enforce morality. Such men, it would seem, were taking a step toward a

William E. Nelson

modern view of criminal law—a view that its purpose is to protect men from unwanted invasions of their rights. At the same time, churchmen and others faithful to the old tradition were abandoning "the dream of theocracy,"[33] as it became "evident that the salvation of the nation . . . had to be won . . . with no assistance from any civil authority." The end result was that criminal law became secularized; its purpose came to be seen not as the preservation of morality, but rather as the protection of social order and property.

With the cessation in the 1790s of anti-governmental violence and prosecutions for immorality, criminal law in fact as well as in theory became concerned primarily with the punishment of theft. During the two decades after 1790, prosecutions for various sorts of theft amounted to forty-seven percent of all cases. This in turn produced a further modification of the theory of criminal law; by 1810 the obsession with mob violence was declining, and the law's purpose was coming to be seen almost entirely as the relief of the public from the "depredations" of thieves.

Meanwhile, the criminal was becoming an outcast of society. Prior to the Revolution, all sorts of men became involved in crime. By 1810, though, the well-to-do rarely became involved with the criminal law, and it was greatly to be regretted "when the offender has some rank in society, with respectable connections who may suffer with him."[34] Such connections were rare, though, for the poverty of most criminals isolated them from the better elements of society on whom they preyed. Criminals in 1810, unlike the mere sinners of old, were different from other men. Nor were their differences and their consequent isolation from society ameliorated by the increasing use of hard labor as a punishment. As some began to observe soon after 1810, long terms of imprisonment did not reform men and enable them to take their place in society, but instead confirmed them in their criminal ways by giving them an opportunity "for corrupting one another."[35] Whereas God could forgive the sinner of old, the villain of 1810 kept returning to crime and was forever condemned to segregation from the society whose peace and prosperity he challenged.

KAI ERIKSON

On the Sociology of Deviance

In 1895 Emile Durkheim wrote a book called
The Rules of Sociological Method which was intended as a
working manual for persons interested in the systematic study
of society. One of the most important themes of Durkheim's
work was that sociologists should formulate a new set of criteria
for distinguishing between "normal" and "pathological" elements
in the life of a society. Behavior which looks abnormal to the
psychiatrist or the judge, he suggested, does not always look
abnormal when viewed through the special lens of the sociologist;
and thus students of the new science should be careful to understand that even the most aberrant forms of individual behavior
may still be considered normal from this broader point of view.
To illustrate his argument, Durkheim made the surprising observation that crime was really a natural kind of social activity, "an
integral part of all healthy societies."[1]

Durkheim's interest in this subject had been expressed several
years before when *The Division of Labor in Society* was first
published.[2] In that important book, he had suggested that crime
(and by extension other forms of deviation) may actually perform a needed service to society by drawing people together in

Reprinted with permission from *The Wayward Puritans*, pp. 3-18 (Wiley,
1966).

Notes to this Selection will be found on page 425.

Erikson is Professor of Sociology at Yale University.

Kai Erikson

a common posture of anger and indignation. The deviant individual violates rules of conduct which the rest of the community holds in high respect; and when these people come together to express their outrage over the offense and to bear witness against the offender, they develop a tighter bond of solidarity than existed earlier. The excitement generated by the crime, in other words, quickens the tempo of interaction in the group and creates a climate in which the private sentiments of many separate persons are fused together into a common sense of morality.

. . .

The deviant act, then, creates a sense of mutuality among the people of a community by supplying a focus for group feeling. Like a war, a flood, or some other emergency, deviance makes people more alert to the interests they share in common and draws attention to those values which constitute the "collective conscience" of the community. Unless the rhythm of group life is punctuated by occasional moments of deviant behavior, presumably, social organization would be impossible.

This brief argument has been regarded a classic of sociological thinking ever since it was first presented, even though it has not inspired much in the way of empirical work. . . . The pages to follow may range far afield from the starting point recommended by Durkheim, but they are addressed to the question he originally posed: does it make any sense to assert that deviant forms of behavior are a natural and even beneficial part of social life?

One of the earliest problems the sociologist encounters in his search for a meaningful approach to deviant behavior is that the subject itself does not seem to have any natural boundaries. Like people in any field, sociologists find it convenient to assume that the deviant person is somehow "different" from those of his fellows who manage to conform, but years of research into the problem have not yielded any important evidence as to what, if anything, this difference might be. Investigators have studied the character of the deviant's background, the content of his dreams, the shape of his skull, the substance of his thoughts—yet none of this information has enabled us to draw a clear line between the kind of person who commits deviant acts and the kind of person who does not. Nor can we gain a better perspective on the matter by shifting our attention away from the individual deviant and looking instead at the behavior he enacts. Definitions of deviance vary widely as we range over the various classes found in a single society or across the various cultures into which mankind is divided, and it soon becomes apparent that there are no objective properties which all deviant acts can be said to share in common —even within the confines of a given group. Behavior which qualifies one man for prison may qualify another for sainthood, since the quality of the act itself depends so much on the circumstances under which it was performed and the temper of the audience which witnessed it.

This being the case, many sociologists employ a far simpler tactic in their approach to the problem—namely, to let each social group in question provide its own definitions of deviant behavior. In this study, as in others dealing with the same general subject; the term "deviance" refers to conduct which the people of a group consider so dangerous or embarrassing or irritating that they bring special sanctions to bear against the persons who exhibit it. Deviance is not a property *inherent in* any particular kind of behavior; it is a property *conferred upon* that behavior by the people who come into direct or indirect contact with it. The only way an observer can tell whether or not a given style of behavior is deviant, then, is to learn something about the standards of the audience which responds to it.

This definition may seem a little awkward in practice, but it has the advantage of bringing a neglected issue into proper focus. When the people of a community decide that it is time to "do something" about the conduct of one of their number, they are involved in a highly intricate process. After all, even the worst miscreant in society conforms most of the time, if only in the sense that he uses the correct silver at dinner, stops obediently at traffic lights, or in a hundred other ways respects the ordinary conventions of his group. And if his fellows elect to bring sanctions against him for the occasions when he does misbehave, they are responding to a few deviant details scattered among a vast array of entirely acceptable conduct. The person who appears in a criminal court and is stamped a "thief" may have spent no more than a passing moment engaged in that activity, and the same can be said for many of the people who pass in review before some agency of control and return from the experience with a deviant label of one sort or another. When the community nominates someone to the deviant class, then, it is sifting a few important details out of the stream of behavior he has emitted and is in effect declaring that these details reflect the kind of person he "really" is. In law as well as in public opinion, the fact that someone has committed a felony or has been known to use narcotics can become the major identifying badge of his person: the very expression "he is a thief" or "he is an addict" seems to provide at once a description of his position in society and a profile of his character.

The manner in which a community sifts these telling details out of a person's overall performance, then, is an important part of its social control apparatus. And it is important to notice that the people of a community take a number of factors into account when they pass judgment on one another which are not immediately related to the deviant act itself: whether or not a person will be considered deviant, for instance, has something to do with his social class, his past record as an offender, the amount of remorse he manages to convey, and many similar concerns which take hold in the shifting mood of the community. Perhaps this is not so apparent in cases of serious crime or desperate illness, where the offending act looms so darkly that it obscures most of the other details of the person's life; but in the day-by-day sifting processes which take place throughout society this feature is always present. Some men who drink heavily are called alcoholics and others are not, some men who behave oddly are committed to hospitals and others are not, some men with no visible means of support are charged with vagrancy and others are not— and the difference between those who earn a deviant title in society and those who go their own way in peace is largely determined by the way in which the community filters out and codes the many details of behavior which come to its attention.

Once the problem is phrased in this manner we can ask: how does a community decide which of these behavioral details are important enough to merit special attention? And why, having made this decision, does it build institutions like prisons and asylums to detain the persons who perform them? The conven-

tional answer to that question, of course, is that a society creates
the machinery of control in order to protect itself against the
"harmful" effects of deviation, in much the same way that an
organism mobilizes its resources to combat an invasion of germs.
Yet this simple view of the matter is apt to pose many more
problems than it actually settles. As both Emile Durkheim and
George Herbert Mead pointed out long ago, it is by no means
evident that all acts considered deviant in society are in fact (or
even in principle) harmful to group life. It is undoubtedly true
that no culture would last long if its members engaged in murder or arson among themselves on any large scale, but there is no
real evidence that many other of the activities considered deviant
throughout the world (certain dietary prohibitions are a promi-
nent example) have any relationship to the group's survival. In
our own day, for instance, we might well ask why prostitution
or marihuana-smoking or homosexuality are thought to endanger
the health of the social order. Perhaps these activities *are* dangerous, but to accept this conclusion without a thoughtful review
of the situation is apt to blind us to the important fact that people
in every corner of the world manage to survive handsomely while
engaged in practices which their neighbors regard as extremely
abhorrent. In the absence of any surer footing, then, it is quite
reasonable for sociologists to return to the most innocent and
yet the most basic question which can be asked about deviation:
why does a community assign one form of behavior rather than
another to the deviant class?

. . .

The only material found in a society for marking boundaries
is the behavior of its members—or rather, the networks of interaction which link these members together in regular social relations. And the interactions which do the most effective job of
locating and publicizing the group's outer edges would seem to
be those which take place between deviant persons on the one
side and official agents of the community on the other. The deviant is a person whose activities have moved outside the margins
of the group, and when the community calls him to account for
that vagrancy it is making a statement about the nature and

placement of its boundaries. It is declaring how much variability and diversity can be tolerated within the group before it begins to lose its distinctive shape, its unique identity. Now there may be other moments in the life of the group which perform a similar service: wars, for instance, can publicize a group's boundaries by drawing attention to the line separating the group from an adversary, and certain kinds of religious ritual, dance ceremony, and other traditional pageantry can dramatize the difference between "we" and "they" by portraying a symbolic encounter between the two. But on the whole, members of a community inform one another about the placement of their boundaries by participating in the confrontations which occur when persons who venture out to the edges of the group are met by policing agents whose special business it is to guard the cultural integrity of the community. Whether these confrontations take the form of criminal trials, excommunication hearings, courts-martial, or even psychiatic case conferences, they act as boundary-maintaining devices in the sense that they demonstrate to whatever audience is concerned where the line is drawn between behavior that belongs in the special universe of the group and behavior that does not. In general, this kind of information is not easily relayed by the straightforward use of language. Most readers of this paragraph, for instance, have a fairly clear idea of the line separating theft from more legitimate forms of commerce, but few of them have ever seen a published statute describing these differences. More likely than not, our information on the subject has been drawn from publicized instances in which the relevant laws were applied—and for that matter, the law itself is largely a collection of past cases and decisions, a synthesis of the various confrontations which have occurred in the life of the legal order.

It may be important to note in this connection that confrontations between deviant offenders and the agents of control have always attracted a good deal of public attention. In our own past, the trial and punishment of offenders were staged in the market place and afforded the crowd a chance to participate in a direct, active way. Today, of course, we no longer parade deviants in the town square or expose them to the carnival atmosphere of a Tyburn, but it is interesting that the "reform" which brought about this change in penal practice coincided almost exactly with the development of newspapers as a medium of mass information. Perhaps this is no more than an accident of history, but it is nonetheless true that newspapers (and now radio and television) offer much the same kind of entertainment as public hangings or a Sunday visit to the local gaol. A considerable portion of what we call "news" is devoted to reports about deviant behavior and its consequences, and it is no simple matter to explain why these items should be considered newsworthy or why they should command the extraordinary attention they do. Perhaps they appeal to a number of psychological perversities among the mass audience, as commentators have suggested, but at the same time they constitute one of our main sources of information about the normative outlines of society. In a figurative sense, at least, morality and immorality meet at the public scaffold, and it is during this meeting that the line between them is drawn.

Boundaries are never a fixed property of any community. They are always shifting as the people of the group find new ways to define the outer limits of their universe, new ways to position themselves on the larger cultural map. Sometimes changes occur within the structure of the group which require its members to make a new survey of their territory—a change of leadership, a shift of mood. Sometimes changes occur in the surrounding environment, altering the background against which the people of the group have measured their own uniqueness. And always, new generations are moving in to take their turn guarding old institutions and need to be informed about the contours of the world they are inheriting. Thus single encounters between the deviant and his community are only fragments of an ongoing social process. Like an article of common law, boundaries remain a meaningful point of reference only so long as they are repeatedly tested by persons on the fringes of the group and repeatedly defended by persons chosen to represent the group's inner morality. Each time the community moves to censure some act of deviation, then, and convenes a formal ceremony to deal with the responsible offender, it sharpens the authority of the violated norm and restates where the boundaries of the group are located.

For these reasons, deviant behavior is not a simple kind of

Kai Erikson

leakage which occurs when the machinery of society is in poor working order, but may be, in controlled quantities, an important condition for preserving the stability of social life. Deviant forms of behavior, by marking the outer edges of group life, give the inner structure its special character and thus supply the framework within which the people of the group develop an orderly sense of their own cultural identity.

. . .

This raises a delicate theoretical issue. If we grant that human groups often derive benefit from deviant behavior, can we then assume that they are organized in such a way as to promote this resource? Can we assume, in other words, that forces operate in the social structure to recruit offenders and to commit them to long periods of service in the deviant ranks? This is not a question which can be answered with our present store of empirical data, but one observation can be made which gives the question an interesting perspective—namely, that deviant forms of conduct often seem to derive nourishment from the very agencies devised to inhibit them. Indeed, the agencies built by society for preventing deviance are often so poorly equipped for the task that we might well ask why this is regarded as their "real" function in the first place.

It is by now a thoroughly familiar argument that many of the institutions designed to discourage deviant behavior actually operate in such a way as to perpetuate it. For one thing, prisons, hospitals, and other similar agencies provide aid and shelter to large numbers of deviant persons, sometimes giving them a certain advantage in the competition for social resources. But beyond this, such institutions gather marginal people into tightly segregated groups, give them an opportunity to teach one another the skills and attitudes of a deviant career, and even provoke them into using these skills by reinforcing their sense of alienation from the rest of society.

. . .

Perhaps we find it difficult to change the worst of our penal practices because we *expect* the prison to harden the inmate's commitment to deviant forms of behavior and draw him more deeply into the deviant ranks. On the whole, we are a people who do not really expect deviants to change very much as they are processed through the control agencies we provide for them, and we are often reluctant to devote much of the community's resources to the job of rehabilitation. In this sense, the prison which graduates long rows of accomplished criminals (or, for that matter, the state asylum which stores its most severe cases away in some back ward) may do serious violence to the aims of its founders, but it does very little violence to the expectations of the population it serves.

These expectations, moreover, are found in every corner of society and constitute an important part of the climate in which we deal with deviant forms of behavior.

To begin with, the community's decision to bring deviant sanctions against one of its members is not a simple act of censure. It is an intricate rite of transition, at once moving the individual out of his ordinary place in society and transferring him into a special deviant position. The ceremonies which mark this change of status, generally, have a number of related phases. They supply a formal stage on which the deviant and his community can confront one another (as in the criminal trial); they make an announcement about the nature of his deviancy (a verdict or diagnosis, for example); and they place him in a particular role which is thought to neutralize the harmful effects of his misconduct (like the role of prisoner or patient). These commitment ceremonies tend to be occasions of wide public interest and ordinarily take place in a highly dramatic setting. Perhaps the most obvious example of a commitment ceremony is the criminal trial, with its elaborate formality and exaggerated ritual, but more modest equivalents can be found wherever procedures are set up to judge whether or not someone is legitimately deviant.

Now an important feature of these ceremonies in our own culture is that they are almost irreversible. Most provisional roles conferred by society—those of the student or conscripted soldier, for example—include some kind of terminal ceremony to mark the individual's movement back out of the role once its temporary advantages have been exhausted. But the roles allotted the deviant seldom make allowance for this type of passage. He is ushered

Kai Erikson

into the deviant position by a decisive and often dramatic ceremony, yet is retired from it with scarcely a word of public notice.
And as a result, the deviant often returns home with no proper
license to resume a normal life in the community. Nothing has
happened to cancel out the stigmas imposed upon him by earlier
commitment ceremonies; nothing has happened to revoke the
verdict or diagnosis pronounced upon him at that time. It should
not be surprising, then, that the people of the community are apt
to greet the returning deviant with a considerable degree of apprehension and distrust, for in a very real sense they are not at all
sure who he is.

A circularity is thus set into motion which has all the earmarks
of a "self-fulfilling prophesy," to use Merton's fine phrase. On the
one hand, it seems quite obvious that the community's apprehensions help reduce whatever chances the deviant might otherwise
have had for a successful return home. Yet at the same time,
everyday experience seems to show that these suspicions are
wholly reasonable, for it is a well-known and highly publicized
fact that many if not most ex-convicts return to crime after leaving prison and that large numbers of mental patients require further treatment after an initial hospitalization. The common feeling
that deviant persons never really change, then, may derive from
a faulty premise; but the feeling is expressed so frequently and
with such conviction that it eventually creates the facts which
later "prove" it to be correct. If the returning deviant encounters
this circularity often enough, it is quite understandable that he,
too, may begin to wonder whether he has fully graduated from
the deviant role, and he may respond to the uncertainty by re-
suming some kind of deviant activity. In many respects, this may
be the only way for the individual and his community to agree
what kind of person he is.

Moreover this prophesy is found in the official policies of even
the most responsible agencies of control. Police departments could
not operate with any real effectiveness if they did not regard
ex-convicts as a ready pool of suspects to be tapped in the event of
trouble, and psychiatric clinics could not do a successful job in
the community if they were not always alert to the possibility of
former patients suffering relapses. Thus the prophesy gains currency at many levels within the social order, not only in the

poorly informed attitudes of the community at large, but in the best informed theories of most control agencies as well.

In one form or another this problem has been recognized in the West for many hundreds of years, and this simple fact has a curious implication. For if our culture has supported a steady flow of deviation throughout long periods of historical change, the rules which apply to any kind of evolutionary thinking would suggest that strong forces must be at work to keep the flow intact—and this because it contributes in some important way to the survival of the culture as a whole. This does not furnish us with sufficient warrant to declare that deviance is "functional" (in any of the many senses of that term), but it should certainly make us wary of the assumption so often made in sociological circles that any well-structured society is somehow designed to prevent deviant behavior from occurring.

PART TWO

Process

ROSCOE POUND

Criminal Justice in the American City

We may say that the three chief factors in the administration of justice are: (1) the men by whom it is administered; (2) the machinery of legal and political institutions by means of which they administer justice; and (3) the environment in which they do so. One who surveys the workings of a legal system with these three things in mind will not go far wrong. Yet his picture will not be complete nor wholly accurate. He must take account also of certain practical limitations and practical difficulties inherent in the legal ordering of human relations, at least by any legal institutions thus far devised. The purposes of law, as we know them, and the very nature of legal institutions as we have received and fashioned them, involve certain obstacles to our doing everything which we should like to do by means thereof, and even to our doing well many things which we have been trying to do thereby for generations. These

Reprinted with permission from Pound et al., Criminal Justice in Cleveland, pp. 559–82 (Cleveland Foundation, 1922).

Pound was Professor of Law at Harvard University and the author of many books, among them Criminal Justice in America (1945) and An Introduction to the Philosophy of Law (1954).

Roscoe Pound

practical limitations on effective legal action explain much that, on a superficial view, is ascribed to bad men or bad legal machinery. Hence a fourth factor must be added, namely, (4) the bounds within which the law may function effectively as a practical system.

The Function of Law

We look to the physical and biological sciences to augment the means of satisfying human wants and to teach us to conserve those means. We look to the social sciences to teach us how we may apply those means to the purpose of satisfying human wants with a minimum of friction and waste. Thus we may think of the legal order as a piece of social engineering; as a human attempt to conserve values and eliminate friction and preclude waste in the process of satisfying human wants. That part of the whole process of social engineering which has to do with the ordering of human relations and of human conduct through applying to men the force of politically organized society is the domain of law.

. . .

In this process of adjusting and ordering human relations and ordering human conduct in order to eliminate friction and waste, the legal order deals, on the one hand, with controversies between individuals. Where their claims or wants or desires overlap, it seeks to harmonize and reconcile those claims or wants or desires by a system of rules and principles administered in tribunals. On the other hand, it has to deal with certain acts or courses of conduct which run counter to the interests involved in the existence and functioning of civilized society. Civilized society rests upon the general security, including the general safety, the general health, peace, and good order, and the security of the economic order. It is maintained through social institutions, domestic, religious and political. It involves a moral life and hence calls for protection of the general morals. In a crowded world it presupposes conservation of social resources. It is a society of individual human beings, and hence its proper functioning presupposes the moral and social life of each individual therein according to its standards. These social interests, as they may be called, namely, the general security, the security of social institutions, the general morals, the conservation of social resources, and the individual moral or social life, are threatened by the anti-social acts or anti-social conduct or even anti-social mode of life of particular individuals. To restrain these persons, to deter others who might follow their example, to correct such anti-social mode of life as far as possible, and to give effect to these social interests, the law imposes a system of duties upon all persons in society, enforced through administrative and police supervision, through prosecution and through penal treatment. The part of the legal system that defines these duties and prescribes how they shall be enforced by means of prosecutions and penal treatment is the criminal law.

It is important to bear in mind that the law is only one of many regulative agencies whereby human conduct is ordered for the securing of social interests. The household, religious organizations, fraternal organizations, social, professional, and trade organizations may operate also, through their internal discipline, to order the conduct of their members and to restrain them from anti-social conduct. In the past these organizations, whereby the force of the opinions of one's fellow-members may be brought to bear upon him, have played a large part in maintaining civilized society. When the law seems to break down in whole or in part we may well inquire, among other things, how far it is supported or is interfered with by some or all of these organizations, and how far they also or some of them must bear the blame. Obviously the number and vitality of these organizations in any society and the manner in which and ends for which they are conducted are important items in the environment of the administration of justice.

To think of the legal order functionally, in terms of engineering, is especially important in such a survey as the present. Here we are not concerned with legal rules in their abstract nature, but in their concrete workings. We are not seeking to know what the law is. We seek to know what the legal system does and how what it does measures up to the requirements of the ends for

Roscoe Pound

which it is done. Hence the purpose of the law must be before us as a critique of its achievements in action, not some criterion drawn from the law itself.

. . .

Dissatisfaction with the Administration of Justice

Dissatisfaction with the administration of justice is as old as law. As long as there have been laws and lawyers conscientious men have believed that laws were but arbitrary technicalities, and that the attempt to govern the relations of men in accordance with them resulted largely in injustice. From the beginning others have asserted that, so far as laws were good, they were perverted in their application, and that the actual administration of justice was unequal or inefficient or corrupt. . . . We must not allow this perennial and perhaps inevitable discontent with all law to blind us to serious and well-founded complaints as to the actual operation of the legal system today. But it may give us a needed warning that some discontent is unavoidable, that we may not hope to obviate all grounds of complaint, and that we must begin by taking account of the inherent difficulties, because of which a certain amount of dissatisfaction must always be discounted.

Inherent Difficulties in All Justice According to Law

I. THE MECHANICAL OPERATION OF LEGAL RULES

To a certain extent legal rules must operate mechanically and the most important and most constant cause of dissatisfaction with all law in all times grows out of this circumstance. A proper balance between strict rule and magisterial discretion is one of the most difficult problems of the science of law. Throughout the history of law men have turned from an extreme of the one to an extreme of the other and then back again, without being able to attain a satisfactory administration of justice through either. Sometimes, as in the strict law of the late medieval courts in England, or as in the maturity of American law in the last half of the nineteenth century, men put their faith in strict confinement of the magistrate by minute and detailed rules or by a mechanical process of application of law through logical deduction from fixed principles. By way of reaction at other times men pin their faith in a wide magisterial power to fit justice to the facts of the particular case through judicial discretion, as in the administrative tribunals of sixteenth- and seventeenth-century England, the executive and legislative justice of the American colonies, and the executive boards and commissions which are setting up in this country today on every hand. But these reactions are followed by new periods of fixed rules. Thus experience seems to show that the mechanical action of law may be tempered but may not be obviated.

We seek to administer justice according to law. That is, we seek just results by means of a machinery of legal rules. But a certain sacrifice of justice is involved in the very attainment of it through rules, which yet are, on the whole, the best and most certain method of attaining it which we have discovered. Legal rules are general rules. In order to make them general we must eliminate what by and large are the immaterial elements of particular controversies. This would be of no consequence if all cases were alike, or if it were possible to foresee or to reckon precisely the degree in which actual cases approach or depart from the types which the law defines. In practice they approximate to these types in endless gradations, the one often shading into the next, so that in difficult cases choice of the proper type is not easy and often gives rise to judicial disagreement. As a result, when the law eliminates what are taken to be immaterial factors in order to frame a general rule, it can never avoid entirely elimination of factors which may have an important bearing upon some particular controversy.

There are three ways of meeting this difficulty: One is to provide a judicial or magisterial dispensing power, or even a series of devices for introducing discretion into the administration of justice. In American administration of criminal justice today there is a long series of such devices, one imposed upon the other. There is the discretion of the police as to who and what shall be brought before the tribunals. There are wide and substantially uncontrolled powers in prosecuting attorneys to ignore offenses

Roscoe Pound

or offenders, to dismiss proceedings in their earlier stages, to present them to grand juries in such a way that no indictment follows, to decline to prosecute after indictment, or to agree to accept a plea of guilty of a lesser offense. There is the power of the grand jury to ignore the charge. There is the power of the trial jury to exercise a dispensing power through a general verdict of not guilty. Next comes judicial discretion as to sentence or suspension of sentence or mitigation of sentence. Finally there is administrative parole or probation, and in the last resort executive pardon. All these involve uncertainty—opportunity for perversion of the device intended to meet exceptional cases into a means of enabling the typical offender to escape, and a sometimes intolerable scope for the personal equation of the official.

A second way of meeting this difficulty is to eliminate all discretion and seek to meet exceptional cases by an elaborate series of legal exceptions and qualifications and detailed provisos. But human foresight has not proved equal to foreseeing all the varieties of exception for which provision must be made, and the attempt to cover everything by special provisions makes the legal system cumbrous and unworkable.

Hence the law usually ends by adopting a third method of compromising between wide discretion and over-minute law making. But in order to reach a middle ground between rule and discretion some sacrifice of flexibility of application to individual cases is necessary. And this sacrifice cannot go far without a danger of occasional injustice. Moreover, the slightest sacrifice, necessary as it is, makes legal rules appear arbitrary and brings the application of them more or less into conflict with the moral ideas of individual citizens. Whenever, in a complex and crowded society containing heterogeneous elements, groups and classes and interests have conflicting ideas of justice, this cause of dissatisfaction is likely to become acute. The individual citizen looks only at single cases, and measures them by his individual sense of right and wrong. The courts must look at cases by types or classes and must measure them by what is necessarily to some extent an artificial standard. If discretion is given the judge, his exercise of it may reflect the view of the element of society from which he comes or with which he associates. If his hands are tied by law, he may be forced to apply the ethical ideas of the past as formulated in common law and legislation. In either event there are many chances that judicial standards and the ethical standards of individual critics will diverge. Herein lies a fruitful cause of popular dissatisfaction with the administration of justice.

2. DIFFERENCE IN RATE OF PROGRESS BETWEEN LAW AND PUBLIC OPINION

In seeking to maintain the interests of civilized society through public administration of justice we risk a certain sacrifice of those interests through corruption or the personal prejudices of magistrates or individual incompetency of those to whom administration is committed. To make this risk as small as possible, to preclude corruption, restrain personal prejudices, and minimize the scope of incompetency, the law formulates the moral ideas of the community in rules and requires the tribunals to apply those rules. So far as they are formulations of public opinion, legal rules cannot exist until public opinion has become fixed and settled, and cannot well change until public opinion has definitely changed. It follows that law is likely to lag somewhat behind public opinion whenever the latter is active and growing.

Many devices have been resorted to in order to make the law more immediately sensitive and responsive to public opinion. Some of these are frequent and copious legislation upon legal subjects, deprofessionalizing the practice of law by opening it to all, regardless of education and special training, putting of the courts into politics through making judges elective for short terms, conferring wide powers upon juries at the expense of courts, setting up of administrative tribunals with large jurisdiction, to be exercised in a non-technical fashion, and recall of judges or of judicial decisions. The first four of these expedients were tried in the fore part of the last century, and many jurisdictions carried some or even all of them to extremes. The last three have been urged in the present century, and a tendency to commit enforcement of law to administrative agencies and tribunals has gone far. But none of them has succeeded in its purpose, and many of them in action have subjected the administration of justice not to public opinion, but to influences destructive of the interests which law seeks to maintain. We must recognize that this difficulty in justice according to law may be minimized, but

Roscoe Pound

not wholly obviated. We must make a practical compromise. Experience has shown that public opinion must affect the administration of justice through the rules by which justice is administered rather than through direct pressure upon those who apply them. Interference with the uniform and scientific application of them, when actual controversies arise, introduces elements of uncertainty, caprice, and deference to aggressive interests which defeat the general security. But if public opinion affects tribunals through the rules by which they decide, as these rules, once established, stand till abrogated or altered, it follows that the law will not respond quickly to new conditions. It will not change until ill effects are felt—often not until they are felt acutely. The economic or political or moral change must come first. While it is coming and until it is so definite and complete as to affect the law and formulate itself therein, divergence between law and a growing public opinion is likely to be acute and to create much dissatisfaction. We must pay this price for the certainty and uniformity demanded by the general security. It should be said, however, that consciousness of this inherent difficulty easily leads lawyers to neglect the importance of reducing this difference in rate of growth between law and public opinion so far as possible.

3. POPULAR UNDERESTIMATION OF THE DIFFICULTIES IN ADMINISTERING JUSTICE

Much popular dissatisfaction with justice according to law arises from a popular assumption that the administration of justice is an easy task to which anyone is competent. If the task of law may be described in terms of social engineering, laws may be compared to the formulas of engineers. They sum up the experience of many courts with many cases and enable the magistrate to apply that experience without being aware of it. In the same way the formula enables the engineer to utilize the accumulated experience of past builders even though he could not of himself work out a step in its evolution. The lay public are no more competent to construct and apply the one formula than the other. Each requires special knowledge and special preparation. But the notion that anyone is competent to understand what justice requires in the intricate controversies and complicated relations of a modern urban community leads to all manner of obstacles to proper standards of training for the bar, to low standards of qualification for judicial office, and to impatience of scientific methods and a high measure of technical skill. This notion was especially strong in pioneer America, and its influence may be seen in extravagant powers of juries, lay judges of probate, and legislative or judicial attacks upon the authority of precedents in most of the states of the South and West. In criminal law it is usually manifest in legislation committing the fixing of penalties to trial juries, not perceiving that the trier, in order to determine the facts fairly, ought not to know certain things without which, on the other hand, the penalty cannot be fixed intelligently. Popular judgments are reached by labeling acts according to certain obvious characteristics. A judge, on the other hand, must examine carefully into all the details of the act, the conditions, internal and external, under which it was done, its motive and its consequences. Hence his judgment may well differ from that of the man in the street, although they apply the same moral standard. The man in the street is likely to regard this disagreement as proof of defects in the administration of justice. Yet courts do not sit to register his judgment on such data as he has but to do what the sober judgment of the community would dictate upon the basis of all the facts.

It is not generally realized how much the public is interested in maintaining the highest scientific standards in the administration of justice. It is the most certain protection against corruption, prejudice, class feeling, and incompetence. Publicity is important, but it is impossible to invoke public indignation in every case, nor is it always evoked in the right cases. Our main reliance must be put in the training of bench and bar, whereby the judges form habits of seeking and applying principles when called upon to act, and the lawyers are able to subject their decisions to expert criticism. The latter is especially important. The daily criticism of trained minds, the knowledge that nothing which does not conform to the principles and received doctrines of scientific law will escape notice, will do more than any other agency for the everyday purity and efficiency of courts of justice. But as things are today the best trained element of the bar more and more does its chief work out of court, and wholly avoids criminal cases. Thus in our large cities the most effective check upon the administration of justice becomes inoperative, and this special difficulty is added to the inherent difficulty involved in public reluctance to admit the necessity of scientific justice and the training of bench and bar which it presupposes.

4. POPULAR IMPATIENCE OF RESTRAINT

Law involves restraint and regulation with the sheriff and his posse or the police force in the background to enforce it. As a society becomes more complex, as it carries further the division of labor, as it becomes more crowded and more diversified in race and in habits of life and thought, the amount of restraint and regulation must increase enormously. But however necessary and salutary this restraint, men have never been reconciled to it entirely; and most American communities are still so close to the frontier that pioneer hostility toward discipline, good order, and obedience is still often a latent instinct in the better class of citizens. The very fact that the restraint of the legal order is in some sort a compromise between the individual and his fellows makes the individual, who must abate some part of his activities in the interest of his fellows, more or less restive. In a time of absolute democratic theories this restiveness may be acute. The feeling that each individual, as an organ of the sovereign democracy, is above the law which he helps to make, fosters disrespect for legal methods and legal institutions and a spirit of resistance to them. Thus the administration of justice according to law is made more difficult. Whether the law is enforced or is not enforced, dissatisfaction will result.

Popular impatience of restraint is aggravated in the United States by political and legal theories of "natural law." As a political doctrine, they lead individuals to put into action a conviction that conformity to the dictates of the individual conscience is a test of the validity of a law. Accordingly, jurors will disregard statutes in perfect good faith, as in the Sunday-closing prosecutions in Chicago in 1908. In the same spirit a well-known preacher wrote not long since that a prime cause of lawlessness was enactment of legislation at variance with the law of nature. In the same spirit a sincere and, as he believed, a law-abiding labor leader declared in a Labor Day address that he would not obey mandates of the courts which deprived him of his natural "rights." In the same spirit the business man may regard evasion of statutes which interfere with his carrying on business as he chooses as something entirely legitimate.

. . .

5. INHERENT LIMITATIONS ON EFFECTIVE LEGAL ACTION

There are certain limitations inherent in the administration of justice through legal machinery—at least, through any of which we have knowledge—which prevent the law from securing all interests which ethical considerations or social ideals indicate as proper or even desirable to be secured. Five such limitations are of much importance in connection with the criminal law. These are: (1) Difficulties involved in ascertainment of the facts to which legal rules are to be applied, so that, especially in certain types of case, it is difficult to discover the offender or there is danger of convicting the innocent; (2) the intangibleness of certain duties which morally are of much moment but legally defy enforcement, as, for instance, many duties involved in the family relation to which courts of domestic relations or juvenile courts seek to give effect; (3) the subtlety of certain modes of inflicting injury and of modes of infringing important interests which the legal order would be glad to secure effectively if it might; (4) the inapplicability of the legal machinery of rule and sanction to many human relations and to some serious wrongs, and (5) the necessity of relying upon individuals to set the law in motion.

Three of the limitations just enumerated call for some notice. Intrigue may seriously disturb the peace of a household. The subtle methods by which grievous wrongs may be done in this way have been the theme of playwright and novelist for generations. One court, indeed, has tried the experiment of enjoining a defendant from flirting with a plaintiff's wife. But the futility of legal interference in such cases is obvious and is generally recognized. In no other cases is self-redress so persistently resorted to nor so commonly approved by the public. Again, many cases are too small for the ponderous machinery of prosecution and yet may involve undoubted and serious wrongs to individuals. How to deal with the small annoyances and neighborhood quarrels and petty depredations and small-scale predatory activities which irritate the mass of an urban population but do not seem to involve enough to justify the expensive process of the law is by no means the least of the problems of the legal order in the modern city. Here as elsewhere we must make a practical compromise, and whatever the compromise, many will need be dissatisfied. Finally, law will not enforce itself. We must in some way stimulate individals to go to the trouble of vindicating it; and yet we must not suffer them to use it as a means of extortion or of gratifying spite. Our rules must obtain in action, not merely lie dormant in the books. But if they are to obtain in action, the authority which prescribes them must be so backed by social-psychological power as to be in a position to give them effect as motives for action in spite of countervailing individual motives. Hence the notorious futility of two sorts of lawmaking which are very common: (1) Lawmaking which has nothing behind it but the sovereign imperative, in which the mere words "be it enacted" are relied upon to accomplish the end sought, and (2) lawmaking which is intended to "educate"—to set up an ideal of what men ought to do rather than a rule of what they shall do. To a large extent law depends for its enforcement upon the extent to which it can identify social interests with individual interests, and can give rise to or rely upon individual desire to enforce its rules. In criminal law the desire of the offender to escape and the desire of his friends and relatives that he escape are strong and active. Unless the desires of other individuals may be enlisted in the service of the law, administrative machinery is likely to fall into an easygoing routine, readily manipulated in the interest of offenders, and the law in the books to become wholly academic, while something quite different obtains in action.

Few appreciate the far-reaching operation of the foregoing limitations upon legal action. There is constant pressure upon the law to "do something," whether it may do anything worth-while or not. In periods of expansion the tendency to call upon law to do more than it is adapted to do is especially strong. The result is sure to be failure and the failure affects the whole legal order injuriously.

Inherent Difficulties in All Criminal Justice

I. PUBLIC DESIRE FOR VENGEANCE

Historically, one of the origins of criminal law is in summary community self-help, in offhand public vengeance by a more or less orderly mob. Regulation of this public vengeance, giving rise to a sort of orderly lynch law, is one of the earliest forms of criminal law. The spirit which gave rise to this institution of summary mob self-help in primitive society is still active. It has its roots in a deep-seated instinct, and must be reckoned with in all administration of criminal justice. Moralists and sociologists no longer regard revenge or satisfaction of a desire for vengeance as a legitimate end of penal treatment. But jurists are not agreed. Many insist upon the retributive theory in one form or another, and Anglo-American lawyers commonly regard satisfaction of public desire for vengeance as both a legitimate and a practically necessary end. This disagreement is reflected in all our criminal legislation. Statutes enacted at different times proceed upon different theories. Indeed, the usual course is that adherents of one theory of penal treatment will procure one measure, and adherents of a different theory another, from lawmakers who have no theory of their own. For nothing is done with so little of scientific or orderly method as the legislative making of laws.

Administration is necessarily affected by the fundamental conflict with respect to aims and purposes which pervades our penal legislation. But apart from this, the conflicting theories are also at work in administration. One magistrate paroles freely; another may condemn the system of parole. One executive pardons freely, another not at all. One jury is stern and as like as not acts upon the revenge theory; another jury is soft-hearted. One judge is systematically severe and holds that crime must inevitably be followed by retribution; another is systematically lenient, and many others have no system or policy whatever. Thus the fact that we are not all agreed, nor are we ourselves agreed in all our moods, infects both legislation and administration with uncertainty, inconsistency, and in consequence inefficiency. All attempts to better this situation must reckon with a deep-seated popular desire for vengeance in crimes appealing to the emotions, or in times when crimes against the general security are numerous. Lawyers know well that the average client is apt to be eager to begin a criminal prosecution. He is not satisfied to sue civilly and obtain compensation for an injury. He insists upon something that will hurt the wrongdoer, and is willing to pay liberally to that end. It has taken a long time to eliminate the revenge element from the civil side of the law. Indeed, traces still remain there. On the criminal side this element is still vigorous. The general security requires us to repress self-help, especially mob or mass self-help. Also we must strive to meet the demands of the moral sentiment of the community. These considerations constrain us to keep many things in the criminal law which are purely retributive, and thus serve to preserve a condition of fundamental conflict between different parts of the system. Undoubtedly the law and its administration should reflect the sober views of the community, not its views when momentarily inflamed. But the sober views of the average citizen are by no means so advanced on this subject as to make a wholly scientific system possible.

2. A CONDITION OF INTERNAL OPPOSITION IN CRIMINAL LAW DUE TO HISTORICAL CAUSES

As has been said, criminal law exists to maintain social interests as such; but the social interest in the general security and the social interest in the individual life continually come into conflict, and in criminal law, as everywhere else in law, the problem is one of compromise; of balancing conflicting interests and of securing as much as may be with the least sacrifice of other interests. The most insistent and fundamental of social interests are involved in criminal law. Civilized society presupposes peace and good order, security of social institutions, security of the general morals, and conservation and intelligent use of social resources. But it demands no less that free individual initiative which is the basis of economic progress, that freedom of criticism without which political progress is impossible, and that free mental activity which is a prerequisite of cultural progress. Above all it demands that the individual be able to live a moral and social life as a human being. These claims, which may be put broadly as a social interest in the individual life, continually trench upon the interest in the security of social institutions, and often, in appearance at least, run counter to the paramount interest in the general security. Compromise of such claims for the purpose of securing as much as we may is peculiarly difficult. For historical reasons this difficulty has taken the form of a condition of internal opposition in criminal law which has always impaired its efficiency. As a result there has been a continual movement back and forth between an extreme solicitude for the general security, leading to a minimum of regard for the individual accused and reliance upon summary, unhampered, arbitrary, administrative punitive justice, and at the other extreme excessive solicitude for the social interest in the individual life, leading to a minimum of regard for the general security and security of social institutions and reliance upon strictly regulated judicial punitive justice, hampered at all points by checks and balances and technical obstacles. In England the medieval legal checks upon punitive justice were followed by the rise of the Star Chamber and other forms of executive criminal administration. This was followed by the exaggerated legalism of a common-law prosecution. The latter, carried to an extreme in nineteenth-century America, is being followed hard today by the rise of administrative justice through boards and commissions. The over-technical tenderness for the offender in our criminal law of the last century is giving way to carelessness of violation of the constitutional rights of accused persons and callousness as to administrative methods of dealing with criminals, real or supposed, in the supposed interest of efficient enforcement of penal laws.

.   .   .

Criminal law has its origin, historically, in legal regulation of certain crude forms of social control. Thus it has two sides from the beginning. On the one hand, it is made up of prohibitions addressed to the individual in order to secure social interests. On the other hand, it is made up of limitations upon the enforcement

Roscoe Pound

of these prohibitions in order to secure the social interest in the individual life. In Anglo-American criminal law, as a result of the contests between courts and king in seventeenth-century England, the accused came to be thought of not as an offender pursued by the justice of society, but as a presumably innocent person pursued by the potentially oppressive power of the king. The common law, declared in bills of rights, came to be thought of as standing between the individual and the state, and as protecting the individual from oppression by the agents of the state. No efficient administration of criminal law in a large urban population is possible under the reign of such a theory. But we have abandoned it in places only. Despite an obvious reaction, it still determines many features of American criminal prosecution. Moreover, we must not forget that it is but a historical form of one of the two elements of which criminal law is made up.

3. THE CLOSE CONNECTION OF CRIMINAL LAW AND ADMINISTRATION WITH POLITICS

Criminal law has a much closer connection with politics than the civil side of the law, and this operates to its disadvantage, particularly in respect of administration. There is relatively little danger of oppression through civil litigation. On the other hand, there has been constant fear of oppression through the criminal law. In history drastic enforcement of severe penal laws has been employed notoriously to keep a people or a class in subjection. Not only is one class suspicious of attempts by another to force its ideas upon the community under penalty of prosecution, but the power of a majority or even a plurality to visit with punishment practices which a strong minority consider in no way objectionable is liable to abuse. Whether rightly or wrongly used, this power puts a strain upon criminal law and administration. Also criminal prosecutions are possible weapons of offense and defense in class and industrial conflicts. Hence suspicion arises that one side or the other may get an advantage through abuse of the prosecuting machinery, giving rise to political struggles to get control of that machinery. Thus considerations of efficient securing of social interests are pushed into the background, and the atmosphere in which prosecutions are conducted becomes political. In practice the result is, when the public conscience is active or public indignation is roused, to be spectacular at the expense of efficiency. When the public conscience is sluggish and public attention is focused elsewhere, the temptation is to be lax for fear of offending dominant or militant political groups.

4. THE INHERENT UNRELIABILITY OF EVIDENCE IN CRIMINAL CASES

Inherent unrelaibility of evidence upon which tribunals must proceed affects all departments of judicial administration of justice. But in criminal law, where passions are aroused, where the consequences are so serious, where unscrupulous persons are so apt to be arrayed on one side or the other, the difficulties growing out of the necessity of relying upon human testimony are grave. Psychologists have demonstrated abundantly the extent to which errors of observation and unsuspected suggestion affect the testimony of the most conscientious. Undoubtedly there is much practical psychology and trained intuition behind the common-law rules of evidence; but they are based largely on the psychology of the jury rather than on that of the witness. The problem of lying witnesses, defective observation, and suggestion, as affecting proof in criminal cases, has yet to be studied scientifically by American lawyers. The maxims and presumptions in which we express our practical experience in these connections are too much of the rule-of-thumb type, and are apt to be merely pieces to move in the procedural game between prosecutor and accused. . . .

5. THE WIDER SCOPE FOR ADMINISTRATIVE DISCRETION REQUIRED IN CRIMINAL LAW

As compared with the adjustment of civil relations, criminal law involves a much greater scope for discretion. Much that may be done mechanically in matters of property and contract, and hence with assurance that improper influences are excluded by the perfection of the machinery, must be done by the individual judgment of judges or public officers when we are dealing with human conduct, and hence is open to all the disturbing influences that may be brought to bear upon the individual human being. It is one of the difficult problems of all law to maintain a due pro-

Roscoe Pound

portion between detailed rules and judicial or administrative discretion. In criminal law the dangers involved in such discretion
are obvious. The power which it involves is large and is peculiarly
liable to abuse. Moreover, the consequences of abuse are serious
involving life and liberty, where on the civil side of the law the
effects extend rather to property. But there are two circumstances
in criminal law that require a wide discretion on the part of prosecutors and magistrates: (1) In the administration of criminal law
the moral or ethical element plays a large part, and purely moral
or ethical matters do not lend themselves to strict rules. (2) As
we now think, penal treatment is to fit the criminal rather than
punishment to fit the crime. Hence whether there shall be a prosecution and what shall be done to and with the convicted offender
after prosecution must be left largely to the discretion of someone. . . . Even when we sought to make the punishment fit the
crime, the impossibility of a mathematically constructed system
of penalties became manifest, and sentence, within wide limits,
was a matter for the discretion of the trial judge. In those days
notorious inequalities in sentences bore constant witness to the
liability of unfettered discretion to abuse, even in the best of
hands. In England, review of sentences by the Court of Criminal
Appeal is relied upon to meet this particular danger. In the United
States the tendency is to entrust the nature and duration of penal
treatment to some administrative board. But whichever course is
taken the beginning and continuation as well as the details of the
ultimate result of a criminal prosecution must be left largely to
the discretion of someone, with all which that may imply.

6. INHERENT INADEQUACY OF PENAL METHODS

On the civil side of the law the modes of enforcement have
become very efficacious. If A dispossesses B of land, the sheriff
may put A out and B back in possession. If A dispossesses B of a
chattel, the sheriff may take it from A and give it back to B. If A
does not convey to B as he promised, an officer of the court may
make a deed to which the law gives the effect of the promised
conveyance. If A does not pay a debt he owes B, the sheriff may
sell A's goods and pay B out of the proceeds. No such thoroughgoing remedies are available in criminal law. To guard against
further harm from a particular offender, and to guard against

others who might repeat the offense, society relies upon fear as a deterrent. It attempts to create a widespread fear of punishment and to bring this fear home to the particular offender. Preventive justice, in such matters as are dealt with by the criminal law, must be confined within narrow limits, since it involves undue interference with the freedom of action of individuals. Accordingly, in the great mass of cases the criminal law can only step in after an offense has been committed. But the system of protecting society by creating a general fear of punishment encounters two inherent difficulties: (1) Experience has shown that fear is never a complete deterrent. The venturesome will believe they can escape. The fearless will be indifferent whether they escape. The crafty will believe they can evade, and enough will succeed to encourage others. (2) Threats of punishment are often likely to defeat themselves. The zeal of lawmakers frequently imposes penalties to which juries will not agree that offenders should be subjected. It sometimes defines acts as criminal for which juries will not agree to see men punished. Thus we get so-called dead-letter laws, which weaken the authority of law and destroy the efficacy of fear as a deterrent. Sometimes, indeed, it has happened that courts did not have sympathy with over-severe laws or extreme penalties and warped the law to prevent conviction. Our criminal procedure still suffers from the astuteness of judges in the past to avoid convictions at a time when all felonies were punishable with death. However efficient the administration of criminal law, it will be necessary to make some allowance for this inherent difficulty.

7. THE TENDENCY TO PUT TOO GREAT A BURDEN ON THE CRIMINAL LAW

It is a great disadvantage to the criminal law that it is so interesting in action to the layman. Criminal law is the type of law which figures chiefly in the morning papers; hence when the layman thinks of law, he is almost certain to think of criminal law. Moreover, because of a well-known human instinct, the layman's short and simple cure for all ills is to hurt somebody. Hence every lay lawmaker turns instinctively to the criminal law when he comes to provide a sanction for his new measure, and every new statute adds one more to the mass of prescribed penalties for

Roscoe Pound

which a criminal prosecution may be invoked. It is impossible for any legal machinery to do all which our voluminous penal legislation expects of it. Serious study of how to make our huge annual output of legislation effective for its purpose without prosecutions and giving up the naïve faith that finds expression in the common phrase, "there ought to be a law against it," as an article in the legislative creed, would do much for the efficiency of criminal law.

JEROME FRANK

Facts Are Guesses

If you scrutinize a legal rule, you will see that it is a conditional statement referring to facts. Such a rule seems to say, in effect, "If such and such a fact exists, then this or that legal consequence should follow." It seems to say, for example, "If a trustee, for his own purposes, uses money he holds in trust, he must repay it." Or, "If a man, without provocation, kills another, the killer must be punished."

. . .

For convenience, let us symbolize a legal rule by the letter R, the facts of a case by the letter F, and the court's decision of that case by the letter D. We can then crudely schematize the conventional theory of how courts operate by saying

$$R \times F = D.$$

In other words, according to the conventional theory, a decision is a product of an R and an F. If, as to any lawsuit, you know the R and the F, you should, then, know what the D will be.

Reprinted by permission of Princeton University Press from *Courts on Trial*, pp. 14–36 (Princeton, 1950).

Frank was a member of the U.S. Securities and Exchange Commission, a Judge of the United States Court of Appeals for the Second Circuit and a Lecturer at the Yale Law School. His other books include Law and the Modern Mind *(1930) and* Not Guilty *(1957) (with Barbara Frank).*

Jerome Frank

In a simple, stable society, most of the R's are moderately well stabilized. Which legal rules that society will enforce it is not difficult for men—or at any rate, for the lawyer, the professional court-man—to know in advance of any trial. In such a society, the R—one of the two factors in the $R \times F = D$ formula—is usually fixed.

In our society, however, with the rapid changes brought about by modern life, many of the R's have become unstable. Accordingly, in our times, legal uncertainty—uncertainty about future decisions and therefore about legal rights—is generally ascribed to the indefiniteness of the R's. The increasing multiplicity of the rules, the conflicts between rules, and the flexibility of some of the rules, have arrested the attention of most legal thinkers. Those thinkers, perceiving the absence of rigidity in some rules, have assumed that the certainty or uncertainty of the D's, in the $R \times F = D$ equation, stems principally from the certainty or uncertainty of the R's.

That assumption leads to a grave miscomprehension of court-house government and to the neglect by most legal scholars of the more difficult part of the courts' undertaking. I refer to the courts' task with respect to the other factor in the $R \times F = D$ formula, the F. The courts are supposed to ascertain the facts in the disputes which become law-suits. That is, a court is supposed to determine the actual, objective acts of the parties, to find out just what they did or did not do, before the law-suit began, so far as those facts bear on the compliance with, or the violation of, some legal rule. If there is uncertainty as to whether the court will find the true relevant facts—if it is uncertain whether the court's F will match the real, objective F—then what? Then, since the decision, the D, is presumably the joint product of an R and an F, the D is bound to be uncertain. To put it differently: No matter how certain the legal rules may be, the decisions remain at the mercy of the courts' fact-finding. If there is doubt about what a court, in a law-suit, will find were the facts, then there is at least equal doubt about its decision.

. . .

What is the F? Is it what actually happened between Sensible and Smart? Most emphatically not. At best, it is only what the trial court—the trial judge or jury—thinks happened. What the trial court thinks happened may, however, be hopelessly incorrect. But that does not matter—legally speaking. For court purposes, what the court thinks about the facts is all that matters. The actual events, the real objective acts and words of Sensible and Smart, happened in the past. They do not walk into court. The court usually learns about these real, objective, past facts only through the oral testimony of fallible witnesses. Accordingly, the court, from hearing the testimony, must guess at the actual, past facts. Judicially, the facts consist of the reaction of the judge or jury to the testimony. The F is merely a guess about the actual facts. There can be no assurance that the F, that guess, will coincide with those actual, past facts.

To be sure, this difficulty becomes of no importance when the parties to the suit do not dispute about the facts, when their sole difference concerns the proper R. Then the R will settle the court fight.

. . .

But usually, when men "go to law," the facts are not admitted, and the testimony is oral and in conflict. For convenience, call such suits "contested" cases. It cannot be known in advance which cases will be "contested." To predict a decision in a suit not yet begun, about a dispute which has not yet occurred, requires, then, the most extensive guessing. For whenever there is a question of the credibility of witnesses—of the believability, the reliability, of their testimony—then, unavoidably, the trial judge or jury must make a guess about the facts. The lawyer, accordingly, must make a guess about those guesses. The uncertainty of many "legal rights" corresponds to the correctness or incorrectness of such lawyer-guesses.

1

Let me bring out that point more sharply. When, in 1946, the Sensible-Smart contract is signed, no dispute has yet arisen. The lawyer, in making his guess at that time, must attempt to take into

Jerome Frank

account what may be the future acts of Sensible and Smart, the acts they may do in the interval between 1946 and the date of a future law-suit. Patently, that contingency makes the guessing pretty difficult.

Suppose, however, that Sensible consults his lawyer in 1948, after a dispute has arisen, so that all the actual facts have already happened. It may seem to you that if the client, Sensible, accurately reports all those facts to his lawyer, the latter can undoubtedly tell his client just what a court will decide. I'm sorry to say you are wrong. The lawyer must still cope with many elusive, uncontrollable, wayward factors which may upset any prediction. Trials are often full of surprises. The adversary introduces unanticipated testimony. Witnesses, on whom the lawyer relied, change their stories when they take the witness-stand. The facts as they appeared to the lawyer when, before a trial, he conferred with his client and his witnesses, frequently are not at all like the facts as they later show up in the court-room.

But perhaps you believe that the trial judge or jury will surely learn the truth about the facts. If so, you are adopting an axiom, implied in the conventional theory of how courts decide cases, the "Truth-Will-Out axiom." But often that "axiom" does not jibe with reality. For reflect on the following: When a witness testifies, what is he doing? He is reporting his present memory of something he observed in the past, something he saw or heard. A witness is not a photographic plate or phonographic disc. Let us suppose that he is entirely honest. Nevertheless, note these sources of possible error:

1. The witness may erroneously have observed the past event at the time it occurred. The rankest amateur in psychology knows how faulty observation is, knows that what a man thinks he observes may not accord with what actually happened. Human observation is obviously fallible, subjective. It is affected by defects of sight, or hearing, or by the observer's emotional state or physiological condition, and by his preconceived notions. "Men," say the courts, "often think they see when they did not see, . . . misinterpret what they hear." As hundreds of experiments have demonstrated, two observers of the same happening frequently disagree.

2. But suppose a witness made no error in his original observa-

tion of an event. He may, nevertheless, erroneously remember that correct observation. The faulty, subjective, nature of human memory is notorious. Many a witness has an imaginative memory. "Even a conscientious person," said a court, "in trying to narrate a transaction which exists in his memory in a faded or fragmentary state, will, in his effort to make the reproduction seem complete and natural, substitute fancy for fact, or fabricate the missing or forgotten facts."

"When," writes Paton, "a witness makes a simple statement—'the prisoner is the man who drove the car after the robbery'—he is really asserting: (a) that he observed the car; (b) that the impression became fixed in his mind; (c) that the impression has not been confused or obliterated; (d) that the resemblance between the original impression and the prisoner is sufficient to base a judgment not of resemblance but of identity. Scientific research into the nature of the eye has shown how easy it is for vision to be mistaken; lack of observation and faulty memory add to the difficulties. Borchard, in discussing established cases of error in criminal convictions, points out that many of those errors arose from faulty identification and that in eight of the cases there was not the slightest resemblance between the real criminal and the person who was falsely convicted."

3. Now we come to the stage where the witness reports in the court-room his present recollection of his original observation. Here, again, error may enter. The honest witness, due to a variety of causes, may inadvertently misstate his recollection, may inaccurately report his story. Ram, writing of witnesses, notes that "it happens to all persons occasionally to use one word for another, making the sense very different from what was intended; unconsciously we say what we did not mean to say. . . ."

. . .

Thus far, I have posited an honest and unprejudiced witness. But many witnesses are neither. Some are downright liars. Aside from perjurers, there are the innumerous biased witnesses, whose narratives, although honest, have been markedly affected by their prejudices for or against one of the parties to the suit. A court has said that a biased witness, out of sympathy for a litigant he regards as having been wronged, "with entire innocence may recall things that have never occurred, or forget important instances that have occurred. . . ." "Perhaps the most subtle and prolific of all the 'fallacies of testimony' arises out of unconscious partisanship," writes Wellman. "It is rare that one comes across a witness in court who is so candid and fair that he will testify as fully and favorably for the one side as the other. . . . Witnesses usually feel more or less complimented by the confidence that is placed in them by the party calling them to prove a certain state of facts, and it is human nature to prove worthy of this confidence.". . . "The liar . . . is far less dangerous than the honest but mistaken witness who draws upon his imagination," Moore remarks. It is difficult to "determine in the case of an honestly intentioned witness how much of his evidence should be discarded as unreliable, and how much accepted as true. . . . Nothing is more deceitful than half the truth, and biased witnesses are much addicted to half-truths and coloring of facts. . . . Such a witness is more dangerous than one who commits a gross perjury. . . ."

. . .

The axiom or assumption that, in all or most trials, the truth will out, ignores, then, the several elements of subjectivity and chance. It ignores perjury and bias; ignores the false impression made on the judge or jury by the honest witness who seems untruthful because he is frightened in the court-room or because he is irascible or over-scrupulous or given to exaggeration. It ignores the mistaken witness who honestly and convincingly testifies that he remembers acts or conversations that happened quite differently than as he narrates them in court. It neglects, also, the dead or missing witness without whose testimony a crucial fact cannot be brought out, or an important opposing witness cannot be successfully contradicted. Finally it neglects the missing or destroyed letter, or receipt, or cancelled check.

Nor is it true that trial courts will be sure to detect lies or mistakes in testimony. That is clearly not so when a jury tries a case. Many experienced persons believe that of all the possible ways that could be devised to get at the falsity or truth of testimony, none could be conceived that would be more ineffective than trial by jury.

Judges, too, when they try cases without juries, are often fallible in getting at the true facts of a "contested" case. Partly that is due to our faulty way of trying cases in which we hamstring the judge. But even with the best system that could be devised, there would be no way to ensure that the judge will know infallibly which witnesses are accurately reporting the facts. As yet we have no lie-detector for which all responsible psychologists will vouch and which most courts will regard as reliable. But even a perfect lie-detector will not reveal mistakes in a witness' original observation of the facts to which he testifies, and probably will not disclose his mistakes due to his unconscious prejudices.

Lacking any adequate mechanical means of detecting such matters, the courts resort to a common-sense technique: All of us know that, in every-day life, the way a man behaves when he tells a story—his intonations, his fidgetings or composure, his yawns, the use of his eyes, his air of candor or of evasiveness—may furnish valuable clues to his reliability. Such clues are by no means impeccable guides, but they are often immensely helpful. So the courts have concluded. "The appearance and manner of a witness," many courts have said, "is often a complete antidote to what he testifies." The "witness' demeanor," notes Wigmore, "is always . . . in evidence."

. . .

2

Having in mind this significance properly attached to close observation of the witnesses, I now must emphasize an element in the decisional process which, curiously, has seldom been considered: Trial judges and juries, in trying to get at the past facts through the witnesses, are themselves witnesses of what goes on in court-rooms. They must determine the facts from what they see and hear, from the gestures and other conduct of the testifying witnesses as well as from their words. Now, as silent witnesses of the witnesses, the trial judges and juries suffer from the same human weaknesses as other witnesses. They, too, are not photo-

Jerome Frank

graphic plates or phonographic discs. If the testifying witnesses make errors of observation, are subject to lapses of memory, or contrive mistaken, imaginative reconstruction of events they observed, in the same way trial judges or juries are subject to defects in their apprehension and their recollection of what the witnesses said and how they behaved.

The facts as they actually happened are therefore twice refracted—first by the witnesses, and second by those who must "find" the facts. The reactions of trial judges or juries to the testimony are shot through with subjectivity. Thus we have subjectivity piled on subjectivity. It is surely proper, then, to say that the facts as "found" by a trial court are subjective.

. . .

3

And now I come to a major matter, one which most non-lawyers do not understand, and one which puts the trial courts at the heart of our judicial system: An upper court can seldom do anything to correct a trial court's mistaken belief about the facts. Where, as happens in most cases, the testimony at the trial was oral, the upper court usually feels obliged to adopt the trial court's determination of the facts. Why? Because in such a case the trial court heard and saw the witnesses as they testified, but the upper court did not. The upper court has only a typewritten or printed record of the testimony. The trial court alone is in a position to interpret the demeanor-clues, this "language without words." An upper court, to use Judge Kennison's phrase, "has to operate in the partial vacuum of the printed record." A "stenographic transcript," wrote Judge Ulman, ". . . fails to reproduce tones of voice and hesitations of speech that often make a sentence mean the reverse of what the mere words signify. The best and most accurate record [of oral testimony] is like a dehydrated peach; it has neither the substance nor the flavor of the peach before it was dried." That is why, when testimony is taken in a trial court, an upper court, on appeal, in most instances accepts the facts as found by the trial court, when those findings can be supported by reasonable inferences from some witness's testimony, even if it is flatly contradicted in the testimony of other witnesses.

Considering how a trial court reaches its determination as to the facts, it is most misleading to talk, as we lawyers do, of a trial court "finding" the facts. The trial court's facts are not "data," not something that is "given"; they are not waiting somewhere, ready made, for the court to discover, to "find." More accurately, they are processed by the trial court—are, so to speak, "made" by it, on the basis of its subjective reactions to the witnesses' stories. Most legal scholars fail to consider that subjectivity, because, when they think of courts, they think almost exclusively of upper courts and of their written opinions. For, in these opinions, the facts are largely "given" to the upper courts—given to those courts by the trial courts.

It should now be obvious that the conventional description of the decisional process needs alteration. For that description implies that the F, in the $R \times F = D$ equation, is an objective fact—what might be called an OF—so that, seemingly, $R \times OF = D$. But, as the F is subjective—what might therefore be called an SF—the formula should read: $R \times SF = D$.

4

. . . Recently I read a book written for laymen by a lawyer. The author says that, should you lose a law suit, because the court misapprehended the facts, and should you leave the court-room complaining of injustice, you would be an unreasonable, small-minded critic. For, he explains, in every suit there must be a loser, and you must learn to appreciate that no legal system can be perfect.

That not uncommon patronizing lawyer's way of brushing off laymen leaves me indignant. Of course, no legal system can be perfect. But think of this: A man is accused of killing another man and is tried for murder. If the accused is convicted, the government will kill him. The government's killing is lawful and therefore not murder. But if the government's killing follows a conviction brought about by the trial court's mistaken belief about the facts, so that the government, although acting according to legal forms, kills an innocent man—what then? Then a shocking act of judicial injustice has occurred. Yet our author writes, "Such a contingency does not justify condemnation of a system which is necessarily subject to human judgment; and if this complacent view exasperates a victim who has been found guilty of a crime which he has never committed, it is an incontrovertible fact," it is inevitable, like an "Act of God," as when a stroke of lightning kills a man.

That defense of grave miscarriages of justice is legitimate only if they are inevitable—that is, only if everything practical has been done to avoid such injustices. But, often, everything practical has not been done. Thanks to avoidable court-room errors, innocent men are convicted of crimes; and every week, for similar reasons, someone loses his life's savings, his livelihood, his job. Most of such injustices stem not from lack of justice in the legal rules but from mistakes in fact-finding. And a high percentage of those mistakes derive from needless defects in the court-house methods of getting at the facts.

It is up to the nonlawyers to demand a reform of those methods. They should not, I repeat, demand perfection. Perfect justice lies beyond human reach. But the unattainability of the ideal is no excuse for shirking the effort to obtain the best available. . . .

STANTON WHEELER

Criminal Statistics:
A Reformulation of the Problem

The history of papers on criminal statistics is rather discouraging. The basis for pessimism . . . does not lie with the absence of intelligent critical work. Rather, there is an absence of any follow-through that attempts to solve the problems pointed up in the various critiques.

. . .

In this paper I want to suggest that our inability to utilize and interpret criminal statistics is a result not of the technical deficiencies that have been pointed to before, but rather is a result of the way in which the original problem has been put.

. . .

The problem has to do with the underlying conception of crime, and therefore with the nature of the materials that are

Reprinted by permission from *Journal of Criminal Law, Criminology and Police Science*, Vol. 58, pp. 17–24 (1967).

Notes to this Selection will be found on page 425.

Wheeler is Professor of Law and Sociology at Yale University. He is co-author (with Brim) of Socialization After Childhood (1967) *and editor of* Controlling Delinquents (1968).

gathered as a result of this underlying conception. Put briefly, the underlying conception is that *the data of criminal statistics are mere records of response to the actions of criminals.* A person commits an act that is defined as illegal by statute. When the police department is notified of the act we have an offense known to police. If the department also finds someone and arrests him for the act we have a unit that enters arrest statistics. In either case the assumption is that the units reflect the passive responses of officials to the active behavior of criminals. Differential tendencies to report crimes, or failures to catch offenders, are seen as mere unreliability, and efforts may be made to stamp out such problems, since unreliability is bad. Efforts are made to achieve uniformity in crime reporting, to assure that all officials are handling the acts in similar ways. And efforts are made to improve the efficiency and reliability of the actual coding and classifying operations themselves, through the work of the research bureau of the police department, of those processing the data at the FBI or elsewhere.

Is it feasible, however, to sustain this conception of the nature of criminal statistics? The assumptions hold true only in very important but extremely rare limiting cases. We can treat the record of criminal acts as the record of criminals only when we have indeed achieved a precise uniformity in the reporting of such acts to the police, and in the processing of such acts by the police. Now, of course, we approach this ideal more or less closely with differing types of crime, as the early classification into part 1 and part 2 offenses by the FBI suggests. But the important point is that there is still great room for variability in reporting and processing, and the ideal is only rarely approached. Thus the conception of criminal statistics solely as records of response to the actions of criminals may not be the most useful way to conceive of the underlying problem.

The alternative is to conceive of three elements as *inherently* a part of the rate producing process, and of the resulting rate as an interaction of all three. The three categories include: 1) the offender who commits an act specified by statute to be illegal, 2) pool of citizens who may be either victims or reporters of the acts of the offenders, and 3) officers of the law who are formally charged with the obligation to respond to the action. We would then express offenses as a function of the interaction of these

three elements, any one of which might be more or less important in a particular instance.

It should be noted immediately that this is in no way a radical
reformulation of the problem. All who work with criminal statistics are aware of the great sources of variability that lie in
differential values of the community and in differential police
actions. This proposed change simply introduces these concerns
as a legitimate and inherent part of the model of criminal statistics, rather than conceiving of them as external and unwanted
sources of error and unreliability. The principal gain from making this transition is that variations in citizen and police actions
become important events to be explained, just as we make efforts
to explain why some commit crimes and some do not.

Each of these three categories can be looked at both individ-
ually and collectively. Thus we have single criminals, or in some
cases criminal organizations. We can conceive of the police
system as a whole as the responding agency, where variation in
police policies, technology, and so forth are the relevant aspects.
Or we could concentrate on individual officers, relating their
characteristics to their arrest behavior just as we now relate the
offender's characteristics to his criminal behavior. Finally, we can
think of the community as a pool of separate residents or as an
organized whole with shared sentiments in response to crime. But
before passing to several specific consequences that would flow
from such a reformulation, more should be said by way of an
operational and theoretical justification for this shift.

THE OPERATIONAL JUSTIFICATION

Consider how the records of crime are in fact produced. In
most cases they do indeed begin with an act of an offender, but
they never end there. As is obviously the case, they must be reported by someone or they never end up in our statistics. We
have usually assumed, as indicated in a quote by Sellin which is
perhaps the most oft-quoted remark about criminal statistics: "the
value of a crime rate for index purposes decreases as the distance
from the crime itself, in terms of procedure, increases."[1] But as
that very wording suggests, even the immediate reports themselves may be subject to great error, and it is that error which
is so troublesome to those who wish to use official data to test
theories of crime causation. While there is certainly no reason to

quarrel with the general wisdom of Sellin's statement, neither should we let it hide the fact that the greatest gap of all is likely to occur between the crime itself and the initiating procedure.

There are very few detailed accounts of the actual procedures used by police agencies in the processing of cases and the reporting of crime statistics. Where there are really full and detailed statements (as in the . . . Sellin and Wolfgang volume where a full chapter is devoted to the method of reporting delinquency by a division of the Philadelphia police),[2] two things seem abundantly clear.

First, standardizing decision-making at the initial stage, particularly in areas such as delinquency, is very difficult and requires a great deal of effort and attention to detail. For example, cases may come to the attention of a juvenile bureau either directly in the course of the juvenile officer's duties, or indirectly by referral. In addition to possible effects of these differences, there are different criteria used in the decision to arrest or report. In Philadelphia these include the juvenile's previous contacts with police, the type of offense, the attitude of the complainant, the offender's family situation, and potential community sources. It seems quite evident that individual officers might resolve these matters in somewhat different ways, despite a good deal of training.

The second point, however, is more important. These are procedures worked out by the Philadelphia department for the processing of Philadelphia cases. Quite clearly other principles may be utilized in other cities. How, then, are we to compare the figures in any sensible way? Even though each department may end up with reasonably uniform data for its area, comparability across towns, cities, or regions will be missing, as will comparability over time in the same jurisdiction if any further changes occur. The operational justification, then, is that these sources of variability appear built into the problem. It seems a wise course of action to attempt to understand them, since we are unlikely to get rid of them.

THE THEORETICAL JUSTIFICATION

The theoretical justification for treating crime statistics as a result of three-way interaction between an offender, victims or citizens, and official agents, is that deviation itself is increasingly recognized as a social process that depends heavily on social definition. Acts become deviant when they are so defined by members of the collectivities in which they occur. Whether a given pattern of behavior will be labeled deviant is itself problematic, and is likely to vary from community to community, or from policeman to policeman, at least within certain fairly broad limits. Why emphasize only the person who might commit an act, and not those who might label it as deviant, or those who might officially respond?

The concept here is close to that suggested decades ago by VanVechten: The tolerance quotient of a community.[3] This has to do with how much "trouble" the community will put up with before it acts, or in other words how much deviant behavior it will permit before either citizens or official agents take offense and respond in some systematic way.

Evidence in support of this orientation is found increasingly in the study of forms of deviation close to but not identical with criminality. Consider, for example, mental retardation. A recent study shows that the mentally retarded from families with lower educational background spend a shorter time in institutions and are released more readily than are those from higher educational background.[4] This is true even when they are matched carefully by IQ. The suggested explanation is that families of lower educational level are less likely to define their offspring as mentally retarded, and are therefore more ready to accept them back into the home. A related study shows that families of higher socio-economic status are able to get their children accepted into institutions for the mentally retarded more quickly than are those of lower socio-economic status, and this appears in part to be because they are more insistent about the need of the child in question.[5] In other words, they think of this behavior as more deviant than do those of lower socio-economic levels. It appears likely that both entry and release from the hospital are functions of the social characteristics of those who are attempting to get them in or out, and are not mere reflections of intelligence as measured by standardized tests.

Consider further some of the evidence regarding mental illness. Several recent studies suggest that rates of commitment bear a close correspondence to the paths of entry to hospitals. In one instance, that of a child guidance clinic where the concern is for which children are accepted among all those referred, the evidence is that those referred by doctors are more likely to be accepted than those referred by family members.[6] The further evidence is that the acceptance is more closely related to the source of referral than to the nature of the symptoms of the individual who is being referred.

In these areas of social deviation, therefore, it makes good sense to think of the deviation itself as a social process involving not only the person who commits deviant acts, but also those who choose to label them as deviant and those who are officially charged with acting upon them as such. Indeed, a full understanding of rates of institutionalization or rates of retardation and illness seems to require that we consider more than simply the mental or intellectual status of the person in question.

THE SPECIAL CASE OF CRIME

It can be argued that a mistake is made in attempting to treat crime in the same category as the foregoing forms of deviance. The criminal law is primarily statutory law, and the specification of conditions necessary to convict one of the commission of the crime is certainly more detailed and specific than is the case for mental subnormality or mental illness. Criminal statutes typically specify in some detail the nature of the offense, and we have well worked out techniques which, in the case of pleas of not guilty, may be utilized by juries to assess guilt or innocence. Therefore, we might expect somewhat more objectivity in the collection and analysis of data on crime than is true for other forms of deviation.

This argument is certainly true to a point, and it would be a mistake to equate crime overly readily with other forms of deviation. There is a sizeable difference between the behavioral specification of acts, for example, of burglary or arson, and the much more general, abstract, and judgmental character of the process of diagnosis of a person as psychotic. But again, two features of crime remain important to note in this context. First, enforcement of all statutes is not attempted. Diligence in some areas is matched by negligence in others. In fact, our policing and detection policies introduce new sources of variation that are not encompassed in the definition of the statutes, as Daniel Bell's article on the myths of crime waves reminds us.[7] Policies to "crack down" on all narcotics users or pushers, while "tolerating" organized prostitution, are likely to be found within the same police jurisdiction. This simply indicates that the clarity of the specification of law-violating behavior in the statutes is often not repeated by the policies in fact enforced by the policing agencies.

Even more important than this, however, is the fact that some of the forms of crime that are becoming increasingly important no longer have the clear-cut statutory form of definition. A principal case, of course, is delinquency. Most legal definitions of delinquency are so broad and vague as to make it roughly synonymous with juvenile trouble making. In addition to including offenses that also hold for adults, there are such things as being truant, willful disobeying of parental commands, and staying out after curfew. The lack of specification in these instances approaches that of the case of mental illness, which of course is not surprising in that many see forms of delinquency and forms of mental illness as synonymous.

For these reasons, I think it can be effectively argued that a model stressing the social definition of crime, and especially the actions of other social agents as well as those of presumed offenders, is pragmatically useful as well as being highly realistic.

Some Practical Consequences

The most immediate effect that would flow from adoption of this rationale is that we might be able to learn something more about systematic variations in the crime rate than we learn by examination of the characteristics of criminals. Consider each of the following four consequences:

I. IMPROVED UNDERSTANDING OF POLICE AND OFFICIAL AGENTS

Remembering the distinction between the collective and individual forms, and beginning with the collective, we might ask: What are characteristics of *police systems* where high crime or arrest rates prevail? Here is a problem eminently worthy of study, and we might almost refer to it, . . . as the Los Angeles police problem. Some years ago Ronald Beattie wanted to argue that the high rate of offenses known to the police in Los Angeles was a result, not of the law-violating behavior of Angelenos, but of the good deeds of Chief Parker and his force. The Los Angeles police department, he argued, was a superior force in terms of efficiency and dedication. The high rate of arrests was a result of efficiency, rather than the result of a high rate of offenses. This example at least suggests that we should be able to find some stable and reliable differences between police departments that report high rates of offenses and those that report relatively low rates. What are those differences? Suppose we introduce controls for the nature of the social composition of the community, would we still find stable differentials based upon differences in the police function?

Clearly, to answer these questions requires that we establish differential degrees of police efficiency in crime reporting, and differentials in types of police organization. Conceivably the arrest rate is a function of the number of motorcycles versus police cars on the road, a function of the proportion of the total police force that is civilian, a function of the average educational attainment of the individual officers, a function of whether or not there is a police academy that serves to train policemen for this particular department, and so on. The whole point is that introducing the official actions of the police, not as mere passive response to the criminal, but rather as an inherent part of the production of a crime rate, forces us to ask these questions, and hence ultimately to understand better the workings of police organization.

I shall cite two studies, of radically different styles, where this sort of contribution seems to be forthcoming. One is interesting work by the political scientist James Q. Wilson.[8] Wilson has compared a relatively non-professionalized police force in an Eastern city with a highly professionalized force in a West Coast city. His interest was in seeing whether the nature of the professional organization of the police is related to modes of handling delinquents and to the rate of arrest of juvenile offenders; and his findings suggest that it is indeed. The old-line force, fraternal in organization, recruits its members largely on grounds of locale, provides little training for them, and little professional esprit.

The result is that while they are punitive toward youthful offenders, there is no strong sense of urgency about police work and hence relatively low rates of official actions with regard to youthful offenders. The force in the West Coast city, in contrast, is one that is recruited nationwide, places a high premium on education, pays better, and in other ways appears to fit the model of a professional as distinguished from fraternal system. In the West Coast city youths are more likely to be picked up for minor offenses, minor offenses are more likely to be treated as major infractions, and the arrest rate tends to be much higher than in the East Coast city. This example merely serves to illustrate that the crime rate may vary in close correspondence with the nature of police organization, and conceivably quite independently from the nature of delinquent activity.

The second example comes from an ecological study by W. F. Greenhaigh of the British Home Office.[9] He had the wisdom to include as a relevant variable in his analysis the number of police per capita in various social units. He finds that the number of officers is related to the number of offenses reported, and while this of course raises a neat problem as to cause and effect, it serves to emphasize the potential role of the structure of the police systems themselves.

We may also find important sources of variation in individual differences *within* police departments. There is certainly good reason to imagine that there are sizeable differences in policemen in terms of the number of individuals they arrest or take official action upon. A police officer who has had many years of experience once related to me an incident from one of his early days on the force. He was in a squad car when they received a radio call from central headquarters to proceed rapidly to the scene of a particular offense. He was driving the car with his partner in the automobile, a much older and wiser policemen, sitting next to him. As my young, "gung ho" friend roared to the scene of the crime with the siren wailing, his older colleague turned to him and said "For crying out loud, slow down and turn off the siren. You're makin me noivous." The point is fairly clear: there is little more reason to expect age, training, ethnic background, and other characteristics to be irrelevent in this context than there is to expect them to disappear when we study offenders.

Stanton Wheeler

The necessary first step is to begin collecting data on policemen and police departments similar in form if not in content with what we gather on criminals. This is already done to some extent by the FBI, which annually publishes, for example, the list of the number of uniformed and civilian police employees for every reporting city over 2,500 population. Because this is thought to be relevant for policing, but not for crime, there have been no analyses, to my knowledge, of the possible correlation between number of police and either the number of criminals, or the number of offenses cleared by arrest.

The chief practical consequence of adopting a new rationale is that we would begin to understand the dynamics of police systems in relation to offenders. So long as we treat the police as mere reactors to the actions of criminals, this whole area will remain hidden from our view. My argument is simply that if we transform the degree of police efficiency into a variable to be explained, rather than one to be eliminated by the production of uniformity in procedure, we will enhance our understanding of crime.

2. IMPROVED UNDERSTANDING OF CITIZENS AND SOCIAL CONTROL

The pool of conventional persons in the community, either victims of crimes or citizens who observe them, often initiate the production of crime rates by being the first reporters of criminal events. There appear to be relatively vast communitywide differences in the rate at which persons call the police for help with problems. In Nathan Goldman's study of differential selection of juvenile offenders for court appearance, he suggests that official agents are highly responsive to the definition of deviation on the part of the citizens of the community, and that some of his communities have high rates of delinquency because the officials feel that the citizens will complain if they do not take official action, whereas other ones have low rates because the citizens simply do not complain.[10]

Another example of the possibilities here is provided in a study by Eleanor Maccoby and others.[11] They interviewed members of two communities, one of which had a high rate of delinquency and the other a low rate, where socio-economic characteristics were held constant insofar as possible. One of the things they found is that the community that had a low rate of official offenses had a high rate of community cohesion. That is, friends, neighbors and others would intervene when they saw kids getting into trouble. In the community with the high official delinquency, there was very little interaction among members, and little intervention at these early stages. The strong suggestion here is that informal social controls operate effectively in one community to obviate the need for official actions, whereas in the other they did not. The low official rates were due to prompt intervention in cases of incipient deviation; in the other community incipient deviation was not responded to at all, and it grew in seriousness until official actions occurred.

Although the evidence in these two cases is not entirely clear, the general point is certainly not to be debated: different types of neighborhoods and communities may respond to deviant behavior in radically different ways, and their responses become the initiation of the official reporting system. Unless we understand them we will not be led to a full understanding of the rate production process.

As in the case of police systems, we may find individual variation within the neighborhood or community, just as we find systematic variations between them. Either as victim or as observer, we are likely to find many important differences in the role of the citizenry in the production of crime rates. There are of course several studies focusing on the victim, but usually these have been separate investigations that have little relation to routine police reporting. And there is folk knowledge, though little systematic evidence, of individual differences in willingness to report offenses to the police. Older single women living alone are thought by some to be inordinately observant of potential criminal situations. One police captain once told me that the rate of telepone calls reporting crimes in progress dropped substantially with the growth of television. The implication was that people who used to mind other's business, and hence keep their eyes on the street below, were now absorbed watching crime dramas on TV and did not see the real thing anymore.

Although these examples may be of dubious validity, they serve to illustrate the main point: whether a person gets treated officially as an offender depends on which citizen he happened to meet and which community he happened to be in when the act occurred; and our explanation of variations in crime rates will have to do in part with area variations in the nature of communities and their law-abiding citizens.

3. THE DEVELOPMENT OF CONSUMER-ORIENTED CRIME STATISTICS

A third practical consequence is that we could begin to express crime rates in ways that would have more meaning for the public. The police system itself exists for the protection of the community, but so far we have done extremely little to provide data that is directly relevant to community members. This is apparent by examining the denominators that typically are used in construction of crime rates. If one is diligent, one can find arrest rates for Negroes, for Puerto Ricans, for whites. Or one can find age-specific rates of offense. In a handful of cases, one can find cohort analysis tables indicating the probability that a person will ever be arrested between, say, ages 7 to 18.

All of these figures have a curious cast. They tell us much more about who commits the offense than about the person against whom it is committed. Yet if we think now as citizens, and not as persons interested solely in offenders or policing, it seems that we might ask rather different questions. Personally, I am more concerned whether my wife and children are likely to be assaulted at all, than whether, if the deed is done, they are assaulted by a Caucasian, a Puerto Rican, or a Negro. Yet I can find figures on the latter topic but not on the former. Similarly, one may wonder what New York City residents would make of the fact that the reportedly rising crime rate in the City could be explained as a function of the increased number of persons of juvenile age, which is of course the age at which most crimes are committed (so far as we can tell from official statistics). Certainly it is important theoretically to understand that the rising rate does not appear to be a response to new forces and fears in mass society, but rather can be explained fairly directly as a function of the age structure of the population. But for the typical resident, the important question would seem to be whether or not the rate has gone up for victims in his category.

This is simply to suggest that a useful way of reporting crime data would be to use as a denominator not some characteristic that might describe offenders, but one that will describe their victims. Apartment dwellers might well want to know what the probability is that their apartment will be burgled within the next five years. Others might want to know what the probability is that they will be robbed. In principle, it should not be difficult to prepare such statistics. We take the number of offenses appearing in a particular area against a particular type of victim, and express it as a proportion of all persons who have the social characteristics that the victim happens to hold. In this way we have victim-specific rather than offender-specific crime rates—in effect, a box score which the citizen can use to keep tabs on differing areas in his community, and hopefully on differing communities. It would become abundantly clear, for example, which areas of the city are most dangerous at night, and for what categories of persons they are most dangerous. Such consumer-oriented statistics would seem to be more important as a public service than are offender-oriented statistics such as those we now produce.

The issues are clearly more complicated than suggested here. One problem is the necessity of correcting for the daytime and nighttime populations of the areas. And in order to get detailed victim-specific rates, we would have to learn more now than we normally do about the nature of the victim. In the latest *Uniform Crime Report* available to me (for the year 1963) only one out of some 49 tables tells us anything about the victim. This one has to do with the victims of homicides, and classifies the victims according to their age, sex, and race.[12] At least, I would argue, it is an effort in a much needed direction.

4. IMPROVED UNDERSTANDING OF CRIMINALS AND CRIMINAL ACTS

The fourth and final consequence is that adopting the frame of reference outlined here might enable us to approach what we have always traditionally desired, namely, better descriptive and explanatory accounts of the actions of criminals. Paradoxically, it is only by first directing our attention to the citizens and the police that we can begin making headway on the initial problem of sources of variation in crime rates.

At the moment, any community-wide comparisons of crime data are subject to possible unreliability, and certainly debate as to the interpretation of meaning, because of possible differentials in the functioning of the citizens and the police. A higher rate of crime for community A than for community B cannot be guaranteed to tell us something about the actual level of law violations in the two communities, for all the reasons we have already re-

Stanton Wheeler

viewed. Any efforts aimed at assessing the actual rate of legal violations, or differentials in the rate that are related to differential characteristics of the offenders, must of necessity take into account the variation due to citizens and policing. We can do so, of course, only if we have studied such variations and have evidence with regard to them.

THE NECESSARY FIRST STEP

The most essential first step is that there must be new sources of input to the official collections of data. If the position argued here is correct, it will no longer be enough for the established reporting agencies such as the FBI to collect data simply on the number of crimes reported in the various jurisdictions. It will be essential that they also collect systematic data on a) the complaining witnesses, b) the social characteristics of the community, c) the reporting or arresting officer, and d) the nature of the police system as a whole. Just as there is a reporting form for crime, there must be a reporting form for complainants, for the community, for officers, and for police departments. This would enable us to gather systematic data on the other possible sources of variation in crime rates. The details for such reporting forms would of course have to be worked out, and problems of uniformity would be sure to arise. But there is no reason why they should be any more severe than those now plaguing the reporting of crimes. Also, it would be necessary for us to think about more creative denominators for crime rates, along the lines suggested above. But here too, the technical task is not overwhelming, and much of the work has already been done by the Bureau of the Census.

If prestigious organizations such as the FBI were to begin collecting such data routinely, we could begin to close in on the haunting problems of biases in criminal statistics. We could at least compare jurisdictions whose police procedures were roughly similar, and where the types of complaining witnesses were not simply a function of the demographic structure of the community. More importantly, we could begin to examine the interactions between the three major sources of variation: the offender, the citizenry, and the police system.

JOSEPH GOLDSTEIN

Police Discretion Not to Invoke the Criminal Process: Low-visibility Decisions in the Administration of Justice

Police decisions not to invoke the criminal process largely determine the outer limits of law enforcement. By such decisions, the police define the ambit of discretion throughout the process of other decisionmakers—prosecutor, grand and petit jury, judge, probation officer, correction authority, and parole and pardon boards. These police decisions, unlike their decisions to invoke the law, are generally of extremely low visibility and consequently are seldom the subject of review. Yet an opportunity for review and appraisal of nonenforcement decisions is essential to the functioning of the rule of law in our system of criminal justice. This Article will therefore be an attempt

Reprinted by permission of the Yale Law Journal Company and Fred B. Rothman & Company from the *Yale Law Journal*, vol. 69, pp. 543–89 (1960).

Notes to this Selection will be found on pages 425–426.

Goldstein is Hamilton Professor of Law, Science, and Social Policy at Yale University. He is the author, inter alia, *of* The Government of A British Trade Union (1952) *and coauthor (with Donnelly and Schwartz) of* Criminal Law (1961).

Joseph Goldstein

to determine how the visibility of such police decisions may be increased and what procedures should be established to evaluate them on a continuing basis, in the light of the complex of objectives of the criminal law and of the paradoxes toward which the administration of criminal justice inclines.

1

The criminal law is one of many intertwined mechanisms for the social control of human behavior. It defines behavior which is deemed intolerably disturbing to or destructive of community values and prescribes sanctions which the state is authorized to impose upon persons convicted or suspected of engaging in prohibited conduct. Following a plea or verdict of guilty, the state deprives offenders of life, liberty, dignity, or property through convictions, fines, imprisonments, killings, and supervised releases, and thus seeks to punish, restrain, and rehabilitate them, as well as to deter others from engaging in proscribed activity. Before verdict, and despite the presumption of innocence which halos every person, the state deprives the suspect of life, liberty, dignity, or property through the imposition of deadly force, search and seizure of persons and possessions, accusation, imprisonment, and bail, and thus seeks to facilitate the enforcement of the criminal law.

These authorized sanctions reflect the multiple and often conflicting purposes which now surround and confuse criminal law administration at and between key decision points in the process. The stigma which accompanies conviction, for example, while serving a deterrent, and possibly retributive, function, becomes operative upon the offender's release and thus impedes the rehabilitation objective of probation and parole.† Similarly, the re-

---

† The criminal process, from arrest through release, is comprised of a series of "status degradation ceremonies." A status degradation ceremony is "any communicative work between persons whereby the public identity of an actor is transformed into something looked on as lower in the local scheme of social types." Garfinkel, *Conditions of Successful Degradation Ceremonies*, 61 AM. J. SOCIOLOGY 420 (1956). As a result of the

straint function of imprisonment involves the application of rules and procedures which, while minimizing escape opportunities, contributes to the deterioration of offenders confined for reformation. Since police decisions not to invoke the criminal process may likewise further some objectives while hindering others, or, indeed, run counter to all, any meaningful appraisal of these decisions should include an evaluation of their impact throughout the process on the various objectives reflected in authorized sanctions and in the decisions of other administrators of criminal justice.

Under the rule of law, the criminal law has both a fair-warning function for the public and a power-restricting function for officials. Both post- and preverdict sanctions, therefore, may be imposed only in accord with authorized procedures. No sanctions are to be inflicted other than those which have been prospectively prescribed by the constitution, legislation, or judicial decision for a particular crime or a particular kind of offender. These concepts, of course, do not preclude differential disposition, within the authorized limits, of persons suspected or convicted of the same or similar offenses. In an ideal system differential handling, individualized justice, would result, but only from an equal application of officially approved criteria designed to implement officially approved objectives. And finally a system which presumes innocence requires that preconviction sanctions be kept at a minimum

---

redefinition of individual status which accompanies being labelled "accused," "convict," or "exconvict," many releasees pay the penalty for their offenses and suspected offenses on a never ending installment plan.

One of the crucial problems facing the administration of criminal justice is how to establish release procedures which in practice become *status-elevation* ceremonies. Discharge from parole or from prison should carry with it, in appropriate situations, the kinds of redefinitions upward that are associated, for example, with graduation from high school or college, honorable discharge from the armed services, successful completion of apprenticeship in a trade or admission to a profession. Some ceremony or series of ceremonies must be devised to redefine the social status of releasees so that the public will begin to entertain a presumption that a person honorably discharged (as opposed to neutrally discharged or possibly even dishonorably discharged) from the correctional service is ready to take his place as a law-abiding citizen in the community. Were such a ceremony or ceremonies created, effective pressure might be placed on correctional authorities to test and carry out rehabilitation programs and to develop a meaningful system of communication with the public.

consistent with assuring an opportunity for the process to run its course.

A regularized system of review is a requisite for insuring substantial compliance by the administrators of criminal justice with these rule-of-law principles. Implicit in the word "review" and obviously essential to the operation of any review procedure is the visibility of the decisions and conduct to be scrutinized. Pretrial hearings on motions, the trial, appeal and the writ of habeas corpus constitute a formal system for evaluating the actions of officials invoking the criminal process. The public hearing, the record of proceedings, and the publication of court opinions—all features of the formal system—preserve and increase the visibility of official enforcement activity and facilitate and encourage the development of an informal system of appraisal. These proceedings and documents are widely reported and subjected to analysis and comment by legislative, professional, and other interested groups and individuals.

But police decisions not to invoke the criminal process, except when reflected in gross failures of service, are not visible to the community. Nor are they likely to be visible to official state reviewing agencies, even those within the police department. Failure to tag illegally parked cars is an example of gross failure of service, open to public view and recognized for what it is. An officer's decision, however, not to investigate or report adequately a disturbing event which he has reason to believe constitutes a violation of the criminal law does not ordinarily carry with it consequences sufficiently visible to make the community, the legislature, the prosecutor, or the courts aware of a possible failure of service. The police officer, the suspect, the police department, and frequently even the victim, when directly concerned with a decision not to invoke, unlike the same parties when responsible for or subject to a decision to invoke, generally have neither the incentive nor the opportunity to obtain review of that decision or the police conduct associated with it. Furthermore, official police records are usually too incomplete to permit evaluations of nonenforcement decisions in the light of the purposes of the criminal law. Consequently, such decisions, unlike decisions to enforce, are generally not subject to the control which would follow from administrative, judicial, legislative, or community review and appraisal.

Confidential reports detailing the day to day decisions and activities of a large municipal police force have been made available to the author by the American Bar Foundation. These reports give limited visiblity to a wide variety of police decisions not to invoke the criminal process.[1] Three groups of such decisions will be described and analyzed. Each constitutes a police "program" of nonenforcement either based on affirmative departmental policy or condoned by default. All of the decisions, to the extent that the officers concerned thought about them at all, represent well-intentioned, honest judgments, which seem to reflect the police officer's conception of his job. None of the decisions involve bribery or corruption, nor do they concern "obsolete," though unrepealed, criminal laws. Specifically, these programs involve police decisions (1) not to enforce the narcotics laws against certain violators who inform against other "more serious" violators; (2) not to enforce the felonious assault laws against an assailant whose victim does not sign a complaint; and (3) not to enforce gambling laws against persons engaged in the numbers racket, but instead to harass them. Each of these decisions are made even though the police "know" a crime has been committed, and even though they may "know" who the offender is and may, in fact, have apprehended him. But before describing and evaluating these nonenforcement programs, as an agency of review might do, it is necessary to determine what discretion, if any, the police, as invoking agents, have, and conceptually to locate the police in relation to other principal decisionmakers in the criminal law process.

II

The police have a duty not to enforce the substantive law of crimes unless invocation of the process can be achieved within bounds set by constitution, statute, court decision, and possibly official pronouncements of the prosecutor. *Total enforcement,*

Joseph Goldstein

were it possible, is thus precluded, by generally applicable due-process restrictions on such police procedures as arrest, search, seizure, and interrogation. *Total enforcement* is further precluded by such specific procedural restrictions as prohibitions on invoking an adultery statute unless the spouse of one of the parties complains, or an unlawful-possession-of-firearms statute if the offender surrenders his dangerous weapons during a statutory period of amnesty. Such restrictions of general and specific application mark the bounds, often ambiguously, of an area of *full enforcement* in which the police are not only authorized but expected to enforce fully the law of crimes. An area of *no enforcement* lies, therefore, between the perimeter of *total enforcement* and the outer limits of *full enforcement*. In this *no enforcement* area, the police have no authority to invoke the criminal process.

Within the area of *full enforcement*, the police have not been delegated discretion not to invoke the criminal process. On the contrary, those state statutes providing for municipal police departments which define the responsibility of police provide:

> "It shall be the duty of the police . . . under the direction of the mayor and chief of police and in conformity with the ordinances of the city, and the laws of the state, . . . to pursue and arrest any persons fleeing from justice . . . to apprehend any and all persons in the act of committing any offense against the laws of the state . . . and to take the offender forthwith before the proper court or magistrate, to be dealt with for the offense; to make complaints to the proper officers and magistrates of any person known or believed by them to be guilty of the violation of the ordinances of the city or the penal laws of the state; and at all times diligently and faithfully to enforce all such laws . . ."[2]

Even in jurisdictions without such a specific statutory definition, declarations of the *full enforcement* mandate generally appear in municipal charters, ordinances or police manuals. Police manuals, for example, commonly provide, in sections detailing the duties at each level of the police hierarchy, that the captain, superintendent, lieutenant, or patrolman shall be responsible, so far as is in his power, for the prevention and detection of crime and the enforcement of all criminal laws and ordinances.[3] Illustrative of the spirit and policy of *full enforcement* is this protestation from the introduction to the Rules and Regulations of the Atlanta, Georgia, Police Department:

> "Enforcement of all Criminal Laws and City Ordinances, is my obligation. There are no specialties under the Law. My eyes must be open to traffic problems and disorders, though I move on other assignments, to slinking vice in back streets and dives though I have been directed elsewhere, to the suspicious appearance of evil wherever it is encountered. . . . I must be impartial because the Law surrounds, protects and applies to all alike, rich and poor, low and high, black and white. . . ."

Minimally, then, *full enforcement*, so far as the police are concerned, means (1) the investigation of every disturbing event which is reported to or observed by them and which they have reason to suspect may be a violation of the criminal law; (2) following a determination that some crime has been committed, an effort to discover its perpetrators; and (3) the presentation of all information collected by them to the prosecutor for his determination of the appropriateness of further invoking the criminal process.

Full enforcement, however, is not a realistic expectation. In addition to ambiguities in the definitions of both substantive offenses and due-process boundaries, countless limitations and pressures preclude the possibility of the police seeking or achieving *full enforcement*. Limitations of time, personnel, and investigative devices—all in part but not entirely functions of budget—force the development, by plan or default, of priorities of enforcement. Even if there were "enough police" adequately equipped and trained, pressures from within and without the department, which is after all a human institution, may force the police to invoke the criminal process selectively. By decisions not to invoke within the area of *full enforcement*, the police largely determine the outer limits of *actual enforcement* throughout the criminal process.

Joseph Goldstein

This relationship of the police to the total administration of criminal justice can be seen in the diagram opposite this page. They may reinforce, or they may undermine, the legislature's objectives in designating certain conduct "criminal" and in authorizing the imposition of certain sanctions following conviction. A police decision to ignore a felonious assault "because the victim will not sign a complaint," usually precludes the prosecutor or grand jury from deciding whether to accuse, judge or jury from determining guilt or innocence, judge from imposing the most "appropriate" sentence, probation or correctional authorities from instituting the most "appropriate" restraint and rehabilitation programs, and finally parole or pardon authorities from determining the offender's readiness for release to the community. This example is drawn from one of the three programs of nonenforcement about to be discussed.

III

Trading enforcement against a narcotics suspect for information about another narcotics offense or offender may involve two types of police decisions not to invoke fully the criminal process. First, there may be a decision to ask for the dismissal or reduction of the charge for which the informant is held; second, there may be a decision to overlook future violations while the suspect serves as an informer. The second type is an example of a relatively pure police decision not to invoke the criminal process while the first requires, at a minimum, tacit approval by prosecutor or judge. But examination of only the pure types of decisions would oversimplify the problem. They fail to illustrate the extent to which police nonenforcement decisions may permeate the process as well as influence, and be influenced by, prosecutor and court action in settings which fail to prompt appraisal of such decisions in light of the purposes of the criminal law. Both types of decisions, pure and conglomerate, are nonetheless primarily police decisions. They are distingishable from a prosecutor's or court's decision to trade information for enforcement under an immunity statute and from such parliamentary decisions as the now-repealed seventeenth and eighteenth century English statutes which gave a con-

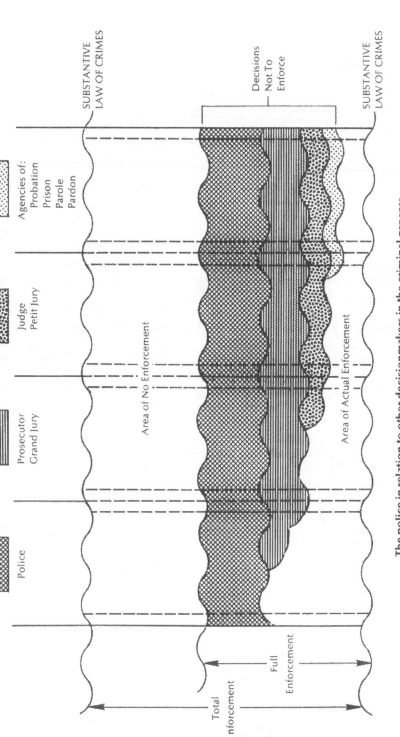

The police in relation to other decisionmakers in the criminal process

Joseph Goldstein

victed offender who secured the conviction of his accomplice an absolute right to pardon. Such prosecutor and parliamentary decisions to trade information for enforcement, unlike the police decisions to be described, have not only been authorized by a legislative body, but have also been made sufficiently visible to permit review.

In the municipality studied, regular uniformed officers, with general law enforcement duties on precinct assignments, and a special narcotics squad of detectives, with citywide jurisdiction, are responsible for enforcement of the state narcotics laws. The existence of the special squad acts as a pressure on the uniformed officer to be the first to discover any sale, possession, or use of narcotics in his precinct. Careful preparation of a case for prosecution may thus become secondary to this objective. Indeed, approximately eighty percent of those apprehended for narcotics violations during one year were discharged. In the opinion of the special squad, which processes each arrested narcotics suspect, either the search was illegal or the evidence obtained inadequate. The precinct officer's lack of interest in carefully developing a narcotics case for prosecution often amounts in effect to a police decision not to enforce but rather to harass.

But we are concerned here primarily with the decisions of the narcotics squad, which, like the Federal Narcotics Bureau, has established a policy of concentrating enforcement efforts against the "big supplier." The chief of the squad claimed that informers must be utilized to implement that policy, and that in order to get informants it is necessary to trade "little ones for big ones." Informers are used to arrange and make purchases of narcotics, to elicit information from suspects, including persons in custody, and to recruit additional informants.

Following arrest, a suspect will generally offer to serve as an informer to "do himself some good." If an arrestee fails to initiate such negotiations, the interrogating officer will suggest that something may be gained by disclosing sources of supply and by serving as an informer. A high mandatory minimum sentence for selling, a high maximum sentence for possession, and, where users are involved, a strong desire on their part to avoid the agonies of withdrawal, combine to place the police in an excellent bargaining position to recruit informers. To assure performance, each informer is charged with a narcotics violation, and final disposition is postponed until the defendant has fulfilled his part of the bargain. To protect the informer, the special squad seeks to camouflage him in the large body of releasees by not disclosing his identity even to the arresting precinct officer, who is given no explanation for release. Thus persons encountered on the street by a uniformed patrolman the day after their arrest may have been discharged, or they may have been officially charged and then released on bail or personal recognizance to await trail or to serve as informers.

While serving as informers, suspects are allowed to engage in illegal activity. Continued use of narcotics is condoned; the narcotics detective generally is not concerned with the problem of informants who make buys and use some of the evidence themselves. Though informers are usually warned that their status does not give them a "license to peddle," possession of a substantial amount of narcotics may be excused. In one case, a defendant found guilty of possession of *marijuana* argued that she was entitled to be placed on probation since she had cooperated with the police by testifying against three persons charged with sale of narcotics. The sentencing judge denied her request because he discovered that her cooperation was related to the possession of a substantial amount of *heroin*, an offense for which she was arrested (but never charged) while on bail for the marijuana violation. A narcotics squad inspector, in response to an inquiry from the judge, revealed that the defendant had not been charged with possession of *heroin* because she had been cooperative with the police on that offense.

In addition to granting such outright immunity for some violations, the police will recommend to the prosecutor either that an informer's case be *nolle prossed* or, more frequently, that the charge be reduced to a lesser offense. And, if the latter course is followed, the police usually recommend to the judge, either in response to his request for information or in the presentence report, that informers be placed on probation or given relatively light sentences. Both the prosecutor and judge willingly respond to police requests for reducing a charge of sale to a lesser offense because they consider the mandatory minimum too severe. As a result, during a four year period in this jurisdiction, less than two

Joseph Goldstein

and one-half percent of all persons charged with the sale of narcotics were convicted of that offense.

The narcotics squad's policy of trading *full enforcement* for information is justified on the grounds that apprehension and prosecution of the "big supplier" is facilitated. The absence of any in the city is attributed to this policy. As one member of the squad said, "[The city] is too hot. There are too many informants." A basic, though untested, assumption of the policy is that ridding the city of the "big supplier" is the key to solving its narcotics problem. Even if this assumption were empirically validated, the desirability of continuing such a policy cannot be established without taking into account its total impact on the administration of criminal justice in the city, the state, and the nation. Yet no procedure has been designed to enable the police and other key administrators of criminal justice to obtain such an appraisal. The extent and nature of the need for such a procedure can be illustrated, despite the limitations of available data, by presenting in the form of a mock report some of the questions, some of the answers, and some of the proposals a Policy Appraisal and Review Board might consider.

Following a description of the informer program, a report might ask:

To what extent, if at all, has the legislature delegated to the police the authority to grant, or obtain a grant of, complete or partial immunity from prosecution, in exchange for information about narcotics suppliers? No provisions of the general immunity or narcotics statutes authorize the police to exercise such discretion. The general immunity statute requires a high degree of visibility by providing that immunity be allowed only on a written motion by the prosecuting attorney to the court and that the information given be reduced to writing under the direction of the judge to preclude future prosecution for the traded offense or offenses. The narcotics statutes, unlike comparable legislation concerning other specific crimes, make no provision for obtaining information by awarding immunity from prosecution. Nor is there any indication, other than possibly in the maximum sentences authorized, that the legislature intended that certain narcotics offenses be given high priority or be enforced at the expense of other offenses. What evidence there is of legislative intent suggests the contrary; this fact is recognized by the local police manual. And nothing in the statute providing for the establishment of local police departments can be construed to authorize the policy of trading enforcement for information. That statute makes *full enforcement* a duty of the police. The narcotics squad has ignored this mandate and adopted an informer policy which appears to constitute a usurpation of legislative function. It does not follow that the police must discontinue employing informers, but they ought to discontinue trading enforcement for information until the legislature, the court, or the prosecutor explicitly initiates such a program. Whether the police policy of trading enforcement for information should be proposed for legislative consideration would depend upon the answers to some of the questions which follow.

Does trading enforcement for information fulfill the retributive, restraining, and reformative functions of the state's narcotics laws? By in effect licensing the user-informer to satisfy his addiction and assuring the peddler-informer, who may also be a user, that he will obtain dismissal or reduction of the pending charge to a lesser offense, the police undermine, if not negate, the retributive and restraining functions of the narcotics laws. In addition, the community is deprived of an opportunity to subject these offenders, particularly the addicts, to treatment aimed at reformation. In fact, the police ironically acknowledge the inconsistency of their program with the goal of treatment; "cured" addicts are not used as informers for fear that exposure to narcotics might cause their relapse. A comparison of the addict-release policies of the police, sentencing judge, and probation and parole authorities demonstrates the extent to which the administration of criminal justice can be set awry by a police nonenforcement program. At one point on the continuum, the police release the addict to informer status so that he can maintain his association with peddlers and users. The addict accepts such status on the tacit condition that continued use will be condoned. At other points on the continuum, the judge and probation and parole authorities make treatment a condition of an addict's release and continued use or even association with narcotics users the basis for revoking probation or parole. Thus the inherent conflict between basic purposes of the criminal law is compounded by conflicts among key decision-points in the process.

Does trading enforcement for information implement the deterrent function of criminal law administration? If deterrence depends—and little if anything is really known about the deterrent impact of the criminal law—in part at least, upon the potential offender's perception of law enforcement, the informer policy can have only a negative effect. In addition to the chance of nondetection which accompanies the commission of all crimes in varying degrees, the narcotics suspect has four-to-one odds that he will not be charged following detection and arrest. And he has a high expectation, even if charged, of obtaining a reduction or dismissal of an accurate charge. These figures reflect and reinforce the offender's view of the administration of criminal justice as a bargaining process initiated either by offering information "to do himself some good" or by a member of the narcotics squad advising the uninformed suspect, the "new offender," of the advantages of disclosing his narcotics "connections." Such law enforcement can have little, if any, deterrent impact.

That the "big supplier," an undefined entity, has been discouraged from using the city as a headquarters was confirmed by a local federal agent and a United States attorney in testimony before a Senate committee investigating illicit narcotics traffic. They attributed the result, however, to the state's high mandatory minimum sentence for selling, not to the informer policy. In fact, that municipal police policy was not made visible at the hearings. It was neither mentioned in their testimony nor in the testimony of the chief of police and the head of the narcotics squad. These local authorities may have reasoned that since the mandatory sentence facilitates the recruitment of informers who, in turn, are essential to keeping the "big supplier" outside city limits, the legislature's sentencing policy could be credited with the "achievement."

Whether the police informer program, the legislature's sentencing policy, both, or neither, caused the "big supplier" to locate elsewhere is not too significant; the traffic and use of narcotics in the city remain major problems. Since user-demand is maintained, if not increased, by trading enforcement for information, potential and actual peddlers are encouraged to supply the city's addicts. Testimony before the Senate committee indicates that although the "big suppliers" have moved their headquarters to other cities, there are now in the city a large number of small peddlers serving a minimum of 1,500 and in all probability a total of 2,500 users, and that the annual expenditure for illicit narcotics in the city is estimated at not lower than ten and probably as high as eighteen million dollars. Evaluated in terms of deterrent effect, the program of trading enforcement for information to reach the "big supplier" has failed to implement locally the ultimate objective of the narcotics laws—reducing addiction. Furthermore, the business of the "big supplier" has not been effectively deterred. At best suppliers have been discouraged from basing their operations in the city, which continues to be a lucrative market. Thus by maintaining the market, local policy, although a copy of national policy, may very well hinder the efforts of the Federal Narcotics Bureau.

A report of a Policy Appraisal and Review Board might find: "Trading little ones for big ones" is outside the ambit of municipal police discretion and should continue to remain so because it conflicts with the basic objectives of the criminal law. Retribution, restraint, and reformation are subverted by a policy which condones the use and possession of narcotics. And deterrence cannot be enhanced by a police program which provides potential and actual suppliers and users with more illustrations of nonenforcement than enforcement.

A report might conclude by exploring and suggesting alternative programs for coping with the narcotics problem. No attempt will be made here to exhaust or detail all possible alternatives. An obvious one would be a rigorous program of *full enforcement* designed to dry up, or at least drastically reduce, local consumer and peddler demand for illicit narcotics. If information currently obtained from suspects is essential and worth a price, compensation might be given to informers, with payments deferred until a suspect's final release. Such a program would neither undermine the retributive and restraining objectives of the criminal law nor deprive the community of an opportunity to impose rehabilitation regimes on the offender. Funds provided by deferred payments might enhance an offender's chances of getting off to a

Joseph Goldstein

good start upon release. Moreover, changing the picture presently perceived by potential violators from nonenforcement to enforcement would at least not preclude the possibility of deterrence. Such a program might even facilitate the apprehension of "big suppliers" who, faced with decreasing demand, might either be forced to discontinue serving the city because sales would no longer be profitable or to adopt bolder sales methods which would expose them to easier detection.

Full enforcement will place the legislature in a position to evaluate its narcotics laws by providing a basis for answering such questions as: Will *full enforcement* increase the price of narcotics to the user? Will such inflation increase the frequency of crimes committed to finance narcotics purchases? Or will *full enforcement* reduce the number of users and the frequency of connected crimes? Will too great or too costly an administrative burden be placed on the prosecutor's office and the courts by *full enforcement?* Will correctional institutions be filled beyond "effective" capacity? The answers to these questions are now buried or obscured by decisions not to invoke the criminal process.

Failure of a *full enforcement* program might prompt a board recommendation to increase treatment or correctional personnel and facilities. Or a board, recognizing that *full enforcement* would be either too costly or inherently ineffective, might propose the repeal of statutes prohibiting the use and sale of narcotics and/or the enactment, as part of a treatment program, of legislation authorizing sales to users at a low price. Such legislative action would be designed to reduce use and connected offenses to a minimum. By taking profits out of sales it would lessen peddler incentive to create new addicts and eliminate the need to support the habit by the commission of crimes.

These then are the kinds of questions, answers, and proposals a Policy Appraisal and Review Board might explore in its report examining this particular type of police decision not to invoke the criminal process.

IV

Another low visibility situation which an Appraisal and Review Board might uncover in this municipality stems from police decisions not to invoke the felonious assault laws unless the victim signs a complaint. Like the addict-informer, the potential complainant in an assault case is both the victim of an offense and a key source of information. But unlike him, the complainant, who is not a suspect, and whose initial contact with the police is generally self-imposed, is not placed under pressure to bargain. And in contrast with the informer program, the police assault program was clearly not designed, if designed at all, to effectuate an identifiable policy.

During one month under the nonenforcement program of a single precinct, thirty-eight out of forty-three felonious assault cases, the great majority involving stabbings and cuttings, were cleared "because the victim refused to prosecute." This program, which is coupled with a practice of not encouraging victims to sign complaints, reduces the pressure of working by eliminating such tasks as apprehending and detaining suspects, writing detailed reports, applying for warrants to prefer charges and appearing in court at inconvenient times for long periods without adequate compensation. As one officer explained, "run-of-the-mill" felonious assaults are so common in his precinct that prosecution of each case would force patrolmen to spend too much time in court and leave too little time for investigating other offenses. This rationalization exposes the private value system of individual officers as another policy-shaping factor. Some policemen feel, for example, that assault is an acceptable means of settling disputes among Negroes, and that when both assailant and victim are Negro, there is no immediately discernible harm to the public which justifies a decision to invoke the criminal process. Anticipation of dismissal by judge and district attorney of cases in which the victim is an uncooperative witness, the police claim, has been another operative factor in the development of the assault policy. A Policy Appraisal and Review Board, whose investigators had been specifically directed to examine the assault policy, should be able to identify these or other policy-shaping factors more precisely. Yet on the basis of the data available, a board could tentatively conclude that court and prosecutor responses do not explain why the police have failed to adopt a policy of encouraging assault victims to sign complaints, and, therefore, that the private value system of department members, as reflected in their

Joseph Goldstein

attitude toward workload and in a stereotypical view of the Negro, is of primary significance.

Once some of the major policy-shaping factors have been identified, an Appraisal and Review Board might formulate and attempt to answer the following or similar questions: Would it be consistent with any of the purposes of the criminal law to authorize police discretion in cases of felonious assaults as well as other specified offenses? Assuming that it would be consistent or at least more realistic to authorize police discretion in some cases, what limitations and guides, if any, should the legislature provide? Should legislation provide that factors such as workload, willingness of victims or certain victims to sign a complaint, the degree of violence and attitude of prosecutor and judge be taken into account in the exercise of police discretion? If workload is to be recognized, should the legislature establish priorities of enforcement designed to assist the police in deciding which offenses among equally pressing ones are to be ignored or enforced? If assaults are made criminal in order to reduce threats to community peace and individual security, should a victim's willingness to prosecute, if he happens to live, be relevant to the exercise of police discretion? Does resting prosecution in the hands of the victim encourage him to "get even" with the assailant through retaliatory lawlessness? Or does such a policy place the decision in the hands of the assailant whose use of force has already demonstrated an ability and willingness to fulfill a threat?

Can the individual police officer, despite his own value system, sufficiently respond to officially articulated community values to be delegated broad powers of discretion? If not, can or should procedures be designed to enable the police department to translate these values into rules and regulations for individual policemen? Can police officers or the department be trained to evaluate the extent to which current practice undermines a major criminal law objective of imposing upon all persons officially recognized minimum standards of human behavior? For example, can the individual officer of the department be trained to evaluate the effect of decisions in cases of felonious assault among Negroes on local programs for implementing national or state policies of integration in school, employment, and housing, and to determine the extent to which current policy weakens or reinforces stereotypes which are used to justify not only police policy, but more importantly, opposition to desegregation programs? Or should legislation provide that the police invoke the process in all felonious assault cases unless the prosecutor or court publicly provide them in recorded documents with authority and guides for exercising discretion, and thus make visible both the policy of nonenforcement and the agency or agencies responsible for it?

Some of these issues were considered and resolved by the Oakland, California, Police Department in 1957 when, after consultation with prosecutors and judges, it decided to abandon a similar assault policy and seek *full enforcement*. Chief of Police W. W. Vernon, describing Oakland's new program, wrote:

> "In our assault cases for years we had followed this policy of releasing the defendant if the complainant did not feel aggrieved to the point of being willing to testify. . . . [Since] World War II . . . our assault cases increased tremendously to the point where we decided to do something about the increase. . . ."[4]

Training materials prepared by the Oakland Police Academy disclose that between 1952 and 1956, while the decision to prosecute was vested in the victim, the rate of reported felonious assaults rose from 93 to 161 per 100,000 population and the annual number of misdemeanor assaults rose from 618 to 2,630.[5] The materials emphasize that these statistics mean a workload of "nearly 10 assault reports a day every day of the year." But they stress:

> "The important point about these figures is not so much that they represent a substantial police workload, which they do, but more important, that they indicate an increasing lack of respect for the laws of society by a measurable segment of our population, and a corresponding threat to the rest of the citizens of our city. The police have a clear responsibility to develop respect for the law among those who disregard

Joseph Goldstein

it in order to insure the physical safety and well-being of those who do.

. . .

"We recognize that the problem exists mainly because the injured person has refused to sign a complaint against the perpetrator. The injured person has usually refused to sign for two reasons: first, because of threats of future bodily harm or other action by the perpetrator and, secondly, because it has been a way of life among some people to adjust grievances by physical assaults and not by the recognized laws of society which are available to them.

"We, the police, have condoned these practices to some extent by not taking advantage of the means at our disposal; that is, by not gathering sufficient evidence and signing complaints on information and belief in those cases where the complainant refuses to prosecute. The policy and procedure of gathering sufficient evidence and signing complaints on information and belief should instill in these groups the realization that the laws of society must be resorted to in settling disputes. When it is realized by many of these people that we will sign complaints ourselves and will not condone fighting and cuttings, many of them will stop such practices."

Following conferences with the police, the local prosecutors and judges pledged their support for the new assault program. The district attorney's office will deny a complainant's request that a case be dropped and suggest that it be addressed to the judge in open court. The judge, in turn, will advise the complainant that the case cannot be dismissed, and that a perjury, contempt, or false-report complaint will be issued in "appropriate cases" against the victim who denies facts originally alleged. The police have been advised that the court and prosecutor will actively cooperate in the implementation of the new program, but that every case will not result in a complaint since it is the "job [of the police] to turn in the evidence and it's the Prosecuting Attorney's job to determine when a complaint will be issued." Thus the role of each of the key decisionmaking agencies with preconviction invoking authority is clearly delineated and integrated.

With the inauguration of a new assault policy, an Appraisal and Review Board might establish procedures for determining how effectively the objectives of the policy are fulfilled in practice. A board might design intelligence retrieving devices which would provide more complete data than the following, termed by Chief Vernon "the best evidence that our program is accomplishing the purpose for which it was developed. . . ." Prior to the adoption of the new policy, eighty percent of the felonious assault cases "cleared" were cleared because "Complainant Refuses To Prosecute," while only thirty-two and two-tenths percent of the clearances made during the first three months in 1958 were for that reason, even though the overall clearance rate rose during that period.[6] And "during the first quarter of this year Felony Assaults dropped 11.1 percent below the same period last year, and in March they were 35.6 percent below March of last year. Battery cases were down 19.0 percent for the first three months of 1958."[7] An Appraisal and Review Board might attempt to determine the extent to which the police in cases formerly dropped because "Complainant Refused To Testify" have consciously or otherwise substituted another reason for "case cleared." And it might estimate the extent to which the decrease in assaults *reported* reflects, if it does, a decrease in the *actual* number of assaults or only a decrease in the number of victims willing to report assaults. Such followup investigations and what actually took place in Oakland on an informal basis between police, prosecutor, and judge illustrate some of the functions an Appraisal and Review Board might regularly perform.

V

Police decisions to harass, though generally perceived as over-zealous enforcement, constitute another body of nonenforcement activities meriting investigation by an Appraisal and Review Board. Harassment is the imposition by the police, acting under color of law, of sanctions prior to conviction as a means of ultimate punishment, rather than as a device for the invocation of criminal proceedings. Characteristic of harassment are efforts to annoy certain "offenders," both by temporarily detaining or arresting them without intention to seek prosecution and by destroying or illegally seizing their property without any intention to use it as evidence. Like other police decisions not to invoke the criminal process, harassment is generally of extremely low visibility, probably because the police ordinarily restrict such activity to persons who are unable to afford the costs of litigation, who would, or think they would, command little respect even if they were to complain, or who wish to keep themselves out of public view in order to continue their illicit activities. Like the informer program, harassment is conducted by the police in an atmosphere of cooperation with other administrators of criminal justice. Since harassment, by definition, is outside the rule of law, any benefits attributed to such police activity cannot justify its continuation. An Appraisal and Review Board, however, would not limit its investigations to making such a finding. It would be expected to identify and analyze factors underlying harassment and to formulate proposals for replacing harassment—lawless nonenforcement—with enforcement of the criminal law.

Investigators for an Appraisal and Review Board in this jurisdiction would discover, for example, a mixture of enforcement and harassment in a police program designed to regulate the gambling operations of mutual-numbers syndicates. The enforcement phase is conducted by a highly trained unit of less than a dozen men who diligently gather evidence in order to prosecute and convict syndicate operators of conspiracy to violate the gambling laws. This specialized unit, which operates independently of and without the knowledge of other officers, conducts all its work within the due-process boundaries of *full enforcement*. Consequently, the conviction rate is high for charges based upon its investigations. The harassment phase is conducted by approximately sixty officers who tour the city and search on sight, because of prior information, or such telltale actions as carrying a paper bag, a symbol of the trade, persons who they suspect are collecting bets. They question the "suspect" and proceed to search him, his car, or home without first making a valid arrest to legalize the search. If gambling paraphernalia are found, the police, fully aware that the exclusionary rule prohibits its use as evidence in this jurisdiction, confiscate the "contraband" and arrest the individual without any intention of seeking application of the criminal law.

Gambling operators treat the harassment program as a cost of doing business, "a risk of the trade." Each syndicate retains a bonding firm and an attorney to service members who are arrested. When a "runner" or "bagman" is absent from his scheduled rounds, routine release procedures are initiated. The bondsman, sometimes prematurely, checks with the police to determine if a syndicate man has been detained. If the missing man is in custody, the syndicate's attorney files an application for a writ of habeas corpus and appears before a magistrate who usually sets bail at a nominal amount and adjourns hearing the writ, at the request of the police, until the following day. Prior to the scheduled hearing, the police usually advise the court that they have no intention of proceeding, and the case is closed. Despite the harassee's release, the police retain the money and gambling paraphernalia. If the items seized are found in a car, the car is confiscated, with the cooperation of the prosecutor, under a nuisance abatement statute. Cars are returned, however, after the harassee signs a "consent decree" and, pursuant to it, pays "court costs"—a fee which is based on the car's value and which the prosecutor calls "the real meat of the harassment program." The "decree," entered under a procedure devised by the court and prosecutor's office, enjoins the defendant from engaging in illegal activity and, on paper, frees the police from any tort liability by an acknowledgment that seizure of the vehicle was lawful and justified—even though one prosecutor has estimated that approximately eighty percent of the searches and seizures were illegal. A prosecuting attorney responsible for car confiscation initially felt that such procedures "in the ordinary practice of law would be unethical, revolting, and shameful," but explained that he now understands why he acted as he did:

"To begin with . . . the laws in . . . [this state] with respect to gambling are most inadequate. This is equally true of the punishment feature of the law. To illustrate . . . a well-organized and productive gambling house or numbers

Joseph Goldstein

racket would take in one quarter of a million dollars each week. If, after a long and vigorous period of investigation and observation, the defendant was charged with violating the gambling laws and convicted therefore, the resulting punishment is so obviously weak and unprohibitive that the defendants are willing to shell out a relatively small fine or serve a relatively short time in prison. The . . . [city's] gamblers and numbers men confidently feel that the odds are in their favor. If they operate for six months or a year, and accumulate untold thousands of dollars from the illegal activity, then the meager punishment imposed upon them if they are caught is well worth it. Then, too, because of the search and seizure laws in . . . [this state], especially in regard to gambling and the number rackets, the hands of the police are tied. Unless a search can be made prior to an arrest so that the defendant can be caught in the act of violating the gambling laws, or a search warrant issued, there is no other earthly way of apprehending such people along with evidence sufficient to convict them that is admissible in court.

"Because of these two inadequacies of the law (slight punishment and conservative search and seizure laws with regard to gambling) the prosecutor's office and the police department are forced to find other means of punishing, harassing and generally making life uneasy for gamblers."

This position, fantastic as it is to be that of a law-trained official, a guardian of the rule of law, illustrates how extensively only one of many police harassment programs in this jurisdiction can permeate the process and be tolerated by other decisionmakers in a system of criminal administration where decisions not to enforce are of extremely low visibility.

Having uncovered such a gambling-control program, an Appraisal and Review Board should recommend that the police abandon such harassment activities because they are antagonistic to the rule of law. In addition, the board might advance secondary reasons for eliminating harassment by exposing the inconsistencies between this program and departmental justifications for its narcotics and assault policies. While unnecessary to the condemnation of what is fundamentally lawless nonenforcement, such exposure might cause the police to question the wisdom of actions based on a personal or departmental belief that the legislature has authorized excessively lenient sanctions and restrictive enforcement procedures. The comparison might emphasize the inconsistencies of police policy toward organized crime by exposing the clash between an informer program designed to rid the city of the "big supplier" and a harassment program which tends to consolidate control of the numbers racket in a few syndicates "big" enough to sustain the legal, bonding, and other "business" costs of continued interruptions and the confiscation of property. More importantly, it should cause a reexamination and redefinition of "workload" which was so significant in the rationalization of the assault policy. A cost accounting would no doubt reveal that a significant part of "workload," as presently defined by the police, includes expenditures of public funds for personnel and equipment employed in unlawful activities. Once harassment is perceived by municipal officials concerned with budgets as an unauthorized expenditure of public funds, consideration for increased awards to the police department might be conditioned upon a showing that existing resources are now deployed for authorized purposes. Such action should stimulate police cooperation in implementing the board's proposal for curtailing harassment.

Further to effectuate its recommendation, the board might attempt to clarify and redefine the duties of the police by a reclassification of crimes which would emphasize the mandate that no more than full enforcement of the existing criminal law as defined by the legislature is expected. For many crimes, this may mean little or no actual enforcement because the values protected by procedural limitations are more important than the values which may be infringed by a particular offense. A board might propose, for example, that crimes be classified not only as felonies and misdemeanors, but in terms of active and passive police enforcement. An active-enforcement designation for an offense would mean that individual police officers or specialized squads are to be assigned the task of ferreting out and even triggering violations. Passive enforcement would mean that the police are to assume a sit-back-and-wait posture, *i.e.*, that they invoke the criminal process only when the disturbing event is brought to

Joseph Goldstein

their attention by personal observation during a routine tour of duty or by someone outside the police force registering a complaint. Designation of gambling, for example, as a passive-enforcement offense would officially apprise the police that substantial expenditures of personnel and equipment for enforcement are not contemplated unless the local community expresses a low tolerance for such disturbing events by constantly bringing them to police attention. The adoption of this or a similar classification scheme might not only aid in training the police to understand that harassment is unlawful, but it may also provide the legislature with a device for officially allowing local differences in attitude toward certain offenses to be reflected in police practice and for testing the desirability of removing criminal sanctions from certain kinds of currently proscribed behavior.

VI

The mandate of *full enforcement*, under circumstances which compel selective enforcement, has placed the municipal police in an intolerable position. As a result, nonenforcement programs have developed undercover, in a hit-or-miss fashion, and without regard to impact on the overall administration of justice or the basic objectives of the criminal law. Legislatures, therefore, ought to reconsider what discretion, if any, the police must or should have in invoking the criminal process, and what devices, if any, should be designed to increase visibility and hence reviewability of these police decisions.

The ultimate answer is that the police should not be delegated discretion not to invoke the criminal law. It is recognized, of course, that the exercise of discretion cannot be completely eliminated where human beings are involved. The frailties of human language and human perception will always admit of borderline cases (although none of the situations analyzed in this Article are "borderline"). But nonetheless, outside this margin of ambiguity, the police should operate in an atmosphere which exhorts and commands them to invoke impartially all criminal laws within the bounds of full enforcement. If a criminal law is ill-advised, poorly defined, or too costly to enforce, efforts by the police to achieve full enforcement should generate pressures for legislative action. Responsibility for the enactment, amendment, and repeal of the criminal laws will not, then, be abandoned to the whim of each police officer or department, but retained where it belongs in a democracy—with elected representatives.

Equating actual enforcement with full enforcement, however, would be neither workable nor humane nor humanly possible under present conditions in most, if not all, jurisdictions. Even if there were "enough police" (and there are not) to enforce all of the criminal laws, too many people have come to rely on the nonenforcement of too many "obsolete" laws to justify the embarrassment, discomfort, and misery which would follow implementation of full enforcement programs for every crime. Full enforcement is a program for the future, a program which could be initiated with the least hardship when the states, perhaps stimulated by the work of the American Law Institute, enact new criminal codes clearing the books of obsolete offenses.

In the interim, legislatures should establish Policy Appraisal and Review Boards not only to facilitate coordination of municipal police policies with those of other key criminal law administrators, but also to assist commissions drafting new codes in reappraising basic objectives of the criminal law and in identifying laws which have become obsolete. To ensure that board appraisals and recommendations facilitate the integration of police policies with overall state policies and to ensure the cooperation of local authorities, board membership might include the state's attorney general, the chief justice of the supreme court, the chairman of the department of correction, the chairman of the board of parole and the chief of parole supervision, the chairman of the department of probation, the chairmen of the judiciary committees of the legislature, the chief of the state police, the local chief of police, the local prosecutor, and the chief judge of each of the local trial courts. In order regularly and systematically to cull and retrieve information, the board should be assisted by a full-time director who has a staff of investigators well-trained in social science research techniques. It should be given power to subpoena persons and records and to assign investigators to observe all phases of police activity including routine patrols, bookings, raids, and contacts with both the courts

Joseph Goldstein

and the prosecutor's office. To clarify its functions, develop procedures, determine personnel requirements and test the idea itself, the board's jurisdiction should initially be restricted to one or two major municipalities in the state. The board would review, appraise, and make recommendations concerning municipal police nonenforcement policies as well as follow up and review the consequences of implemented proposals. In order to make its job both manageable and less subject to attack by those who cherish local autonomy and who may see the establishment of a board as a step toward centralization, it would have solely an advisory function and limit its investigations to the enforcement of state laws, not municipal ordinances. And to ensure that board activity will not compromise current enforcement campaigns or place offenders on notice of new techniques of detection or sources of information, boards should be authorized, with court approval, to withhold specified reports from general publication for a limited and fixed time.

Like other administrative agencies, a Policy Appraisal and Review Board will in time no doubt suffer from marasmus and outlive its usefulness. But while viable, such a board has an enormous potential for uncovering in a very dramatic fashion basic inadequacies in the administration of criminal justice and for prompting a thorough community reexamination of the why of a law of crimes.

ABRAHAM S. GOLDSTEIN

The State and the Accused: Balance of Advantage in Criminal Procedure

The principal objective of criminal procedure, like that of procedure generally, is to assure a just disposition of the dispute before the court. But because time, resources and the ability to determine what is just are limited, a procedural system inevitably represents a series of compromises. Justice to society is sometimes taken to require that a given case be used not only to deal with the situation immediately before the court but also to serve a larger public interest. In criminal cases, the accused may get relief, not so much out of concern for him or for the "truth," but because he is strategically located, and motivated, to call the attention of the courts to excesses in the administration of criminal justice. The underlying premise is that of a social utilitarianism. If the criminal goes free in order to serve a larger and more

Reprinted by permission of The Yale Law Journal Company and Fred B. Rothman & Company from the *Yale Law Journal*, vol. 69, pp. 1149–99 (1960).

Notes to this Selection will be found on pages 426–427.

Goldstein is Dean of the Law School and Cromwell Professor of Law at Yale University. He is the author of The Insanity Defense (1967).

Abraham S. Goldstein

important end, then social justice is done, even if individual justice is not. For example, if the police beat an offender in order to extract a confession, the social interest is held to require that the confession be excluded from evidence, even if amply corroborated. The same [may be] true . . . when evidence is illegally seized, or telephones "tapped," or counsel denied, or jurors selected improperly, or judges biased. In each of these cases, terminating the proceeding against the accused, regardless of his guilt or innocence, shifts the focus of deterrence from the accused to his prosecutors.

Though this idealized conception of procedure, as a means of shaping institutions involved in the administration of substantive law, has a place in civil cases as well as in criminal, it shows up most clearly and dramatically in the criminal cases. The reasons are several: the threat of imprisonment makes the criminal sanction an especially grave and terrifying one; an inherited tradition, reflected in constitutional law, makes more specific requirements for criminal cases than it does for civil; there is a general feeling that most cases find state and defendant mismatched—with the state having far the better of it in prestige and resources; and perhaps most important of all, the criminal trial serves complex psychological functions. In addition to satisfying the public demand for retribution and deterrence, it permits the ready identification of the same public, now in another mood, with the plight of the accused. Both demand and identification root deep in the view that all men are offenders, at least on a psychological level. And from the moment the offender is perceived as a surrogate self, this identification calls for a "fair trial" for him before he is punished, as we would have it for ourselves.

For centuries, the criminal trial has been held out as the most distinctive embodiment of societal interest in the "process" of administering law. In the presumption of innocence accorded the accused, in the requirement that the state prove him guilty beyond reasonable doubt, in the elaborate pretrial evidentiary screens—arrest, preliminary hearing, and grand jury—through which the charge had to pass, in the rigorous pleading and evidentiary standards of the trial itself, it had given detailed content to an accusatorial system. By doing so, this formal system of criminal procedure had effectively resisted the seemingly inexorable logic which had, on the Continent, made state control of prosecution synonymous with reliance upon the accused as the principal source of the evidence against himself.

In the past generation, perhaps out of a feeling that our formal system of criminal procedure is more than adequate, the interest of the courts and commentators has shifted to other areas, usually constitutional in nature. Chief among them have been the problems of police excess in interrogation, search and seizure and wiretapping; the assurance of counsel to all; and the creation of an effective system of appeal for the indigent. Unfortunately, during the very period when tremendous strides were being made in dealing with these newly recognized problems, the bastion itself—the formal system of criminal procedure—was being eroded. In a series of "technical" decisions, each dealing in fragmentary fashion with limited parts of the total process, widespread changes were being wrought. These changes were designed to correct a serious imbalance allegedly existing in a process which gave to the accused "every advantage."[1] In the words of a leading spokesman for the position, Judge Learned Hand in *United States v. Garsson:*

> "While the prosecution is held rigidly to the charge, [the accused] need not disclose the barest outline of his defense. He is immune from question or comment on his silence; he cannot be convicted when there is the least fair doubt in the minds of any one of the twelve. . . . Our dangers do not lie in too little tenderness to the accused. Our procedure has been always haunted by the ghost of the innocent man convicted. It is an unreal dream. What we need to fear is the archaic formalism and the watery sentiment that obstructs, delays, and defeats the prosecution of crime."[2] †

This "hard-boiled" and "modern" view of criminal procedure has come to affect a myriad of issues in criminal cases, such as the place of the presumption of innocence; how much variance is

† The view is widely held and, indeed, serves in considerable part as a model of the total criminal process. See, e.g., State v. Tune, 13 N.J., 203, 210–11, 98 A.2d, 881, 884–85 (1953) (opinion of Chief Judge Vanderbilt). . . .

Abraham S. Goldstein

fatal and how much not; how closely the grand and petit jury should be supervised by the courts; the scope of harmless error and plain error; and, perhaps most important, the availability of pretrial discovery of issues and evidence. It has done so principally by measuring the "formal" criminal procedure against its more efficient and flexible civil counterpart.

If Judge Hand's view represented an accurate appraisal of the formal system of criminal procedure, it would be difficult to join issue with his conclusion, except on broad philosophical grounds. But the fact is that his view does not accurately represent the process. Both doctrinally and practically, criminal procedure, as presently constituted, does not give the accused "every advantage" but, instead, gives overwhelming advantage to the prosecution. The real effect of the "modern" approach has been to aggravate this condition by loosening standards of pleading and proof without introducing compensatory safeguards earlier in the process. Underlying this development has been an inarticulate, albeit clearly operative, rejection of the presumption of innocence in favor of a presumption of guilt.

The purpose of this Article is to examine in some detail the two major problems of the criminal trial following indictment—that of the sufficiency of evidence to take a criminal case to the jury and that of disclosure, by prosecution and defense, of the issues and evidence to be presented by them at the trial. Each of the problems will be placed in the context of the entire process, principally in order to determine the lines which reform should take before it can become realistic to talk of removing "advantage" to the accused from the system.

Proof Beyond Reasonable Doubt

When the jury system first evolved in the seventeenth century into a method of trial by fact-witnesses, the procedural rights of the defendant were few in number. He had no right to counsel or even to a copy of the indictment against him. The freest use was made by the state of admissions elicited from him before trial, often under torture or the threat of it. And hearsay was regularly used as a means of establishing guilt. Before the century was out, there was added to these disadvantages the incompetency, because of interest, of the accused as a witness in his own behalf. Fairly clearly, the dominant strain in such a system of trial was the assumption that the accused was guilty and that it was of great importance to the state to prove him so.

Such an approach may well have served the needs of an expanding national state seeking to conserve its new gains and to deter as forcefully as possible any and all challenges to its authority. But with the consolidation of those gains in the eighteenth century, what had previously seemed essential instruments became oppressive ones. Grand and petit juries stepped into the breach. By refusing to return indictments or to find defendants guilty, they succeeded in considerable part in forcing a redress of the imbalance in favor of the state. And their actions directed attention to the substantive and procedural inadequacies of the criminal law. A whole series of institutions and practices, designed to safeguard the person accused of crime, appeared in response, principally in the nineteenth century. The spirit underlying these new developments was perhaps best reflected in the rule that the accused brought with him a "presumption of innocence" and that his guilt must be proved "beyond a reasonable doubt." Those two phrases symbolize today, as they did in their beginnings, the special place of the accused in our system of criminal procedure. They cast in evocative language the deeply-held feeling that the combination of all-to-fallible witnesses and serious sanctions requires that the sanctions should be imposed only where guilt seems virtually certain. They also suggest substantial advantage to the defendant and disadvantage to the prosecution. Yet, on analysis, it soon becomes clear that the degree of advantage or disadvantage depends upon the use to which those words are put. Those uses have been undergoing substantial change.

Conventionally, the phrases appear in the trial judge's instructions to the jury, much as they did a century ago. The jury is told that the defendant is presumed innocent; that the mere fact that he has been charged with crime is not to be taken as evidence against him; and that his guilt must be proved beyond reasonable doubt. Now and then, controversy has arisen about whether the presumption of innocence is to be treated by the

Abraham S. Goldstein

jury as "evidence," or whether it is reversible error to omit all reference to the presumption or to water it down, or whether "proof beyond reasonable doubt" may be entirely eliminated from the charge. For the most part, however, there has been little tampering with either phrase at the jury stage. Whatever inroads have been made are found in the criteria fashioned by the courts to decide the question of sufficiency of evidence to take the case to the jury.

These criteria are applied by the trial judge in passing upon the motion for a judgment of acquittal at the close of the prosecution's case, or at the close of the entire case, or after the jury has returned its verdict. With rare exceptions, they are also used by the appellate court in deciding whether the trial judge erred in sending the case to the jury. The decision of trial and appellate judge is ordinarily described as a decision on a matter of law: Did the prosecution offer "enough" evidence to enable the jury to act rationally? Or, to use Judge Frank's terminology, is there enough F (facts) to permit application of R (rule of law)? The jury's decision is contrasted to that of the judge and is said to be on an issue of fact. Yet both, fairly clearly, involve a sifting of the evidence.

The judge sifts to delimit a zone within which the jury may act. He must take all facts offered in evidence by the prosecution as true and from those facts he must draw all reasonable inferences in favor of the prosecution. When, therefore, X testifies that he saw the accused aim at and shoot Y, and there is no question of defense or justification, the trial judge has no alternative but to submit the case to the jury, unless X or his testimony are inherently incredible. In this context of direct evidence of each element of the offense, the presumption of innocence means no more than that the prosecution must go forward first with the evidence and that the fact of indictment should not be taken as in any way determinative of guilt. "Proof beyond a reasonable doubt" can then mean only that the jury should be very certain that X is telling the truth—though it may also be viewed as a form of words inviting the jury to exercise its inherent power to dispense with law.

But when the prosecution's case, or any essential element of it, is built on circumstantial evidence, the role of the trial judge (and of the appellate court on review) in passing upon the sufficiency of evidence becomes much more significant. By definition, circumstantial evidence requires the assistance of an inference to make it probative of guilt. The handkerchief located at the scene of the crime must first be found to belong to the defendant; it must then be inferred, or proved, that it was in his possession at the time of the crime. There then remain the problems of placing the defendant at the scene of the crime at the time it was committed; and of making him the criminal, rather than a casual bystander. To the extent that a case is built up of a series of fragments of this kind, the trial judge may follow one of several courses: he may leave for the jury the problem of drawing inferences from each item of evidence, limiting his role to little more than ascertaining that there is "some" evidence of each element of the offense; or he may make an effort to trace inferences, or a sequence of inferences, flowing from each item of evidence to the point of determining whether it could be adopted by a rational man; or he may incorporate the standard of ultimate persuasion into the legal test of sufficiency of evidence. For example, in the civil context, he would try to assess whether the evidence is such that a reasonable jury could find it preponderates in favor of the party bearing the burden of proof; in the criminal case, he would test the evidence to determine whether a reasonable jury could find that guilt had been proved beyond reasonable doubt.

Whichever approach is adopted, it seeems fairly clear that none of the tests can be applied with precision or with confidence that any of them will materially affect the decision in any given case. Judges are too varied in personality, in perception, in analytical ability, and in their conception of themselves to make such abstract tests serve reliably in the many fact situations to which they will be applied. "The authoritative language of nice and scientific precision in which such conclusions are cast is after all only the language of delusive exactness. . . . [T]hroughout the field of circumstantial proof there is not a little room for considerations of policy and expediency to play a part in choosing between two very fallible and equally undemonstrable generalizations about the balance of probability."[3]

It is precisely because "policy and expediency" do play a part

Abraham S. Goldstein

in the decision whether to keep cases from the jury that the forms of words in which the legal tests are cast can be said to be important. The shade of meaning connoted by a word or phrase is itself a statement of policy which may tip the scales in the direction of acquittal or of further exposure to conviction. Whether the shades inherent in either the "presumption of innocence" or "proof beyond a reasonable doubt" shall be used is the substantive problem posed by cases dealing with sufficiency of evidence.

Almost from the time judges began to determine the sufficiency of the evidence in criminal cases, a development little more than a century old, they have included the standard of ultimate persuasion as part of their criterion of sufficiency. The earliest and the most common of the formulae is that set out in *Isbell v. United States,* holding it to be the trial judge's function to assure that the jury could reasonably find that the evidence of the prosecution negated "every other hypothesis but that of guilt."[4] In effect, such a formula places both "presumption of innocence" and "proof beyond reasonable doubt" in the legal test and invites trial judges to give them a place among the "considerations of policy and expediency" inevitably accompanying their decisions in cases based on circumstantial evidence. A formula seemingly less strict, but inclining in the same direction, was set forth in *Curley v. United States.*[5] It imposed upon the judge the obligation to decide whether the prosecution's case would permit reasonable jurymen to conclude guilt beyond reasonable doubt.

The newest look, which promises to be an influential one because of the preeminence of its sponsors, has been developed most systematically by the judges of the Court of Appeals for the Second Circuit. Apparently a part of the correcting process foreshadowed in *Garsson,* it would eliminate from the judge's determination of when a case should be kept from the jury both the concept of "proof beyond reasonable doubt" and the presumption of innocence. Briefly stated, the Second Circuit rule, already followed in several other federal and state jurisdictions, confines "proof beyond a reasonable doubt" to the role of an admonition to the jury regarding the assurance it should have before finding a man guilty. The *Isbell* language is permissible so long as its use is confined to the court's instructions to the jury.

For the judge ruling on the sufficiency of the evidence, however, there is to be no distinction between civil and criminal cases.[6] If there is substantial circumstantial evidence of each element of the offense, the case is to go to the jury. . . .

The potential difference of the various tests, in application to similar facts, is illustrated by *Barton v. United States*[7] and *Girgenti v. United States*,[8] both of which involved charges of illicit possession or operation of a still. In *Barton*, the defendant and others were arrested just after arriving at the scene of an illegal distillery. Federal officers testified that they had heard the defendants discuss operation of a still, though it was uncertain whether they were discussing this one. In *Girgenti* too, the defendants were arrested when they arrived at the scene of the still. They had in their possession a hydrometer, old clothes and a revolver. The hydrometer was of the type used in testing the specific gravity of liquids heavier than water, particularly alcohol from mash.

The *Barton* court, adopting an approach similar to that of the Second Circuit and affirming a verdict against the defendant, said:

"[T]he proximity of the accused to the place of the crime and [to] the unlawful apparatus used in the perpetration, may by a reasonable inference raise the presumption of possession, and that the party so found was guilty of a participation in the crime charged, which required the possession and use of the property. It is entirely a question for a jury whether this inference is . . . sufficient to convict the defendant beyond a reasonable doubt."[9]

The *Girgenti* court, apparently following *Isbell*, reversed the conviction and ordered acquittal, saying:

"[T]he presence of the appellants at or near the premises where the still was in operation is not sufficient to sustain a conviction on counts charging them with possession of an unregistered still or the manufacture of mash, in the absence of any testimony that they were in charge of, or were doing work in connection with, the still. The possession of old

Abraham S. Goldstein

clothes . . . and a revolver is as consistent with innocence of
the offenses charged as with guilt. . . . The unexplained possession of the hydrometer supports an inference that the
appellants were concerned with testing liquor in some form,
but was not in itself sufficient evidence to warrant the conclusion that they were connected with the operation of the
still in question. To mention but a few of the possibilities,
the appellants might have been purchasers of liquor, or sold
liquor, or even had some connection with a still other than
the one described in the indictment."[10]

If words in opinions can be said to reflect or to shape attitudes, it seems fair to say that the *Isbell* rule, or the *Curley* rule,
invite more careful judicial scrutiny of evidence in criminal
cases than in civil. In contrast, the Second Circuit rule tells trial
judges they are under no obligation to approach criminal cases
as involving especially opprobrious or painful sanctions. Criminal
prosecutions are not to be viewed as qualitatively different from
the usual civil cases, even though society's interest in civil litigation may be no more than to provide an orderly means of resolving disputes.

By removing "proof beyond a reasonable doubt" from the
legal test of the sufficiency of evidence, the Second Circuit rule
has gone a long way toward completing the work begun by
Thayer and Wigmore when they decreed that the "presumption
of innocence" was no longer to have any evidentiary significance.[11] For, if that presumption is to be more than a requirement that he who charges liability must prove it, it must be given
content by judges in areas subject to their control. The instructions to the jury are, of course, one such area. But far more important, because far more subject to judicial control, is the
power to keep cases from the jury. Assertion of that power,
with its insistence upon a "fact" role for court as well as jury,
serves not only to minimize "convicting the innocent" but also
to keep the pressure on judge, prosecutor, and police to act as
responsibly as possible in screening out cases not fit for trial.
Placing the prestige of the judiciary directly on the scales in
favor of strict standards of proof, it announces that the sufficiency of evidence will be ruled upon, deliberately, by a judge

and will not simply pass into the anonymity of the general verdict.

Even if societal interests were put to one side and attention confined to the particular case, the serious nature of the criminal sanction would seem to be ample reason for insisting upon standards of proof more rigorous than those which prevail in civil cases. It has already been pointed out that no finding of fact in a case based upon circumstantial evidence is simply an exercise in computing whether there is "enough" evidence. Inevitably, mood and inclination play a considerable part. The perceptions of judge and jury, as witnesses of the witnesses, are as much influenced by the manner of men they are and the attitudes with which they set out to perceive as are the impressions of the witnesses themselves. Why, then, the seeming refusal to concede that the criminal case, being more serious, calls for an admonition to the judge comparable to that addressed to the jury?

The explanation which appears most plausible is that intimated by Thayer.[12] It rests upon the assumption that "natural inference" indicates that he who is charged is guilty. This is, in turn, based upon the seeming plenitude of screens through which the charge against an accused must pass before he can be brought to trial. The large numbers of persons who do not pass through the screens—either because they have pleaded guilty or because there have been findings of insufficient evidence—appear to leave for the trial process only the guilty—indeed, those who are most adamant in denying their guilt. To accord this residuary group the benefit of a standard of proof more rigorous than in civil cases would seem, under the Thayer view, to be both inappropriate and undeserved.

This image represents only a small part of the reality. Largely overlooked in this "model" of the accused at trial are those defendants who deal in "good faith" with the system—those who have factual or legal defenses reasonably believed by them to be valid. From their ranks are drawn a substantial portion of the twenty-three to thirty-six percent of defendants who actually stand trial and are acquitted. But even more important, in assessing the image, are the very limited protections afforded by the pretrial screening agencies—police, prosecutor, magistrate, and grand jury. The minimal standards of proof employed by these

Abraham S. Goldstein

agencies give very little assurance that persons passed on by them to a later screen are indeed guilty of the offenses charged against them.

ARREST. The screening process begins the moment evidence of conduct designated criminal is discovered by policeman or private party. In the decision to make such conduct the basis of a formal charge, there exists the initial *de facto* screen which passes some persons further along the path towards ultimate adjudication of guilt or innocence, while taking others out of it. This decision first finds itself subjected to judicial scrutiny when the police officer seeks a warrant of arrest from a magistrate. If the officer arrests without a warrant, as he may for serious offenses, his decision will not be reviewed until the arrest has been consummated and its legality challenged. In both situations, the nature of the showing required of the officer is substantially the same. The arrest is legal if it is made upon "probable cause" —information which would have moved a reasonable man, under the circumstances, to believe that the crime in question had occurred and that it was committed by the accused. When the arresting officer is himself an eye-witness, no substantial problem arises. But when he acts on the basis of information supplied by others, his decision involves an embryo adjudication. He must weigh the probative value of the information, make judgments about the credibility of his informants, balance the probabilities, and determine the extent to which deviational conduct should be tolerated and law nullified.

The courts take note of the preliminary nature of the policeman's adjudication by requiring less formal, and less credible, evidence to validate his judgment than they require of the subsequent, more formal, screens. The word of the unidentified informer suffices, for example, if he has been shown to be reliable in the past. The lateness of the hour, the shape of the bag being carried, the reports of crimes in the neighborhood, the criminal records of the persons involved—all are permitted a weight in this determination which they would not receive at the trial itself. Such loose standards are entirely consistent with the primary concern of the police, at this early stage, which is to investigate, not adjudicate. But for that very reason, even the best enforced police evidentiary "screen" cannot be treated as a substantial one.

What makes the process of arrest even less rigorous a screen than it might be is the extent to which the illegal arrest may go unchallenged. Between the time of arrest and the appearance before a magistrate at a preliminary hearing (on the question of bail and of "probable cause" to hold for further proceedings), the alleged offender ordinarily need not be informed of his right to counsel, nor allowed access to counsel if he asks for it, nor supplied with counsel if he is indigent.† If he does have counsel who knows of his arrest, a petition for habeas corpus might conceivably bring his release; but it is far more likely that he will have to defer his challenge until the preliminary hearing. In any event, since most persons arrested for crime neither know their rights nor have ready access to a lawyer, the deterent effect of this remedy upon the illegal arrest is bound to be slight. The same is true, for a variety of reasons, of the civil suit for false arrest.

THE PRELIMINARY HEARING. Pressure on the arresting officer to act responsibly in screening the charges of crime would ordinarily come in the preliminary hearing before the magistrate. It is the magistrate who must determine whether the policeman's "reasonable belief," when made visible, constitutes "probable cause" to believe a crime has been committed; or a "prima facie" case; or sufficient evidence to warrant a jury's finding the accused guilty. Almost everywhere, however, the showing is held to be sufficient if the prosecution presents a skeletal outline of evidence admissible in court to support each element of the offense. This skeletal quality is virtually assured by certain grim facts. In most jurisdictions, no provision is made for appointment of counsel at this stage. Neither the due process clause of the fourteenth amendment nor state constitutional provisions have been held to require it. And most states make no statutory provision for appointment of counsel, though a considerable

† [Ed. note: Miranda v. Arizona, 384 U.S. 436 (1966) holds that a person suspected of crime and subjected to "custodial interrogation" must be advised of his right to counsel and, if he is indigent and asks for counsel, must be provided with one as a condition of lawful interrogation. The holding is not applicable unless interrogation is involved. See note 27, p. 427 infra.]

Abraham S. Goldstein

number require that he be advised of his right to retain counsel. Since, therefore, defense counsel is usually either not present, or insufficiently informed to play his role properly, it ordinarily falls to the magistrate, almost alone, to test the sufficiency of the evidence to warrant holding the accused for the grand jury, or for trial where there is no grand jury. Yet most magistrates are either unskilled, or too busy, or too closely linked with police or prosecutor, or insufficiently mindful of the "judicial" nature of their role to perform this function adequately. And the sole review of the sufficiency of the evidence before them is the limited one afforded by habeas corpus, which looks only for some "legally competent evidence" to support the order committing the accused for trial. But even that is a limited safeguard because the unrepresented, or poorly represented, defendant may not learn until after his trial that there was insufficient evidence at the preliminary hearing to warrant passing the case on to trial. If the case has proceeded to trial, no remedy is available to the accused for the defect in the preliminary hearing. He must then look, on appeal, solely to the inadequacy of the evidence at trial.

In practical effect, therefore, the preliminary hearing in the United States does not add significantly to the police evidentiary screen which has preceded it. As in the case of arrest, the point is not to suggest that the screening function of the preliminary hearing should be made more rigorous; or that every "error" requires a remedy. It is merely to indicate first, that the institutions empowered to do the screening job do it in quite limited fashion and, second, that the cumulation of noninterventionist attitudes serves to make very slight indeed the external pressures on policeman, prosecutor and magistrate to act as responsible screens. Entirely too much is left to self-discipline and tradition, which have been notoriously slow in developing in most American police forces and magistracies.

It would be misleading to leave the inference that there are not a substantial number of drop-outs at the arrest and preliminary hearing stages. What is not at all clear, however, is whether they are the result of the formal evidentiary screen, thereby reinforcing the probability of guilt, or whether they derive from something else—for example, the virtually undefined and unreviewable exercise of discretion by police and prosecutor not to proceed further, in accordance with criteria so subjective as to afford no assurance that the rule of law is being applied equally to all.

THE GRAND JURY. In perhaps half the states, mostly in the West, the preliminary hearing is the last formal screening device before trial. But in the remaining states and in the federal system, the grand jury stands as yet another screen. Though it may serve as an initiator of investigation and accusation, by far the greatest proportion of matters coming before it has already passed through arrest and preliminary hearing.

The grand jury is unquestionably the most celebrated of the pre-trial screening devices. Originally conceived as an extension of the royal authority over the citizen, it reached its greatest glory as a barrier against the state, refusing to indict for crime where the evidence was inadequate or the law creating the crime unpopular. During the nineteenth century, a great many jurisdictions set about to "judicialize" the grand jury proceeding, principally because the return of an indictment, without more, was recognized as bringing serious extra-legal sanctions with it. Beginning with a hearing restricted to the prosecution's case alone, with a firm ban on calling the defendant or his witnesses, most states soon authorized the grand jury to hear them if it chose. A considerable number enacted statutes providing that the grand jury was to hear only "legal evidence," or that it "ought" to indict only on the basis of such evidence. And those requirements were frequently enforced through the granting of motions to quash indictments based on no evidence at all, or no evidence as to an element of the crime, or "utterly insufficient" evidence. The nature of the judicial inquiry tended to resemble the manner in which courts now review the action of administrative agencies—to ascertain whether they are acting within the limits of their authority. The net effect of this development was to impose upon the prosecution the obligation to proceed more cautiously and circumspectly with the business of prosecuting crime than it might otherwise have done.

In the late '20's and early '30's, a complete change in judicial attitude toward the grand jury took place. There came to be increasing feeling, manifested most clearly in the report of the Wickersham Commission, that the grand jury was an inefficient

Abraham S. Goldstein

"rubber stamp" for the prosecutor who conceived its investigations, directed its secret proceedings, and drafted its indictment. Apart from its subpoena authority, which could conceivably be better lodged with the prosecutor who exercised the power *de facto,* the grand jury hearing seemed to serve no useful purpose.[13] The adjudication of probable guilt would have to be made again by a petit jury after a fuller and fairer hearing than the grand jury could possibly provide. And besides, there was the preliminary hearing, which could be used to do the screening job hitherto done by the grand jury. There came to be increasing reluctance on the part of the courts to examine the sufficiency of the evidence before the grand jury. That body became its own judge of the kind of evidence it would hear and the amount and quality of evidence it would require for indictment.

United States v. Costello[14] placed the imprimatur of the Supreme Court upon this conception of the grand jury. The Court held that an indictment based completely upon hearsay evidence is neither defective, dismissible on motion, nor ground for reversal of a conviction. The attempt by Justice Burton to place his concurrence on a narrower ground—that the hearsay was clearly reliable[15]—and the failure of the Court to incorporate that ground into its opinion, indicated strongly that, henceforth, the federal grand jury was to police itself. Except for their very limited relationship to it before and during the proceedings, courts were no longer to interfere if the grand jury was "legally constituted and unbiased."[16] The reason for this approach, fairly clearly stated in *Costello,* is that the accused will get his fair, "judicial," hearing at his trial. Due process, and the Supreme Court, require no more. Stated in somewhat more rhetorical fashion, why protect the defendant at the grand jury stage against an indictment based on little or no evidence when the exacting standards of the trial process will make such indictments meaningless?

THE RELATIONSHIPS AMONG THE SCREENS. In sum, the evidentiary standards of the pretrial screening process, implicitly relied upon by trial and appellate courts as a basis for relaxing trial standards, have themselves been relaxed in reliance upon the assumed vigor of the trial process. It by no means follows, however, that the pretrial process should be "judicialized" to

assure that only the "really guilty" come to trial. Though a tightening of the screens might well decrease the danger that innocent men would be convicted, it might also distort other functions, such as investigation, which are perhaps equally important.

The point, simply stated, is this: the looseness of the pretrial screens makes questionable the move toward abandonment of the traditionally strict trial standards called for in *Isbell* and *Curley*. Only if the criminal sanction were to lose the special stigma associated with it in our society, or if the threat of imprisonment did not loom ominously in the background, or if there had been fewer instances in our history of conviction of innocent persons, would it be appropriate to treat the question of sufficiency of evidence in criminal trials in the same manner as in civil trials.

Disclosure

Increased reliance upon the trial as the principal device for protecting the accused makes it imperative that the defense come to trial as well equipped as the prosecution to raise "doubt in the minds of any one of the twelve" men in the jury box.[17] Particularly in a system based, as is ours, upon a single trial held on a single occasion, the parties must come to trial prepared to make the most of their presentation on that occasion.[18] It is crucial, therefore, to determine which of the parties is specially advantaged by the system of disclosure currently employed. In Judge Hand's view, it will be recalled, the accused enjoys every advantage. Not only is the prosecution handicapped by the obligation to prove guilt beyond "the least fair doubt," [19] it is further hampered in assembling the evidence to satisfy the obligation. "While the prosecution is held rigidly to the charge, . . . [the accused] need not disclose the barest outline of his defense. He is immune from question or comment on his silence. . . ."[20]

Judge Hand is undoubtedly correct in tying proof of guilt or innocence to the problem of disclosure of issues and evidence. But he is quite wrong in his assessment of where the advantage lies. It has probably always been with the state, and is becoming even more so. Increasingly, the prosecution is being freed from restrictions on pleading and proof while the defendant and his

Abraham S. Goldstein

case are, and always have been, far more accessible to the prosecution than Judge Hand's polemic would have it. To evaluate argument and counter-argument, it will be necessary to place the problem of disclosure in the perspective of the entire criminal procedural process, much as has been done with the problem of screening baseless charges.

"THE PROSECUTION IS HELD RIGIDLY TO THE CHARGE"

That persons accused of crime should be put on notice of the charge against them is fundamental in both a procedural and a substantive sense. Notice serves not only to assure maximal participation by the parties in the adversary trial but also to aid in fulfilling the function of that trial—deterring others from committing like crimes and instilling remorse in persons found guilty of the crime charged. Until fairly recently, notice (or disclosure) was afforded the accused by a series of devices. The indictment had to be drawn with precision; it could neither be explicitly amended nor would any variance be permitted between its allegations and the proof offered to support them. Only one offense could be charged in each count. If there were more, the count was "bad for duplicity."

These technical doctrines represented fairly crude devices for assuring that the decision of the magistrate or grand jury would be given effect—that, for example, the decision not to charge for larceny by trick but instead to charge for obtaining property by false pretenses would be respected. Moreover, defendants would be given as clear an idea of what they would have to meet at trial as could be supplied by pleadings alone. This heavy reliance on the pleadings was made necessary, of course, because there was virtually no other way in which the defendant could compel disclosure of the prosecution's case. An examination of pleading in modern criminal cases will show that the pleadings have lost their rigidity, and their specificity with it, while no compensatory increase has taken place in the amount of pretrial disclosure available to the defendant.

INDICTMENT OR INFORMATION. The Hand view of criminal pleading is, in large part, a reaction against the ridiculous lengths to which courts, armed with a constitutional principle, often carried the requirement that the indictment furnish the accused with notice of the charge against him. It has become a commonplace to inveigh against the pleading of that day by referring to dismissals of indictments because names were spelled incorrectly, or times and places stated inaccurately. Because of these "horribles," and because of the impact of legal realism on legal thinking generally, criminal pleading was made looser and more flexible. Indictments could now follow the language of the statute creating the crime, provided the statute contained the "essential elements of the offense." Though the cases continued to pay lip service to constitutional doctrine regarding specificity, indictments came to be drafted in more general terms. Any loss to the defendant in the way of notice could be made up to him when he moved for a bill of particulars.

But here, as in the analogous erosion of the preindictment screens, the implicit dependence upon the ready availability of particulars has proved to be unwarranted. Court after court has undercut the notice-giving function of the bill of particulars by refusing to grant it. Most often, the grounds for refusal have been that the defendant is not entitled to obtain the government's "evidence" in advance of trial; or to embark on a "fishing expedition"; or, ironically, to get details when he knows very well "what he did." Almost invariably, the shield for refusal has been the awareness of trial judges, because appellate courts have said it so often, that the application for a bill of particulars is "addressed to the sound discretion of the [trial] court."

DUPLICITY AND VARIANCE. In the wake of the indictment's decline in specificity has come the demise of the doctrine holding "bad for duplicity" any count which charged more than one offense. That doctrine had as its principal rationale the need for precise statement of the charge so that the accused could prepare his defense. Inevitably, however, the logic of the position that defects in the indictment could be "cured" brought with it the willingness to accept as a remedy for the "error" of duplicity something less than dismissal of the indictment. Not only were fewer pleadings classed as duplicitous, but in most jurisdictions, once the trial had begun, prosecutors were permitted to elect the one offense on which they intended to rely for conviction; in others, the indictment could be amended.

The concept of postindictment "cure" of an unfortunate

Abraham S. Goldstein

pleading by the prosecution has also had an impact upon the doctrine of fatal variance between allegation and proof. Until recently, that doctrine prohibited any departure in the course of trial from the single offense alleged in each count; the prosecution was to be held strictly to the theory announced in the charging document. If the proof did vary, the prohibition against "amendment" of indictments, which denied to prosecutor or judge the power to add to what the grand jury had charged, prevented correction of the error.[21]

Within the past generation, the rigors of both "variance" and "amendment" doctrine have been considerably relaxed. The Supreme Court held in *Berger v. United States* that the charge of one conspiracy, and the proof of more than one, was "harmless error" so long as the defendant was not "surprised"—that is, that the departure from the allegation had not materially prejudiced the accused in making his defense.[22] Though the Supreme Court has not been altogether consistent in its decisions, this reasoning has been extended by the courts and legislatures to a wide variety of cases. Amendments as to form have been held permissible. And, in many jurisdictions, amendments as to substance are authorized by special statutory or constitutional provision. Evidencing the same trend are the cases holding that the prosecution may prove any "offense" of which the indictment does in fact give notice, even if the indictment indicates, on its face, that it is dealing with another, similar offense category.

EFFECTIVE NOTICE TO THE ACCUSED. Does this developing trend prejudice the defendant's preparation and trial of his case? There can be no question that notice of the facts and legal theories to be litigated is essential to the effective operation of an adversary system. Without such notice, each party is precluded from making the most of the facts potentially at his disposal or of legal research. If, for example, defense counsel does not learn until late in the trial that two conspiracies are involved rather than one, he faces the problem of belatedly mustering his proofs or of having to re-call witnesses—at best inefficient procedures making for disjointed testimony. Difficulties also arise with respect to objections by counsel to the admissibility of evidence, or cross-examination, or the preparation of instructions to the jury. What is the criterion of relevance by which counsel can object, and the trial judge rule, on admissibility? Toward what version of the facts should defense counsel's examination press the witnesses for the prosecution? What "law" should the parties seek to have the judge pass to the jury in his instructions? Only some "theory of the case" can furnish such a guide.

Perhaps in a system of "trial by intervals," such as characterizes German civil procedure and some of our own administrative proceedings, the importance of initial notice is minimized. Notice wanting on one occasion can be supplied on another. But in the single event trial, initial notice is essential. This does not mean, of course, that all the rigors of the early "issue" pleading need be revived, or that the "theory of the case" need be restricted to a single offense category. Indeed, a decent respect for the grand jury would seem to require that its indictment be taken to refer to any "legal theory," or "offense category," reasonably encompassed by the operative facts recorded in the indictment. Too strict an adherence to the initial pleading is probably more likely to frustrate the intention of the grand jury than to effectuate it. But notice of issues and facts adequate to enable the defense to prepare for trial is made all the more essential if such a view of pleading is adopted. The real question is: How is notice to be afforded the parties?

The reasonably expansible pleading, recognizing as it does the difficulties of precise initial statement of either facts or legal theories, moves in an inevitable direction. But unless it is accompanied by the means to prepare for the shifts in prosecution theories, factual and legal, the expansible pleading significantly aggravates the plight of the accused. Unfortunately, no such means is ordinarily available.

DISCOVERY BY THE DEFENDANT

The elimination of precise pleading, the general unavailability of particulars, and the increasing elasticity given to indictments all leave a good deal of room for "surprise" at trial. And not all such "surprise" is readily curable by granting a continuance. Civil procedure seeks to minimize this problem by permitting each party to inform himself to the utmost about the other's case—to sift legal issues and evidence in detail before trial through depositions, requests for admissions, and discovery of documents. This

Abraham S. Goldstein

process has as its object the harnessing of the full creative potential of the adversary process, bringing each party to trial as aware of what he must meet as his finances and his lawyer's energy and intelligence permit.

Yet virtually no such machinery exists for the defendant accused of a crime. No deposition or admissions procedure is ordinarily available to him. Though a motion for discovery of documents before trial is technically available, attempts to invoke it are rarely successful. When they are, they usually enable the defendant to get only materials which are not central to his task of preparing a defense. For example, motions for leave to subpoena before trial commercial records of various sorts—in short, materials in the hands of nongovernmental persons involved in the prosecution—are often granted. Confessions, guns, bullets, chemical analyses and autopsy reports are also beginning to be made available, albeit reluctantly and in only a few jurisdictions. But the statement of a government witness—at best, a poor substitute for a deposition, since defense counsel was not there to crossexamine when it was made—is virtually unobtainable. The few federal cases making such statements available before trial, such as *Fryer v. United States*,[23] have probably been overruled by the legislation which followed in the wake of *United States v. Jencks*.[24] Even before that legislation was enacted, *Jencks* had done little to open the government's files. It said no more than that defense counsel, *at trial*, must be given access to prior statements of a witness *on the stand* regarding the subject matter of that witness's testimony. The case did not address itself either to the pretrial stage or to the statements, in government files at time of trial, of witnesses not testifying but potentially helpful to the defense. Only a handful of fairly limited due process cases deal with the latter problem—and none of them explicitly with the right to obtain such materials before trial.

If the defendant should wish to use his own resources in searching out those witnesses who have spoken to police, prosecutor, or grand jury, he will, more often than not, find that they have been advised not to discuss their testimony with him. Without the subpoena, he can do nothing effective to break the wall of silence. If he should try, he runs the risk of being charged with tampering with witnesses. Even his search for evidence at large is inevitably restricted because he has neither a crime laboratory nor vast identification and fingerprint files available to him. Most often, he has no investigative assistance whatever.

The one institution on the scene which might be used to afford the accused effective pretrail discovery of the prosecution's case is the preliminary hearing. But American courts have consistently refused to shape it in the mold of its British counterpart, in which the prosecution is obligated to make complete disclosure of the evidence it will use at trial. In its present form, the American preliminary hearing provides a minimal opportunity to discover the government's case and to confront and cross-examine witnesses. It requires only so much disclosure as is necessary to make out "probable cause" to believe that defendant committed the crime, or a "prima facie" case, or some other formulation of a minimal evidentiary burden.

Even this obligation can be evaded through subtle pressures designed to maximize waiver—for example, through failure to provide for appointment of counsel at this stage, thereby making it less likely that a hearing will be requested by the defendant. Where indictment by grand jury remains the general rule, continuance of the preliminary hearing until the grand jury has returned an indictment withdraws the limited opportunity for discovery at the preliminary hearing. For he who has already been indicted by a grand jury is not "entitled" to a preliminary hearing.[25]

Once the case is placed in the grand jury's hands, it is shrouded with secrecy. Only under the most extraordinary circumstances may the defendant obtain the minutes of that body, though the government may use them for many purposes. And neither defendant nor his counsel sees, nor is given the opportunity to examine, the witnesses against him. True, in many states the names of witnesses before the grand jury are required by statute to be endorsed on the ensuing indictment. But, in most of them, witnesses whose names are not endorsed will be permitted to testify. And in the others, there is nothing the defendant can do to make the named witnesses talk to him or to get copies of their statements to the prosecutor.

In sum, if police or prosecution choose to withhold from the defendant their evidence or legal theories, or if they continue the preliminary hearing until indictment, the defendant has only the notice given him by the indictment, the occasional bill of particulars, and the even more occasional pretrial discovery. Is the prosecution similarly handicapped?

Denial of pretrial discovery to the defendant is justified most often as a necessary counterweight to the alleged fact that the accused "need not disclose the barest outline of his defense [and] . . . is immune from question or comment on his silence."[26] The justification is unsatisfactory for two entirely separate reasons. First, by assigning a central tenet of our accusatorial procedure to the bargain-counter, the defendant is made to pay dearly for his privilege of silence, whether or not he makes use of it. Second, and more immediately relevant, the Hand view grossly exaggerates the protection which this "immunity" affords.

Though the defendant still need not file a detailed responsive pleading in most states, more and more require that the defenses of alibi and insanity be pleaded specially before trial. Even at the trial, where the accused is most clearly immune from being called by the prosecution as its witness (or, in most jurisdictions, from having his failure to testify made the subject of comment by the prosecution), the protection means less to the defendant than appears: first, the accused will testify in his own behalf in most cases and thus subject himself to cross-examination; second, the prosecutor will rarely wish to make the accused his witness; third, the failure of the accused to testify is so conspicuous, particularly in this day of frequent invocation of the fifth amendment, that he is under the utmost pressure to take the stand to rebut the inference of guilt which will likely be drawn by the jury, whether or not his silence is explicitly called to their attention; finally, admissions made by the accused to the police before trial are freely and regularly used at the trial, placing defendants under pressure to take the stand to explain the admissions away.

If the accused's immunity at trial were all it is reputed to be, there would still remain his considerable amenability to interrogation before trial. Ordinarily, an accused person may be interrogated by the police up to the point of "coercion." † So long as certain kinds of pressures—such as violence, threats of violence, in-

---

† [Ed. note: For description of major developments on this issue, see note 27, p. 427.]

tensive interrogation continuing over long periods of time, or promises of immunity—are not utilized, the ensuing admissions or confessions can ordinarily be used at trial. This remains true even where the accused has neither been advised of his right to remain silent nor permitted access to counsel. The *McNabb-Mallory* rule, excluding confessions obtained during the period before arraignment at a preliminary hearing, has had a mitigating effect in the federal courts. But no state court has followed it. Moreover, in both state and federal courts, leads obtained as a result of concededly inadmissable confessions or admissions may be used to find evidence which does not share the infection of the original source.

In state prosecutions, and in federal prosecutions in which the accused has been brought promptly before a magistrate, the police may use methods of interrogation involving trickery, fabricated evidence, subtle threats, violations of confidence, and a myriad other techniques for manipulating the fearful or suggestible. None of these conventional methods of interrogation is prohibited by law. None of them, alone, suffices to invalidate confessions or admissions following from its use. Each constitutes one among many factors to be considered in determining the complex issue of the "trustworthiness" or "voluntariness" of the confession. And because that issue has been arbitrarily limited to permit just such methods, police are invited to press to the limits of interrogation.[27] Nor does the preliminary hearing, with its advice of rights to counsel and to silence, necessarily end exposure of the accused to these pressures. In most states, the accused apparently remains accessible to the police for questioning until final disposition of the case. The most impressive indication that our criminal procedure regularly acts on the assumption that the defendant is very much available and usable for self-incrimination is the overwhelming proportion of cases (75 to 90 percent) which are decided by pleas of guilty. Such pleas quite obviously follow in considerable part from a breach in the wall of silence allegedly surrounding the defendant—whether because he has been cajoled to do so, or because he sees his interest best served in that way, or for more obscure reasons, is very difficult to say.

The availability of the accused for self-incrimination does not end with police interrogation. For, if he is that unusual accused

Abraham S. Goldstein

who obstinately persists in remaining silent in the face of accusation at the police station, a substantial number of jurisdictions take his silence . . . as an adoptive admission—an admission by silence—the theory being that an innocent man must be expected to cry out his innocence in the face of accusation. And, virtually everywhere, the body of the accused may be used fairly freely to incriminate him. Although, on a theoretical level, such use of the body is not within the concept of self-incrimination, it remains a significant factor in assessing the total balance, or lack of it, between prosecution and accused. The accused's fingerprints and footprints may be taken; his blood and urine may be removed, provided the job is done scientifically; his handwriting and his voice may be used in most jurisdictions; he may be required to exhibit himself, in a line-up or otherwise, wearing particular kinds of clothing, though such exhibition may well increase the likelihood that he will be identified as the culprit.[28]

When the grand jury investigation begins, most jurisdictions recognize the immunity of the accused from interrogation only if he has already been named a defendant by arrest, by information, or by earlier indictment. If the prosecutor chooses to defer arrest or formal charge and hales the target of his investigation before the grand jury as a "witness," that target need not, except in a few jurisdictions, be advised that it is he whose conduct is under scrutiny. As a result, he may testify where otherwise he might refrain from doing so. If he should assert complete immunity (for example, a privilege not to appear, or not to be sworn) on the ground that he is the accused *de facto*, most jurisdictions would deny the claim, thereby compelling him to testify or to virtually concede his indictment by invoking his privilege against self-incrimination.

Not only is the accused himself subject to considerable use by police and prosecution before trial, but every witness, his as well as the prosecution's, may be subjected to similar interrogation before trial. This may be done formally before a grand jury, which affords a full-fledged deposition procedure for the prosecution without the embarrassing presence of defendant or his counsel. Or it may be done informally at the police station, where the specter of being held as a material witness—or of being charged with one of many vaguely defined crimes as a means of detaining for questioning—offers a considerable inducement for cooperation. As if all this were not enough, extensive legislative and administrative subpoena power exists to assist the government in investigating virtually every major field of regulatory activity. These too may serve as discovery and trial preparation devices available to the government and unavailable to the defense.

Fairly clearly, pretrial discovery by the prosecution is farreaching. And it cannot in any sense be said to be matched by what is available to the defendant or by what he can keep from the prosecution—even when his "immunity" from self-incrimination is thrown into the scales. While the possibility that the defendant may produce a hitherto undisclosed witness or theory of defense is always present, the opportunity for surprise is rendered practically illusory by the government's broad investigatory powers and by the requirement in many states that the defenses of alibi and insanity must be specially pleaded. The sum of the matter is that the defendant is not an effective participant in the pretrial criminal process. It is to the trial alone that he must look for justice. Yet the imbalance of the pretrial period may prevent him from making the utmost of the critical trial date. And the trial, in turn, has been refashioned so that it is increasingly unlikely that it will compensate for the imbalance before trial.

IMPLICATIONS FOR REFORM

If a procedural system is to be fair and just, it must give each of the participants to a dispute the opportunity to sustain his position. It must not create conditions which add to any essential inequality of position between the parties but rather must assure that such inequality will be minimized as much as human ingenuity can do so. In the case of enforcement of the criminal law, it seems quite clear that our existing institutional arrangements, as construed by the courts, aggravate the tendencies toward inequality between state and accused. How can a halt be called to these tendencies?

Several tiers of solutions are neceessary—some within the scope of this article and some without. Among the latter are the various measures now being taken to make the indigent accused "equal

Abraham S. Goldstein

before the law"—such as providing him with counsel and trial transcripts—and those which should be taken, such as making public investigative resources available to the accused.

Most immediately relevant, however, is the creation of a free deposition and discovery procedure. For this would afford the accused the ability to draw upon all that the prosecution has gathered, compensating in part for all that the prosecution has learned from the accused and his witnesses. Every one of the many excellent arguments which carried the day for pretrial discovery in civil cases is equally applicable on the criminal side. If the trial is to be the occasion at which well prepared adversaries test each other's evidence and legal contentions in the best tradition of the adversary system, there can be no substitute for a deposition, discovery, and pretrial procedure. Whether this is accomplished through an expansion of the preliminary hearing, following the English model, or through incorporation of the discovery provisions of the Federal Rules of Civil Procedure, as in Professor Donnelly's proposed Puerto Rican Penal Code, is less important than that the job be done. If a choice is to be made, however, it should probably be for the Donnelly proposal since it draws upon a body of rules with which our courts are thoroughly familiar.

The argument customarily advanced in opposition to such a reform is that advice to the accused as to the details of the case against him will be an invitation to him to fabricate evidence, to suborn others to do so, or to intimidate the witnesses against him. Such a view implies that the presumption of innocence is inapplicable before trial. Indeed, its operational assumption is that all persons are guilty; since they expect to be convicted "for what they did," they can be expected to take any measures necessary to prevent conviction. This view builds a procedural system upon the assumption that virtually all are guilty when some twenty-three percent to thirty-six percent of persons who actually stand trial are acquitted. Moreover, it treats existing laws against lying, bribing, and intimidating witnesses as ineffective to deter persons charged with crime. In place of such assumedly ineffective criminal sanctions, it attaches a crippling procedural handicap to all defendants.

Since there is good reason to believe that the amount of perjury in civil cases is considerable, it seems questionable at best to allow full discovery in civil cases and deny it in criminal cases. It could, of course, be said that the severity of criminal sanctions is so much greater than civil ones that the accused is more likely to tamper with the process than is the party to a civil case, or that the criminal "class" includes more persons disposed to violence than does the civil litigant class. But a moment's reflection indicates how suspect such hypotheses are. Even if we assume the accused to be more motivated or more disposed by personality to engage in such conduct, he, unlike his civil analogue, is already marked by the state as a criminal and hence is more likely to be under scrutiny. Moreover, the very real likelihood that charges of such misconduct against criminal defendants will be believed makes it all the more obvious that they must behave with the utmost circumspection.

But perhaps the most significant reason of all is the fact that the range of civil and criminal substantive law is too broad to permit the generalization that one involved in civil litigation is far less likely to suborn perjury or intimidate witnesses. It is difficult to believe that the defendant to charges of income tax evasion, false advertising, mail fraud, etc., will regularly tamper with justice on the criminal side of the court but that he will not do so when defending against the same or comparable charges on the civil side. Or that the petty thief accused of shoplifting will lie or intimidate but that the same person suing for an injury from an automobile collision will behave properly. Far more likely, "bad" people will do bad things on both sides of the court; the kind of people involved in litigation, and the stakes at issue, are central to the intimidation-bribery-perjury nexus, not their involvement on any one side of the court. It must be conceded, of course, that, at the margins, the pressure of a serious criminal charge may cause a given individual to engage in conduct which he would not consider if he were faced with a less serious civil charge, and that the personality types brought within certain criminal categories may present a significantly greater threat to the process. But since generalizations are necessary if systems of procedure are to be built, it seems fairly obvious that in most instances, the only approach to disclosure consonant with equality of opportunity and with the presumption of innocence is that

Abraham S. Goldstein

used on the civil side of the court. It places its faith in the freest possible discovery as an aid to truth and as a means of searching out falsehood. But most important, it leaves to a more selective process than a blanket distinction between civil and criminal cases the development of techniques for coping with the special problems which may arise in some criminal cases.

THE PROTECTIVE ORDER. A number of problems will undoubtedly arise in the creation of such a system. Most important is the fear, well founded in certain limited classes of cases, that the defendant is dangerous and poses a real threat to the prosecution's witnesses. The almost identical problem is posed whenever a defendant who knows the identity of the complaining witness is released on bail pending trial; or when he sees several of the prosecution's witnesses at a preliminary hearing; or when the nature of events leading up to the charge of crime informs him to the utmost about the nature of the case against him; or when, after a full trial, he is released on bail pending appeal. The law of bail stands four-square across the path to the easy assumption that he who is charged with crime is indiscriminately dangerous. It refuses to deny to all their liberty and their right to assist in preparing their defense because there are a few who may interfere with the process while it is at work. Even where the ban on excessive bail is manipulated to keep in prison those perceived as dangerous to public or process, the justification ordinarily reflects an attempt to cope with the incredibly complex problems of predicting the behavior of the accused while on bail.

It is likely, however, despite all that has been said, that there will arise cases in which free discovery by the defendant may be too dangerous. In such cases, it may be desirable to borrow from the Federal Rules of Civil Procedure the concept of the "protective order." This would authorize a trial court upon a proper showing to seal off information or identity of witnesses. It would do explicitly what is now done covertly at the bail stage. And in time it would undoubtedly lead to a more selective and discriminating case law than any we now have.

Special problems will surely follow in the wake of the "protective order." Where its effect is merely to seal off the identity of documents or of material which will eventually be disclosed at trial, the only interference with the defendant is that he will have to defer until trial the preparation of defensive matter responsive to, or discoverable from, such previously undisclosed material. Allowance of limited continuances may, of course, be necessary to enable the defendant to make use of such material.

Where, on the other hand, the effect of the protective order is to deny defendant access to material which the government is not likely to introduce at trial—for example, materials helpful to the defense—the prosecution's contentions will undoubtedly resemble those now regularly urged to support a claim of "government privilege." Disclosure will either make known the identity of an informer who would preferably remain unidentified; or it will involve "secrets" of some kind or other; or it will intrude upon the "work-product" of the government attorney; or it will interfere with the administration of justice in some undefined way. Here, the range of solutions developed in the case law generally for "government privilege" would seem adequate. If the court were persuaded that the matter should be privileged, and that nondisclosure would not seriously injure the defendant, then no price need be paid by the government. Where there is both a valid claim of privilege *and* injury to the defendant, the present case law makes the government pay a price—either of dismissing the case or of having an issue taken as decided against it. Where the claim of privilege is held to be invalid, disclosure could be compelled under penalty of contempt.

DISCOVERY BY THE DEFENDANT—RIGHT OR PRIVILEGE. If full discovery were adopted, it would perhaps be open to the prosecution to claim that it would not have as much access to the defendant himself as he would have to all the prosecution's witnesses. This would, of course, be true—subject to all of the qualifications on the extent of that inaccessibility. Three responses may be made to this line of argument—none of which consigns all defendants to outer darkness, as does the present approach.

The first, and probably the most desirable, would allow the defendant his immunity—as a mark of the maturity of our state and the consummate respect it pays to the dignity of the individual, both for his own sake and for the benefit of a society seeking

Abraham S. Goldstein

to impress upon its police and prosecutors the high obligation to proceed against a citizen only when they have independent evidence of his crime. History teaches that too ready availability of the accused as the source of the evidence against him inevitably tempts the state to intrude too much. And the inherent inequality in investigative resources, as between state and accused, suggests also that the defendant does not get so much on the total scale when his limited immunity is left him.

The second response would demand of the accused who wishes to participate in a balanced and intelligent procedural system that he pay a price for such participation: that he waive his special status as an accused, though not his status as witness, in return for full rights of discovery. He would still have the privilege of the witness to refuse to answer particular incriminating questions. But the questions could be put to him at depositions or at trial. And his refusal to answer, or to take the stand, could be made the subject of comment.

Yet a third response remains. As a condition of enjoying full rights of discovery, the accused could be required to waive all immunity from self-incrimination regarding the crime charged, at the time he enters his plea of not guilty. He would then become as much subject to deposition, discovery and testimony at trial as is any witness in a civil case. The choice would be his to make—to participate in either a civil or criminal type procedural system. In all three approaches, the remedy of the protective order would remain to deal with the exceptionally threatening situation.

About all that can reasonably be said against the second or third suggestions is that the mere existence of the option may make for invidious comparison between those defendants who elect the civil-type procedure and those who insist upon their privilege or immunity. The argument is reminiscent of another day when some resisted the restoration of competency to defendants. Then, too, it was urged that if any defendant were permitted to take the stand, it would create an adverse effect upon those defendants who did not choose to do so. The second and third suggestions seem to call for less in the way of invidious comparison. And in both cases, there is too much to be gained by defendants as a class to warrant denying them the opportunity to get the fairest and most efficient trial our procedural reformers have been able to develop.

Conclusion

The "procedural revolution" of the twentieth century followed inevitably from the legal realists' attack upon the procedural formalism of the prior century. Uncritical reverence for the forms of another day was supplanted by a more discriminating and instrumental view of procedure as an integral part of the substantive law. It became clear that the effectiveness of a court's statement of "the law" is a function of many variables—chief among them the manner in which relevant institutions channel to them the materials for decision, the forms of words in which legal criteria are stated, and the vigor with which those criteria are worked out at each stage by all those concerned with the process. In the field of civil procedure, the heritage left by the legal realists was a happy one—flexibility, concern for the substantive ends to be served by a procedural system, discriminating efficiency, and maximal opportunity to all to make use of the legal process to obtain the information necessary for resolving the dispute between the parties.

But when those who did so much to shape the procedural revolution on the civil side turned their attention to criminal procedure, albeit as writers of case law not of codes, the results were unfortunate. The modifications fashioned by them on the basis of allegedly rigorous analysis and in the interest of flexibility and efficiency have all worked to the very serious disadvantage of the defendant. This has occurred not because the modifications are intrinsically undesirable but rather because they have been fragmentary in nature and were introduced without any real appreciation of the requirements of the total procedural system.

If the flexibility of pleading and proof introduced by the procedural reformers at the trial stage were matched by a compensatory zeal for improving the pretrial disclosure devices, or if the pretrial screens could be expected to leave for trial only those who are guilty, it would be difficult to avoid joining the "mod-

Abraham S. Goldstein

ernizers," though there would still remain the question why the state could not afford to try the obviously guilty by the strictest possible standards of proof; or whether it is not as important that the process be "fair" as that the guilty be brought to book. Unfortunately, however, the relationships among the parts remain unnoticed in entirely too much of the case law. Judicial supervision of the quantum of proof necessary to convict is being relaxed at the very time when pretrial standards of proof are being removed from meaningful judicially enforced standards. And pleading is being loosened at the very time that judicial attitudes toward pretrial discovery and bills of particulars remain hard.

However much he can be said to benefit from the widely publicized decisions in certain areas of constitutional law, the hypothetical "accused" can find little to please him in current developments in the criminal trial process. Those developments reflect entirely too little concern about the inherent inequality of litigating position between the expanding state and even the most resourceful individual, much less the vast majority of resourceless ones. And even more fundamentally, they reflect subtle erosion of the accusatorial system, relieving police and prosecutor in many instances of the pressures necessary to maintain their actions at the optimum level of responsibility.

HERBERT L. PACKER

Two Models of the Criminal Process

$\mathbf{P}$eople who commit crimes appear to share the prevalent impression that punishment is an unpleasantness that is best avoided. They ordinarily take care to avoid being caught. If arrested, they ordinarily deny their guilt and otherwise try not to cooperate with the police. If brought to trial, they do whatever their resources permit to resist being convicted. And even after they have been convicted and sent to prison, their efforts to secure their freedom do not cease. It is a struggle from start to finish. This struggle is often referred to as the criminal process, a compendious term that stands for all the complexes of activity that operate to bring the substantive law of crime to bear (or to keep it from coming to bear) on persons who are suspected of having committed crimes. It can be described, but only partially and inadequately, by referring to the rules of law that govern the apprehension, screening, and trial of persons suspected of crime. It consists at least as importantly of patterns of official activity that correspond only in the roughest kind of

Reprinted with permission of the publishers from Packer, *The Limits of the Criminal Sanction*, pp. 149–173 (Stanford: Stanford University Press; London: Oxford University Press, 1968).

Notes to this Selection will be found on page 428.

Packer is Professor of Law at Stanford University and author of Ex-Communist Witnesses (1962).

Herbert L. Packer

way to the prescriptions of procedural rules. As a result of recent emphasis on empirical research into the administration of criminal justice, we are just beginning to be aware how very rough the correspondence is.

At the same time, and perhaps in part as a result of this new accretion of knowledge, some of our lawmaking institutions—particularly the Supreme Court of the United States—have begun to add measurably to the prescriptions of law that are meant to govern the operation of the criminal process. This accretion has become, in the last few years, exponential in extent and velocity. We are faced with an interesting paradox: the more we learn about the Is of the criminal process, the more we are instructed about its Ought and the greater the gulf between Is and Ought appears to become. We learn that very few people get adequate legal representation in the criminal process; we are simultaneously told that the Constitution requires people to be afforded adequate legal representation in the criminal process. We learn that coercion is often used to extract confessions from suspected criminals; we are then told that convictions based on coerced confessions may not be permitted to stand. We discover that the police often use methods in gathering evidence that violate the norms of privacy protected by the Fourth Amendment; we are told that evidence obtained in this way must be excluded from the criminal trial. But these prescriptions about how the process ought to operate do not automatically become part of the patterns of official behavior in the criminal process. Is and Ought share an increasingly uneasy coexistence. Doubts are stirred about the kind of criminal process we want to have.

The kind of criminal process we have is an important determinant of the kind of behavior content that the criminal law ought rationally to comprise. Logically, the substantive question may appear to be prior: decide what kinds of conduct one wants to reach through the criminal process, and then decide what kind of process is best calculated to deal with those kinds of conduct. It has not worked that way. On the whole, the process has been at least as much a given as the content of the criminal law. But it is far from being a given in any rigid sense.

The shape of the criminal process affects the substance of the criminal law in two general ways. First, one would want to know, before adding a new category of behavior to the list of crimes and therefore placing an additional burden on the process, whether it is easy or hard to employ the criminal process. The more expeditious the process, the greater the number of people with whom it can deal and, therefore, the greater the variety of antisocial conduct that can be confided in whole or in part to the criminal law for inhibition. On the other hand, the harder the process is to use, the smaller the number of people who can be handled by it at any given level of resources for staffing and operating it. The harder it is to put a suspected criminal in jail, the fewer the number of cases that can be handled in a year by a given number of policemen, prosecutors, defense lawyers, judges and jurymen, probation officers, etc., etc. A second and subtler relationship exists between the characteristic functioning of the process and the kinds of conduct with which it can efficiently deal. Perhaps the clearest example, but by no means the only one, is in the area of what have been referred to as victimless crimes, i.e., offenses that do not result in anyone's feeling that he has been injured so as to impel him to bring the offense to the attention of the authorities. The offense of fornication is an example. In a jurisdiction where it is illegal for two persons not married to each other to have sexual intercourse, there is a substantial enforcement problem (or would be, if the law were taken seriously) because people who voluntarily have sexual intercourse with each other often do not feel that they have been victimized and therefore often do not complain to the police. Consensual transactions in gambling and narcotics present the same problem, somewhat exacerbated by the fact that we take these forms of conduct rather more seriously than fornication. To the difficulties of apprehending a criminal when it is known that he has committed a crime are added the difficulties of knowing that a crime has been committed. In this sense, the victimless crime always presents a greater problem to the criminal process than does the crime with an ascertainable victim. But this problem may be minimized if the criminal process has at its disposal measures designed to increase the probability that the commission of such offenses will become known. If suspects may be entrapped into committing offenses, if the police may arrest and search a suspect without evidence that he has committed an of-

Herbert L. Packer

fense, if wiretaps and other forms of electronic surveillance are permitted, it becomes easier to detect the commission of offenses of this sort. But if these measures are prohibited and if the prohibitions are observed in practice, it becomes more difficult, and eventually there may come a point at which the capacity of the criminal process to deal with victimless offenses becomes so attenuated that a failure of enforcement occurs.

Thus, a pragmatic approach to the central question of what the criminal law is good for would require both a general assessment of whether the criminal process is a high-speed or a low-speed instrument of social control, and a series of specific assessments of its fitness for handling particular kinds of antisocial behavior. Such assessments are necessary if we are to have a basis for elaborating the criteria that ought to affect legislative invocation of the criminal sanction. How can we provide ourselves with an understanding of the criminal process that pays due regard to its static and dynamic elements? There are, to be sure, aspects of the criminal process that vary only inconsequentially from place to place and from time to time. But its dynamism is clear—clearer today, perhaps, than ever before. We need to have an idea of the potentialities for change in the system and the probable direction that change is taking and may be expected to take in the future. We need to detach ourselves from the welter of more or less connected details that describe the myriad ways in which the criminal process does operate or may be likely to operate in mid-twentieth-century America, so that we can begin to see how the system as a whole might be able to deal with the variety of missions we confide to it.

One way to do this kind of job is to abstract from reality, to build a model. In a sense, a model is just what an examination of the constitutional and statutory provisions that govern the operation of the criminal process would produce. This in effect is the way analysis of the legal system has traditionally proceeded. It has considerable utility as an index of current value choices; but it produces a model that will not tell us very much about some important problems that the system encounters and that will only fortuitously tell us anything useful about how the system actually operates. On the other hand, the kind of model that might emerge from an attempt to cut loose from the law on the books and to describe, as accurately as possible, what actually goes on in the real-life world of the criminal process would so subordinate the inquiry to the tyranny of the actual that the existence of competing value choices would be obscured. The kind of criminal process we have depends importantly on certain value choices that are reflected, explicitly or implicitly, in its habitual functioning. The kind of model we need is one that permits us to recognize explicitly the value choices that underlie the details of the criminal process. In a word, what we need is a *normative* model or models. It will take more than one model, but it will not take more than two.

Two models of the criminal process will let us perceive the normative antinomy at the heart of the criminal law. These models are not labeled Is and Ought, nor are they to be taken in that sense. Rather, they represent an attempt to abstract two separate value systems that compete for priority in the operation of the criminal process. Neither is presented as either corresponding to reality or representing the ideal to the exclusion of the other. The two models merely afford a convenient way to talk about the operation of a process whose day-to-day functioning involves a constant series of minute adjustments between the competing demands of two value systems and whose normative future likewise involves a series of resolutions of the tensions between competing claims.

I call these two models the Due Process Model and the Crime Control Model. . . . The weighty questions of public policy that inhere in any attempt to discern where on the spectrum of normative choice the "right" answer lies are beyond the scope of the present inquiry. The attempt here is primarily to clarify the terms of discussion by isolating the assumptions that underlie competing policy claims and examining the conclusions that those claims, if fully accepted, would lead to.

.   .   .

Each of the two models we are about to examine is an attempt to give operational content to a complex of values underlying the criminal law. As I have suggested earlier, it is possible to identify two competing systems of values, the tension between which ac-

Herbert L. Packer

counts for the intense activity now observable in the development of the criminal process. The actors in this development—
lawmakers, judges, police, prosecutors, defense lawyers—do not
often pause to articulate the values that underlie the positions
that they take on any given issue. Indeed, it would be a gross over-
simplification to ascribe a coherent and consistent set of values
to any of these actors. Each of the two competing schemes of
values we will be developing in this section contains components
that are demonstrably present some of the time in some of the
actors' preferences regarding the criminal process. No one person
has ever identified himself as holding all of the values that underlie these two models. The models are polarities, and so are the
schemes of value that underlie them. A person who subscribed
to all of the values underlying one model to the exclusion of all
of the values underlying the other would be rightly viewed as a
fanatic. The values are presented here as an aid to analysis, not
as a program for action.

Some Common Ground

. . . A model of the criminal process that left out of account
relatively stable and enduring features of the American legal system would not have much relevance to our central inquiry. For
convenience, these elements of stability and continuity can be
roughly equated with minimal agreed limits expressed in the
Constitution of the United States and, more importantly, with
unarticulated assumptions that can be perceived to underlie
those limits. Of course, it is true that the Constitution is constantly appealed to by proponents and opponents of many measures that affect the criminal process. And only the naive would
deny that there are few conclusive positions that can be reached
by appeal to the Constitution. Yet there are assumptions about
the criminal process that are widely shared and that may be
viewed as common ground for the operation of any model of the
criminal process. Our first task is to clarify these assumptions.

First, there is the assumption, implicit in the ex post facto
clause of the Constitution, that the function of defining conduct
that may be treated as criminal is separate from and prior to the

process of identifying and dealing with persons as criminals. How wide or narrow the definition of criminal conduct must be is an important question of policy that yields highly variable results depending on the values held by those making the relevant decisions. But that there must be a means of definition that is in some sense separate from and prior to the operation of the process is clear. If this were not so, our efforts to deal with the phenomenon of organized crime would appear ludicrous indeed (which is not to say that we have by any means exhausted the possibilities for dealing with that problem within the limits of this basic assumption).

A related assumption that limits the area of controversy is that the criminal process ordinarily ought to be invoked by those charged with the responsibility for doing so when it appears that a crime has been committed and that there is a reasonable prospect of apprehending and convicting its perpetrator. Although police and prosecutors are allowed broad discretion for deciding not to invoke the criminal process, it is commonly agreed that these officials have no general dispensing power. If the legislature has decided that certain conduct is to be treated as criminal, the decision-makers at every level of the criminal process are expected to accept that basic decision as a premise for action. The controversial nature of the occasional case in which the relevant decision-makers appear not to have played their appointed role only serves to highlight the strength with which the premise holds. This assumption may be viewed as the other side of the ex post facto coin. Just as conduct that is not proscribed as criminal may not be dealt with in the criminal process, so conduct that has been denominated as criminal must be treated as such by the participants in the criminal process acting within their respective competences.

Next, there is the assumption that there are limits to the powers of government to investigate and apprehend persons suspected of committing crimes. I do not refer to the controversy (settled, at least in broad outline) as to whether the Fourth Amendment's prohibition against unreasonable searches and seizures applies to the states with the same force with which it applies to the federal government.[1] Rather, I am talking about the general assumption that a degree of scrutiny and control must be exercised with re-

Herbert L. Packer

spect to the activities of law enforcement officers, that the security and privacy of the individual may not be invaded at will. It is possible to imagine a society in which even lip service is not paid to this assumption. Nazi Germany approached but never quite reached this position. But no one in our society would maintain that any individual may be taken into custody at any time and held without any limitation of time during the process of investigating his possible commission of crimes, or would argue that there should be no form of redress for violation of at least some standards for official investigative conduct. Although this assumption may not appear to have much in the way of positive content, its absence would render moot some of our most hotly controverted problems. If there were not general agreement that there must be some limits on police power to detain and investigate, the highly controversial provisions of the Uniform Arrest Act, permitting the police to detain a person for questioning for a short period even though they do not have grounds for making an arrest, would be a magnanimous concession by the all-powerful state rather than, as it is now perceived, a substantial expansion of police power.

Finally, there is a complex of assumptions embraced by terms such as "the adversary system," "procedural due process," "notice and an opportunity to be heard," and "day in court." Common to them all is the notion that the alleged criminal is not merely an object to be acted upon but an independent entity in the process who may, if he so desires, force the operators of the process to demonstrate to an independent authority (judge and jury) that he is guilty of the charges against him. It is a minimal assumption. It speaks in terms of "may" rather than "must." It permits but does not require the accused, acting by himself or through his own agent, to play an active role in the process. By virtue of that fact the process becomes or has the capacity to become a contest between, if not equals, at least independent actors. As we shall see, much of the space between the two models is occupied by stronger or weaker notions of how this contest is to be arranged, in what cases it is to be played, and by what rules. The Crime Control Model tends to de-emphasize this adversary aspect of the process; the Due Process Model tends to make it central. The common ground, and it is important, is the agreement that the process has, for everyone subjected to it, at least the potentiality of becoming to some extent an adversary struggle.

. . .

Crime Control Values

The value system that underlies the Crime Control Model is based on the proposition that the repression of criminal conduct is by far the most important function to be performed by the criminal process. The failure of law enforcement to bring criminal conduct under tight control is viewed as leading to the breakdown of public order and thence to the disappearance of an important condition of human freedom. If the laws go unenforced—which is to say, if it is perceived that there is a high percentage of failure to apprehend and convict in the criminal process—a general disregard for legal controls tends to develop. The law-abiding citizen then becomes the victim of all sorts of unjustifiable invasions of his interests. His security of person and property is sharply diminished, and, therefore, so is his liberty to function as a member of society. The claim ultimately is that the criminal process is a positive guarantor of social freedom. In order to achieve this high purpose, the Crime Control Model requires that primary attention be paid to the efficiency with which the criminal process operates to screen suspects, determine guilt, and secure appropriate dispositions of persons convicted of crime.

Efficiency of operation is not, of course, a criterion that can be applied in a vacuum. By "efficiency" we mean the system's capacity to apprehend, try, convict, and dispose of a high proportion of criminal offenders whose offenses become known. In a society in which only the grossest forms of antisocial behavior were made criminal and in which the crime rate was exceedingly low, the criminal process might require the devotion of many more man-hours of police, prosecutorial, and judicial time per case than ours does, and still operate with tolerable efficiency. A society that was prepared to increase even further the resources

Herbert L. Packer

devoted to the suppression of crime might cope with a rising crime rate without sacrifice of efficiency while continuing to maintain an elaborate and time-consuming set of criminal processes. However, neither of these possible characteristics corresponds with social reality in this country. We use the criminal sanction to cover an increasingly wide spectrum of behavior thought to be antisocial, and the amount of crime is very high indeed, although both level and trend are hard to assess.[2] At the same time, although precise measures are not available, it does not appear that we are disposed in the public sector of the economy to increase very drastically the quantity, much less the quality, of the resources devoted to the suppression of criminal activity through the operation of the criminal process. These factors have an important bearing on the criteria of efficiency, and therefore on the nature of the Crime Control Model.

The model, in order to operate successfully, must produce a high rate of apprehension and conviction, and must do so in a context where the magnitudes being dealt with are very large and the resources for dealing with them are very limited. There must then be a premium on speed and finality. Speed, in turn, depends on informality and on uniformity; finality depends on minimizing the occasions for challenge. The process must not be cluttered up with ceremonious rituals that do not advance the progress of a case. Facts can be established more quickly through interrogation in a police station than through the formal process of examination and cross-examination in a court. It follows that extra-judicial processes should be preferred to judicial processes, informal operations to formal ones. But informality is not enough; there must also be uniformity. Routine, stereotyped procedures are essential if large numbers are being handled. The model that will operate successfully on these presuppositions must be an administrative, almost a managerial, model. The image that comes to mind is an assembly-line conveyor belt down which moves an endless stream of cases, never stopping, carrying the cases to workers who stand at fixed stations and who perform on each case as it comes by the same small but essential operation that brings it one step closer to being a finished product, or, to exchange the metaphor for the reality, a closed file. The criminal process, in this model, is seen as a screening process in which each successive stage—pre-arrest investigation, arrest, post-arrest investigation, preparation for trial, trial or entry of plea, conviction, disposition—involves a series of routinized operations whose success is gauged primarily by their tendency to pass the case along to a successful conclusion.

What is a successful conclusion? One that throws off at an early stage those cases in which it appears unlikely that the person apprehended is an offender and then secures, as expeditiously as possible, the conviction of the rest, with a minimum of occasions for challenge, let alone post-audit. By the application of administrative expertness, primarily that of the police and prosecutors, an early determination of probable innocence or guilt emerges. Those who are probably innocent are screened out. Those who are probably guilty are passed quickly through the remaining stages of the process. The key to the operation of the model regarding those who are not screened out is what I shall call a presumption of guilt. The concept requires some explanation, since it may appear startling to assert that what appears to be the precise converse of our generally accepted ideology of a presumption of innocence can be an essential element of a model that does correspond in some respects to the actual operation of the criminal process.

The presumption of guilt is what makes it possible for the system to deal efficiently with large numbers, as the Crime Control Model demands. The supposition is that the screening processes operated by police and prosecutors are reliable indicators of probable guilt. Once a man has been arrested and investigated without being found to be probably innocent, or, to put it differently, once a determination has been made that there is enough evidence of guilt to permit holding him for further action, then all subsequent activity directed toward him is based on the view that he is probably guilty. The precise point at which this occurs will vary from case to case; in many cases it will occur as soon as the suspect is arrested, or even before, if the evidence of probable guilt that has come to the attention of the authorities is sufficiently strong. But in any case the presumption of guilt will begin to operate well before the "suspect" becomes a "defendant."

The presumption of guilt is not, of course, a thing. Nor is it even a rule of law in the usual sense. It simply is the consequence of a complex of attitudes, a mood. If there is confidence in the reliability of informal administrative fact-finding activities that take place in the early stages of the criminal process, the remaining stages of the process can be relatively perfunctory without any loss in operating efficiency. The presumption of guilt, as it operates in the Crime Control Model, is the operational expression of that confidence.

It would be a mistake to think of the presumption of guilt as the opposite of the presumption of innocence that we are so used to thinking of as the polestar of the criminal process and that, as we shall see, occupies an important position in the Due Process Model. The presumption of innocence is not its opposite; it is irrelevant to the presumption of guilt; the two concepts are different rather than opposite ideas. The difference can perhaps be epitomized by an example. A murderer, for reasons best known to himself, chooses to shoot his victim in plain view of a large number of people. When the police arrive, he hands them his gun and says, "I did it and I'm glad." His account of what happened is corroborated by several eyewitnesses. He is placed under arrest and led off to jail. Under these circumstances, which may seem extreme but which in fact characterize with rough accuracy the evidentiary situation in a large proportion of criminal cases, it would be plainly absurd to maintain that more probably than not the suspect did not commit the killing. But that is not what the presumption of innocence means. It means that until there has been an adjudication of guilt by an authority legally competent to make such an adjudication, the suspect is to be treated, for reasons that have nothing whatever to do with the probable outcome of the case, as if his guilt is an open question.

The presumption of innocence is a direction to officials about how they are to proceed, not a prediction of outcome. The presumption of guilt, however, is purely and simply a prediction of outcome. The presumption of innocence is, then, a direction to the authorities to ignore the presumption of guilt in their treatment of the suspect. It tells them, in effect, to close their eyes to what will frequently seem to be factual probabilities. The reasons why it tells them this are among the animating presuppositions of the Due Process Model, and we will come to them shortly. It is enough to note at this point that the presumption of guilt is descriptive and factual; the presumption of innocence is normative and legal. The pure Crime Control Model has no truck with the presumption of innocence, although its real-life emanations are, as we shall see, brought into uneasy compromise with the dictates of this dominant ideological position. In the presumption of guilt this model finds a factual predicate for the position that the dominant goal of repressing crime can be achieved through highly summary processes without any great loss of efficiency (as previously defined), because of the probability that, in the run of cases, the preliminary screening processes operated by the police and the prosecuting officials contain adequate guarantees of reliable fact-finding. Indeed, the model takes an even stronger position. It is that subsequent processes, particularly those of a formal adjudicatory nature, are unlikely to produce as reliable fact-finding as the expert administrative process that precedes them is capable of. The criminal process thus must put special weight on the quality of administrative fact-finding. It becomes important, then, to place as few restrictions as possible on the character of the administrative fact-finding processes and to limit restrictions to such as enhance reliability, excluding those designed for other purposes. As we shall see, this view of restrictions on administrative fact-finding is a consistent theme in the development of the Crime Control Model.

In this model, as I have suggested, the center of gravity for the process lies in the early, administrative fact-finding stages. The complementary proposition is that the subsequent stages are relatively unimportant and should be truncated as much as possible. This, too, produces tensions with presently dominant ideology. The pure Crime Control Model has very little use for many conspicuous features of the adjudicative process, and in real life works out a number of ingenious compromises with them. Even in the pure model, however, there have to be devices for dealing with the suspect after the preliminary screening process has resulted in a determination of probable guilt. The focal device, as we shall see, is the plea of guilty; through its use, adjudicative fact-finding is reduced to a minimum. It might be said of the Crime Control Model that, when reduced to its barest essentials and operating at its most successful pitch, it offers two possibilities: an administrative fact-finding process leading (1) to exoneration of the suspect or (2) to the entry of a plea of guilty.

Herbert L. Packer

Due Process Values

If the Crime Control Model resembles an assembly line, the Due Process Model looks very much like an obstacle course. Each of its successive stages is designed to present formidable impediments to carrying the accused any further along in the process. Its ideology is not the converse of that underlying the Crime Control Model. It does not rest on the idea that it is not socially desirable to repress crime, although critics of its application have been known to claim so. Its ideology is composed of a complex of ideas, some of them based on judgments about the efficacy of crime control devices, others having to do with quite different considerations. The ideology of due process is far more deeply impressed on the formal structure of the law than is the ideology of crime control; yet an accurate tracing of the strands that make it up is strangely difficult. What follows is only an attempt at an approximation.

The Due Process Model encounters its rival on the Crime Control Model's own ground in respect to the reliability of fact-finding processes. The Crime Control Model, as we have suggested, places heavy reliance on the ability of investigative and prosecutorial officers, acting in an informal setting in which their distinctive skills are given full sway, to elicit and reconstruct a tolerably accurate account of what actually took place in an alleged criminal event. The Due Process Model rejects this premise and substitutes for it a view of informal, nonadjudicative fact-finding that stresses the possibility of error. People are notoriously poor observers of disturbing events—the more emotion-arousing the context, the greater the possibility that recollection will be incorrect; confessions and admissions by persons in police custody may be induced by physical or psychological coercion so that the police end up hearing what the suspect thinks they want to hear rather than the truth; witnesses may be animated by a bias or interest that no one would trouble to discover except one specially charged with protecting the interests of the accused (as the police are not). Considerations of this kind all lead to a rejection of informal fact-finding processes as definitive of factual guilt and to an insistence on formal, adjudicative, adversary fact-finding processes in which the factual case against the accused is publicly heard by an impartial tribunal and is evaluated only after the accused has had a full opportunity to discredit the case against him. Even then, the distrust of fact-finding processes that animates the Due Process Model is not dissipated. The possibilities of human error being what they are, further scrutiny is necessary, or at least must be available, in case facts have been overlooked or suppressed in the heat of battle. How far this subsequent scrutiny must be available is a hotly controverted issue today. In the pure Due Process Model the answer would be: at least as long as there is an allegation of factual error that has not received an adjudicative hearing in a fact-finding context. The demand for finality is thus very low in the Due Process Model.

This strand of due process ideology is not enough to sustain the model. If all that were at issue between the two models was a series of questions about the reliability of fact-finding processes, we would have but one model of the criminal process, the nature of whose constituent elements would pose questions of fact not of value. Even if the discussion is confined, for the moment, to the question of reliability, it is apparent that more is at stake than simply an evalution of what kinds of fact-finding processes, alone or in combination, are likely to produce the most nearly reliable results. The stumbling block is this: how much reliability is compatible with efficiency? Granted that informal fact-finding will make some mistakes that can be remedied if backed up by adjudicative fact-finding, the desirability of providing this backup is not affirmed or negated by factual demonstrations or predictions that the increase in reliability will be x percent or x plus n percent. It still remains to ask how much weight is to be given to the competing demands of reliability (a high degree of probability in each case that factual guilt has been accurately determined) and efficiency (expeditious handling of the large numbers of cases that the process ingests). The Crime Control Model is more optimistic about the improbability of error in a significant number of cases; but it is also, though only in part therefore, more tolerant about the amount of error that it will put up with. The Due Process Model insists on the prevention and elimination of mistakes to the extent possible; the Crime Control Model accepts the probability of mistakes up to the level at which they interfere with the goal of repressing crime, either

Herbert L. Packer

because too many guilty people are escaping or, more subtly, because general awareness of the unreliability of the process leads to a decrease in the deterrent efficacy of the criminal law. In this view, reliability and efficiency are not polar opposites but rather complementary characteristics. The system is reliable *because* efficient; reliability becomes a matter of independent concern only when it becomes so attenuated as to impair efficiency. All of this the Due Process Model rejects. If efficiency demands short-cuts around reliability, then absolute efficiency must be rejected. The aim of the process is at least as much to protect the factually innocent as it is to convict the factually guilty. It is a little like quality control in industrial technology: tolerable deviation from standard varies with the importance of conformity to standard in the destined uses of the product. The Due Process Model resembles a factory that has to devote a substantial part of its input to quality control. This necessarily cuts down on quantitative output.

All of this is only the beginning of the ideological difference between the two models. The Due Process Model could disclaim any attempt to provide enhanced reliability for the fact-finding process and still produce a set of institutions and processes that would differ sharply from those demanded by the Crime Control Model. Indeed, it may not be too great an oversimplification to assert that in point of historical development the doctrinal pressures emanating from the demands of the Due Process Model have tended to evolve from an original matrix of concern for the maximization of reliability into values quite different and more far-reaching. These values can be expressed in, although not adequately described by, the concept of the primacy of the individual and the complementary concept of limitation on official power.

The combination of stigma and loss of liberty that is embodied in the end result of the criminal process is viewed as being the heaviest deprivation that government can inflict on the individual. Furthermore, the processes that culminate in these highly afflictive sanctions are seen as in themselves coercive, restricting, and demeaning. Power is always subject to abuse—sometimes subtle, other times, as in the criminal process, open and ugly. Precisely because of its potency in subjecting the individual to the coercive power of the state, the criminal process must, in this model, be subjected to controls that prevent it from operating with maximal efficiency. According to this ideology, maximal efficiency means maximal tyranny. And, although no one would assert that minimal efficiency means minimal tyranny, the proponents of the Due Process Model would accept with considerable equanimity a substantial diminution in the efficiency with which the criminal process operates in the interest of preventing official oppression of the individual.

The most modest-seeming but potentially far-reaching mechanism by which the Due Process Model implements these anti-authoritarian values is the doctrine of legal guilt. According to this doctrine, a person is not to be held guilty of crime merely on a showing that in all probability, based upon reliable evidence, he did factually what he is said to have done. Instead, he is to be held guilty if and only if these factual determinations are made in procedurally regular fashion and by authorities acting within competences duly allocated to them. Furthermore, he is not to be held guilty, even though the factual determination is or might be adverse to him, if various rules designed to protect him and to safeguard the integrity of the process are not given effect: the tribunal that convicts him must have the power to deal with his kind of case ("jurisdiction") and must be geographically appropriate ("venue"); too long a time must not have elapsed since the offense was committed ("statute of limitations"); he must not have been previously convicted or acquitted of the same or a substantially similar offense ("double jeopardy"); he must not fall within a category of persons, such as children or the insane, who are legally immune to conviction (" criminal responsibility"); and so on. None of these requirements has anything to do with the factual question of whether the person did or did not engage in the conduct that is charged as the offense against him; yet favorable answers to any of them will mean that he is legally innocent. Wherever the competence to make adequate factual determinations lies, it is apparent that only a tribunal that is aware of these guilt-defeating doctrines and is willing to apply them can be viewed as competent to make determinations of legal guilt. The police and the prosecutors are ruled out by lack of competence, in the first instance, and by lack of assurance of willingness, in

Herbert L. Packer

the second. Only an impartial tribunal can be trusted to make determinations of legal as opposed to factual guilt.

In this concept of legal guilt lies the explanation for the apparently quixotic presumption of innocence of which we spoke earlier. A man who, after police investigation, is charged with having committed a crime can hardly be said to be presumptively innocent, if what we mean is factual innocence. But if what we mean is that it has yet to be determined if any of the myriad legal doctrines that serve in one way or another the end of limiting official power through the observance of certain substantive and procedural regularities may be appropriately invoked to exculpate the accused man, it is apparent that as a matter of prediction it cannot be said with confidence that more probably than not he will be found guilty.

Beyond the question of predictability this model posits a functional reason for observing the presumption of innocence: by forcing the state to prove its case against the accused in an adjudicative context, the presumption of innocence serves to force into play all the qualifying and disabling doctrines that limit the use of the criminal sanction against the individual, thereby enhancing his opportunity to secure a favorable outcome. In this sense, the presumption of innocence may be seen to operate as a kind of self-fulfilling prophecy. By opening up a procedural situation that permits the successful assertion of defenses having nothing to do with factual guilt, it vindicates the proposition that the factually guilty may nonetheless be legally innocent and should therefore be given a chance to qualify for that kind of treatment.

The possibility of legal innocence is expanded enormously when the criminal process is viewed as the appropriate forum for correcting its own abuses. This notion may well account for a greater amount of the distance between the two models than any other. In theory the Crime Control Model can tolerate rules that forbid illegal arrests, unreasonable searches, coercive interrogations, and the like. What it cannot tolerate is the vindication of those rules in the criminal process itself through the exclusion of evidence illegally obtained or through the reversal of convictions in cases where the criminal process has breached the rules laid down for its observance. And the Due Process Model, although it may in the first instance be addressed to the maintenance of reliable fact-finding techniques, comes eventually to incorporate prophylactic and deterrent rules that result in the release of the factually guilty even in cases in which blotting out the illegality would still leave an adjudicative fact-finder convinced of the accused person's guilt. Only by penalizing errant police and prosecutors within the criminal process itself can adequate pressure be maintained, so the argument runs, to induce conformity with the Due Process Model.

Another strand in the complex of attitudes underlying the Due Process Model is the idea—itself a shorthand statement for a complex of attitudes—of equality. This notion has only recently emerged as an explicit basis for pressing the demands of the Due Process Model, but it appears to represent, at least in its potential, a most powerful norm for influencing official conduct. Stated most starkly, the ideal of equality holds that "there can be no equal justice where the kind of trial a man gets depends on the amount of money he has."[3] The factual predicate underlying this assertion is that there are gross inequalities in the financial means of criminal defendants as a class, that in an adversary system of criminal justice an effective defense is largely a function of the resources that can be mustered on behalf of the accused, and that the very large proportion of criminal defendants who are, operationally speaking, "indigent" will thus be denied an effective defense. This factual premise has been strongly reinforced by recent studies that in turn have been both a cause and an effect of an increasing emphasis upon norms for the criminal process based on the premise.

The norms derived from the premise do not take the form of an insistence upon governmental responsibility to provide literally equal opportunities for all criminal defendants to challenge the process. Rather, they take as their point of departure the notion that the criminal process, initiated as it is by government and containing as it does the likelihood of severe deprivations at the hands of government, imposes some kind of public obligation to ensure that financial inability does not destroy the capacity of an accused to assert what may be meritorious challenges to the processes being invoked against him. At its most gross, the norm of equality would act to prevent situations in which financial in-

Herbert L. Packer

ability forms an absolute barrier to the assertion of a right that is in theory generally available, as where there is a right to appeal that is, however, effectively conditional upon the filing of a trial transcript obtained at the defendant's expense. Beyond this, it may provide the basis for a claim whenever the system theoretically makes some kind of challenge available to an accused who has the means to press it. If, for example, a defendant who is adequately represented has the opportunity to prevent the case against him from coming to the trial stage by forcing the state to its proof in a preliminary hearing, the norm of equality may be invoked to assert that the same kind of opportunity must be available to others as well. In a sense the system as it functions for the small minority whose resources permit them to exploit all its defensive possibilities provides a benchmark by which its functioning in all other cases is to be tested: not, perhaps, to guarantee literal identity but rather to provide a measure of whether the process as a whole is recognizably of the same general order. The demands made by a norm of this kind are likely by their very nature to be quite sweeping. Although the norm's imperatives may be initially limited to determining whether in a particular case the accused was injured or prejudiced by his relative inability to make an appropriate challenge, the norm of equality very quickly moves to another level on which the demand is that the process in general be adapted to minimize discriminations rather than that a mere series of post hoc determinations of discrimination be made or makeable.

It should be observed that the impact of the equality norm will vary greatly depending upon the point in time at which it is introduced into a model of the criminal process. If one were starting from scratch to decide how the process ought to work, the norm of equality would have nothing very important to say on such questions as, for example, whether an accused should have the effective assistance of counsel in deciding whether to enter a plea of guilty. One could decide, on quite independent considerations, that it is or is not a good thing to afford that facility to the generality of persons accused of crime. But the impact of the equality norm becomes far greater when it is brought to bear on a process whose contours have already been shaped. If our model of the criminal process affords defendants who are in a financial position to do so the right to consult a lawyer before entering a plea, then the equality norm exerts powerful pressure to provide such an opportunity to all defendants and to regard the failure to do so as a malfunctioning of the process of whose consequences the accused is entitled to be relieved. In a sense, this has been the role of the equality norm in affecting the real-world criminal process. It has made its appearance on the scene comparatively late, and has therefore encountered a system in which the relative financial inability of most persons accused of crime results in treatment very different from that accorded the small minority of the financially capable. For this reason, its impact has already been substantial and may be expected to be even more so in the future.

There is a final strand of thought in the Due Process Model that is often ignored but that needs to be candidly faced if thought on the subject is not to be obscured. This is a mood of skepticism about the morality and utility of the criminal sanction, taken either as a whole or in some of its applications. The subject is a large and complicated one, comprehending as it does much of the intellectual history of our times. It is properly the subject of another essay altogether. To put the matter briefly, one cannot improve upon the statement by Professor Paul Bator: "In summary we are told that the criminal law's notion of just condemnation and punishment is a cruel hypocrisy visited by a smug society on the psychologically and economically crippled; that its premise of a morally autonomous will with at least some measure of choice whether to comply with the values expressed in a penal code is unscientific and outmoded; that its reliance on punishment as an educational and deterrent agent is misplaced, particularly in the case of the very members of society most likely to engage in criminal conduct; and that its failure to provide for individualized and humane rehabilitation of offenders is inhuman and wasteful."[4]

This skepticism, which may be fairly said to be widespread among the most influential and articulate contemporary leaders of informed opinion, leads to an attitude toward the processes of the criminal law that, to quote Mr. Bator again, engenders "a peculiar receptivity toward claims of injustice which arise within the traditional structure of the system itself; fundamental disagreement and unease about the very bases of the criminal law has, inevitably, created acute pressure at least to expand and liberalize those of its processes and doctrines which serve to make more tentative its judgments or limit its power." In short, doubts about the ends for which power is being exercised create pressure to limit the discretion with which that power is exercised.

The point need not be pressed to the extreme of doubts about or rejection of the premises upon which the criminal sanction in general rests. Unease may be stirred simply by reflection on the variety of uses to which the criminal sanction is put and by a judgment that an increasingly large proportion of those uses may represent an unwise invocation of so extreme a sanction. It would be an interesting irony if doubts about the propriety of certain uses of the criminal sanction prove to contribute to a restrictive trend in the criminal process that in the end requires a choice among uses and finally an abandonment of some of the very uses that stirred the original doubts, but for a reason quite unrelated to those doubts.

There are two kinds of problems that need to be dealt with in any model of the criminal process. One is what the rules shall be. The other is how the rules shall be implemented. The second is at least as important as the first. . . . The distinctive difference between the two models is not only in the rules of conduct that they lay down but also in the sanctions that are to be invoked when a claim is presented that the rules have been breached and, no less importantly, in the timing that is permitted or required for the invocation of those sanctions.

As I have already suggested, the Due Process Model locates at least some of the sanctions for breach of the operative rules in the criminal process itself. The relation between these two aspects of the process—the rules and the sanctions for their breach—is a purely formal one unless there is some mechanism for bringing them into play with each other. The hinge between them in the Due Process Model is the availability of legal counsel. This has a double aspect. Many of the rules that the model requires are couched in terms of the availability of counsel to do various things at various stages of the process—this is the conventionally recognized aspect; beyond it, there is a pervasive assumption that counsel is necessary in order to invoke sanctions for breach of any of the rules. The more freely available these sanctions are, the more important is the role of counsel in seeing to it that the sanctions are appropriately invoked. If the process is seen as a series of occasions for checking its own operation, the role of counsel is a much more nearly central one than is the case in a process that is seen as primarily concerned with expeditious determination of factual guilt. And if equality of operation is a governing norm, the availability of counsel to some is seen as requiring it for all. Of all the controverted aspects of the criminal process, the right to counsel, including the role of government in its provision, is the most dependent on what one's model of the process looks like, and the least susceptible of resolution unless one has confronted the antinomies of the two models.

I do not mean to suggest that questions about the right to counsel disappear if one adopts a model of the process that conforms more or less closely to the Crime Control Model, but only that such questions become absolutely central if one's model moves very far down the spectrum of possibilities toward the pure Due Process Model. The reason for this centrality is to be found in the assumption underlying both models that the process is an adversary one in which the initiative in invoking relevant rules rests primarily on the parties concerned, the state, and the accused. One could construct models that placed central responsibility on adjudicative agents such as committing magistrates and trial judges. And there are . . . marginal but nonetheless important adjustments in the role of the adjudicative agents that enter into the models with which we are concerned. For present purposes it is enough to say that these adjustments are marginal, that the animating presuppositions that underlie both models in the context of the American criminal system relegate the adjudicative agents to a relatively passive role, and therefore place central importance on the role of counsel.

. . . What assumptions do we make about the sources of authority to shape the real-world operations of the criminal process? Recognizing that our models are only models, what agencies of government have the power to pick and choose between their competing demands? Once again, the limiting features of the American context come into play. Ours is not a system of legislative supremacy. The distinctively American institution of

Herbert L. Packer

judicial review exercises a limiting and ultimately a shaping influence on the criminal process. Because the Crime Control Model is basically an affirmative model, emphasizing at every turn the existence and exercise of official power, its validating authority is ultimately legislative (although proximately administrative). Because the Due Process Model is basically a negative model, asserting limits on the nature of official power and on the modes of its exercise, its validating authority is judicial and requires an appeal to supra-legislative law, to the law of the Constitution. To the extent that tensions between the two models are resolved by deference to the Due Process Model, the authoritative force at work is the judicial power, working in the distinctively judicial mode of invoking the sanction of nullity. That is at once the strength and the weakness of the Due Process Model: its strength because in our system the appeal to the Constitution provides the last and the overriding word; its weakness because saying no in specific cases is an exercise in futility unless there is a general willingness on the part of the officials who operate the process to apply negative prescriptions across the board. It is no accident that statements reinforcing the Due Process Model come from the courts, while at the same time facts denying it are established by the police and prosecutors.

JEROME HALL

The Basic Dilemma of Criminal Procedure

The most important single generalization that can be made about American criminal procedure or for that matter about any civilized criminal procedure is that its ultimate ends are dual and conflicting. It must be designed from inception to end, to acquit the innocent as readily, at least, as to convict the guilty. This presents the inescapable dilemma of criminal procedure which Bentham failed to recognize. For a procedure that does not assume guilt, but seeks to determine it rationally, by its basic hypothesis provides for innocence.

The dilemma consists in the fact that the easier it is made to prove guilt, the more difficult does it become to establish innocence. Lack of appreciation of the dual character of our criminal procedure is apparent in much of the criminological reform movement in the recent past which reflects hardly any suspicion that police and prosecutors are not omniscient. The presumption that to be charged means to be guilty has been tenaciously, if unconsciously, entertained by well-intentioned reformers lulled

Reprinted by permission of The Yale Law Journal Company and Fred B. Rothman & Co. from Hall, *Objectives of Federal Criminal Procedural Revision*, *Yale Law Journal*, vol. 51, pp. 723, 728–34 (1942).

Notes to this Selection will be found on page 428.

Hall *is Professor of Law at Indiana University and the author of* Criminal Law (1960) *and* Theft, Law and Society (1952).

into complacency by humanitarian motives to substitute "treatment" for punishment, and enlightened by negligible insight into the functions of criminal procedure. It can be demonstrated that their agitation parallels Enrico Ferri's almost to the word: one has but to read his condemnation of any presumption of innocence and of civil liberties generally to know where such reform leads. The problem is of paramount importance because of the challenge to elementary democratic values embodied in the Constitution and the Bill of Rights—largely a document of criminal procedure, and because, in conjunction with the guarantees of the written instrument, criminal law and procedure provide the most perfected inclusive safeguard against oppression available. The danger here is especially great because most of the competent members of the bar are so utterly uninformed in this branch of the law that the lawyers' criticism that can normally be expected concerning important proposed legal changes is non-existent.

Failure to appreciate the dual nature of American criminal procedure is represented in a number of fallacies. The degree of error in the fallacy that indictment means guilt is not reduced by the fact that the police are honest and competent and that the probabilities are therefore great that the accused committed the crimes charged against them. Admittedly, under such conditions a generous and circumspect attitude is required to give the presumption of innocence effect. Admittedly, also, the presumption of innocence does not rest solely on ethical principle; it equally represents stability of institutions, public confidence and the probability that most guilty persons are convicted. But the overriding considerations are that reliance is on rational procedure to determine guilt or innocence, and that, whatever police competence and the statistics suggest, we cannot form any intelligent judgment on this basis with reference to any particular case. Statistical generalizations hold true only for large numbers; even if 99% of all persons charged were convicted, this should not make the slightest difference in the judging of any particular case.

. . .

There is also the fallacy of arguing that because the accused had so few rights in the 16th and 17th centuries, therefore he has too many rights now. This view is not novel, and Stephen writing in 1863 noted that "one of the commonest arguments against allowing prisoners to be defended by counsel always was, that rogues had too many chances of escape already."[1] The present form of this argument points to the fact that until about 1700 an accused person could not testify in his own behalf, be represented by counsel, have access to books, have a copy of the indictment or other means of knowing the charge or the witnesses who would testify against him. There were few restrictions on the evidence that could be used against him; he could not call sworn witnesses in his behalf. The trials were extraordinarily efficient, "never extending beyond a day."[2] It may be wise to place certain restrictions on the present mode of criminal defense but it is obviously fallacious to pretend that the necessity or wisdom results because the pendulum has swung too far already in favor of the accused. We know that under present safeguards, innocent persons are convicted, and the recent federal provision for compensation[3] implies that their number is not negligible. Anyone with actual experience in the administration of criminal law realizes that in the vast majority of cases the handicaps of fortune and intelligence are so great as to make "equality" of the parties hardly more than a humbug. The professional criminal undoubtedly has many advantages but they result from his greater knowledge, financial and political support, as well as from deficiencies in the substantive law. There is wisdom in the observation that the substantive criminal law should be designed for criminals, the procedural for honest people. Certainly any revision in criminal procedure constructed with professional offenders particularly in mind, or on the supposition that "the rogues have too many chances of escape" because of the 18th and 19th century progress in safeguards, would result in a ritual whose efficiency would be equalled only by its terror.

There is [another] fallacy fetchingly described as "protection of society against criminals." Group security is opposed to individual liberty, with the clear implication that we must choose between them. This separation of group from individual, of society from offender, is one of the most vicious fallacies ever invented. Again it begins with the presumption of guilt. It implies that any method of "social defense" is permissible after one has

Jerome Hall

been thus prejudged, and that any measures of "prevention" are proper. Society is composed of individuals, but the logic of the above authoritarian ideology would place every individual outside the pale—should the occasion, as created by the logicians in political control, arise. As a matter of fact, group security is a function of individual security. If criminal procedure is designed to facilitate convictions, public security is imperilled. Pro tanto does "protection of society" increase when each individual is protected from indiscriminate and irrational exercise of official power. . . .

All of the above fallacies result from failure to comprehend the immanent conflicting ends of any civilized criminal procedure. This duality of objectives can be expressed mathematically, and it should be possible to construct a calculus of the probabilities of decision as functions of the conditions of trial, present or proposed; the range of variables would be complete abandonment of any prosecution for criminal behavior, on the one extreme, to treating every complaint as equivalent to conviction, on the other. In the absence of a forensic sociology, such objectivity would be hypothetical, but such a deliberate exercise would accentuate the implications of the basic axiom of criminal procedure. It might even provide the bare outlines of a future empirical science of procedure. Fortunately there is little likelihood of any present drastic curtailment of the basic guarantees of the Constitution and Bill of Rights. What lies closer at hand is the possible ignoring of the nicer ramifications of the above principles, the temptation to remedy substantive defects by procedural reforms, and to compensate for incompetent administration, e.g., in prosecution, by loading additional burdens on the accused, or in sentencing, by radical curtailment of judicial functions.

. . .

But the major consideration that gives pause to the wholesale adoption of reforms designed to facilitate conviction results from a judgment on the total situation, one that is characterized normally by a powerful state with practically unlimited resources arrayed against an impotent individual. Hence a great many informed persons, who would readily concede the abstract fairness of many reforms if the parties were evenly matched, are loath to increase the resources of an already vastly superior litigant. . . . One of the most generously motivated measures in recent years, the public defender, illustrates the impasse. The statistics on the increased pleas of guilty and on huge "savings to the taxpayers,"[4] reveal only too clearly that, at best, the plan represents a lesser of existing evils. Perhaps the most that can be hoped for is that a sympathetic understanding of actual conditions will temper paper plans for relentless application of logic to criminal procedure.

Certainly sound revision will employ logic to discard useless ritual and advance rational procedure. Certainly such revision must employ all relevant science and scientific method, *e.g.*, in analysis of the rules of evidence. But revision will not only miss its mark, it will be positively harmful if it does not subject each proposal to analysis in light of the basic duality of criminal procedure, in effect, if it does not weigh the ethical import of any proposed measure of reform, and do so in full awareness of the actualities that determine the outcome of criminal prosecutions. The formula is simple: logic and science must be limited by policy; but the application is difficult and calls for the nicest integration of experience in actual criminal administration with the subtlest comprehension of the ethical implications of criminal procedure. Under such conditions and with such objectives, revision will frequently eschew science for less effective methods. The existing preference is apparent when we consider that a criminal trial turns almost exclusively on human testimony. *Homo sapiens* talks and there is accordingly available the best possible evidence of human conduct—communication by the actor. Hence the insistence of the mediaeval inquisitor upon "confession or else" was no less logical and scientific than grim. In our books and in the courts, we abjure torture (though the police are not always so unscientific!); in effect, we even tell suspects not to talk because their statements will be held against them. We have constitutional guarantees against self-incrimination; we make some sincere effort to provide counsel to guard against indiscretions. All of this is illogical in the extreme, considering that disclosure by the defendant would be the simplest, the cheapest and very frequently the best evidence of what we

Jerome Hall

seek to know. The point here is not that we must accept every existing limitation on trial methods as an absolute value—for example, it is at least debatable whether comment on the defendant's failure to testify should not be permitted—but that we must recognize as fully as possible that we do impose such limitations, and that each involves a basic question of policy that operates directly contra the relevant logic.

There are other considerations regarding the application of scientific methods in criminal procedure. Indeed the most perplexing of all problems of legal reform is presented by demands for total logicality, for such a streamlining of procedure as to extract completely the game, the drama, the battle. Insistence on business efficiency, total condemnation of the jury, appeals for decision by experts and for scientific investigation as opposed to "trial by battle" are the familiar proposals. Their initial persuasiveness cannot be denied; but their relevance to and utility for criminal trials must be carefully weighed nonetheless. It is submitted that criminal procedure serves other functions than purely logical and scientific decision; that, indeed, in light of the facts, there are and, for an unforseeable future, will continue to be, sharp limits on the availability and utility of scientific methods in criminal procedure. The argument in support cannot be elaborated here but the outlines of the thesis must be briefly indicated.

Criminal law is people's law in a sense that applies to no other department of law. Indeed, for most persons criminal law is the only very familiar law because of almost daily actual and vicarious participation in its process. Most persons may know little of the technicality of either substantive or procedural law, but they can follow the rational outline of the conduct of the trial; a sense of security results that could never be provided by an expert operating in secret chambers or by little known formulas.[5] Hence criminal procedure constitutes a social situation which finds little counterpart in the administration of complicated property interests or other relatively impersonal affairs. Certainly the differentiation of such matters from more simple human rights, intuitively understood in the light of our history of civil liberties, supplies one clue to the recent direction of important judicial decisions. Beyond popular understanding of and participation in the processes of criminal law, there are other reasons for ques-

tioning the unmitigated application of science and scientific methods to criminal procedure. The criminal law in large measure represents an intimate self-government. The supplanting of popular institutions, especially those productive of confidence against abuse, with government by scientists would challenge public opinion, especially if effected by the recommendations of persons appointed by officials who were themselves appointees. We must recognize that the axioms of self-government and the democratic process imply that the best methods may temporarily, at least, be rejected although it is certainly defensible to maintain that in the long run social problems are best solved by consensuses freely arrived at rather than by imposition—even by disinterested specialists.

Finally, it is evident, also, that criminal procedure discharges non-rational functions which cannot presently be ignored. The thesis in this regard may be stated somewhat paradoxically: it is rational to employ criminal procedure, in part, to satisfy non-rational needs. The confidence aroused by the order, publicity and rationality of criminal procedure has been noted. But there are even deeper instinctual needs that cannot soon be modified. No reform of criminal procedure may lightly ignore the public "sense of justice," the interminable conflict between conscience and animal desire, or the criminal trial as a vicarious avenue of emotional release which supports the delicate balance of adjustment to social restraint. It is one thing to damn such emotional need and to look for a wiser direction of it; nonetheless it must be recognized that the present form of criminal procedure does take it into account in appreciable degree. . . .

ERVING GOFFMAN

Characteristics of Total Institutions

Every institution captures something of the time and interest of its members and provides something of a world for them; in brief, every institution has encompassing tendencies. When we review the different institutions in our Western society we find a class of them which seems to be encompassing to a degree discontinuously greater than the ones next in line. Their encompassing or total character is symbolized by the barrier to a social intercourse with the outside that is often built right into the physical plant: locked doors, high walls, barbed wire, cliffs and water, open terrain, and so forth. These I am calling total institutions, and it is their general characteristics I want to explore. This exploration will be phrased as if securely based on findings, but will in fact be speculative.

The total institutions of our society can be listed for convenience in five rough groupings. First, there are institutions established to care for persons thought to be both incapable and

Reprinted by permission from Symposium on Preventive and Social Psychiatry, Walter Reed Army Institute of Research, U.S. Govt. Printing Office (1958).

Notes to this Selection will be found on page 428.

Goffman is Benjamin Franklin Professor of Sociology at the University of Pennsylvania. He is the author of Presentation of Self in Everyday Life *(1959) and* Asylums *(1961).*

Erving Goffman

harmless; these are the homes for the blind, the aged, the orphaned, and the indigent. Second, there are places established to care for persons thought to be at once incapable of looking after themselves and a threat to the community, albeit an unintended one: TB sanitariums, mental hospitals, and leprosoriums. Third, another type of total institution is organized to protect the community against what are thought to be intentional dangers to it; here the welfare of the persons thus sequestered is not the immediate issue. Examples are: Jails, penitentiaries, POW camps, and concentration camps. Fourth, we find institutions purportedly established the better to pursue some technical task and justifying themselves only on these instrumental grounds: Army barracks, shops, boarding schools, work camps, colonial compounds, large mansions from the point of view of those who live in the servants' quarters, and so forth. Finally, there are those establishments designed as retreats from the world or as training stations for the religious: Abbeys, monasteries, convents, and other cloisters. This sublisting of total institutions is neither neat nor exhaustive, but the listing itself provides an empirical starting point for a purely denotative definition of the category. By anchoring the initial definition of total institutions in this way, I hope to be able to discuss the general characteristics of the type without becoming tautological.

. . .

A basic social arrangement in modern society is that we tend to sleep, play, and work in different places, in each case with a different set of coparticipants, under a different authority, and without an over-all rational plan. The central feature of total institutions can be described as a breakdown of the kinds of barriers ordinarily separating these three spheres of life. First, all aspects of life are conducted in the same place and under the same single authority. Second, each phase of the member's daily activity will be carried out in the immediate company of a large batch of others, all of whom are treated alike and required to do the same thing together. Third, all phases of the day's activities are tightly scheduled, with one activity leading at a prearranged time into the next, the whole circle of activities being imposed from above through a system of explicit formal rulings and a body of officials. Finally, the contents of the various enforced activities are brought together as parts of a single over-all rational plan purportedly designed to fulfill the official aims of the institution.

.   .   .

The handling of many human needs by the bureaucratic organization of whole blocks of people—whether or not this is a necessary or effective means of social organization in the circumstances—can be taken, then, as the key fact of total institutions. From this, certain important implications can be drawn.

Given the fact that blocks of people are caused to move in time, it becomes possible to use a relatively small number of supervisory personnel where the central relationship is not guidance or periodic checking, as in many employer-employee relations, but rather surveillance—a seeing to it that everyone does what he has been clearly told is required of him, and this under conditions where one person's infraction is likely to stand out in relief against the visible, constantly examined, compliance of the others. Which comes first, the large block of managed people or the small supervisory staff, is not here at issue; the point is that each is made for the other.

In total institutions, as we would then suspect, there is a basic split between a large class of individuals who live in and who have restricted contact with the world outside the walls, conveniently called *inmates,* and the small class that supervises them, conveniently called *staff,* who often operate on an eight-hour day and are socially integrated into the outside world. Each grouping tends to conceive of members of the other in terms of narrow hostile stereotypes, staff often seeing inmates as bitter, secretive, and untrustworthy, while inmates often see staff as condescending, highhanded, and mean. Staff tends to feel superior and righteous; inmates tend, in some ways at least, to feel inferior, weak, blameworthy, and guilty. Social mobility between the two strata is grossly restricted; social distance is typically great and often formally prescribed; even talk across the boundaries may be conducted in a special tone of voice. These restrictions on contact presumably help to maintain the antagonistic stereotypes. In any case, two different social and cultural worlds develop, tending to

Erving Goffman

jog along beside each other, with points of official contact but little mutual penetration. It is important to add that the institutional plant and name comes to be identified by both staff and inmates as somehow belonging to staff, so that when either grouping refers to the views or interests of "the institution," by implication they are referring (as I shall also) to the views and concerns of the staff.

The staff-inmate split is one major implication of the central features of total institutions; a second one pertains to work. In the ordinary arrangements of living in our society, the authority of the workplace stops with the worker's receipt of a money payment; the spending of this in a domestic and recreational setting is at the discretion of the worker and is the mechanism through which the authority of the workplace is kept within strict bounds. However, to say that inmates in total institutions have their full day scheduled for them is to say that some version of all basic needs will have to be planned for, too. In other words, total institutions take over "responsibility" for the inmate and must guarantee to have everything that is defined as essential "layed on." It follows, then, that whatever incentive is given for work, this will not have the structural significance it has on the outside. Different attitudes and incentives regarding this central feature of our life will have to prevail.

Here, then, is one basic adjustment required of those who work in total institutions and of those who must induce these people to work. In some cases, no work or little is required, and inmates, untrained often in leisurely ways of life, suffer extremes of boredom. In other cases, some work is required but is carried on at an extremely slow pace, being geared into a system of minor, often ceremonial payments, as in the case of weekly tobacco ration and annual Christmas presents, which cause some mental patients to stay on their job. In some total institutions, such as logging camps and merchant ships, something of the usual relation to the world that money can buy is obtained through the practice of "forced saving"; all needs are organized by the institution, and payment is given only after a work session is over and the men leave the premises. And in some total institutions, of course, more than a full day's work is required and is induced not by reward, but by threat of dire punishment. In all such cases, the work-oriented individual may tend to become somewhat demoralized by the system.

In addition to the fact that total institutions are incompatible with the basic work-payment structure of our society, it must be seen that these establishments are also incompatible with another crucial element of our society, the family. The family is sometimes contrasted to solitary living, but in fact the more pertinent contrast to family life might be with batch living. For it seems that those who eat and sleep at work, with a group of fellow workers, can hardly sustain a meaningful domestic existence. Correspondingly, the extent to which a staff retains its integration in the outside community and escapes the encompassing tendencies of total institutions is often linked up with the maintenance of a family off the grounds.

Whether a particular total institution acts as a good or bad force in civil society, force it may well have, and this will depend on the suppression of a whole circle of actual or potential households. Conversely, the formation of households provides a structural guarantee that total institutions will not arise. The incompatibility between these two forms of social organization should tell us, then, something about the wider social functions of them both.

Total institutions, then, are social hybrids, part residential community, part formal organization, and therein lies their special sociological interest. There are other reasons, alas, for being interested in them, too. These establishments are the forcing houses for changing persons in our society. Each is a natural experiment, typically harsh, on what can be done to the self.

The Inmate World

It is characteristic of inmates that they come to the institution as members, already full-fledged, of a home world, that is, a way of life and a round of activities taken for granted up to the point of admission to the institution. It is useful to look at this culture that the recruit brings with him to the institution's door—his presenting culture, to modify a psychiatric phrase—in terms especially designed to highlight what it is the total institution will do to

Erving Goffman

him. Whatever the stability of his personal organization, we can assume it was part of a wider supporting framework lodged in his current social environment, a round of experience that somewhat confirms a conception of self that is somewhat acceptable to him and a set of defensive maneuvers exercisable at his own discretion as a means of coping with conflicts, discreditings and failures.

Now it appears that total institutions do not substitute their own unique culture for something already formed. We do not deal with acculturation or assimilation but with something more restricted than these. In a sense, total institutions do not look for cultural victory. They effectively create and sustain a particular kind of tension between the home world and the institutional world and use this persistent tension as strategic leverage in the management of men. The full meaning for the inmate of being "in" or "on the inside" does not exist apart from the special meaning to him of "getting out" or "getting on the outside."

The recruit comes into the institution with a self and with attachments to supports which had allowed this self to survive. Upon entrance, he is immediately stripped of his wonted supports, and his self is systematically, if often unintentionally, mortified. In the accurate language of some of our oldest total institutions, he is led into a series of abasements, degradations, humiliations, and profanations of self. He begins, in other words, some radical shifts in his moral career, a career laying out the progressive changes that occur in the beliefs that he has concerning himself and significant others.

The stripping processes through which mortification of the self occurs are fairly standard in our total institutions. Personal identity equipment is removed, as well as other possessions with which the inmate may have identified himself, there typically being a system of nonaccessible storage from which the inmate can only reobtain his effects should he leave the institution. As a substitute for what has been taken away, institutional issue is provided, but this will be the same for large categories of inmates and will be regularly repossessed by the institution. In brief, standardized defacement will occur. In addition, ego-invested separateness from fellow inmates is significantly diminished in many areas of activity, and tasks are prescribed that are infra dignitatem. Family, occupational, and educational career lines are chopped off, and a stigmatized status is submitted. Sources of fantasy materials which had meant momentary releases from stress in the home world are denied. Areas of autonomous decision are eliminated through the process of collective scheduling of daily activity. Many channels of communication with the outside are restricted or closed off completely. Verbal discreditings occur in many forms as a matter of course. Expressive signs of respect for the staff are coercively and continuously demanded. And the effect of each of these conditions is multiplied by having to witness the mortification of one's fellow inmates.

We must expect to find different official reasons given for these assaults upon the self. In mental hospitals there is the matter of protecting the patient from himself and from other patients. In jails there is the issue of "security" and frank punishment. In religious institutions we may find sociologically sophisticated theories about the soul's need for purification and penance through disciplining of the flesh. What all of these rationales share is the extent to which they are merely rationalizations, for the underlying force in many cases is unwittingly generated by efforts to manage the daily activity of a large number of persons in a small space with a small expenditure of resources.

In the background of the sociological stripping process, we find a characteristic authority system with three distinctive elements, each basic to total institutions.

First, to a degree, authority is of the echelon kind. Any member of the staff class has certain rights to discipline any member of the inmate class. This arrangement, it may be noted, is similar to the one which gives any adult in some small American towns certain rights to correct and demand small services from any child not in the immediate presence of his parents. In our society, the adult himself, however, is typically under the authority of a *single* immediate superior in connection with his work or under authority of one spouse in connection with domestic duties. The only echelon authority he must face—the police—typically are neither constantly nor relevantly present, except perhaps in the case of traffic-law enforcement.

Second, the authority of corrective sanctions is directed to a great multitude of items of conduct of the kind that are constantly occurring and constantly coming up for judgment; in brief, authority is directed to matters of dress, deportment, social intercourse, manners, and the like. In prisons these regulations regarding situational properties may even extend to a point where silence during mealtime is enforced, while in some convents explicit demands may be made concerning the custody of the eyes during prayer.

The third feature of authority in total institutions is that misbehaviors in one sphere of life are held against one's standing in other spheres. Thus, an individual who fails to participate with proper enthusiasm in sports may be brought to the attention of the person who determines where he will sleep and what kind of work task will be accorded to him.

When we combine these three aspects of authority in total institutions, we see that the inmate cannot easily escape from the press of judgmental officials and from the enveloping tissue of constraint. The system of authority undermines the basis for control that adults in our society expect to exert over their interpersonal environment and may produce the terror of feeling that one is being radically demoted in the age-grading system. On the outside, rules are sufficiently lax and the individual sufficiently agreeable to required self-discipline to insure that others will rarely have cause for pouncing on him. He need not constantly look over his shoulder to see if criticism and other sanctions are coming. On the inside, however, rulings are abundant, novel, and closely enforced so that, quite characteristically, inmates live with chronic anxiety about breaking the rules and chronic worry about the consequences of breaking them. The desire to "stay out of trouble" in a total institution is likely to require persistent conscious effort and may lead the inmate to abjure certain levels of sociability with his fellows in order to avoid the incidents that may occur in these circumstances.

It should be noted finally that the mortifications to be suffered by the inmate may be purposely brought home to him in an exaggerated way during the first few days after entrance, in a form of initiation that has been called the welcome. Both staff and fellow inmates may go out of their way to give the neophyte a clear notion of where he stands. As part of this rite de passage, he may find himself called by a term such as "fish," "swab," etc., through which older inmates tell him that he is not only merely an inmate but that even within this lowly group he has a low status.

While the process of mortification is in progress, the inmate begins to receive formal and informal instruction in what will here be called the privilege system. Insofar as the inmate's self has been unsettled a little by the stripping action of the institution, it is largely around this framework that pressures are exerted, making for a reorganization of self. Three basic elements of the system may be mentioned.

First, there are the house rules, a relatively explicit and formal set of prescriptions and proscriptions which lay out the main requirements of inmate conduct. These regulations spell out the austere round of life in which the inmate will operate. Thus, the admission procedures through which the recruit is initially stripped of his self-supporting context can be seen as the institution's way of getting him in the position to start living by the house rules.

Second, against the stark background, a small number of clearly defined rewards or privileges are held out in exchange for obedience to staff in action and spirit. It is important to see that these potential gratifications are not unique to the institution but rather are ones carved out of the flow of support that the inmate previously had quite taken for granted. On the outside, for example, the inmate was likely to be able to unthinkingly exercise autonomy by deciding how much sugar and milk he wanted in his coffee, if any, or when to light up a cigarette; on the inside, this right may become quite problematic and a matter of a great deal of conscious concern. Held up to the inmate as possibilities, these few recapturings seem to have a reintegrative effect, re-establishing relationships with the whole lost world and assuaging withdrawal symptoms from it and from one's lost self.

The inmate's run of attention, then, especially at first, comes to be fixated on these supplies and obsessed with them. In the most fanatic way, he can spend the day in devoted thoughts concerning the possibility of acquiring these gratifications or the approach of the hour at which they are scheduled to be granted. The building of a world around these minor privileges is perhaps the most important feature of inmate culture and yet is something

Erving Goffman

that cannot easily be appreciated by an outsider, even one who has lived through the experience himself. This situation sometimes leads to generous sharing and almost always to a willingness to beg for things such as cigarettes, candy, and newspapers. It will be understandable, then, that a constant feature of inmate discussion is the release binge fantasy, namely, recitals of what one will do during leave or upon release from the institution.

House rules and privileges provide the functional requirements of the third element in the privilege system: punishments. These are designated as the consequence of breaking the rules. One set of these punishments consists of the temporary or permanent withdrawal of privileges or abrogation of the right to try to earn them. In general, the punishments meted out in total institutions are of an order more severe than anything encountered by the inmate in his home world. An institutional arrangement which causes a small number of easily controlled privileges to have a massive significance is the same arrangement which lends a terrible significance to their withdrawal.

There are some special features of the privilege system which should be noted.

First, punishments and privileges are themselves modes of organization peculiar to total institutions. Whatever their severity, punishments are largely known in the inmate's home world as something applied to animals and children. For adults this conditioning, behavioristic model is actually not widely applied, since failure to maintain required standards typically leads to indirect disadvantageous consequences and not to specific immediate punishment at all. And privileges, it should be emphasized, are not the same as perquisites, indulgences, or values, but merely the absence of deprivations one ordinarily expects one would not have to sustain. The very notions, then, of punishments and privileges are not ones that are cut from civilian cloth.

Second, it is important to see that the question of release from the total institution is elaborated into the privilege system. Some acts will become known as ones that mean an increase or no decrease in length of stay, while others become known as means for lessening the sentence.

Third, we should also note that punishments and privileges come to be geared into a residential work system. Places to work and places to sleep become clearly defined as places where certain kinds and levels of privilege obtain, and inmates are shifted very rapidly and visibly from one place to another as the mechanisms for giving them the punishment or privilege their co-operativeness has warranted. The inmates are moved, the system is not.

This, then, is the privilege system: a relatively few components put together with some rational intent and clearly proclaimed to the participants. The over-all consequence is that co-operativeness is obtained from persons who often have cause to be unco-operative.

. . .

Immediately associated with the privilege system we find some standard social processes important in the life of total institutions.

We find that an institutional lingo develops through which inmates express the events that are crucial in their particular world. Staff too, especially its lower levels, will know this language, using it when talking to inmates, while reverting to more standardized speech when talking to superiors and outsiders. Related to this special argot, inmates will possess knowledge of the various ranks and officials, an accumulation of lore about the establishment, and some comparative information about life in other similar total institutions.

Also found among staff and inmates will be a clear awareness of the phenomenon of messing up, so called in mental hospitals, prisons, and barracks. This involves a complex process of engaging in forbidden activity, getting caught doing so, and receiving something like the full punishment accorded this. An alteration in privilege status is usually implied and is categorized by a phrase such as "getting busted." Typical infractions which can eventuate in messing up are: fights, drunkenness, attempted suicide, failure at examinations, gambling, insubordination, homosexuality, improper taking of leave, and participation in collective riots. While these punished infractions are typically ascribed to the offender's cussedness, villainy, or "sickness," they do in fact constitute a vocabulary of institutionalized actions, limited in such a way that the same messing up may occur for quite different reasons. Informally, inmates and staff may understand,

Erving Goffman

for example, that a given messing up is a way for inmates to show resentment against a current situation felt to be unjust in terms of the informal agreements between staff and inmates, or a way of postponing release without having to admit to one's fellow inmates that one really does not want to go.

In total institutions there will also be a system of what might be called secondary adjustments, namely, techniques which do not directly challenge staff management but which allow inmates to obtain disallowed satisfactions or allowed ones by disallowed means. These practices are variously referred to as: the angles, knowing the ropes, conniving, gimmicks, deals, ins, etc. Such adaptations apparently reach their finest flower in prisons, but of course other total institutions are overrun with them too. It seems apparent that an important aspect of secondary adjustments is that they provide the inmate with some evidence that he is still, as it were, his own man and still has some protective distance, under his own control, between himself and the institution. In some cases, then, a secondary adjustment becomes almost a kind of lodgment for the self, a churinga in which the soul is felt to reside.

The occurrence of secondary adjustments correctly allows us to assume that the inmate group will have some kind of a *code* and some means of informal social control evolved to prevent one inmate from informing staff about the secondary adjustments of another. On the same grounds we can expect that one dimension of social typing among inmates will turn upon this question of security, leading to persons defined as "squealers," "finks," or "stoolies" on one hand, and persons defined as "right guys" on the other. It should be added that where new inmates can play a role in the system of secondary adjustments, as in providing new faction members or new sexual objects, then their "welcome" may indeed be a sequence of initial indulgences and enticements, instead of exaggerated deprivations. Because of secondary adjustments we also find kitchen strata, namely, a kind of rudimentary, largely informal, stratification of inmates on the basis of each one's differential access to disposable illicit commodities; so also we find social typing to designate the powerful persons in the informal market system.

While the privilege system provides the chief framework within which reassembly of the self takes place, other factors characteristically lead by different routes in the same general direction. Relief from economic and social responsibilities—much touted as part of the therapy in mental hospitals—is one, although in many cases it would seem that the disorganizing effect of this moratorium is more significant than its organizing effect. More important as a reorganizing influence is the *fraternalization process*, namely, the process through which socially distant persons find themselves developing mutual support and common *counter-mores* in opposition to a system that has forced them into intimacy and into a single, equalitarian community of fate. It seems that the new recruit frequently starts out with something like the staff's popular misconceptions of the character of the inmates and then comes to find that most of his fellows have all the properties of ordinary decent human beings and that the stereotypes associated with their condition or offense are not a reasonable ground for judgment of inmates.

If the inmates are persons who are accused by staff and society of having committed some kind of a crime against society, then the new inmate, even though sometimes in fact quite guiltless, may come to share the guilty feelings of his fellows and, thereafter, their well-elaborated defenses against these feelings. A sense of common injustice and a sense of bitterness against the outside world tends to develop, marking an important movement in the inmate's moral career. This response to felt guilt and massive deprivation is most clearly illustrated perhaps in prison life:

> "By their reasoning, after an offender has been subjected to unfair or excessive punishment and treatment more degrading than that prescribed by law, he comes to justify his act which he could not have justified when he committed it. He decides to "get even" for his unjust treatment in prison and takes reprisals through further crime at the first opportunity. *With that decision he becomes a criminal.*"[1]

A more general statement may be taken from two other students of the same kind of total institution:

> "In many ways, the inmate social system may be viewed as providing a way of life which enables the inmates to avoid the devastating psychological effects of internalizing and con-

Erving Goffman

verting social rejection into self rejection. In effect, it permits the inmate to reject his rejectors rather than himself." [2]

The mortifying processes that have been discussed and the privilege system represent the conditions that the inmate must adapt to in some way, but however pressing, these conditions allow for different ways of meeting them. We find, in fact, that the same inmate will employ different lines of adaptation or tacks at different phases in his moral career and may even fluctuate between different tacks at the same time.

First, there is the process of situational withdrawal. The inmate withdraws apparent attention from everything except events immediately around his body and sees these in a perspective not employed by others present. This drastic curtailment of involvement in interactional events is best known, of course, in mental hospitals, under the title of "regression." Aspects of "prison psychosis" or "stir simpleness" represent the same adjustment, as do some forms of "acute depersonalization" described in concentration camps. I do not think it is known whether this line of adaptation forms a single continuum of varying degrees of withdrawal or whether there are standard discontinuous plateaus of disinvolvement. It does seem to be the case, however, that, given the pressures apparently required to dislodge an inmate from this status, as well as the currently limited facilities for doing so, we frequently find here, effectively speaking, an irreversible line of adaptation.

Second, there is the rebellious line. The inmate intentionally challenges the institution by flagrantly refusing to co-operate with staff in almost any way. The result is a constantly communicated intransigency and sometimes high rebel-morale. Most large mental hospitals, for example, seem to have wards where this spirit strongly prevails. Interestingly enough, there are many circumstances in which sustained rejection of a total institution requires sustained orientation to its formal organization and hence, paradoxically, a deep kind of commitment to the establishment. Similarly, when total institutions take the line (as they sometimes do in the case of mental hospitals prescribing lobotomy or army barracks prescribing the stockade) that the recalcitrant inmate must be broken, then, in their way, they must show as much special devotion to the rebel as he has shown to them. It should be added, finally, that while prisoners of war have been known staunchly to take a rebellious stance throughout their incarceration, this stance is typically a temporary and initial phase of reaction, emerging from this to situational withdrawal or some other line of adaptation.

Third, another standard alignment in the institutional world takes the form of a kind of colonization. The sampling of the outside world provided by the establishment is taken by the inmate as the whole, and a stable, relatively contented existence is built up out of the maximum satisfactions procurable within the institution. Experience of the outside world is used as a point of reference to demonstrate the desirability of life on the inside; and the usual tension between the two worlds collapses, thwarting the social arrangements based upon this felt discrepancy. Characteristically, the individual who too obviously takes this line may be accused by his fellow inmates of "having found a home" or of "never having had it so good." Staff itself may become vaguely embarrassed by this use that is being made of the institution, sensing that the benign possibilities in the situation are somehow being misused. Colonizers themselves may feel obliged to deny their satisfaction with the institution, if only in the interest of sustaining the counter-mores supporting inmate solidarity. They may find it necessary to mess up just prior to their slated discharge, thereby allowing themselves to present involuntary reasons for continued incarceration. It should be incidentally noted that any humanistic effort to make life in total institutions more bearable must face the possibility that doing so may increase the attractiveness and likelihood of colonization.

Fourth, one mode of adaptation to the setting of a total institution is that of *conversion*. The inmate appears to take over completely the official or staff view of himself and tries to act out the role of the perfect inmate. While the colonized inmate builds as much of a free community as possible for himself by using the limited facilities available, the convert takes a more disciplined, moralistic, monochromatic line, presenting himself as someone whose institutional enthusiasm is always at the disposal of the staff. In Chinese POW camps, we find Americans who became "pros" and fully espoused the Communist view of the world. In army

Erving Goffman

barracks there are enlisted men who give the impression that they are always "sucking around" and always "bucking for promotion." In prison there are "square johns." In German concentration camps, longtime prisoners sometimes came to adapt the vocabulary, recreation, posture, expressions of aggression, and clothing style of the Gestapo, executing their role of straw-boss with military strictness. Some mental hospitals have the distinction of providing two quite different conversion possibilities—one for the new admission who can see the light after an appropriate struggle and adapt the psychiatric view of himself, and another for the chronic ward patient who adopts the manner and dress of attendants while helping them to manage the other ward patients with a stringency excelling that of the attendants themselves.

Here, it should be noted, is a significant way in which total institutions differ. Many, like progressive mental hospitals, merchant ships, TB sanitariums and brainwashing camps, offer the inmate an opportunity to live up to a model of conduct that is at once ideal and staff-sponsored—a model felt by its advocates to be in the supreme interests of the very persons to whom it is applied. Other total institutions, like some concentration camps and some prisons, do not officially sponsor an ideal that the inmate is expected to incorporate as a means of judging himself.

While the alignments that have been mentioned represent coherent courses to pursue, few inmates, it seems, carry these pursuits very far. In most total institutions, what we seem to find is that most inmates take the tack of what they call playing it cool. This involves a somewhat opportunistic combination of secondary adjustments, conversion, colonization, and loyalty to the inmate group, so that in the particular circumstances the inmate will have a maximum chance of eventually getting out physically and psychically undamaged. Typically, the inmate will support the counter-mores when with fellow inmates and be silent to them on how tractably he acts when alone in the presence of staff. Inmates taking this line tend to subordinate contacts with their fellows to the higher claim of "keeping out of trouble." They tend to volunteer for nothing, and they may even learn to cut their ties to the outside world sufficiently to give cultural reality to the world inside but not enough to lead to colonization.

I have suggested some of the lines of adaptation that inmates can take to the pressures that play in total institutions. Each represents a way of managing the tension between the home world and the institutional world. However, there are circumstances in which the home world of the inmate was such, in fact, as to immunize him against the bleak world on the inside, and for such persons no particular scheme of adaptation need be carried very far. Thus, some lower-class mental hospital patients who have lived all their previous life in orphanages, reformatories and jails, tend to see the hospital as just another total institution to which it is possible to apply the adaptive techniques learned and perfected in other total institutions. "Playing it cool" represents for such persons, not a shift in their moral career, but an alignment that is already second nature.

. . .

A note should be added here concerning some of the more dominant themes of inmate culture.

First, in the inmate group of many total institutions there is a strong feeling that time spent in the establishment is time wasted or destroyed or taken from one's life; it is time that must be written off. It is something that must be "done" or "marked" or "put in" or "built" or "pulled." (Thus, in prisons and mental hospitals a general statement of how well one is adapting to the institution may be phrased in terms of how one is doing time, whether easily or hard.) As such, this time is something that its doers have bracketed off for constant conscious consideration in a way not quite found on the outside. And as a result, the inmate tends to feel that for the duration of his required stay—his sentence—he has been totally exiled from living. It is in this context that we can appreciate something of the demoralizing influence of an indefinite sentence or a very long one. We should also note that however hard the conditions of life may become in total institutions, harshness alone cannot account for this quality of life wasted. Rather we must look to the social disconnections caused by entrance and to the usual failure to acquire within the institution gains that can be transferred to outside life—gains such as money earned, or marital relations formed, or certified training received.

Erving Goffman

Second, it seems that in many total institutions a peculiar kind and level of self-concern is engendered. The low position of inmates relative to their station on the outside, as established initially through the mortifying processes, seems to make for a milieu of personal failure and a round of life in which one's fall from grace is continuously pressed home. In response, the inmate tends to develop a story, a line, a sad tale—a kind of lamentation and apologia—which he constantly tells to his fellows as a means of creditably accounting for his present low estate. While staff constantly discredit these lines, inmate audiences tend to employ tact, suppressing at least some of the disbelief and boredom engendered by these recitations. In consequence, the inmate's own self may become even more of a focus for his conversation than it does on the outside.

Perhaps the high level of ruminative self-concern found among inmates in total institutions is a way of handling the sense of wasted time that prevails in these places. If so, then perhaps another interesting aspect of inmate culture can be related to the same factor. I refer here to the fact that in total institutions we characteristically find a premium placed on what might be called removal activities, namely, voluntary unserious pursuits which are sufficiently engrossing and exciting to lift the participant out of himself, making him oblivious for the time to his actual situation. If the ordinary activities in total institutions can be said to torture time, these activities mercifully kill it.

Some removal activities are collective, such as ball games, woodwork, lectures, choral singing, and card playing; some are individual but rely on public materials, as in the case of reading, solitary TV watching, etc. No doubt, private fantasy ought to be included too. Some of these activities may be officially sponsored by staff; and some, not officially sponsored, may constitute secondary adjustments. In any case, there seems to be no total institution which cannot be seen as a kind of Dead Sea in which appear little islands of vivid, enrapturing activity.

. . .

Total institutions frequently claim to be concerned with rehabilitation, that is, with resetting the inmate's self-regulatory mechanisms so that he will maintain the standards of the establishment of his own accord after he leaves the setting. In fact, it seems this claim is seldom realized and even when permanent alteration occurs, these changes are often not of the kind intended by the staff. With the possible exception presented by the great resocialization efficiency of religious institutions, neither the stripping processes nor the reorganizing ones seem to have a lasting effect. No doubt the availability of secondary adjustments helps to account for this, as do the presence of counter-mores and the tendency for inmates to combine all strategies and "play it cool." In any case, it seems that shortly after release, the ex-inmate will have forgotten a great deal of what life was like on the inside and will have once again begun to take for granted the privileges around which life in the institution was organized. The sense of injustice, bitterness, and alienation, so typically engendered by the inmate's experience and so definitely marking a stage in his moral career, seems to weaken upon graduation, even in those cases where a permanent stigma has resulted.

But what the ex-inmate does retain of his institutional experience tells us important things about total institutions. Often entrance will mean for the recruit that he has taken on what might be called a *proactive status*. Not only is his relative social position within the walls radically different from what it was on the outside, but, as he comes to learn, if and when he gets out, his social position on the outside will never again be quite what it was prior to entrance. Where the proactive status is a relatively favorable one, as it is for those who graduate from officers' training schools, elite boarding schools, ranking monastaries, etc., then the permanent alteration will be favorable, and jubilant official reunions announcing pride in one's "school" can be expected. When, as seems usually the case, the proactive status is unfavorable, as it is for those in prisons or mental hospitals, we popularly employ the term "stigmatization" and expect that the ex-inmate may make an effort to conceal his past and try to "pass."

The Staff World

Most total institutions, most of the time, seem to function merely as storage dumps for inmates, but as previously suggested,

Erving Goffman

they usually present themselves to the public as rational organizations designed consciously, through and through, as effective machines for producing a few officially avowed and officially approved ends. It was also suggested that one frequent official objective is the reformation of inmates in the direction of some ideal standard. This contradiction, then, between what the instituation does and what its officials must say that it does, forms the central context of the staff's daily activity.

Within this context, perhaps the first thing to say about staff is that their work, and hence their world, has uniquely to do with people. This people-work is not quite like personnel work nor the work of those involved in service relationships. Staffs, after all, have objects and products to work upon, not relationships, but these objects and products are people.

. . .

Given the physiological characteristics of the human organism, it is obvious that certain requirements must be met if any continued use is to be made of people. But this, of course, is the case with inanimate objects, too; the temperature of any storehouse must be regulated, regardless of whether people or things are stored. However, persons are almost always considered to be ends in themselves, as reflected in the broad moral principles of a total institution's environing society. Almost always, then, we find that some technically unnecessary standards of handling must be maintained with human materials. This maintenance of what we can call humane standards comes to be defined as one part of the "responsibility" of the institution and presumably is one of the things the institution guarantees the inmate in exchange for his liberty. Thus, prison officials are obliged to thwart suicidal efforts of the prisoner and to give him full medical attention even though in some cases this may require postponement of his date of execution. Something similar has been reported in German concentration camps, where inmates were sometimes given medical attention to tidy them up into a healthier shape for the gas chamber.

A second special contingency in the work-world of staff is the fact that inmates typically have statuses and relationships in the outside world that must be taken into consideration. (This consideration, of course, is related to the previously mentioned fact that the institution must respect some of the rights of inmates qua persons.) Even in the case of the committed mental patient whose civil rights are largely taken from him, a tremendous amount of mere paper work will be involved. Of course, the rights that are denied a mental patient are usually transferred to a relation, to a committee, or to the superintendent of the hospital itself, who then becomes the legal person whose authorization must be obtained for many matters. Many issues originating outside the institution will arise: Social Security benefits, income taxes, upkeep of properties, insurance payments, old age pension, stock dividends, dental bills, legal obligations incurred prior to commitment, permission to release psychiatric case records to insurance companies or attorneys, permission for special visits from persons other than next of kin, etc. All of these issues have to be dealt with by the institution, even if only to pass the decisions on to those legally empowered to make them.

It should be noted that staff is reminded of its obligations in these matters of standards and rights, not only by its own internal superordinates, by various watchdog agencies in the wider society, and by the material itself, but also by persons on the outside who have kin ties to inmates. The latter group presents a special problem because, while inmates can be educated about the price they will pay for making demands on their own behalf, relations receive less tutoring in this regard and rush in with requests for inmates that inmates would blush to make for themselves.

The multiplicity of ways in which inmates must be considered ends in themselves and the multiplicity of inmates themselves forces upon staff some of the classic dilemmas that must be faced by those who govern men. Since a total institution functions somewhat as a State, its staff must suffer somewhat from the tribulations that beset governors.

In the case of any single inmate, the assurance that certain standards will be maintained in his own interests may require sacrifice of other standards, and implied in this is a difficult weighing of ends. For example, if a suicidal inmate is to be kept alive, staff may feel it necessary to keep him under constant deprivatizing surveillance or even tied to a chair in a small locked room.

Erving Goffman

If a mental patient is to be kept from tearing at grossly irritated sores and repeating time and again a cycle of curing and disorder, staff may feel it necessary to curtail the freedom of his hands. Another patient who refuses to eat may have to be humiliated by forced feeding. If inmates of TB sanitariums are to be given an opportunity to recover, it will be necessary to curtail freedom of recreation.

The standards of treatment that one inmate has a right to expect may conflict, of course, with the standards desired by another, giving rise to another set of governmental problems. Thus, in mental hospitals, if the grounds gate is to be kept open out of respect for those with town parole, then some other patients who otherwise could have been trusted on the grounds may have to be kept on locked wards. And if a canteen and mailbox are to be freely available to those on the grounds, then patients on a strict diet or those who write threatening and obscene letters will have to be denied liberty on the grounds.

The obligation of staff to maintain certain humane standards of treatment for inmates represents problems in itself, as suggested above, but a further set of characteristic problems is found in the constant conflict between humane standards on one hand and institutional efficiency on the other. I will cite only one main example. The personal possessions of an individual are an important part of the materials out of which he builds a self, but as an inmate, the ease with which he can be managed by staff is likely to increase with the degree to which he is dispossessed. Thus, the remarkable efficiency with which a mental hospital ward can adjust to a daily shift in number of resident patients is related to the fact that the comers and leavers do not come or leave with any properties but themselves and do not have any right to choose where they will be located. Further, the efficiency with which the clothes of these patients can be kept clean and fresh is related to the fact that everyone's soiled clothing can be indiscriminately placed in one bundle, and laundered clothing can be redistributed not according to ownership but according to rough size. Similarly, the quickest assurance that patients going on the grounds will be warmly dressed is to march them in file past a pile of the ward's allotment of coats, requiring them for the same purposes of health to throw off these collectivized garments on returning to the ward.

Just as personal possessions may interfere with the smooth running of an institutional operation and be removed for this reason, so parts of the body itself may conflict with efficient management and the conflict resolved in favor of efficiency. If the heads of inmates are to be kept clean and the possessor easily identified, then a complete head shave is efficacious, regardless of the damage this does to appearance. On similar grounds, some mental hospitals have found it useful to extract the teeth of "biters," give hysterectomies to promiscuous female patients, and perform lobotomies on chronic fighters.

. . .

I have suggested that people-work differs from other kinds because of the tangle of statuses and relationships which each inmate brings with him to the institution and because of the humane standards that must be maintained with respect to him. Another difference occurs in cases where inmates have some rights to visit off the grounds, for then the mischief they may do in civil society becomes something for which the institution has some responsibility. Given this responsibility, it is understandable that total institutions tend not to view off-grounds leave favorably. Still another type of difference between people-work and other kinds, and perhaps the most important difference of all, is that by the exercise of threat, reward or persuasion human objects can be given instructions and relied upon to carry them out on their own. The span of time during which these objects can be trusted to carry out planned actions without supervision will vary of course a great deal, but, as the social organization of back wards in mental hospitals teaches us, even in the limiting case of catatonic schizophrenics, a considerable amount of such reliance is possible. Only the most complicated electronic equipment shares this capacity.

While human materials can never be as refractory as inanimate ones, their very capacity to perceive and to follow out the plans of staff insures that they can hinder the staff more effectively than inanimate objects can. Inanimate objects cannot purposely and intelligently thwart our plans, regardless of the fact that we may momentarily react to them as if they had this capacity. Hence, in prison and on "better" wards of mental hospitals, guards have to be ready for organized efforts at escape and must constantly deal with attempts to bait them, "frame" them, and otherwise get them into trouble. This leads to a state of anxiety in the guard that is not alleviated by knowledge that the inmate may be acting thusly merely as a means of gaining self-respect or relieving boredom. Even an old, weak, mental patient has tremendous power in this regard; for example, by the simple expedient of locking his thumbs in his trouser pockets he can remarkably frustrate the efforts of an attendant to undress him.

A third general way in which human materials are different from other kinds and hence present unique problems is that, however distant staff manages to stay from them, they can become objects of fellow-feeling and even affection. Always there is the danger that an inmate will appear human. If what are felt to be hardships must be inflicted on the inmate, then sympathetic staff will suffer. And on the other hand, if an inmate breaks a rule, staff's conceiving of him as a human being may increase their sense that injury has been done to their moral world. Expecting a "reasonable" response from a reasonable creature, staff may feel incensed, affronted, and challenged when this does not occur. Staff thus finds it must maintain face not only before those who examine the product of work but before these very products themselves.

The capacity of inmates to become objects of staff's sympathetic concern is linked to what might be called an involvement cycle sometimes recorded in total institutions. Starting at a point of social distance from inmates, a point from which massive deprivation and institutional trouble cannot easily be seen, the staff person finds he has no reason not to builld up a warm involvement in some inmates. The involvement, however, brings the staff members into a position to be hurt by what inmates do and by what they suffer, and also brings him to a position from which he is likely to threaten the distant stand from inmates taken by his fellow members of the staff. In response, the sympathizing staff member may feel he has been "burnt" and retreat into paper-work, committee work or other staff-enclosed routine. Once removed from the dangers of inmate contact, he may gradually cease to feel he has reason to remain so, and thus the cycle of contact and withdrawal may be repeated again and again.

When we combine together the fact that staff is obliged to maintain certain standards of humane treatment for inmates and may come to view inmates as reasonable, responsible creatures who are fitting objects for emotional involvement, we have the background for some of the quite special difficulties of people-work. In mental hospitals, for example, there always seem to be some patients who dramatically act against their own obvious self-interest. They drink water they have themselves first pol-luted; they rush against the wall with their heads; they tear out their own sutures after a minor operation; they flush false teeth down the toilet, without which they cannot eat and which take months to obtain; or smash glasses, without which they cannot see. In an effort to frustrate these visibly self-destructive acts, staff may find itself forced to manhandle these patients. Staff then is forced to create an image of itself as harsh and coercive, just at the moment that it is attempting to prevent someone from doing to himself what no human being is expected to do to any-one. At such times it is extremely difficult for staff members to keep their own emotions in control, and understandably so.

The special requirements of people-work establish the day's job for staff, but this job must be carried out in a special moral climate. For the staff is charged with meeting the hostility and demands of the inmates, and what it has to meet the inmate with, in general, is the rational perspective espoused by the institution. It is the role of the staff to defend the institution in the name of its avowed rational aims—to the inmate as well as to outsiders of various kinds. Thus, when inmates are allowed to have incidental face-to-face contact with staff, the contact will often take the form of "gripes" or requests on the part of the inmate and of justification for prevailing restrictive treatment on the part of the staff. Such, for example, is the general structure of staff-patient interaction in mental hospitals. Further, the privileges and punishments meted out by staff will often be couched in a language that reflects the legitimated objectives of the institution, even though this may require that inmates or low-level members of staff translate these responses into the verbal language˘ of the privilege system.

Given the inmates over whom it has charge and the processing that must be done to these objects, staff tends to evolve what may be thought of as a theory of human nature. This verbalized perspective rationalizes the scene, provides a subtle means of maintaining social distance from inmates and a stereotyped view of them, and gives sanction to the treatment accorded them. Typically, the theory covers the "good" and "bad" possibilities of inmate conduct, the forms that messing up take, and the instructional value of privileges and punishments. In army barracks, officers will have a theory about the relation between discipline and obedience under fire, about the qualities proper to men, about the "breaking point" of men, and about the difference between mental sickness and malingering. In prisons, we find currently an interesting conflict between the psychiatric and the moral-weakness theory of crime. In convents, we find theories about the way in which the spirit can be weak and strong, and the ways its defects can be combatted. Mental hospitals, it should be noted, are especially interesting in this connection because staff members pointedly establish themselves as specialists in the knowledge of human nature who must diagnose and prescribe on the basis of this philosophy. Hence, in the standard psychiatric textbooks there are chapters on "psychodynamics" and "psychopathology" which provide charmingly explicit formulations of the "nature" of human nature.

Given the fact that the management of inmates is typically rationalized in terms of the ideal aims or functions of the establishment and that certain humane standards will form part of this ideal, we can expect that professionals ostensibly hired to service these functions will likely become dissatisfied, feeling that they are being used as "captives" to add professional sanction to the privilege system and that they cannot here properly practice their calling. And this seems to be a classic cry. At the same time, the category of staff that must keep the institution going through continuous contact with inmates may feel that they too are being set a contradictory task, having to coerce inmates into obedience while at the same time giving the impression that humane standards are being maintained and that the rational goals of the institution are being realized.

Institutional Ceremonies

I have described total institutions from the point of view of inmates and from the point of view of the staff. Each of these two perspectives contains as one crucial element a role-image of the other grouping; but while this role-image of the other is held, it is seldom sympathetically taken, except perhaps on the part of those inmates, previously described, who take a trusty role and seriously "identify with the aggressor." When unusual intimacies and relationships do occur across the staff-inmate line, we know that involvement cycles may follow, and all kinds of awkward reverberations are likely to occur. Every total institution, however, seems to develop—whether spontaneously or by imitation—a set of institutionalized practices through which staff and inmates come together closely enough so that each may have an image of the other that is somewhat favorable and also be able to take the role sympathetically that this image suggests. Instead of differences between the two levels, we will then find that unity, solidarity and joint commitment to the institution are expressed.

In form, these institutionalized get-togethers are characterized by a release from the formalities and task orientation that govern inmate-staff contacts and by a softening of the usual chain of command. Often participation is relatively voluntary. Given the usual roles then, these activities represent "role releases"; of course, given the pervasive effect of inmate-staff distance, any alteration in this breach in the direction of solidarity expressions would automatically represent a role-release. It is possible to speculate on the many functions of these comings-together, but the explanations so far suggested seem much less impressive than the singular way in which these practices keep cropping up in every kind of total institution and in what would seem to be the poor-est possible soil. One is led to feel that there must be a very good reason for these practices even though none has yet been found.

. . .

In all instances of unified ceremonial life that I have men-tioned, staff is likely to play more than a supervisory role. Often a high-ranking officer attends as a symbol of management and (it is hoped) of the whole establishment. He dresses well, is moved by the occasion, and gives smiles, speeches, and handshakes. He dedicates new buildings on the grounds, gives his blessing to new equipment, judges contests, and hands out awards. When acting in this capacity, his interaction with inmates will take a special benign form; inmates are likely to show embarrassment and re-spect, and he is likely to display an avuncular interest in them. In the case of our very large and benevolently oriented mental hospitals, executive officers may be required to spend a goodly portion of their time putting in an appearance at these ceremonial occasions, providing us with some of the last places in modern society in which to observe a lord-of-the-manor feudal role.

A final note should be added about these institutional cere-monies. They tend to occur with well-spaced periodicity and to give rise to some social excitement. All the groupings in the estab-lishment join in and have a place regardless of rank or position, but a place that expresses this position. These ceremonial prac-tices then ought to bear strong witness to the value of a Durk-heimian analysis. A society dangerously split into inmates and staff can through these ceremonies hold itself together. Staff and inmates are the two ends of the arch, and these ceremonies are needed for the keystone.

But, except for the claims sometimes made for the effective-ness of group therapy, in many cases it is a nice question whether these role releases hold up anything at all. Staff, to other members of the staff, typically complain of their boredom with these cere-monies and that they have to participate because of their own noblesse oblige or, worse still, because of that of their superiors. And inmates often participate because, wherever the ceremony is held, they will be more comfortable and less restricted there than where they otherwise would be. A total institution perhaps needs collective ceremonies because it is something more than a formal organization, but its ceremonies are often pious and flat, perhaps because it is something less than a community.

. . .

Conclusion

I have defined total institutions denotatively by listing them and then have tried to suggest some of their common characteristics. We now have a quite sizable literature on these establishments and should be in a position to supplant mere suggestions with a solid framework bearing on the anatomy and functioning of this kind of social animal. Certainly the similarities obtrude so glaringly and persistently that we have a right to suspect that these features have good functional reasons for being present and that it will be possible to tie them together and grasp them by means of a functional explanation. When we have done so, I feel we will then give less praise and blame to particular superintendents, commandants, wardens, and abbots, and tend more to understand the social problems and issues in total institutions by appealing to the underlying structural design common to all of them.

PART THREE

Purpose and Process

FRANCIS A. ALLEN

Criminal Justice, Legal Values and the Rehabilitative Ideal

Although one is sometimes inclined to despair of any constructive changes in the administration of criminal justice, a glance at the history of the past half-century reveals a succession of the most significant developments. Thus, the last fifty years have seen the widespread acceptance of three legal inventions of great importance: the juvenile court, systems of probation and of parole. During the same period, under the inspiration of continental research and writing, scientific criminology became an established field of instruction and inquiry in American universities and in other research agencies. At the same time, psychiatry made its remarkable contributions to the theory of human behavior and, more specifically, of that form of human behavior described as criminal. These developments have been accompanied by nothing less than a revolution in public conceptions of the nature of crime and the criminal, and in public attitudes toward the proper treatment of the convicted offender.

Reprinted by permission from *Journal of Criminal Law, Criminology and Police Science*, vol. 50, pp. 226–232 (1959).

Notes to this Selection will be found on pages 428–429.

Allen was Professor of Law at Harvard and Chicago Universities and is Dean of the Law School at the University of Michigan. He is the author of The Borderland of Criminal Justice *(1964).*

Francis A. Allen

This history with its complex developments of thought, institutional behavior, and public attitudes must be approached gingerly; for in dealing with it we are in peril of committing the sin of oversimplification. Nevertheless, despite the presence of contradictions and paradox, it seems possible to detect one common element in much of this thought and activity which goes far to characterize the history we are considering. This common element or theme I shall describe, for want of a better phrase, as the rise of the rehabilitative ideal.

The rehabilitative ideal is itself a complex of ideas which, perhaps, defies completely precise statement. The essential points, however, can be articulated. It is assumed, first, that human behavior is the product of antecedent causes. These causes can be identified as part of the physical universe, and it is the obligation of the scientist to discover and to describe them with all possible exactitude. Knowledge of the antecedents of human behavior makes possible an approach to the scientific control of human behavior. Finally, and of primary significance for the purposes at hand, it is assumed that measures employed to treat the convicted offender should serve a therapeutic function, that such measures should be designed to effect changes in the behavior of the convicted person in the interests of his own happiness, health, and satisfactions and in the interest of social defense.

Although these ideas are capable of rather simple statement, they have provided the arena for some of the modern world's most acrimonious controversy. And the disagreements among those who adhere in general to these propositions have been hardly less intense than those prompted by the dissenters. This is true, in part, because these ideas possess a delusive simplicity. No idea is more pervaded with ambiguity than the notion of reform or rehabilitation. Assuming, for example, that we have the techniques to accomplish our ends of rehabilitation, are we striving to produce in the convicted offender something called "adjustment" to his social environment or is our objective something different from or more than this? By what scale of values do we determine the ends of therapy?

These are intriguing questions, well worth extended consideration. But it is not my purpose to pursue them in this paper. Rather, I am concerned with describing some of the dilemmas and conflicts of values that have resulted from efforts to impose the rehabilitative ideal on the system of criminal justice. I know of no area in which a more effective demonstration can be made of the necessity for greater mutual understanding between the law and the behavioral disciplines.

There is, of course, nothing new in the notion of reform or rehabilitation of the offender as one objective of the penal process. This idea is given important emphasis, for example, in the thought of the medieval churchmen. The church's position, as described by Sir Francis Palgrave, was that punishment was not to be "thundered in vengeance for the satisfaction of the state, but imposed for the good of the offender: in order to afford the means of amendment and to lead the transgressor to repentance, and to mercy"[1] Even Jeremy Bentham, whose views modern criminology has often scorned and more often ignored, is found saying: "It is a great merit in a punishment to contribute to the reformation of the offender, not only through fear of being punished again, but by a change in his character and habits."[2] But this is far from saying that the modern expression of the rehabilitative ideal is not to be sharply distinguished from earlier expressions. The most important differences, I believe, are two. First, the modern statement of the rehabilitative ideal is accompanied by, and largely stems from, the development of scientific disciplines concerned with human behavior, a development not remotely approximated in earlier periods when notions of reform of the offender were advanced. Second, and of equal importance for the purposes at hand, in no other period has the rehabilitative ideal so completely dominated theoretical and scholarly inquiry, to such an extent that in some quarters it is almost assumed that matters of treatment and reform of the offender are the only questions worthy of serious attention in the whole field of criminal justice and corrections.

The Narrowing of Scientific Interests

This narrowing of interests prompted by the rise of the rehabilitative ideal during the past half-century should put us on our guard. No social institutions as complex as those involved in the administration of criminal justice serve a single function or pur-

Francis A. Allen

pose. Social institutions are multi-valued and multi-purposed. Values and purposes are likely on occasion to prove inconsistent and to produce internal conflict and tension. A theoretical orientation that evinces concern for only one or a limited number of purposes served by the institution must inevitably prove partial and unsatisfactory. In certain situations it may prove positively dangerous. This stress on the unfortunate consequences of the rise of the rehabilitative ideal need not involve failure to recognize the substantial benefits that have also accompanied its emergence. Its emphasis on the fundamental problems of human behavior, its numerous contributions to the decency of the criminal-law processes are of vital importance. But the limitations and dangers of modern trends of thought need clearly to be identified in the interest, among others, of the rehabilitative ideal itself.

My first proposition is that the rise of the rehabilitative ideal has dictated what questions are to be investigated, with the result that many matters of equal or even greater importance have been ignored or cursorily examined. This tendency can be abundantly illustrated. Thus, the concentration of interest on the nature and needs of the criminal has resulted in a remarkable absence of interest in the nature of crime. This is, indeed, surprising, for on reflection it must be apparent that the question of what is a crime is logically the prior issue: how crime is defined determines in large measure who the criminal is who becomes eligible for treatment and therapy. A related observation was made some years ago by Professor Karl Llewellyn, who has done as much as any man to develop sensible interdisciplinary inquiry involving law and the behavioral disciplines: "When I was younger I used to hear smuggish assertions among my sociological friends, such as: 'I take the sociological, *not* the legal, approach to crime'; and I suspect an inquiring reporter could still hear much the same (perhaps with 'psychiatric' often substituted for 'sociological')—though it is surely somewhat obvious that when you take 'the legal' out, you also take out 'crime.' "[3] This disinterest in the definition of criminal behavior has afflicted the lawyers quite as much as the behavioral scientists. Even the criminal law scholar has tended, until recently, to assume that problems of procedure and treatment are the things that "really matter." Only the issue of criminal responsibility as affected by mental disorder has attracted the consistent attention of the non-lawyer, and the literature reflecting this interest is not remarkable for its cogency or its wisdom. In general, the behavioral sciences have left other issues relevant to crime definition largely in default.

. . .

The absence of widespread interest in these areas is not to be explained by any lack of challenging questions. Thus, what may be said of the relationships between legislative efforts to subject certain sorts of human behavior to penal regulation and the persistence of police corruption and abuse of power? Studies of public attitudes toward other sorts of criminal legislation might provide valuable clues as to whether given regulatory objectives are more likely to be attained by the provision of criminal penalties or by other kinds of legal sanctions. It ought to be re-emphasized that the question, what sorts of behavior should be declared criminal, is one to which the behavioral sciences might contribute vital insights. This they have largely failed to do, and we are the poorer for it.

Another example of the narrowing of interests that has accompanied the rise of the rehabilitative ideal is the lack of concern with the idea of deterrence—indeed the hostility evinced by many modern criminologists toward it. This, again, is a most surprising development. It must surely be apparent that the criminal law has a general preventive function to perform in the interests of public order and of security of life, limb, and possessions. Indeed, there is reason to assert that the influence of criminal sanctions on the millions who never engage in serious criminality is of greater social importance than their impact on the hundreds of thousands who do. Certainly, the assumption of those who make our laws is that the denouncing of conduct as criminal and providing the means for the enforcement of the legislative prohibitions will generally have a tendency to prevent or minimize such behavior. Just what the precise mechanisms of deterrence are is not well understood. Perhaps it results, on occasion, from the naked threat of punishment. Perhaps, more frequently, it derives from a more subtle process wherein the mores and moral sense of the community are recruited to advance the attainment of the criminal

Francis A. Allen

law's objectives. The point is that we know very little about these vital matters, and the resources of the behavioral sciences have rarely been employed to contribute knowledge and insight in their investigation. Not only have the criminologists displayed little interest in these matters, some have suggested that the whole idea of general prevention is invalid or worse. Thus, speaking of the deterrent theory of punishment, the authors of a leading textbook in criminology assert: "This is simply a derived rationalization of revenge. Though social revenge is the actual psychological basis of punishment today, the apologists for the punitive regime are likely to bring forward in their defense the more sophisticated, but equally futile, contention that punishment deters from [*sic*] crime."[4] We are thus confronted by a situation in which the dominance of the rehabilitative ideal not only diverts attention from many serious issues, but leads to a denial that these issues even exist.

Debasement of the Rehabilitative Ideal

Now permit me to turn to another sort of difficulty that has accompanied the rise of the rehabilitative ideal in the areas of corrections and criminal justice. It is a familiar observation that an idea once propagated and introduced into the active affairs of life undergoes change. The real significance of an idea as it evolves in actual practice may be quite different from that intended by those who conceived it and gave it initial support. An idea tends to lead a life of its own; and modern history is full of the unintended consequences of seminal ideas. The application of the rehabilitative ideal to the institutions of criminal justice presents a striking example of such a development. My second proposition, then, is that the rehabilitative ideal has been debased in practice and that the consequences resulting from this debasement are serious and, at times, dangerous.

This proposition may be supported, first, by the observation that, under the dominance of the rehabilitative ideal, the language of therapy is frequently employed, wittingly or unwittingly, to disguise the true state of affairs that prevails in our custodial institutions and at other points in the correctional process. Certain measures, like the sexual psychopath laws, have been advanced and supported as therapeutic in nature when, in fact, such a characterization seems highly dubious. Too often the vocabulary of therapy has been exploited to serve a public-relations function. Recently, I visited an institution devoted to the diagnosis and treatment of disturbed children. The institution had been established with high hopes and, for once, with the enthusiastic support of the state legislature. Nevertheless, fifty minutes of an hour's lecture, delivered by a supervising psychiatrist before we toured the building, were devoted to custodial problems. This fixation on problems of custody was reflected in the institutional arrangements which included, under a properly euphemistic label, a cell for solitary confinement. Even more disturbing was the tendency of the staff to justify these custodial measures in therapeutic terms.† Perhaps on occasion the requirements of institutional security and treatment coincide. But all the inducements to self-deception in such situations are strong and all too apparent. In short, the language of therapy has frequently provided a formidable obstacle to a realistic analysis of the conditions that confront us. And realism in considering these problems is the only quality that we require above all others.

There is a second sort of unintended consequence that has resulted from the application of the rehabilitative ideal to the practical administration of criminal justice. Surprisingly enough, the rehabilitative ideal has often led to increased severity of penal measures. This tendency may be seen in the operation of the juvenile court. Although frequently condemned by the popular press as a device of leniency, the juvenile court is authorized to intervene punitively in many situations in which the conduct, were it committed by an adult, would be wholly ignored by the law or would subject the adult to the mildest of sanctions. The tendency of proposals for wholly indeterminate sentences, a clearly identifiable fruit of the rehabilitative ideal, is unmistakably in the direction of lengthened periods of imprisonment. A large variety of statutes authorizing what is called "civil" commitment of persons,

† As I recall, it was referred to as the "quiet room." In another institution the boy was required to stand before a wall while a seventy pound fire hose was played on his back. This procedure went under the name of "hydrotherapy."

Francis A. Allen

but which, except for the reduced protections afforded the parties proceeded against, are essentially criminal in nature, provide for absolutely indeterminate periods of confinement. Experience has demonstrated that, in practice, there is a strong tendency for the rehabilitative ideal to serve purposes that are essentially incapacitative rather than therapeutic in character.

The Rehabilitative Ideal and Individual Liberty

The reference to the tendency of the rehabilitative ideal to encourage increasingly long periods of incarceration brings me to my final proposition. It is that the rise of the rehabilitative ideal has often been accompanied by attitudes and measures that conflict, sometimes seriously, with the values of individual liberty and volition. As I have already observed, the role of the behavioral sciences in the administration of criminal justice and in the areas of public policy lying on the borderland of the criminal law is one of obvious importance. But I suggest that, if the function of criminal justice is considered in its proper dimensions, it will be discovered that the most fundamental problems in these areas are not those of psychiatry, sociology, social case work, or social psychology. On the contrary, the most fundamental problems are those of political philosophy and political science. The administration of the criminal law presents to any community the most extreme issues of the proper relations of the individual citizen to state power. We are concerned here with the perennial issue of political authority: Under what circumstances is the state justified in bringing its force to bear on the individual human being? These issues, of course, are not confined to the criminal law, but it is in the area of penal regulation that they are most dramatically manifested. The criminal law, then, is located somewhere near the center of the political problem, as the history of the twentieth century abundantly reveals. It is no accident, after all, that the agencies of criminal justice and law enforcement are those first seized by an emerging totalitarian regime. In short, a study of criminal justice is most fundamentally a study in the exercise of political power. No such study can properly avoid the problem of the abuse of power.

The obligation of containing power within the limits suggested by a community's political values has been considerably complicated by the rise of the rehabilitative ideal. For the problem today is one of regulating the exercise of power by men of good will, whose motivations are to help not to injure, and whose ambitions are quite different from those of the political adventurer so familiar to history. There is a tendency for such persons to claim immunity from the usual forms of restraint and to insist that professionalism and a devotion to science provide sufficient protections against unwarranted invasion of individual right.

.   .   .

There is one proposition which, if generally understood, would contribute more to clear thinking on these matters than any other. It is not a new insight. Seventy years ago the Italian criminologist, Garafalo, asserted: "The mere deprivation of liberty, however benign the administration of the place of confinement, is undeniably punishment."[5] This proposition may be rephrased as follows: Measures which subject individuals to the substantial and involuntary deprivation of their liberty are essentially punitive in character, and this reality is not altered by the facts that the motivations that prompt incarceration are to provide therapy or otherwise contribute to the person's well-being or reform. As such, these measures must be closely scrutinized to insure that power is being applied consistently with those values of the community that justify interferences with liberty for only the most clear and compelling reasons.

But the point I am making requires more specific and concrete application to be entirely meaningful. It should be pointed out, first, that the values of individual liberty may be imperilled by claims to knowledge and therapeutic technique that we, in fact, do not possess and by failure candidly to concede what we do not know. At times, practitioners of the behavioral sciences have been guilty of these faults. At other times, such errors have supplied the assumptions on which legislators, lawyers and lay people generally have proceeded. Ignorance, in itself, is not disgraceful so long as it is unavoidable. But when we rush to measures affecting human liberty and human dignity on the assumption that we know what we do not know or can do what we cannot do, then the problem of ignorance takes on a more sinister hue. An illustration of these dangers is provided by the sexual psychopath laws, to which I return; for they epitomize admirably some of the worst tendencies of modern practice. These statutes authorize the indefinite incarceration of persons believed to be potentially dangerous in their sexual behavior. But can such persons be accurately identified without substantial danger of placing persons under restraint who, in fact, provide no serious danger to the community? Having once confined them, is there any body of knowledge that tells us how to treat and cure them? If so, as a practical matter, are facilities and therapy available for these purposes in the state institutions provided for the confinement of such persons? Questions almost as serious can be raised as to a whole range of other measures. The laws providing for commitment of persons displaying the classic symptoms of psychosis and advanced mental disorder have proved a seductive analogy for other proposals. But does our knowledge of human behavior really justify the extension of these measures to provide for the indefinite commitment of persons otherwise afflicted? We who represent the disciplines that in some measure are concerned with the control of human behavior are required to act under weighty responsibilities. It is no paradox to assert that the real utility of scientific technique in the fields under discussion depends on an accurate realization of the limits of scientific knowledge.

There are other ways in which the modern tendencies of thought accompanying the rise of the rehabilitative ideal have imperiled the basic political values. The most important of these is the encouragement of procedural laxness and irregularity. . . . Our increased knowledge of the functioning of totalitarian regimes makes it more difficult to assert that the insistence on decent and orderly procedure represents simply a lawyer's quibble or devotion to outworn ritual. Nevertheless, in our courts of so-called "socialized justice" one may still observe, on occasion, a tendency to assume that, since the purpose of the proceeding is to "help" rather than to "punish", some lack of concern in establishing the charges against the person before the court may be justified. This position is self-defeating and otherwise indefensible. A child brought before the court has a right to demand, not only the benevolent concern of the tribunal, but justice. And one may rightly wonder as to the value of therapy purchased at the expense of justice. The essential point is that the issues of treatment and therapy be kept clearly distinct from the quesion of whether the person committed the acts which authorize the intervention of state power in the first instance. This is a principle often violated. Thus, in some courts the judge is supplied a report on the offender by the psychiatric clinic before the judgment of guilt or acquittal is announced. Such reports, while they may be relevant to the defendant's need for therapy or confinement, ordinarily are wholly irrelevant to the issue of his guilt of the particular offense charged. Yet it asks too much of human nature to assume that the judge is never influenced on the issue of guilt or innocence by a strongly adverse psychiatric report.

Let me give one final illustration of the problems that have accompanied the rise of the rehabilitative ideal. Some time ago we encountered a man in his eighties incarcerated in a state institution. He had been confined for some thirty years under a statute calling for the automatic commitment of defendants acquitted on grounds of insanity in criminal trials. It was generally agreed by the institution's personnel that he was not then psychotic and probably had never been psychotic. The fact seemed to be that he had killed his wife while drunk. An elderly sister of the old man was able and willing to provide him with a home, and he was understandably eager to leave the institution. When we asked the director of the institution why the old man was not released, he gave two significant answers. In the first place, he said, the statute requires me to find that this inmate is no longer a danger to the community; this I cannot do, for he may kill again. And of course the director was right. However unlikely commission of homicide by such a man in his eighties might appear, the director could not be certain. But, as far as that goes, he also could not be certain about himself or about you or me. The second answer was equally interesting. The old man, he said, is better off here. To understand the full significance of this reply it is necessary to know something about the place of confinement. Although called a hospital, it was in fact a prison, and not at all a progressive prison. Nothing worthy of the name of therapy was provided and very little by way of recreational facilities.

This case points several morals. It illustrates, first, a failure of the law to deal adequately with the new requirements being placed upon it. The statute, as a condition to the release of the inmate, required the director of the institution virtually to warrant the future good behavior of the inmate, and, in so doing, made unrealistic and impossible demands on expert judgment. This might be remedied by the formulation of release criteria more consonant with actuality. Provisions for conditional release to test the inmate's reaction to the free community would considerably reduce the strain on administrative decision-making. But there is more here. Perhaps the case reflects that arrogance and insensitivity to human values to which men who have no reason to doubt their own motives appear peculiarly susceptible.

Conclusion

. . . I have attempted to describe certain of the continuing problems and difficulties associated with, what I have called, the rise of the rehabilitative ideal. In so doing, I have not sought to cast doubt on the substantial benefits associated with that movement. It has exposed some of the most intractable problems of our time to the solvent properties of human intelligence. Moreover, the devotion to the ideal of empirical investigation provides the movement with a self-correcting mechanism of great importance, and justifies hopes for constructive future development.

Nevertheless, no intellectual movement produces only unmixed blessings. It has been suggested in these remarks that the ascendency of the rehabilitative ideal has, as one of its unfortunate consequences, diverted attention from other questions of great criminological importance. This has operated unfavorably to the full development of criminological science. Not only is this true, but the failure of many students and practitioners in the relevant areas to concern themselves with the full context of criminal justice has produced measures dangerous to basic political values and has, on occasion, encouraged the debasement of the rehabilitative ideal to produce results, unsupportable whether measured by the objectives of therapy or of corrections. The worst manifestations of these tendencies are undoubtedly deplored as sincerely by competent therapists as by other persons. But the occurrences are neither so infrequent nor so trivial that they can be safely ignored.

H. L. A. HART

The Use and Abuse
of the Criminal Law

1

Should the criminal law be used to enforce
sexual morality? To anyone anxious to clear his mind on this
question, I recommend the following simple exercise, which will
serve to focus attention on some neglected essentials. Let him
consult a short survey of American laws concerning sexual
offences such as is to be found in the American Law Institute's
Commentary on its Model Penal Code. There, to his astonishment, he will find that though the laws of the different states vary
very much, between them they make punishable almost every
conceivable form of sexual conduct except "normal" intercourse
between husband and wife and solitary acts of masturbation.

Reprinted with permission from *Lawyer* (Trinity & Michaelmas), vol. 8,
pp. 7–12 (Oct. 1965).

*Hart is Professor Emeritus of Jurisprudence at Oxford University. He is
the author,* inter alia, *of* The Concept of Law (1961) *and* Punishment and
Responsibility (1968).

Moreover, he will find that thirty-seven of the states still make fornication or adultery a penal offence; only in a few states is the penalty limited to a fine; and in some states the maximum penalty is as high as five years' imprisonment.

Astonishment will, however, give way to relief in the mind of the reader of this survey, when he finds that the statutes creating these offences are for the most part not enforced; yet it will be salutary for him to ask himself just *why* he is relieved to find that such laws are virtually dead letters. What precisely is wrong in mid-twentieth century with, for example, the idea of legally enforced chastity and generally with the use of the criminal law to stop freely consenting adults engaging privately in sexual practices, which are commonly spoken of and (more doubtfully) thought of as "immoral"? At first the effort to wake up one's sleeping common sense on these matters may not be successful. The first attempt to say precisely what is wrong with the use of the criminal law to enforce conventional sexual morality may only produce an explosive reiteration of the conviction that it is "wrong" or "absurd" or "not the law's business." But, a little patient reflection on some plain facts, as well as the law, will soon bring something more specific to light. Most people who are prepared to think dispassionately about deviant sexual behaviour and its control by law will find, when they probe their own re-actions to the law's interference in such matters, that their objections range from quite humble matters of economy to fundamental principles which are themselves moral.

II

One might arrange such objections to the law's interference in a scale of increasing importance, somewhat as follows:

1. ECONOMY. How much law enforcement can a society afford? Surely not enough to warrant turning the police onto the detection of fornication, adultery or homosexual behavior between consenting adults in private. And surely this will be a bad use of existing resources, so long as thieves and murderers remain uncaught.

2. IMPRACTICALITY OF GENERAL CONTROL. The sexual needs in which fornication, adultery and homosexual behaviour originate

are very strong, and even in the case of homosexuality are felt by very many; yet concealment is relatively so easy that only a negligible proportion of offenders against laws proscribing such behaviour are ever likely to be detected or deterred by the law's threats, or by actual punishment. This situation could only be changed if the punishment were made immensely more severe than would in fact be tolerated, and even that might have very little effect.

3. INEQUALITIES OF TREATMENT. Two forms of inequality must arise from the attempt to punish by law deviant sexual behaviour even if it takes place between freely consenting adults in private. The first arises because the numbers involved and the difficulties of detection are so great; for it must be a mere matter of chance that enables evidence to be obtained in some cases and not in others equally "bad." Secondly, though together with much empty lip-service, there may be a quite genuine conviction that all sexual intercourse except normal intercourse between the married is "immoral," people disagree very much in their estimate of the moral gravity of deviation from the standard and the punishment which it deserves. If the moral offence is made punishable by law, there will be wide variations in the actual punishments meted out in similar cases.

4. MORALITY MORALLY VALUELESS IF ENFORCED. Where the aim of the criminal law is, as in the case of murder, to protect individuals from harm, this aim is achieved even if criminals abstain from murder solely out of fear of the law. But, if the aim of the law is not to protect individuals but "to maintain morality," matters are different. What *moral* value is secured if people abstain from sexual intercourse simply out of fear of punishment?

5. LAW-CREATED MISERY: CUI BONO? All criminal law providing for punishment creates suffering in different ways: first, for the guilty, by the punishment actually inflicted; secondly, for the guilty person's family and friends; thirdly, for the guilty again, in the difficulties of regaining his place in social life after punishment. But, laws against deviant sexual behaviour create misery in quite special ways and in a special degree. For the difficulties involved in an adult's repression of sex impulses and the consequences of repression are of a quite different order from

those involved in the abstention from "ordinary" crimes. Very rarely, except in the mentally diseased, is the impulse to defraud, steal or even kill a continually recurrent and insistent part of daily experience. Resistance to the temptation to commit these crimes is not often, as the suppression of sexual instincts generally is, something which affects the whole emotional life and the development of the personality. Further the existence of laws punishing deviant forms of sexual behaviour has always provided special opportunities for one of the most potent instruments of human misery: blackmail.

Of these five objections, the three last are matters which most people would recognise as themselves matters of moral principle; and of them, the last objection, *viz.*, that the law regulating sexual behaviour creates great misery for many, is the most important, though it is also very simple. I shall devote the rest of this article to considering the question whether there is anything which outweighs this objection. I do this because I think that this is a crucial question, and contemporary, more sophisticated, discussions of the enforcement of morality by the criminal law appear to me not to have answered this crucial question, but instead to have obscured it.

III

Few people have denied that it is *an* objection, though not a conclusive one, to the use of the criminal law that it will create great and widespread misery. This is indeed one of the strongest reasons for entrusting control of certain types of conduct to agencies other than the criminal law; to educators, moralists, social workers or religious teachers. So very few defenders of the legal enforcement of morality are likely to say "I don't see why the human misery matters: it doesn't appeal to me as an objection at all." And, of course, if this is not *an* objection, it is difficult to imagine what could be. The diminution of human misery at least for some, the making of *some* human lives less nasty, less brutish and less short, is a common concern of all legal systems and all moral codes, however much they differ in other respects and however barbarous, unequal and repressive in those other respects they may be. What are laws for, if not (among other things) for this?

But, although no one is likely to contest the simple principle that the creation of great misery is an objection to the law which creates it, the principle may be silently ignored. There is, for example, no mention of this objection in Sir Patrick Devlin's lecture *The Enforcement of Morals*. If this is an oversight, it is surely an extraordinary one.

What then is there to set off against the misery which such laws create, as a justification for creating it? Do such laws avert from others some misery greater than the misery which they cause? Or do they produce for others happiness on a scale which outweighs this misery? It is surely not possible to regard the disappointment or indignation of those whose wish for a legally enforced morality is not gratified, as misery, comparable to that which such laws inflict. Indeed, it is very doubtful whether they suffer anything which could be called *misery* at all. Nor, where such laws do exist, can the satisfaction of those who want them be ranked as happiness which could outweigh the misery caused. No one, I think, has ever argued in these terms in defence of such laws, or attempted to show that the misery caused is balanced by the avoidance of greater misery or the production of greater happiness.

Indeed, the question whether there is anything to outweigh the misery caused by the legal enforcement of sexual morality is seldom faced in this stark and simple form, as it should be. Instead, the issue is usually said to be whether sexual morality "as such" (*i.e.*, even if its breach causes no harm to other individuals) may be enforced by the criminal law. Of course, if the answer to this question is "Yes," this strongly suggests, and perhaps strictly entails, that there is something in a legally enforced morality of such value that it outweighs the misery it causes. So, we must inquire what this value is.

IV

Here an important ambiguity is to be noticed. The contention that a legally enforced morality is a valuable thing may mean that it is merely in itself or "intrinsically" a good thing. Or, it may

H. L. A. Hart

mean that although not "intrinsically" a good thing, it is good "instrumentally," that is, because it promotes or maintains something else which is of value: perhaps because, as is sometimes urged, it preserves society from dissolution. And, of course, it may mean that a legally enforced morality is a good thing in both of these ways.

Sir Patrick Devlin, indeed, sets out to show that it is justifiable to enforce morality "as such"; but the only arguments which he deploys are directed to showing that the legal enforcement of morality is justified because the existence of morality is necessary for the existence of society. It is, indeed, not surprising that he does not show that a legally enforced sexual morality is a good thing intrinsically, that is, independently of its preservation of society; for even if the accepted sexual morality of a society (assuming, as Sir Patrick does, that it has *one* morality) is conceived of as a set of Divine Commands, it is very difficult to see how its enforcement by law could be a thing of value in itself. Of course, we often admire those who master their passions in pursuit of some ideal of chastity or out of respect for what they accept as a moral law; but, conformity with sexual morality from fear of the law's punishment seems destitute of moral significance or value. In any case, the argument that a society's conventional sexual morality is of intrinsic value because it has the status of Divine Commands is one which will only have force for those who find it possible to believe that they have that status and many do not believe this. Sir Patrick's defence of the legal enforcement of morality does not rest on this view of morality. The morality which he argues may be enforced is what Austin called "positive morality": a man made, not a Divine, affair. It is to be identified by the feelings (indignation, intolerance and disgust) which certain types of conduct evoke generally in society, and it is articulated by the ordinary reasonable (though "not rational") man to be found on the Clapham omnibus or in the jury box. The enforcement of this morality is justified not because conformity to it or deviation from it is a good thing in itself, but because such a morality is necessary for the existence of society. Deviation from it is like treason—an attack on society itself.

I have criticised elsewhere Sir Patrick's famous analogy of sexual immorality (even between consenting adults in private) and treason. Here, all that needs to be said about this defence of the legal enforcement of morality is that, when we have fought our way through the thickets of his ingenious argument, we find that there is a crucial question of plain fact which he never faces and so never answers. The question simply is: what evidence is there that a failure to enforce by law a society's accepted sexual morality is likely to lead to the destruction of all morality and so jeopardise the existence of society? There is much evidence both from contemporary societies of Western Europe and from the past that the belief is false. The story that homosexual behavior or the failure to make it a criminal offence has led to the ruin of states is a myth which no reputable historian has ever accepted: it has as much support from the facts as Justinian's belief that homosexuality was the cause of earthquakes. It is astonishing in an elaborate discussion such as Sir Patrick's to find this empirical question never faced; for, without the evidence, the argument that the legal enforcement of sexual morality is necessary for the existence of society cannot stand. Throughout, he assumes either that deviation from an accepted sexual morality which is backed by intolerance, indignation and disgust, or the failure to punish such deviation, or perhaps both, *must* jeopardise the existence of society. To which one can only reply in the idiom of contemporary philosophers, what sort of "must" is that?

There are, indeed, other objections to such attempts to show that the legal enforcement of morality is a thing of value such as could outweigh the misery it causes. Why, for example, should we assume that it is a good thing that every society should continue to exist? Why should a society whose principal occupation is torturing a racial minority continue to exist? Unless we think that it should exist however great the misery it causes, surely the argument that certain laws are required to preserve the society is not *per se* sufficient to justify the misery they cause. But, the full development of this objection would involve a critical consideration of the meaning and truth of the belief, shared apparently by Sir Patrick, that every society has a "right" to exist. I shall not undertake this critical task here because it would lead us into some deep (and muddy) philosophical waters, and would obscure those objections to the legal enforcement of sexual morality which appear to me to rest on some very simple truths.

NORVAL MORRIS and GORDON HAWKINS

The Overreach of the Criminal Law

The first principle of our cure for crime is this: we must strip off the moralistic excrescences on our criminal justice system so that it may concentrate on the essential. The prime function of the criminal law is to protect our persons and our property; these purposes are now engulfed in a mass of other distracting, inefficiently performed, legislative duties. When the criminal law invades the spheres of private morality and social welfare, it exceeds its proper limits at the cost of neglecting its primary tasks. This unwarranted extension is expensive, ineffective, and criminogenic.

For the criminal law at least, man has an inalienable right to go to hell in his own fashion, provided he does not directly injure the person or property of another on the way. The criminal law is an inefficient instrument for imposing the good life on others. These principles we take as self-evident, though we shall soon consider

Reprinted with permission from *The Honest Politician's Guide to Crime Control*, pp. 1-28 (University of Chicago Press, 1969).

Morris is Julius Kreeger Professor of Law and Criminology and Director of the Center for Studies in Criminal Justice at the University of Chicago. He is author of The Habitual Criminal *(1950). Hawkins is Senior Lecturer in Criminology at the University of Sydney.*

Norval Morris and Gordon Hawkins

some of the consequences of their neglect. They must receive priority of attention in our cure for crime since only when they are applied will we have both the resources and the clarity of purpose to deal with the serious problems of crime—injury to the person, fear in the streets, burglaries, muggings, and the larger incursions on our property rights.

Hence, our series of dictatorial ukases deals with law reform. They are not an academic refashioning of minutiae of the law; they are rather a determined return to the proper, more modest and realistic role of the criminal law. It is fortunate that we have dictatorial powers, since this type of law reform is distasteful to politicians and probably commands less than majority popular support. Politicians rely heavily on the criminal law and like to invoke criminal sanctions in connection with most social problems, if only to indicate their moral fervor and political virtue. They take little interest in the consequences of the invocation. Moreover, support for the removal of a sanction is often interpreted as support for the behavior previously punished; if you vote for the legalization of consensual adult homosexual conduct you must be either a faggot or a homosexual fellow traveler. Few votes are so gained. Likewise, the public often cherishes criminal sanctions as an expression of their virtuous inclinations as distinct from the squalid realities of their lives.

It is necessary, however, if we are to be serious about the crime problem, to clear the ground of action of the criminal law. This is essential to the police, to the courts, and to the correctional agencies. They must deal only with those problems and those people for whom their services and their capacities are appropriate; not those who are merely being sacrificed to prejudice and taboos. Public sacrifice, throwing virgins off the rocks, to reinforce the group superego, to placate the ancient gods, is not the job of the criminal justice system.

We provide, initially, a bare statement of our program; the rationale follows.

1. *Drunkenness.* Public drunkenness shall cease to be a criminal offense.
2. *Narcotics and drug abuse.* Neither the acquisition, purchase, possession, nor the use of any drug will be a criminal offense. The sale of some drugs other than by a licensed chem-

ist (druggist) and on prescription will be criminally
proscribed; proof of possession of excessive quantities may
be evidence of a sale or of intent to sell.

3. *Gambling.* No form of gambling will be prohibited by the
criminal law; certain fraudulent and cheating gambling
practices will remain criminal.

4. *Disorderly conduct and vagrancy.* Disorderly conduct and
vagrancy laws will be replaced by laws precisely stipulating
the conduct proscribed and defining the circumstances in
which the police should intervene.

5. *Abortion.* Abortion performed by a qualified medical practitioner in a registered hospital shall cease to be a criminal
offense.

6. *Sexual behavior.* Sexual activities between consenting adults
in private will not be subject to the criminal law.

Adultery, fornication, illicit cohabitation, statutory rape
and carnal knowledge, bigamy, incest, sodomy, bestiality,
homosexuality, prostitution, pornography, and obscenity;
in all of these the role of the criminal law is excessive.

7. *Juvenile delinquency.* The juvenile court should retain jurisdiction only over conduct by children which would be
criminal were they adult. . . .

The consequences of our program for adults emerge from the
statistics. There are six million nontraffic arrests of adults per year
in the United States. Counting most conservatively, the reforms
listed above account for three million of those arrests. Indeed, the
report of the President's Commission on Law Enforcement and
the Administration of Justice (hereafter referred to as the President's Crime Commission) states, "Almost half of all arrests are
on charges of drunkenness, disorderly conduct, vagrancy, gambling, and minor sexual deviations." The consequent reduction of
pressure on police, courts, and correctional services would have a
massive impact on the criminal justice system.

"We may start with the obvious observation that not every
standard of conduct that is fit to be observed is also fit to be enforced." Ernst Freund's words define the theme of this [essay].
There are two senses in which the criminal law causes crime. It is
the formal cause of crime. If we had no criminal law we would
have no crime. It is also an efficient cause of crime in that some

Norval Morris and Gordon Hawkins

of our criminal laws foster, encourage, sustain, and protect crime —in particular, organized crime. It is therefore necessary to begin with the question of what constitutes and what ought to constitute a crime? Or to put it another way: when should we use the criminal law in an effort to regulate human conduct?

We are broadly in agreement with the definition of the proper sphere of the criminal law given by Mill in his essay *On Liberty:*

> "The principle is, that the sole end for which mankind are warranted, individually or collectively, in interfering with the liberty of action of any of their members is self-protection. That the only purpose for which power can be rightfully exercised over any member of a civilized community against his will, is to prevent harm to others. His own good, either physical or moral, is not a sufficient warrant, he cannot rightfully be compelled to do or forbear because it would be better for him to do so, because it will make him happier, because, in the opinion of others, to do so would be wise or even right."

The function, as we see it, of the criminal law is to protect the citizen's person and property, and to prevent the exploitation or corruption of the young and others in need of special care or protection. We think it improper, impolitic, and usually socially harmful for the law to intervene or attempt to regulate the private moral conduct of the citizen. In this country we have a highly moralistic criminal law and a long tradition of using it as an instrument for coercing men toward virtue. It is a singularly inept instrument for that purpose. It is also an unduly costly one, both in terms of harm done and in terms of the neglect of the proper tasks of law enforcement.

Most of our legislation concerning drunkenness, narcotics, gambling, and sexual behavior and a good deal of it concerning juvenile delinquency is wholly misguided. It is based on an exaggerated conception of the capacity of the criminal law to influence men. We incur enormous collateral disadvantage costs for that exaggeration and we overload our criminal justice system to a degree which renders it grossly defective as a means of protection in the areas where we really need protection—from violence, incursions into our homes, and depredations of our property.

The present "overreach" of the criminal law contributes to the crime problem in the following ways,

1. Where the supply of goods or services is concerned, such as narcotics, gambling, and prostitution, the criminal law operates as a "crime tariff" which makes the supply of such goods and services profitable for the criminal by driving up prices and at the same time discourages competition by those who might enter the market were it legal.

2. This leads to the development of large-scale organized criminal groups which, as in the field of legitimate business, tend to extend and diversify their operations, thus financing and promoting other criminal activity.

3. The high prices which criminal prohibition and law enforcement help to maintain have a secondary criminogenic effect in cases where demand is inelastic, as for narcotics, by causing persons to resort to crime in order to obtain the money to pay those prices.

4. The proscription of a particular form of behavior (e.g., homosexuality, prostitution, drug addiction) by the criminal law drives those who engage or participate in it into association with those engaged in other criminal activities and leads to the growth of an extensive criminal subculture which is subversive of social order generally. It also leads, in the case of drug addiction, to endowing that pathological condition with the romantic glamour of a rebellion against authority or of some sort of élitist enterprise.

5. The expenditure of police and criminal justice resources involved in attempting to enforce statutes in relation to sexual behavior, drug taking, gambling, and other matters of private morality seriously depletes the time, energy, and manpower available for dealing with the types of crime involving violence and stealing which are the primary concern of the criminal justice system. This diversion and overextension of resources result both in failure to deal adequately with current serious crime and, because of the increased chances of impunity, in encouraging further crime.

6. These crimes lack victims, in the sense of complaints asking for the protection of the criminal law. Where such complainants are absent it is particularly difficult for the police to enforce the

Norval Morris and Gordon Hawkins

law. Bribery tends to flourish; political corruption of the police is invited. It is peculiarly with reference to these victimless crimes that the police are led to employ illegal means of law enforcement.

It follows therefore that any plan to deal with crime in America must first of all face this problem of the overreach of the criminal law, state clearly the nature of its priorities in regard to the use of the criminal sanction, and indicate what kinds of immoral or antisocial conduct should be removed from the current calendar of crime.

Drunkenness

One of every three arrests in America—over two million each year—is for the offense of public drunkenness; more than twice the number of arrests in the combined total for all of the seven serious crimes which the FBI takes as its index crimes (willful homicide, forcible rape, aggravated assault, robbery, burglary, theft of $50 or over, and motor vehicle theft). The cost of handling each drunkenness case involving police, court, and correctional time has been estimated at $50 per arrest. We thus reach a conservative national estimate of annual expenditure for the handling of drunkenness offenders (excluding expenditure for treatment or prevention) of $100 million. In addition, the great volume of these arrests places an enormous burden on the criminal justice system; it overloads the police, clogs the courts, and crowds the jails.

The extent to which drunkenness offenses interfere with other police activities varies from city to city, but in the majority of cities it involves a substantial diversion of resources from serious crime. Thus, in Washington, D.C., during a nine-month period, it was found that 44 percent of the arrests made by the special tactical police force unit used "to combat serious crime" was for drunkenness. A similar situation exists in relation to correctional systems. In one city it was reported that 95 percent of short-term prisoners were drunkenness offenders. One-half of the entire misdemeanant population consists of drunkenness offenders. Yet the criminal justice system is effective neither in deterring drunkenness nor in meeting the problems of the chronic offenders who form a large proportion of those arrested for drunkenness. All that the system appears to accomplish is the temporary removal from view of an unseemly public spectacle.

We think that the use of the police, the courts, and the prisons on this scale to handle unseemliness at a time when one-third of Americans are afraid to walk alone at night in their own neighborhoods is so ludicrously inept and disproportionate that we need no more than point it out to justify the removal of drunkenness from the criminal justice system. This is not to say that if a person while drunk causes damage to property, steals, or assaults another person he should not be arrested under the appropriate statutes dealing with malicious damage, theft, or assault. But there should always be some specific kind of offensive conduct in addition to drunkenness before the criminal law is invoked.

It is sometimes argued that we have a choice between the criminal law model and the medical model in the treatment of drunkenness. And there is a considerable literature which deals with the dangers of medical authoritarianism. To us this is a false dichotomy; our choice need not be so narrowly restricted. A social welfare model may, in the present state of medical knowledge, be preferable to either the criminal law or the medical model.

For the police lockups, courts, and jails we would substitute community-owned overnight houses capable of bedding down insensible or exhausted drunks. For the police and the paddy wagons we would substitute minibuses, each with a woman driver and two men knowledgeable of the local community in which the minibus will move. A woman is preferred to a man as the driver-radio-operator because it is our experience that the presence of a woman has an ameliorative effect on the behavior of males, even drunken males.

The minibus would tour the skid row area, picking up the fallen drunks and offering to help the weaving, near-to-falling drunks. If there be a protest or resistance by a drunk, cowardice and withdrawal must control our team's actions; if there be assaults or other crimes, a police transceiver will call those who will attend to it; if there be unconsciousness or drunken consent, the minibus will deliver the body to the overnight house.

If there be talk by the drunk the next day of treatment for his social or alcoholic problem, let him be referred, or preferably

Norval Morris and Gordon Hawkins

taken, to whatever social assistance and alcoholic treatment facilities are available. Indeed, let such assistance be offered if he fails to mention them; but let them never be coercively pressed.

The saving effected by abolishing the costly and pointless business of processing drunkenness cases through the criminal justice system would vastly exceed the cost of providing such facilities and treatment programs for those willing to accept them.

Narcotics and Drug Abuse

As in the case of drunkenness, so in regard to the use of other drugs, the invocation of the criminal process is wholly inappropriate. Yet at present, although drug addiction itself is not a crime in America, the practical effect of federal and state laws is to define the addict as a criminal. According to FBI arrest data, 162,177 arrests for violations of the narcotic drug laws were made in 1968. As the President's Crime Commission report puts it, ". . . the addict lives in almost perpetual violation of one or several criminal laws." Neither the acquisition nor the purchase nor the possession nor the use of drugs should be a criminal offense. This elimination of criminal prosecution provisions should apply to the narcotics (opiates, synthetic opiates, and cocaine), marihuana, hallucinogens, amphetamines, tranquilizers, barbiturates, and the volatile intoxicants.

Those who support the present laws and the traditional methods of enforcement commonly claim a causal connection between drug use and crime. Yet leaving aside crime to raise funds to support the inflated costs of purchasing legally proscribed drugs, the evidence of a causal connection between drug use and crime is slight and suspect.

As with alcohol, the fact that drugs not only release inhibition but also suppress function is commonly ignored. They may well inhibit more crime than they facilitate; heroin for example has a calming depressant effect, and the "drug crazed sex fiend" of popular journalism has no counterpart in reality although the myth dies hard. The prototypal headline, "Addict Rapes Widow" is misleading—the truth would be "Addict Nods While Widow Burns."

There seems to be no doubt, however, that the policy of

criminalization and the operations of criminal justice agencies in this field have in themselves been criminogenic without measurably diminishing the extent of the drug problem or reducing the supply of narcotics entering the country. There is substantial evidence that organized criminals engaged in drug traffic have made and continue to make high profits. There is evidence, too, that criminalization of the distribution of drugs has caused much collateral crime with drug addicts, "to support their habits," as the President's Crime Commission puts it, "stealing millions of dollars worth of property every year and contributing to the public's fear of robbery and burglary."

The one certain way totally to destroy the criminal organizations engaged in the narcotics trade and to abolish addict crime would be to remove the controls and make narcotics freely available to addicts. . . . the increase, stated as a percentage, seems great, it starts from a base so very much smaller than that in the United States that the figures showing increase misstate the problem. It remains a problem of little social significance. Further, the outlets for medical prescription and administration of drugs need to be better controlled to avoid the development of a black market. But these are details in a scheme of incomparably sounder structure.

With regard to marihuana, it is necessary to say something further. . . .

[T]he law, by treating marihuana as equivalent to opiates, may well foster the belief that there is no difference between them. Yet as marihuana can be relatively easily obtained in most states and found not to have the dramatically deleterious effects advertised, graduation to the use of heroin, which *is* addictive and harmful, could be stimulated by this policy. Worse still, because marihuana is bulky and detection is thereby facilitated, youthful experimenters are encouraged to move to dangerous and addictive drugs which are more easily concealed. As with alcohol, controls relating to the sale or other disposition of the drug to minors are necessary, but that is all.

One of the principal advantages of the decriminalization and the pathologization of addiction is that the "image" of drug taking as an act of adventurous daring conferring status on the taker as a bold challenger of authority, convention, and the Establishment will be destroyed. With punitive laws and the brunt of law en-

Norval Morris and Gordon Hawkins

forcement falling heavily on the user and the addict rather than on traffickers, we have created a persecuted minority with its own self-sustaining myths and ideology. The alcoholic, on the other hand, is nowhere seen as a heroic figure in our culture but quite commonly as a person to be pitied and treated as sick. Consequently, no addict subculture with a morale-enhancing, self-justifying ideology and recruitment process has developed in this area.

Gambling

Gambling is the greatest source of revenue for organized crime. Estimates of the size of the criminal revenue from gambling in the United States vary from $7 to $50 billion, which means that it is huge but nobody knows how huge. Because statutes in every state, except Neveda, prohibit various forms of gambling, criminals operate behind the protection of a crime tariff which guarantees the absence of legitimate competition. This has led to the development of a powerful and influential vested interest opposed to the legalization of gambling.

Despite sporadic prosecution, the laws prohibiting gambling are poorly enforced and there is widespread disregard for the law. We do not face a choice between abolishing or legalizing gambling; the choice is between leaving gambling and the vast profits which accrue from it in the hands of criminals or citizens taking it over and running it for the benefit of society or, by licensing and taxation measures, controlling it. . . .

Disorderly Conduct and Vagrancy

According to the Uniform Crime Reports, there were nearly six hundred thousand arrests for disorderly conduct in 1968. This represents more arrests than for any other crime except drunkenness. Disorderly conduct statutes vary in their formulation, and the conduct dealt with as disorderly includes a wide variety of petty misbehavior including much that is harmless, although annoying, and not properly subject to criminal control.

Criminal codes and statutes should prohibit specific, carefully defined, serious misconduct so that the police can concentrate on enforcing the law in that context. Disorderly conduct statutes allow the police very wide discretion in deciding what conduct to treat as criminal and are conducive to inefficiency, open to abuse, and bad for police-public relations.

Similar considerations apply to vagrancy. It is a criminal offense in all states, with over ninety-nine thousand arrests in 1968. Here, however, it is not a question of more rigorously defining the type of behavior to be prohibited but rather of entirely abandoning the vagrancy concept. The commentary to the American Law Institute's Model Penal Code states: "If disorderly conduct statutes are troublesome because they require so little in the way of misbehavior, the vagrancy statutes offer the astounding spectacle of criminality with no misbehavior at all." And the fact is that those statutes, which frequently make it an offense for any person to wander about without being able to give a "good account of himself," burden defendants with a presumption of criminality and constitute a license for arbitrary arrest without a warrant.

Vagrancy laws are widely used to provide the police with justification for arresting, searching, questioning, and detaining persons whom they suspect may have committed or may commit a crime. . . .

In our view the police need authority to stop any person whom they reasonably suspect is committing, has committed, or is about to commit a crime and to demand his name, address, and an explanation of his behavior—to stop and frisk, now clearly constitutionally permissible. The police need such powers of inquiry to control crime and to protect themselves in dealing with persons encountered in suspicious circumstances, and they should have these powers without having to resort to the subterfuge of vagrancy arrest. . . .

Abortion

It is estimated that a million abortions are performed every year in America and that criminal abortion is the third most remunerative criminal enterprise in the United States—following gambling and narcotics. The arrest rate is certainly less than one per thousand abortions performed. No other felony is as free from punishment as illegal abortion, particularly when it is performed by a medical practitioner.

Nevertheless it would be incorrect to say that the laws relating to abortion have no effect on behavior. The commentary to the American Law Institute's Model Penal Code states that "experience has shown that hundreds of thousands of women, married as well as unmarried, will continue to procure abortions . . . in ways that endanger their lives and subject them to exploitation and degradation. We cannot regard with equanimity a legal pattern which condemns thousands of women to needless death at the hands of criminal abortionists. This is a stiff price to pay for the effort to repress abortion."

The principal effect of the abortion laws appears to be that whereas women of higher socioeconomic status can usually receive competent and even legal termination of pregnancy—"therapeutic abortion on psychiatric grounds"—those less fortunately placed are forced to resort to the backstreet abortion with its grim train of consequential shame, misery, morbidity, and death. It is a law for the poor.

Abortion may be sinful or immoral, but it is not the function of the law to enforce the whole of morality. It is difficult to understand what religious or moral principle, what divine or human purpose, is served by compelling underprivileged women to undergo pregnancy for the full term and to bear unsought and frequently unwanted children or to risk sickness or death at the hands of incompetent and frequently lecherous and importunate abortionists. No doubt the fact that the price of maintaining this principle is paid almost exclusively by the poor has delayed its critical examination.

We, as criminologists, have a professional reason for advocating a rational approach to abortion legislation. We have been impressed by observation in many countries of the disproportionate number of unwanted children we find in orphanages, reformatories, correctional institutions for youth, and on through the correctional treadmill to institutions for habitual criminals. We believe that the single factor most highly correlated with persistent delinquency and crime would be, if properly tested, being unwanted.

The principle which is most often invoked in this connection is that designated by the phrase "the sanctity of life." It is ironical that in defense of the sanctity of life we pursue a policy which tends toward the maximization of maternal mortality. . . .

[I]n view of the fact that human reproduction is a continuum, such questions as "When does life begin?" are unanswerable, except perhaps in metaphysical or theological terms. Nevertheless it is quite practicable to draw objective distinctions between abortion, infanticide, and homicide; and in terms of these well-recognized distinctions we say that abortion should not be regarded as criminal as long as the woman desires its performance. We see no reason to regard some other arbitrarily selected point prior to parturition, in what is a continuous process, as having any particular significance.

In regard to this problem we adopt what Professor Glanville Williams calls "the short and simple solution" of permitting abortions to be conducted by qualified legal practitioners in certified hospitals when requested by the pregnant woman. We believe that the woman herself should have the full right to decide whether she will go through with the pregnancy or not, although there should be formal provisions to ensure that she is protected from undue pressure from other persons and that her request represents what she on some advised reflection really wants. In short, we regard the total legalization of abortion performed by a licensed physician as the answer. . . .

Sexual Behavior

With the possible exception of sixteenth-century Geneva under John Calvin, America has the most moralistic criminal law that the world has yet witnessed. One area in which this moralism is most extensively reflected is that of sexual behavior. In all states the criminal law is used in an egregiously wide-ranging and largely ineffectual attempt to regulate the sexual relationships and activities of citizens. Indeed, it is as if the sex offense laws were designed to provide an enormous legislative chastity belt encompassing the whole population and proscribing everything but solitary and joyless masturbation and "normal coitus" inside wedlock.

It is proper for the criminal law to seek to protect children

Norval Morris and Gordon Hawkins

from the sexual depredations of adults, and adults and children from the use of force, the threat of force, and certain types of fraud in sexual relationships. Further, there is some justification for the use of the criminal law to suppress such kinds of public sexual activity or open sexual solicitation as are widely felt to constitute a nuisance or an affront to decency. But beyond this, in a post-Kinsey and post-Johnson and Masters age, we recognize that the criminal law is largely both unenforceable and ineffective, and we think that in some areas the law itself constitutes a public nuisance. . . .

Sodomy and Crimes against Nature

Statutes concerning sodomy and crimes against nature include within their scope such sexual behavior as bestiality, both homosexual and heterosexual, and oral copulation, and mutual masturbation. These laws receive only capricious and sporadic enforcement, usually, although not exclusively, in regard to such relations outside marriage. Obviously laws of this kind are peculiarly liable to abuse because of the wide discretion involved.

No social interests whatsoever are protected by desultory attempts to impose upon persons adherence to patterns of sexual behavior arbitrarily selected from the great variety which forms our mammalian heritage. Bestiality would be more properly dealt with under statutes relating to cruelty to animals where any cruelty is involved; otherwise, there is no reason to include it within the criminal law.

Homosexual Acts

Homosexual offenses are treated under such titles as sodomy, buggery, perverse or unnatural acts, and crimes against nature; homosexual practices are condemned as criminal in all states but Illinois, usually as a felony. Penalties vary enormously. A consensual homosexual act which is legal in Illinois is a misdemeanor in New York and can be punished as a felony by life imprisonment in some states. The Kinsey report states: "There appears to be no other major culture in the world in which public opinion and the statute law so severely penalize homosexual relationships as they do in the United States today."

Our primacy in this field is purchased at a considerable price. Although the Kinsey report maintains that "perhaps the major portion of the male population has at least some homosexual experience between adolescence and old age," only a small minority are ever prosecuted and convicted. Yet the law in this area, while not significantly controlling the incidence of the proscribed behavior, not only increases unhappiness by humiliating and demoralizing an arbitrarily selected sample of persons every year and threatening numberless others, but at the same time encourages corruption of both the police and others who discover such relationships by providing opportunities for blackmail and extortion.

As far as the police are concerned, a great deal has been written both about corruption in this area and the degrading use of entrapment and decoy methods employed in order to enforce the law. It seems to us that the employment of tight-panted police officers to invite homosexual advances or to spy upon public toilets in the hope of detecting deviant behavior, at a time when police solutions of serious crimes are steadily declining and, to cite one example, less than one-third of robbery crimes are cleared by arrest, is a perversion of public policy both maleficent in itself and calculated to inspire contempt and ridicule.

In brief, our attitude to the function of the law in regard to homosexual behavior is the same as in regard to heterosexual behavior. Apart from providing protection for the young and immature; protection against violence, the threat of violence, and fraud; and protection against affronts to public order and decency, the criminal law should not trespass in this area. If all the law enforcement agents involved in ineffectual efforts to control buggery were to be diverted to an attempt to improve the current 20 percent clearance rate for burglary it is unlikely that there would be an immediate fall in the burglary rate. But it is utterly unlikely that there would be an increase in buggery; for people's sexual proclivities and patterns are among the least labile of their responses, as the almost total failure of "cures" and treatment programs for homosexuals should have taught us. And in the long run such a strategic redeployment of resources could not but be beneficial to society.

. . .

Conclusion: Some Objections and the Eighth Ukase

We are of the opinion that if the employment of the criminal justice system's resources were to be curtailed and restricted along the lines we have suggested in the seven major fields of action indicated, and the means thus made available were devoted to protecting the public from serious crime, such a redeployment would result in a substantial accession of strength to law enforcement which would help appreciably to reduce the crime problem to manageable proportions. . . .

It should be clear, then, that in the light of our definition of the function of the criminal law, in terms of the protection of the lives and property of citizens and the preservation of public order and decency, the sort of restrictions on the use of the criminal sanction we have proposed are not only unobjectionable but desirable. Moreover, we have suggested that even those who do not accept our definition must face the question whether the collateral social costs of endeavoring to preserve the particular prohibitions we have discussed are not excessive.

We have argued that they are excessive, not only in terms of human suffering and the loss of freedom, but also in that in many cases the attempt to use the criminal law to prohibit the supply of goods and services which are constantly demanded by millions of Americans is one of the most powerful criminogenic forces in our society. By enabling criminals to make vast profits from such sources as gambling and narcotics; by maximizing opportunities for bribery and corruption; by attempting to enforce standards which do not command either the respect or compliance of citizens in general; by these and in a variety of other ways, we both encourage disrespect for the law and stimulate the expansion of both individual and organized crime to an extent unparalleled in any other country in the world.

ALAN M. DERSHOWITZ

On Preventive Detention

The conditions giving rise to the call for preventive detention are not difficult to understand. A person suspected of committing a crime cannot stand trial on the day of his arrest; he must be given time to consult with his lawyer and prepare a defense. Although this should rarely take more than a few days the delay between arrest and trial has been growing, until it is now almost as long as two years in some cities and a year in most other cities, including the District of Columbia. This is the consequence primarily of our unwillingness to pay for needed increases in judicial machinery.

At the same time there has been a growing sensitivity to the plight of the indigent accused, who are unable to raise even modest bail; this is reflected in a 1966 bail reform law which authorizes federal judges to release most defendants without requiring money bail. The net result of bail reform and increased delays in court has been that more criminal defendants spend more time out on the street awaiting their trials than ever before. This has led to an increase—or at least the appearance of an increase—in the number of crimes committed by some of these defendants between arrest and trial. And so, in an effort to stem this tide of increasing crime,

Reprinted with permission from the *New York Review of Books*, March 13, 1969. Copyright 1967, The New York Review.

Notes to this Selection will be found on page 429.

Dershowitz is Professor of Law at Harvard University and co-author (with Katz and Goldstein, J.) of Psychoanalysis, Psychiatry, and Law (1967).

Alan M. Dershowitz

many political leaders . . . have focused their attention on the defendant awaiting trial. . . .

The resulting proposals for preventive detention vary: some are limited to the District of Columbia, while others apply to all federal courts; some would seem to authorize the confinement of a very large number of defendants, while others are narrower in their scope; some include methods for shortening the time interval between arrest and trial, while others seem satisfied to leave things pretty much as they are now.

But they all have one point in common: they permit the imprisonment of a defendant who has not been convicted, and who is presumed innocent, of the crime with which he stands charged, on the basis of a prediction that he may commit a crime at some future time. These predictions would be made by judges on the basis of their appraisal of the suspect's dangerousness, after study of his prior record and the crime for which he is being tried. The proponents of preventive detention hope thereby to identify and isolate those defendants awaiting trial who account for the apparently high incidence of serious crime. The opponents of preventive detention . . . maintain that, under our system of criminal justice, which is characterized by "the presumption of innocence," conviction for a past crime is the only legitimate basis for confinement; they are fearful that acceptance of this "novel" approach to crime prevention might be an opening wedge leading to widespread confinement of persons suspected, on the basis of untested predictions, of dangerous propensities.

Before the claims for and against pre-trial preventive detention can be fairly evaluated, this misunderstood device must be placed in its historical and contemporary setting. Predicting who will commit crimes has long fascinated mankind. In the eighteenth century Cesare Lombroso, an Italian criminologist, thought that he could detect the criminal type by observing the configuration of bumps on the head; Sheldon and Eleanor Glueck, my colleagues at Harvard and pioneers in the prediction of juvenile delinquency, maintain that they can spot potential criminals at an early age by observing aspects of their family life; and some biologists now assert, on the basis of rather flimsy evidence, that they can identify potential criminals by examining the chromosomal structure of their cells.

One can sympathize with these efforts to predict and prevent crimes before they occur, rather than to wait until the victim lies dead. Indeed, Lewis Carroll put in the Queen's mouth an argument for preventive detention that Alice found difficult to refute. The Queen says:

> "There's the King's Messenger. He's in prison now, being punished: and the trial doesn't even begin till next Wednesday: and of course the crime comes last of all."
>
> "Suppose he never commits the crime?" asked Alice.
>
> "That would be all the better, wouldn't it?" the Queen responded. . . .
>
> Alice felt there was no denying that. "Of course it would be all the better," she said: "But it wouldn't be all the better his being punished."
>
> "You're wrong. . . ." said the Queen. "Were you ever punished?"
>
> "Only for faults," said Alice.
>
> "And you were all the better for it, I know!" the Queen said triumphantly.
>
> "Yes, but then I had done the things I was punished for," said Alice: "That makes all the difference."
>
> "But if you hadn't done them," the Queen said, "that would have been better still; better, and better, and better!" Her voice went higher with each "better" till it got quite to a squeak. . . .
>
> *Alice thought, "There's a mistake somewhere—"*

And there is a mistake somewhere, but it is not where the opponents of preventive detention have sought to locate it.

The debate over pre-trial preventive detention has proceeded on the assumption that confining people on the basis of predictions of future crime is unprecedented in this country (and throughout the civilized world). . . . [This] is simply incorrect . . . A Justice of the Supreme Court of Burma came closer to the truth when he observed that "preventive justice which consists in restraining a man from committing a crime which he may commit but has not yet committed . . . is common to all systems of jurisprudence."[1]

Alan M. Dershowitz

No system of jurisprudence has ever required that its law enforcers always sit back and wait until the spear has been thrown,
or even until the gun has been loaded. Societies have differed in
their techniques of crime prevention, but for centuries people
throughout the world have been imprisoned "to protect society
from predicted but unconsummated offenses." That preventive
justice was part of the English common-law tradition was a
source of great pride to Blackstone.

. . .

The "preventive justice" to which Blackstone was specifically
referring consisted of confining persons about whom there was
"a probable suspicion that some crime is intended or likely to
happen," unless they could find "pledges or securities for keeping
peace, or for their good behavior." This "humanitarian" device
led to the confinement of large numbers of "vagabonds" and
"strangers."

During both world wars, Great Britain promulgated regulations explicitly authorizing the preventive detention of certain
persons suspected of "hostile origin or association." During the
Second World War the United States employed one of the
grossest forms of preventive detention known to history: the mass
transfer and internment of Americans of Japanese descent, allegedly on the basis of a prediction that otherwise some of them
would sabotage our war effort on the West Coast and become
victims of racial violence. The Supreme Court's approval of that
device[2] laid the foundation for a statute, now on the books, which
authorizes the detention, during a declared internal security emergency, of any person whom "there is reasonable ground to believe
. . . probably will engage in or probably will conspire with others
to engage in acts of espionage or of sabotage."[3]

. . .

Nor is preventive detention limited to Blackstone's England or
to wartime. Indeed, every American jurisdiction permits pre-trial
detention of at least one category of criminal suspects: those

charged with capital offenses. And it should be recalled that at the time of the enactment of the Eighth Amendment—which has been construed to prohibit excessive bail in noncapital cases—many, if not most, felonies were capital; accordingly, many, if not most, accused felons were detained pending completion of their trials.

The most widespread form of preventive detention employed in the United States today is commitment of the mentally ill. More than half a million mentally ill persons who have not been convicted of crime are imprisoned in state hospitals without adequate treatment, and, often, with little hope of eventual release, on the basis of psychiatric predictions that unless confined they would do violence to themselves or to others.

Peace bonds—the Blackstonian technique of "preventive justice"—are still authorized in many parts of the United States. In a Pennsylvania case, a defendant was charged with assault and battery. He stood trial and was acquitted by a jury. Despite this, the judge required him to post a bond of $1,000 "to keep the peace for two years." In its opinion vacating the bond as inconsistent with the right to trial by jury, the State Supreme Court cited data indicating that during ten previous years "478 men, after acquittal of criminal charges, were compelled to serve an aggregate of over 600 years in . . . prison in default of bonds aggregating $613,-200."[4]

Juvenile statutes authorize confinement of young persons who have not yet committed criminal acts, but who are thought likely to become criminals. Indeed, in his separate opinion in the *Gault* case, Mr. Justice Harlan cited figures indicating that between 26 and 48 percent of the 600,000 children brought before juvenile courts "are not in any sense guilty of criminal misconduct."[5] Some sex psychopath laws also authorize detention of persons who have never been convicted of crimes, but are thought likely to engage in sexual misconduct. Many states permit the incarceration of so-called "material witnesses"—that is, persons not themselves charged with crime, who may be important witnesses at another's trial, and who are thought likely to flee the jurisdiction unless confined. An alleged witness to the assassination of Dr. King was recently imprisoned under such a statute.

Another widespread American practice is the so-called "pre-

Alan M. Dershowitz

ventive arrest," recently described in a report to the Commissioners of the District of Columbia as follows:

> ". . . A person trying front doors of stores, or peering into parked cars, in the early hours of the morning; a person "known" to the police as a pickpocket loitering at a crowded bus stop; a "known" Murphy game operator talking to a soldier or a sailor—such persons may be arrested . . . largely in order to eliminate at least temporarily the occasion for any possible criminal activity. The principle upon which such arrests are made appears to be: if the individual is detained until 10 or 11 A.M. the following day, at least he will have committed no crime that night. . . ."[6]

The Courts are beginning to place limits on police discretion in some such situations. For example, the arrest of a person found wandering around toilets on the ground that there is cause to suspect that he is about to perform an act of homosexuality might not be sustained as a justifiable exercise of police discretion. But many legislatures have made it unnecessary for the police to justify such arrests by reference to as yet uncommitted crimes. They make the "suspicious" act itself a crime justifying arrest. Thus a number of states now make it a crime "to loiter in or about public toilets" or "to wander about the streets at late or unusual hours without any visible or lawful business."[7]

A . . . judicial decision has recognized that the "basic design" of vagrancy statutes is one of "preventive conviction imposed upon those who, because of their background and behavior, are more likely than the general public to commit crimes, and that the statute contemplates such convictions even though no overt criminal act has been committed or can be proved." The real issue in the enforcement of vagrancy statutes was viewed as "whether our system tolerates the concept of preventive conviction on suspicion." The United States Court of Appeals for the District of Columbia . . . struck down such statutes as unconstitutional, observing that "statistical likelihood" of a particular person's or group's engaging in criminality "is not permissible as an all out substitute for proof of individual guilt."

But "statistical likelihood"—gross and impersonal as that sounds

—is all we ever have, whether we are predicting the future or reconstructing the past. When we establish rules for convicting the guilty, we do not require certainty; we only require that guilt be proved "beyond a reasonable doubt." And that means that we are willing to tolerate the conviction of some innocent suspects in order to assure the confinement of a vastly larger number of guilty criminals. We insist that the statistical likelihood of guilt be very high: "better ten guilty men go free than one innocent man be wrongly condemned." But we do not—nor could we—insist on certainty; to do so would result in immobility.

What difference is there between imprisoning a man for past crimes on the basis of "statistical likelihood" and detaining him to prevent future crimes on the same kind of less-than-certain information? The important difference may not be one of principle; it may be, as Justice Holmes said all legal issues are, one of degree. The available evidence suggests that our system of determining past guilt results in the erroneous conviction of relatively few innocent people. We really do seem to practice what we preach about preferring the acquittal of guilty men over the conviction of innocent men.

But the indications are that any system of predicting future crimes would result in a vastly larger number of erroneous confinements—that is, confinements of persons predicted to engage in violent crime who would not, in fact, do so. Indeed, all the experience with predicting violent conduct suggests that in order to spot a significant proportion of future violent criminals, we would have to reverse the traditional maxim of the criminal law and adopt a philosophy that it is "better to confine ten people who would not commit predicted crimes, than to release one who would."

It should not be surprising to learn that predictions of the kind relied upon by the proponents of preventive detention are likely to be unreliable. Predictions of human conduct are difficult to make, for man is a complex entity and the world he inhabits is full of unexpected occurrences. Predictions of rare human events are even more difficult. And predictions of rare events occurring within a short span of time are the most difficult of all. Acts of violence by persons released while awaiting trial are relatively rare events (though more frequent among certain categories of sus-

Alan M. Dershowitz

pects), and the relevant time span is short. Accordingly, the kind of predictions under consideration begin with heavy odds against their accuracy. A predictor is likely to be able to spot a large number of persons who would actually commit acts of violence only if he is also willing to imprison a very much larger number of defendants who would not, in fact, engage in violence if released.

This brings me to an obvious fact that is often overlooked in evaluating the accuracy of predictions. In order that the evaluation be fair, there must be information about both sides; we must not only know how many crimes committed by defendants out on bail were prevented; we must also know how many defendants were erroneously imprisoned. Either of these alone tells you very little. It is no trick at all to spot a very high percentage of defendants who would commit acts of violence while awaiting trial: you simply predict that all or almost all will do so. (Of course, the number of erroneous confinements would be extraordinarily high, but most or all of the crimes would have been prevented.) Conversely, it is easy to avoid erroneous confinements if that is your only aim: simply predict that few or none of the defendants will engage in violence pending trial. (In that case, you would prevent very few, if any, of the potential crimes, but the number of erroneous confinements would be minimal or non-existent.)

The difficult task is to select a category which includes the largest number of defendants who would commit violent crimes and the smallest possible number who would not. If it were possible to select a category which included all those and only those, who would commit such crimes, there would be little problem. But since this is impossible, a choice must be made. It must be decided how many defendants we should be willing to confine erroneously in order to prevent how many acts of violence. This will in turn depend on the nature of the violence to be prevented and the duration of the contemplated confinement: we should be willing to tolerate fewer erroneous confinements to prevent predicted purse-snatching than predicted murder; and fewer again if the trial is a year off than if it can be completed within two weeks of the arrest.

Another reason why predictions of the future are less reliable than reconstructions of the past concerns the processes by which human beings make decisions. Participants in judicial decision-making—lawyers, judges, even jurors—have some sense of what it means to decide whether a specifically charged act probably was or probably was not committed. The participants bring to their decisions some basis for sorting out the relevant from the irrelevant, the believable from the incredible, the significant from the trivial. And this basis—though often rough and intuitive—is far more than the judge is likely to bring to the process of predicting the future.

It is true that all judgments about human events, whether past or future, rest upon a superstructure of assumptions about how people behave; all decision-making requires a theory. What I am suggesting is that participants in the judicial process are better equipped by their experience to construct and employ theories about what probably occurred in the past than theories about what is likely to occur in the future. Put another way, we are all historians, but few of us are scientists. Perhaps Lewis Carroll's Queen had a "memory" that worked equally well both ways: she remembered "things that happened the week after next" even better than things that happened yesterday. But Alice spoke for most of us when she said that her memory "only works one way . . . I can't remember things before they happen."

The most serious danger inherent in any system of preventive detention is that it always seems to be working well, even when it is performing dismally; this is so because it is the nature of any system of preventive detention to display its meager successes in preventing crime while it hides its frequent errors. This has been demonstrated in other areas where detention rests on predictions of dangerousness. One such area . . . is the confinement of the mentally ill on the basis of psychiatric predictions of injurious conduct. It has long been assumed that these psychiatric predictions are reasonably accurate; that patients who are diagnosed as dangerous would have engaged in seriously harmful conduct had they not been confined. The accuracy of these predictions has never been systematically tested, since patients predicted to be dangerous are confined and thus do not have the opportunity to demonstrate that they would not have committed the predicted act if they were at liberty.

Accordingly, the psychiatrist almost never learns about his

Alan M. Dershowitz

erroneous predictions of violence. But he almost always learns about his erroneous predictions of non-violence—often from newspaper headlines announcing the crime. The fact that the errors of underestimating the possibilities of violence are more visible than errors of overestimating inclines the psychiatrist—whether consciously or unconsciously—to err on the side of confining rather than of releasing. His *modus operandi* becomes: When in doubt, don't let him out.

The accuracy of psychiatric predictions has been called into considerable question. A decision of the United States Supreme Court in 1966, *Baxtrom v. Herald*,[8] resulted in freeing many mentally ill persons predicted to be dangerous. Grave fear was expressed for the safety of the community. But follow-up studies . . . indicate that the predictions of violence were grossly exaggerated, and that very few of the patients have done what the psychiatrists predicted they would do if released. Similar studies in Baltimore support this conclusion of extreme overprediction.[9]

The same phenomenon is likely to plague efforts to predict violence pending trial if a preventive detention statute is . . . enacted. Judges, like psychiatrists, will rarely learn about their erroneous predictions of violence; for these defendants, being confined, will not have an opportunity to demonstrate that they would *not* have committed the predicted crime. But every time a judge makes an erroneous prediction of *non*-violence—every time he decides to release someone who then does commit a violent act—he learns about his "mistake" swiftly and dramatically.

Thus, if a statute is enacted authorizing pre-trial preventive detention on the basis of judicial predictions of violence, we will never know how many defendants are being erroneously confined. And as more and more information is accumulated, most of it concerning defendants who were erroneously released, judges will keep expanding the category of defendants to be detained. There is evidence that this is already being done.

.   .   .

The Senate Subcommittee on Constitutional Rights considered a study of the decisions of two trial judges in the District of Columbia on pre-trial release and detention; one judge routinely, if unlawfully, detained all suspects whom he regarded as "bad risks"; the other judge routinely released most suspects. Over the period studied, the "tough" judge detained about half the defendants who came before him (144 out of 285); while the "lenient" judge detained only about one fifth (46 out of 226). Of those released by the tough judge, twelve were charged with offenses—either felonies or misdemeanors—while awaiting trial; while of those released by the lenient judge, sixteen were accused of such offenses.

In other words, in order to prevent about four more crimes (some of them misdemeanors), the tough judge had to confine almost a hundred more defendants. Moreover, of the 144 persons detained by the tough judge, thirty-six subsequently had their cases dismissed and another "large percentage of them" were acquitted. Most of the defendants in this latter group were therefore the victims of a compounded legal error: not only did they not commit the predicted crimes; they were not even guilty—or so the process determined—of the past crime with which they stood charged.

Now it may be that eventually criteria for confinement can be refined to the point where such errors are minimized. Perhaps the high rate of violent crime by certain categories of released defendants will permit a high degree of crime prevention without too many erroneous confinements. It is claimed, for example, that a very high percentage of defendants charged with armed robbery in the District of Columbia—some place the figure as high as 34 percent, others as low as 11 percent—commit new felonies while awaiting trial. But if a statute were to be enacted now authorizing the confinement of all persons awaiting trial who, on the basis of specified criteria, were predicted to commit violent crimes, then the development of such refined criteria would be seriously retarded.

It must never be forgotten that many years of experience administering an untested system will not always increase the accuracy of that system. Many years of experience are often only one year of experience repeated many times. The unknown mistake of the past becomes the foundation for a confident, but erroneous, prediction of the future. This was demonstrated many years ago, in a famous "experiment" conducted by the Harvard

Alan M. Dershowitz

psychologist Thorndike, who had a student throw darts repeatedly at a board to test the thesis that aim improves with
experience, but blindfolded the student and never told him when
he hit or missed the target. Needless to say, his aim did not improve with "experience." Nor would the accuracy of judicial
predictions necessarily improve simply as a result of judges spending more and more years meting out preventive detention without
any accurate way to test their predictions.

The time is not yet ripe for resolving definitively by legislation
the dilemma of pre-trial preventive detention. We have just begun
to understand what the problem is, but we do not yet have enough
information to know what the optimal solutions are. We have
not even tried other—less drastic—amelioratives, such as speedier
trials, more supervision for released defendants, and perhaps even
increased penalties for crimes committed while out on bail. If such
solutions were tried, the problem of crimes committed by released
defendants might become a very small one indeed. What must be
avoided is a simple solution that freezes knowledge at its existing
low state.

. . .

What I suggest is that any proposed criteria for confinement
be tested to determine how accurate—or inaccurate—they are in
predicting violence. This could be done in a number of ways.
Judges might be asked to apply the criteria being tested . . . and
to predict on the basis of those criteria which defendants awaiting
trial would engage in violent crimes. All of the defendants would
then be released, even those who the judges think should be detained. Careful studies should then be conducted to determine how
accurate the judges were in their predictions. There is, however, a
serious problem with this kind of test. If the judges know that
everyone will be released and their actions observed, they might
be extremely cautious about predicting violence, more cautious
than if they knew that the predicted criminals would be safely
confined.

This suggests a variation which would increase the accuracy
of the test, but at a substantial cost in human liberty. The judges
would again decide who should be detained on the basis of the

criteria being tested, but, this time, only some—say half—of those selected for detention would be randomly released and observed. The other half would be detained. This suggestion is not free of difficulties either, for the status of experimentation under the law is far from clear. But I am confident that a workable and constitutional approach can be devised.[10] Then we can see how many of these defendants would, in fact, fulfill the predictions.

What we learn about our ability to predict may be discouraging to those who advocate preventive detention. But it is far better to know the discouraging truth than to build a house—especially one with bars—on untested assumptions.

JOHANNES ANDENAES

The General Preventive Effects
of Punishment

I. *The Concept of General Prevention*

In continental theories of criminal law, a basic distinction is made between the effects of punishment on the man being punished—individual prevention or special prevention—and the effects of punishment upon the members of society in general —general prevention. The characteristics of special prevention are termed "deterrence," "reformation" and "incapacitation," and these terms have meanings similar to their meanings in the English speaking world. General prevention, on the other hand, may be described as the *restraining influences emanating from the criminal law and the legal machinery*.

By means of the criminal law, and by means of specific applications of this law, "messages" are sent to members of a society. The criminal law lists those actions which are liable to prosecution, and it specifies the penalties involved. The decisions of the

Reprinted by permission of The *University of Pennsylvania Law Review* from *University of Pennsylvania Law Review*, vol. 114, pp. 949–83 (1966).

Notes to this Selection will be found on pages 429–430.

Andenaes is Professor of Criminal Law at the University of Oslo. He is the author of The General Part of the Criminal Law of Norway (1965).

Johannes Andenaes

courts and actions by the police and prison officials transmit knowledge about the law, underlining the fact that criminal laws are not mere empty threats, and providing detailed information as to what kind of penalty might be expected for violations of specific laws. To the extent that these stimuli restrain citizens from socially undesired actions which they might otherwise have committed, a general preventive effect is secured. While the effects of special prevention depend upon how the law is implemented in each individual case, general prevention occurs as a result of an interplay between the provisions of the law and its enforcement in specific cases. In former times, emphasis was often placed on the physical exhibition of punishment as a deterrent influence, for example, by performing executions in public. Today it is customary to emphasize the *threat* of punishment as such. From this point of view the significance of the individual sentence and the execution of it lies in the support that these actions give to the law. It may be that some people are not particularly sensitive to an abstract threat of penalty, and that these persons can be motivated toward conformity only if the penalties can be demonstrated in concrete sentences which they feel relevant to their own life situations.

The effect of the criminal law and its enforcement may be mere deterrence. Because of the hazards involved, a person who contemplates a punishable offense might not act. But it is not correct to regard general prevention and deterrence as one and the same thing. The concept of general prevention also includes the moral or socio-pedagogical influence of punishment. The "messages" sent by law and the legal processes contain factual information about what would be risked by disobedience, but they also contain proclamations specifying that it is *wrong* to disobey. Some authors extend the concept of deterrence so that it includes the moral influences of the law and is, thus, synonymous with general prevention. In this article, however, the term deterrence is used in the more restrictive sense.

The moral influence of the criminal law may take various forms. It seems to be quite generally accepted among the members of society that the law should be obeyed even though one is dissatisfied with it and wants it changed. If this is true, we may conclude that the law as an institution itself to some extent creates conformity. But more important than this formal respect for the law is respect for the values which the law seeks to protect. It may be said that from law and the legal machinery there emanates a flow of propaganda which favors such respect. Punishment is a means of expressing social disapproval. In this way the criminal law and its enforcement supplement and enhance the moral influence acquired through education and other non-legal processes. Stated negatively, the penalty neutralizes the demoralizing consequences that arise when people witness crimes being perpetrated.

Deterrence and moral influence may both operate on the conscious level. The potential criminal may deliberate about the hazards involved, or he may be influenced by a conscious desire to behave lawfully. However, with fear or moral influence as an intermediate link, it is possible to create unconscious inhibitions against crime, and perhaps to establish a condition of habitual lawfulness. In this case, illegal actions will not present themselves consciously as real alternatives to conformity, even in situations where the potential criminal would run no risk whatsoever of being caught.

General preventive effects do not occur only among those who have been informed about penal provisions and their applications. Through a process of learning and social imitation, norms and taboos may be transmitted to persons who have no idea about their origins—in much the way that innovations in Parisian fashions appear in the clothing of country girls who have never heard of Dior or Lanvin.

Making a distinction between special prevention and general prevention is a useful way of calling attention to the importance of legal punishment in the lives of members of the general public, but the distinction is also to some extent an artificial one. The distinction is simple when one discusses the reformative and incapacitative effects of punishment on the individual criminal. But when one discusses the deterrent effects of punishment the distinction becomes less clear. Suppose a driver is fined ten dollars for disregarding the speed limit. He may be neither reformed nor incapacitated but he might, perhaps, drive more slowly in the future. His motivation in subsequent situations in which he is tempted to drive too rapidly will not differ fundamentally from that of a driver who has not been fined; in other words a general preventive effect will operate. But for the driver who has been fined, this motive has, perhaps, been strengthened by the recollection of his former unpleasant experience. We may say that a general preventive feature and special preventive feature here act together. . . .

II. *A Neglected Field of Research*

General prevention has played a substantial part in the *philosophy of the criminal law*. It is mentioned in Greek philosophy, and it is basic in the writings of Beccaria, Bentham and Feuerbach. According to Feuerbach, for example, the function of punishment is to create a "psychological coercion" among the citizens.[1] The threat of penalty, consequently, had to be specified so that, in the mind of the potential malefactor, the fear of punishment carried more weight than did the sacrifice involved in refraining from the offense. The use of punishment in individual cases could be justified only because punishment was necessary to render the threat effective. The earlier writers were concerned mainly with the purely deterrent effects of punishment, while the moral effect of punishment has been subjected to detailed analysis in more recent theories.

Notions of general prevention also have played a major part in legislative actions. This was especially apparent a hundred or a hundred and fifty years ago when the classical school was dominant. The Bavarian Penal Code of 1813, copied by many countries, was authored by Feuerbach and fashioned on his ideas. In more recent years, there has been an increasing tendency to emphasize special prevention. The judge now has greater discretion in deciding the length of sentences and he has at his disposal several alternatives to the classical prison sentence. But these changes have not altered the basic character of the system. Unlike mental health acts, penal laws are not designed as prescriptions for people who are in need of treatment because of personality troubles. While there are some exceptions, such as sexual psychopath acts and provisions in penal laws about specific measures to be used when dealing with mentally abnormal people or other special groups of delinquents, penal laws are primarily fashioned to establish and defend social norms. As a legislature tries to decide whether to extend or to restrict the area of punishable offenses, or to increase or mitigate the penalty, the focus of attention usually is on the ability of penal laws to modify patterns of behavior. . . . From the point of view of sheer logic one must say that general prevention—*i.e.*, assurance that a minimum number of crimes will be committed—must have priority over special prevention—*i.e.*, impeding a particular criminal from future offenses. If general prevention were one hundred percent effective, there would obviously be no need for the imposition of penalties in individual cases.

. . .

While general prevention has occupied and still occupies a central position in the philosophy of criminal law, in penal legislation and in the sentencing policies of the courts, it is almost totally neglected in criminology and sociology. It is a deplorable fact that practically no empirical research is being carried out on the subject. In both current criminological debates and the literature of criminology, statements about general prevention are often dogmatic and emotional. They are proclamations of faith which are used as arguments either in favor of or in opposition to the prevailing system. On one hand, we find those who favor authority, severity and punishment; on the other hand those who believe in understanding, treatment and measures of social welfare. The vast majority of criminologists seem to have adopted the second position, and sweeping statements are sometimes put forth as scientific facts. . . .

III. *Some Erroneous Inferences About General Prevention*

Certain untenable contentions are frequently introduced in various forms into discussions of general prevention, and it might be helpful to clear them away before we proceed.

1. "*Our knowledge of criminals shows us that the criminal law has no deterrent effects.*"

The fallacy of this argument is obvious. If a man commits a crime, we can only conclude that general prevention has not

Johannes Andenaes

worked *in his case.* If I interview a thousand prisoners, I collect information about a thousand men in whose cases general prevention has failed. But I cannot infer from this data that general prevention is ineffective in the cases of all those who have *not* committed crimes. General prevention is more concerned with the psychology of those obedient to the law than with the psychology of criminals.

2. *"This belief in general prevention rests on an untenable rationalistic theory of behavior."*

It is true that the extreme theories of general prevention worked out by people like Bentham and Feuerbach were based on a shallow psychological model in which the actions of men were regarded as the outcome of a rational choice whereby gains and losses were weighed against each other. Similar simplified theories are sometimes expressed by police officials and by authors of letters to newspaper editors asking for heavier penalties. But if we discard such theories, it does not follow that we have to discard the idea of general prevention.

. . .

3. *"Legal history shows that general prevention has always been overestimated."*

It is true that in the course of history there have been contentions about general prevention which seem fantastic today. There was a time when distinguished members of the House of Lords rose to warn their countrymen that the security of property would be seriously endangered if the administration of justice were weakened by abolition of capital punishment for shoplifting of items having a value of five shillings. . . . But the fact that the general preventive effects of punishment might have been exaggerated does not disprove the existence of such effects.

4. *"Because people generally refrain from crimes on moral grounds, threats of penalty have little influence."*

The premise contains a large measure of truth, but it does not justify the conclusion. Three comments are necessary. (a) Even if people on the whole do not require the criminal law to keep them from committing more serious offenses, this is not true for offenses which are subject to little or no moral reprobation. (b) Even though moral inhibitions today are adequate enough to prevent the bulk of the population from committing serious crimes, it is a debatable question whether this would continue for long if the hazards of punishment were removed or drastically minimized. It is conceivable that only a small number of people would fall victim to temptation when the penalties were first abolished or greatly reduced, but that with the passage of time, crime would attract the weaker souls who had become demoralized by seeing offenses committed with impunity. The effects might gradually spread through the population in a chain reaction.

5. "*To believe in general prevention is to accept brutal penalties.*"

This reasoning is apparent in Zilboorg's statement that "if it is true that the punishment of the criminal must have a deterrent effect, then the abolition of the drawing and quartering of criminals was both a logical and penological mistake. Why make punishment milder and thus diminish the deterrent effect of punishment?"[2]

Here we find a mixture of empirical and ethical issues. It was never a principle of criminal justice that crime should be prevented at all costs. Ethical and social considerations will always determine which measures are considered "proper." As Ball has expressed it: "[A] penalty may be quite effective as a deterrent, yet undesirable."[3] Even if it were possible to prove that cutting off thieves' hands would effectively prevent theft, proposals for such practice would scarcely win many adherents today. This paper, however, is primarily concerned with the empirical questions.

IV. *Some Basic Observations About General Prevention*

There are other varieties of error about general prevention, but the five types discussed are the basic ones. I shall now state in greater detail some facts we must bear in mind when considering general prevention. While most of these points seem fairly self evident, they nevertheless are frequently overlooked.

1. DIFFERENCES BETWEEN TYPES OF OFFENSES. The effect of criminal law on the motivation of individuals is likely to vary substantially, depending on the character of the norm being protected. Criminal law theory has for ages distinguished between actions which are immoral in their own right, *mala per se*, and actions which are illegal merely because they are prohibited by law, *mala quia prohibita*. Although the boundaries between these two types of action are somewhat blurred, the distinction is a fundamental one. In the case of *mala per se*, the law supports the moral codes of society. If the threats of legal punishment were removed, moral feelings and the fear of public judgment would remain as powerful crime prevention forces, at least for a limited period. In the case of *mala quia prohibita*, the law stands alone; conformity is essentially a matter of effective legal sanctions.

But there are variations within each of these two main groups. Let us take the ban on incest and the prohibition of theft, as examples. As a moral matter, the prohibition of incest is nearly universal, but violations are not legally punishable everywhere. I doubt that the absence of a threat of punishment seriously influences the number of cases of incest. The moral prohibition of incest is so closely integrated with family structure that there is little need for the support of the criminal law. Stealing, however, is an entirely different matter. As Leslie Wilkins puts it: "The average normal housewife does not need to be deterred from poisoning her husband, but possibly does need a deterrent from shoplifting."[4] And what applies to stealing applies even more to tax dodging. In this field, experience seems to show that the majority of citizens are potential criminals. Generally speaking, the more rational and normally motivated a specific violation may appear, the greater the importance of criminal sanctions as a means of sustaining lawfulness.

Any realistic discussion of general prevention must be based on a distinction between various types of norms and on an analysis of the circumstances motivating transgression in each particular type. . . .

2. DIFFERENCES BETWEEN PERSONS. Citizens are not equally

receptive to the general preventive effects of the penal system. The intellectual prerequisites to understanding and assessing the threat of punishment may be deficient or totally absent. Children, the insane and those suffering from mental deficiency are, for this reason, poor objects of general prevention. In other cases, the emotional preconditions are missing; some people more than others are slaves of the desires and impulses of the moment, even when realizing that they may have to pay dearly for their self-indulgence. In addition, psychiatrists claim that some people have feelings of guilt and consequent cravings for penance that lead them to commit crimes for the purpose of bringing punishment upon themselves.

Just as intellectual and emotional defects reduce the deterrent effects of punishment, they may also render an individual more or less unsusceptible to the moral influences of the law. While most members of the community will normally be inclined to accept the provisions and prohibitions of the law, this attitude is not uniform. Some people exhibit extreme opposition to authority either in the form of indifference or overaggression and defiance.

3. DIFFERENCES BETWEEN SOCIETIES. The criminal laws do not operate in a cultural vacuum. Their functions and importance vary radically according to the kind of society which they serve. In a small, slowly changing community the informal social pressures are strong enough to stimulate a large measure of conformity without the aid of penal laws. In an expanding urbanized society with a large degree of mobility this social control is weakened, and the mechanisms of legal control assume a far more basic role.

. . .

4. CONFLICTING GROUP NORMS. The motivating influences of the penal law may become more or less neutralized by group norms working in the opposite direction. The group may be a religious organization which opposes compulsory military service, or it may be a criminal gang acting for the sake of profit. It may be organized labor fighting against strike legislation which they regard as unjust, or it may be a prohibited political party

that wants to reform the entire social and political order of the day. It may be a subjugated minority using every means available in its struggle for equality, or the dominating group of society which employs every means available to prevent the minority from enjoying in practice the equality it is promised in law. Or perhaps it may be an ethnic or social group whose traditional patterns of living clash with the laws of society.

In such cases, the result is a conflict between the formalized community laws, which are expressed through the criminal law, and the counteracting norms dominating the group. Against the moral effects of the penal law stands the moral influence of the group; against the fear of legal sanction stands the fear of group sanction, which may range from the loss of social status to economic boycott, violence and even homicide.

5. LAW OBEDIENCE IN LAW ENFORCEMENT AGENCIES. The question of general prevention is normally treated as a matter of the private citizen's obedience of the law. However, a similar question may be raised about law enforcement agencies. All countries have outlawed corruption and neglect of duty within the police and the civil service, but in many places they are serious problems. In all probability, there are few areas in which the crime rates differ so much from country to country. Laxity and corruption in law enforcement in its turn is bound to reduce the general preventive effects of criminal law.

V. *Variations in General Prevention with Changes in Legislation and Enforcement*

It is a matter of basic interest, from a practical point of view, to determine how general prevention varies according to changes in legislation or legal machinery. Such changes may be classified into four different categories.

1. THE RISK OF DETECTION, APPREHENSION AND CONVICTION. The efficiency of the system could be changed, for example, by intensifying or reducing the effort of the police or by altering the rules of criminal procedure so as to increase or lower the

probabilities that criminals will escape punishment. Even the simplest kind of common sense indicates that the degree of risk of detection and conviction is of paramount importance to the preventive effects of the penal law.

. . .

On the other hand there is evidence that the lack of enforcement of penal laws designed to regulate behavior in morally neutral fields may rapidly lead to mass infringements. Parking regulations, currency regulations and price regulations are examples of such laws. The individual's moral reluctance to break the law is not strong enough to secure obedience when the law comes into conflict with his personal interests.

There is an interesting interplay between moral reprobation and legal implementation. At least three conditions combine to prevent an individual from perpetrating a punishable act he is tempted to perform: his moral inhibitions, his fear of the censure of his associates and his fear of punishment. The latter two elements are interwoven in many ways. A law violation may become known to the criminal's family, friends and neighbors even if there is no arrest or prosecution. However, it is frequently the process of arrest, prosecution and trial which brings the affair into the open and exposes the criminal to the censure of his associates. If the criminal can be sure that there will be no police action, he can generally rest assured that there will be no social reprobation. The legal machinery, therefore, is in itself the most effective means of mobilizing that kind of social control which emanates from community condemnation.

Reports on conditions of disorganization following wars, revolutions or mutinies provide ample documentation as to how lawlessness may flourish when the probability of detection, apprehension and conviction is low. In these situations, however, many factors work together. The most clear cut examples of the importance of the risk of detection itself are provided by cases in which society functions normally but all policing activity is paralyzed by a police strike or a similar condition. For example, the following official report was made on lawlessness during a

Johannes Andenaes

1919 police strike, starting at midnight on July 31st, during which nearly half of the Liverpool policemen were out of service:

> "In this district the strike was accompanied by threats, violence and intimidation on the part of lawless persons. Many assaults on the constables who remained on duty were committed. Owing to the sudden nature of the strike the authorities were afforded no opportunity to make adequate provision to cope with the position. Looting of shops commenced about 10 p.m. on August 1st, and continued for some days. In all about 400 shops were looted. Military were requisitioned, special constables sworn in, and police brought from other centers." [5]

The decisive factor in creating the deterrent effect is, of course, not the objective risk of detection but the risk as it is calculated by the potential criminal. We know little about how realistic these calculations are. It is often said that criminals tend to be overly optimistic—they are confident that all will work out well. It is possible that the reverse occurs among many law abiding people; they are deterred because of an over-estimation of the risks. A faulty estimate in one direction or the other may consequently play an important part in determining whether an individual is to become a criminal.

. . .

2. THE SEVERITY OF PENALTIES. At least since the time of Beccaria, it has been commonly accepted that the certainty of detection and punishment is of greater consequence in deterring people from committing crimes than is the severity of the penalty. This notion has undoubtedly contributed significantly to the abolition of brutal penalties, and there is certainly a large measure of truth in it. Part of the explanation is that one who ponders the possibility of detection and punishment before committing a crime must necessarily consider the total social consequences, of which the penalty is but a part. A trusted cashier committing embezzlement, a minister who evades payment of his taxes, a teacher making sexual advances towards minors and a

civil servant who accepts bribes have a fear of detection which is more closely linked with the dread of public scandal and subsequent social ruin than with apprehensions of legal punishment. Whether the punishment is severe or mild thus appears to be rather unimportant. However, in cases of habitual criminals or juvenile delinquents from the slums the situation may be quite different. . . . It is impossible to avoid the question of how important a change in the severity of the punishment may be under standard conditions of detection, apprehension and conviction. For the judge this is the only form in which the problem presents itself.

. . .

Even more complicated than the connection between the magnitude of the penalty and its deterrent effect is the connection between the magnitude of the penalty and its moral effect. Heavy penalties are an expression of strong social condemnation, and prima facie one might assume that the heavier the penalty the greater its moral effect. However, it is not that simple. In fact, we are concerned here with two problems. One problem is that of determining the impact of stronger or lesser severity of the *entire penal system*. In the Scandinavian countries, sentences are on the whole much more lenient than in the United States. A penalty of three years imprisonment in Norway marks the crime as very grave, quite unlike the situation in the United States. Perhaps what takes place is an adjustment between the penalties employed and their evaluation by the public, so that social disapproval may be both expressed and graded almost as efficiently by means of lenient sentences as by severe ones. The second problem is that of determining the impact of stronger or milder penalties for *certain types of offenses*. Is it possible to use legislation and court practice as devices to influence where, on their scale of condemnation, citizens are to place different types of violations? Stephen seemed to have extreme confidence in the power of legislation when he said: "The sentence of the law is to the moral sentiment of the public in relation to any offence what a seal is to hot wax."[6] But it might be maintained with equal justification that while the law certainly serves to strengthen the moral inhibitions against crime in general, it is not very successful in pressing upon the public its own evaluation of various types of conduct.

. . .

It seems reasonable to conclude that as a general rule, though not without exceptions, the general preventive effect of the criminal law increases with the growing severity of penalties. Contemporary dictatorships display with almost frightening clarity the conformity that can be produced by a ruthlessly severe justice.

However, it is necessary to make two important reservations. In the first place, as we indicated when discussing the risk of detection, what is decisive is not the actual practice but how this practice is conceived by the public. Although little research has been done to find out how much the general public knows about the penal system, presumably most people have only vague and unspecified notions. Therefore, only quite substantial changes will be noticed. Only rarely does a single sentence bring about significant preventive effects.

In the second place, the prerequisite of general prevention is that the law be enforced. Experience seems to show that excessively severe penalties may actually reduce the risk of conviction, thereby leading to results contrary to their purpose. When the penalties are not reasonably attuned to the gravity of the violation, the public is less inclined to inform the police, the prosecuting authorities are less disposed to prosecute and juries are less apt to convict.

. . .

VI. *Research Possibilities on the Efficacy of General Prevention*

When for practical reasons it is necessary to estimate the general preventive effects of some specific alternative as opposed to another, the estimate is usually made by means of common psychological reasoning. For example, on the basis of rather cloudy notions of human nature and social conditions, law com-

mittees and judges sometimes try to predict how a certain inno-
vation is likely to function in a particular situation in a given
society. The more realistic the psychology applied, and the more
thorough the knowledge about the activity concerned, the more
probable it is that an estimate is somewhere near the truth.

It is now fashionable to hold that we have no knowledge
whatever about general prevention. As should be apparent from
the preceding material, I believe this to be a considerable exaggeration. In fact, it may well be maintained that we have more
knowledge, at least more useful knowledge, about the general
preventive effects of punishment than about special preventive
effects. A generation ago, prison authorities and psychiatrists believed they knew a good deal about how to treat criminals. Recent
research, especially that conducted in England and California on
the comparative effects of various sanctions, seems to show that,
on the whole, these notions were illusions. This research suggests
that there is little difference between the overall results of various
kinds of treatment when consideration is given to differences in
the composition of the population being treated. Probation shows
almost the same results as institutional treatment; a short period
of treatment about the same results as long one; traditional disciplinary institutional treatment on the whole appears to have
results similar to those produced by treatment in modern, thera-
peutically-oriented institutions. It may be that overall success
rates are improper measures of the effects of different treat-
ments, because one type of treatment may be effective with one
type of offender and not with another. The attempts to work
out a typology with which to verify such an hypothesis have
not gone beyond the "pilot study" stage. The present state of
knowledge does not provide adequate grounds for erecting a
penal system based on special preventive points of view.

Continuing research on treatment is necessary. No less important, however, is research designed to shed more light on
questions of general prevention. . . . Let us examine the methods
at our disposal.

1. COMPARISONS BETWEEN GEOGRAPHIC AREAS. This method
has been employed in discussions of the effects of capital punishment. Areas using the death penalty for murder are compared to
areas where there is no death penalty for this crime, with a view

Johannes Andenaes

to determining whether there is any connection between the punishment and the murder rates. The method certainly has its difficulties. Statistics show only the criminality which has been detected, and it is difficult to obtain full knowledge of the factors which may influence the ratio of undetected crime. Even if the comparative method reveals a real difference in the extent of criminality, we still must judge whether the difference is due to the penal system or to other social conditions. In order to draw definite conclusions we need areas with similar social conditions but drastic differences in legal systems, and such areas are difficult to find. Systems of penal sanctions are usually quite similar in countries which are close to each other in the fields of economic and cultural development. If certain behavior is punishable in one country but not in another, we may face an additional difficulty arising from the fact that in the second country the behavior not regarded as criminal will ordinarily not be investigated or registered.

In certain areas, however, there is hope for fruitful comparisons. By and large, these are fields where sources other than police or court statistics can be utilized to measure the occurrence of a specific type of deviance. Abortion was mentioned previously as a field in which comparisons between differing areas may be both possible and valuable. Beutel compared the operation of Nebraska's bad check laws with the operation of similar laws in Colorado, Vermont and New Hampshire.[7] Information about the number and extent of bad checks was supplied by banks, and information about financial losses for bad checks in various types of businesses was obtained by means of questionnaires.

Intoxication among drivers is another field in which it should be possible to carry out sound geographic comparisons. In this field we find great divergences concerning legislation and legal practice. At the same time the effects of legislation could be studied by using a variety of techniques, for example, by conducting alcohol tests of randomly selected motor car drivers, by interviews or by means of alcohol tests on deceased traffic victims. Many practical and methodological difficulties must be overcome, but I am confident that by expending a reasonable amount of labor and money it will be possible to reach results of great relevance to the solution of a serious social problem in the motor age.

2. COMPARISONS IN TIME. When revisions are made in penal provisions, in the organization of the police and in the practice of the prosecuting authorities or of the courts, the extent of criminality can be examined with a view to assessing the changes. The difficulties here are similar to those encountered when making geographical comparisons. Radical and sudden changes in legal systems and the machinery of justice are rare. As a rule, change takes place through gradual alterations, for example, in the direction of stronger or milder penalties or in the degree of police effectiveness. As these alterations occur, there are changes in other fields bearing upon criminality, and it is extremely difficult to isolate each factor in order to determine what produced the final result. Changes introduced into the system may further influence the registration of crimes, so that the statistics are not comparable.[8] This difficulty is compounded when new penal provisions are introduced or old ones abolished, because generally only violations are recorded—we do not keep records of nonconformity before it becomes a crime or after it ceases to be a crime. Such statistical problems may, however, be overcome in areas where there are objective data on the extent of the nonconformity.

Drastic changes in law enforcement often take place during wars or revolutions, but so many other conditions change simultaneously that it is difficult to draw valid conclusions which apply to normal conditions. The most advantageous basis for conclusions about causal connections is found when great and sudden changes take place in law enforcement while the life of the community proceeds in its normal groove. The police strike, from the point of view of the social scientist, is an ideal situation, but unfortunately for the scientist, society does not permit the strike to continue long enough for exhaustive study.

In spite of the difficulties involved, the method of comparisons in time should not be underestimated. Most of what we know about general prevention comes from what history can tell us. Trade presented a vast amount of material from various countries and periods,[9] while Kinberg concentrated on revolutions and similar conditions.[10] Radzinowicz has provided much material on the importance of a well-organized and effective police.[11] I am sure that a great deal more could become known through systematic exploitation of historical materials. Unfortunately, criminologists ordinarily are not historians, and historians are rarely inclined to concentrate on problems of general prevention.

Even better than to study the past is to watch the changes as they are taking place. This method was employed by Moore and Callahan in their well known study of public reactions to changes in parking regulations, a study more remarkable for its methods and its theoretical basis than for its results.[12] Just as new types of penal institutions should not be introduced unless opportunities are provided for research on the effects of the new measures, important changes in the law or in legal practice should always be correlated with a program of research designed to examine the effects on crime as a whole. The research does not have to be limited to the public legal machinery. Large enterprises producing or marketing easily and widely consumed goods such as tobacco and alcohol have the everlasting problem of preventing theft among their own employees. They have their own system of controls and their own means of sanction. Perhaps research in this area will shed light on how the ordinary citizen resists the temptation to steal and also will show how employees react to changes in risks when control measures are introduced. Studies of the use of lie detector tests in American business enterprises have indicated widespread dishonesty even among those who are ordinarily held above suspicion, and they also have shown that such tests have a deterrent value upon the future conduct of employees.

3. EXPERIMENTS. Any change of a legal provision or a policy of the police, prosecuting authorities or the courts is, in a way, an experiment. Although such alterations are primarily made to gain certain effects, not to increase our knowledge, to a certain degree they may be made with a view to research. Moore and Callahan's study of parking included experiments conducted in concert with the police authorities. Another experiment initiated in Finland attempts to appraise the deterring effect of fines imposed for drunkenness. The local police of three middle-sized towns have agreed to reduce heavily the percentage of prosecutions for persons arrested for drunkenness. The results of the experiment are to be measured principally by comparing the number of arrests for drunkenness before and after the change. Other towns, especially three towns with approximately

the same number of inhabitants and the same number of arrests for drunkenness as the three experiment towns, are to be used as controls. The results of the experiment are not yet available. It seems doubtful, however, that the difference in stimuli in this experiment is sufficiently great to produce conclusive results.

It seems realistic to assume that legal, administrative and economic considerations will impose rather narrow limits for purely research motivated experiments. It is more economical to await alterations which are made for other than experimental reasons and to use the opportunity to promote optimal research conditions with a view to recording the effects.

4. RESEARCH ON MOTIVATION, COMMUNICATION AND PERSONALITY DEVELOPMENT. The kind of research I have been discussing is socio-statistical. It aims at uncovering connections between changes in the function of the legal apparatus and changes in criminality. Even where such connections have been discovered, nothing has been directly revealed about the psychological mechanisms at work, and it is therefore difficult to generalize about the results. Accordingly, research must also probe the individual links in the theories of general prevention. Instead of trying to give direct answers to questions about the effect of the penal law on behavior, one may break the main problem into partial problems accessible to research. . . . I have touched on a good many empirical questions to which we do not know the answers. How widespread and detailed is popular knowledge about legal norms? What are the attitudes toward the legal machinery, and how common is aggression or indifference as opposed to positive support? What proportion of the population has the feelings of guilt and the urge for punishment so often referred to by psychoanalysts? To what extent do criminals think of the risks when they plan or perform a punishable act, and how realistic is their estimate of the risks? How do people at large react to risks? These are questions which focus on the problems already discussed. In addition there are questions related to communication theory. How is knowledge about legislation and the legal machinery transmitted? What is the role of mass media as compared to personal contacts, and what connections exist between the forms of information and their motivating power?

We may also ask how the threat of punishment influences the psychological processes of potential criminals. The following two step hypothesis has been put forward. A person refraining from a desired action because of a penal threat will experience dissonance. Since an effective way of reducing dissonance is by derogating the action, he will then convince himself that he really did not want to do it. In testing this hypothesis, it is essential to determine the manner and degree to which the process depends on the severity of the punishment.

We may also analyze the development and internalization of moral conceptions by individuals. What is the influence of police, punishment and prison in the socialization process? To what extent does the penal law indirectly influence child rearing practices by instilling in parents a desire to prevent their children from coming into conflict with the law and the legal machinery? What defensive mechanisms may be utilized by the criminal to convince himself that his violation is not really a criminal act? What are the psychological effects on the law abiding citizen when he sees crimes committed with impunity? Surely psychologists and sociologists can formulate such questions in a manner that makes them answerable by empirical research and in a manner that attunes them to research already completed.

VII. *Ethical Problems Connected with General Prevention*

The use of any coercive measure raises ethical problems. This is so even when the motive rests upon the need to treat the person in question. To what extent are we justified in imposing upon someone a cure which he does not desire, and how are we to balance considerations in favor of his liberty against the need to eliminate the hazards he inflicts on society? Such problems are encountered in the public health services as well as in the exercise of criminal justice.

The conflict, however, assumes special proportions in connection with general prevention. It has often been said that punishment, in this context, is used not to prevent future violations on the part of the criminal, but in order to instill lawful behavior in others. The individual criminal is merely an instrument; he is sacrificed in a manner which is contrary to our ethical principles. This objection carries least weight in relation to general preventive notions connected with legislation. The law provides, for example, that whoever is found guilty of murder is liable to life imprisonment or that whoever drives a car when he is intoxicated is to be given a prison sentence of thirty days. Such penal provisions have been laid down with an aim to preventing *anyone* from performing the prohibited acts. If we accept the provisions as ethically defensible, we also have to accept the punishment prescribed in each individual case. As H. L. A. Hart has stated:

> "The primary operation of criminal punishment consists simply in announcing certain standards of behavior and attaching penalties for deviation, making it less eligible, and then leaving individuals to choose. This is a method of social control which maximizes individual freedom within the coercive framework of law in a number of different ways." [13]

The question, however, comes to a head when the individual penalty is decided by general prevention considerations, in other words, exemplary penalties.

. . .

Such ethical doubts become even stronger if the individual sentence depends upon the kind of publicity—and hence the kind of preventive effect—which is expected. Suppose a judge is faced with two similar cases within a short interval. In the first case, the courtroom is filled with journalists, and the outcome of the trial is likely to become known to millions of readers. In the second case, the listener's benches are empty and, in all probability, the verdict will not spread far beyond the circles of those who are present in the courtroom. Is it defensible for the judge to pass heavy judgment in the first instance because the sentence is likely to gain much publicity and consequently bring about strong general preventive effects, while the defendant in the second case is merely given a warning because punishment in his case would only mean personal suffering, and would not yield results from a social point of view? Such speculation upon the general preventive effects of the individual sentence easily become tinged with cynicism and for ethical reasons this approach is only acceptable within very narrow limits.

JOSEPH GOLDSTEIN

On the Function of Criminal Law in Riot Control

Whatcan and should be the function of the *criminal law* in the control and regulation of riots? Any response to this narrowly posed legislative question must ultimately be evaluated in the context of answers to such questions as: What are the underlying causes of riots? What are the functions of riots? How can riots be tolerated or prevented without sacrificing values fundamental to a democratic society? For purposes of long-range public and private planning in child care, education, employment, housing, technology, welfare, armed forces recruitment, and civil rights—to identify a few potentially relevant areas of decision—are there meaningful distinctions to be made between, for example, planned and spontaneous riots, between led and apparently leaderless riots, between riots with and without visible goals, or between riots *by* or *against* blacks, veterans, students, police, labor or any other group? All of these questions—questions

Reprinted with permission of International Universities Press from 24 The Psychoanalytic Study of the Child 463 (1969).

Notes to this Selection will be found on pages 430–432.

Goldstein, Hamilton Professor of Law, Science and Social Policy, Yale University, is a lawyer and psychoanalyst. He is coauthor (with Katz and Dershowitz) of Psychoanalysis, Psychiatry and Law (1967).

Joseph Goldstein

to which much in psychoanalytic theory should prove relevant to decisionmakers in law[1]—present too wide a set of issues. In this essay the role and function of only the criminal law in its relationship to riots will be explored.

The criminal law is but a single piece in the mosaic of social controls which constitute our "average expectable environment." It is a last-resort community resource. With riots, as with most criminal conduct, government must rely on other means to reach underlying causes. Lawmakers must avoid the common error of attributing to the criminal process major responsibility for either the occurrence or the absence of riots. At best a law of crimes may reduce a fraction of the frustrations and pent-up forces that are so easily catalyzed into riot. Its maladministration may, however, contribute greatly to the exacerbation of such forces.

In deciding what the criminal law should provide for the purpose of deterring riots, the lawmaker must therefore focus on those characteristics of the event which require proscription and on those means, within the narrow ambit of the law's authorized responses, which are most likely to reduce rather than exacerbate riotous conduct. Recognizing the limit and limitations of the criminal law he must focus, as does this essay, primarily on riots threatened and riots in being—that is on events at a point in time when the underlying causes which give rise to riots have already matured.

This analysis of the role the criminal law can and should play in riot deterrence will draw on traditional law as well as other sources, including psychoanalysis, which seem relevant. The application of psychological knowledge to any sociolegal problem is highly complex. Although law and psychoanalysis converge in their concern for man, his mind, his behavior, and his environment, the two disciplines diverge in purpose, function, and the contexts in which some of their common concerns arise. Further, it must be recognized that the psychoanalytic theory of man as an individual may not be adequate to permit productive explorations of what may be even more complex than an individual—groups of human beings interacting in and with the legal process.

With these caveats in mind about the twin dangers of attributing too much to the criminal law and of overstating the relevance of psychoanalysis to law, I turn to two questions which the promulgators of a criminal code would ask: First, since riot must involve conduct short of revolutionary activity already proscribed by the crimes of treason, insurrection, and mutiny, how is a riot to be distinguished, for criminal law purposes, from legally protected peaceful group conduct? Put another way, is there a need in a criminal code for a special substantive crime of "riot"? Second, whether or not there be such need, should such conventional crimes as assault, arson, or burglary committed during or in furtherance of a riot be subject to the same, greater, lesser, or somehow different sanctions from those authorized by statute for the same offense committed during more "normal" periods? Before turning to the second question, which will be analyzed in some detail, a brief conclusionary response to the first will be made in order to identify some of the socially shared values in issue and in order to define "riot" for criminal law purposes.

I

The never ending challenge to law in a democracy has always been to locate the line past which dissent and protest become intolerable burdens on a minimum need for order. The delegates to the Federal Convention, meeting in Philadelphia in 1787, were men who had rebelled against England and who were themselves plagued with the threat of the rebellion by Shay in Massachusetts. These men were acutely aware of the importance of order on the one hand, and of the value of protest and dissent on the other; the viability of the Union which they hoped to establish would depend on their ability to safeguard these values through law. Accordingly, the Constitution of the United States specifically provides that no law shall be made "abridging the freedom of speech, or of the press; or of the right of the people peaceably to assemble and to petition the Government for a redress of grievance." And the Supreme Court has "fashioned the principle that the constitutional guarantees of free speech and free press do not permit a State to forbid or proscribe advocacy of the use of force or of law violation except where such advocacy is directed to inciting or producing imminent lawless action and is likely to produce such action."[2] The criminal law writes in advance the scenario describing the circumstances under which the government is authorized to arrest and impose other sanctions upon

Joseph Goldstein

persons suspected or convicted of engaging in criminal conduct. In defining specific conduct as offensive, a criminal code thereby excludes from proscription—as is obvious once said—all other conduct and particularly all conduct protected by the Constitution.

The criminal law defines behavior of both the governed and the governors which is deemed intolerably disturbing to and destructive of widely shared community values. Harold Laski described the challenge to law in a way that is particularly relevant to the criminal process:

> "Those who speak of restoring the rule of law forget that respect for law is the condition of its restoration. And respect for law is at least as much a function of what law does as of its formal source. Men break the law not out of an anarchistic hatred for law as such, but because certain ends they deem fundamental cannot be attained within the framework of an existing system of laws. To restore the rule of law means creating the psychological conditions which make men yield allegiance to the law. No limitations upon government can be maintained when society is so insecure that great numbers deny the validity of the very foundations upon which it is based."[3]

Thus the criminal law, in striving to keep our revolutions peaceful, must protect assembly and the free expression of unusual, even deviant, ideas and conduct so essential to the growth of a democratic society.

Riots, whether perceived from a historical, sociological, political or psychological vantage point, are often a form of protest, a dramatic reflection of dissatisfaction with either governmental or private institutions; riots are often an expression of undefined, but nonetheless real frustration and hostility, of the failure or apparent failure of society to provide certain groups of the population with adequate opportunities for hope, for fulfillment, and for equality of treatment.[4]

Since riots are in part a form of group communication, however chaotic and inarticulate, and since the Constitution and the criminal law are designed to protect speech and assembly, lawmakers must determine at what point lawful protest or assembly becomes illegal activity, a crime. Put another way, how is a riot to be distinguished from lawful demonstrations, from the exercise of liberties which require and deserve protection? There must be something more than protest, more than vague or precise expressions of discontent, to justify the imposition of criminal sanctions upon the participants or architects of group, crowd or mob behavior. That "something more" must be either:

(a) *violence*—the forceful exercise of power which results in injury to person or to property, or which seriously threatens such injury or damage; or

(b) *interference with the lawful pursuit of others*—unreasonable interference or serious threats of interference with lawful public or private activity, with constitutionally guaranteed rights or with lawful efforts to safeguard those pursuits and rights.

The essence of a riot, for purposes of the criminal law, then, is a large group of people, civilian or official, organized or not, with or without a leader, engaging over a generally relatively short span of time either in violent conduct, or in other coercive forms of intrusion on legitimate private or public activity.

Any justification for a separate substantive offense of "riot" in a criminal code would require a determination that the conventional body of criminal offenses, of proscribed conduct, in that code did not cover all forms of violent or coercive conduct which constitute the essence of a riot. An illustrative selection of offenses to be found in local, state, and federal codes suggests how wide and all-inclusive is the range of potentially riot-related conduct which is already proscribed: disorderly conduct, breach of the peace, obstruction of traffic, arson, criminal possession of explosives, criminal trespass, burglary, possession of burglar tools, theft, assault, possession of illegal weapons, traffic in unlawful weapons, denial of civil rights, reckless endangerment, creating a hazard, obstructing public officials, giving false alarms or information to authorities, destruction of evidence of a crime, manslaughter, homicide, treason, and finally, conspiracies or attempts to commit all of the above offenses. Although most state codes do make special provision for riot, it is manifest that the arsenal of conventional offenses is sufficiently complete to enable officials to invoke the criminal process against all persons who make, threaten

Joseph Goldstein

to make, or are trying to make a "riot" something more than peaceful protest or assembly. Although this is far too brief an analysis of the question, I submit that there is neither need nor justification for a separate criminal offense of "riot" in local, state, or federal criminal codes.

II

There remains one characteristic of "riot"—a substantially large number of criminal offenses concentrated in a short span of time—which prompts asking the second question: Should a criminal code authorize different sanctions for an individual who commits or is suspected of committing a crime during or in furtherance of a riot than it does for an individual who commits or is suspected of committing the same offense during more "normal" periods?

The law has generally treated "riot" as an aggravating attendant circumstance justifying an increase in both pre- and postconviction sanctions. By permitting police officers physically to assault and even to kill individuals in the course of quelling a "riot" the common law authorized an increase in preconviction sanctions allowing the police to serve as judge, juror, and executioner prior to an orderly determination of guilt or innocence.[5] And the Civil Rights Act of 1968 paradoxically exempts police "engaged in suppressing a riot" from criminal liability for willfully and forcefully injuring or intimidating anyone exercising enumerated federally "protected" civil rights.[6] Thus while under present law "riot" serves as an aggravating factor which legitimizes and increases the preconviction sanctions to which a civilian participant may be subject, it simultaneously serves as a mitigating factor which relieves the police, the official participant, of liability for conduct otherwise criminal—i.e., for his failure to exercise the restraint that would be demanded of him in the "normal" course of his "law enforcement" duties. Illustrative of postconviction sanctions which treat "riot" as an aggravating factor is to authorize increased sentences for offenders found guilty of a crime committed during a riot or, as Congress has done, to make such offenders ineligible for federal employment for a five-year period.

Lawmakers have argued that "committed during the course of a riot" should be treated as an aggravating factor. There seem to be two reasons for this—retribution and deterrence. The retributive purpose often goes unacknowledged and becomes camouflaged by the label and language of deterrence. Increased sanctions for riot-related offenses would undoubtedly serve some as an outlet for the anger aroused against those who provoke with obscenities or who make life more difficult or more dangerous by engaging in criminal activity when protective public resources (police, firemen, prosecutors, defense counsel, and the courts) are overtaxed and at a disadvantage.

In theory, preconviction sanctions are not to serve a retributive function. The presumption of innocence means that there is no place for punishment prior to a finding of guilt. Preconviction sanctions are to be no more severe than is necessary to safeguard any individual from a direct threat to his life, as in self-defense, and to assure an opportunity for the criminal process to run its course until that innocence dissolves into guilt established beyond a reasonable doubt and in accord with due process.

Increasing sanctions for retributive purposes following such a determination of guilt may, however, accord with the general purposes of most criminal codes and thus may be an appropriate response. But even for authorized vengeance there must be some collective point of diminishing returns—i.e., a point at which the sanction no longer serves its function. That assertion contains a prediction about the impact of an external event—the sanction—on conduct and thus moves this analysis away from an evaluation solely in terms of conflicts between the multiple purposes of a sanction and constitutionally protected values. Such speculations about the capacity of a sanction to fulfill its purpose—about the impact of external events on conduct—are, as psychoanalysis teaches, extremely risky and of doubtful validity. And since the analysis of whether sanctions for riot-related offenses should for deterrent purposes be different from sanctions for the same offense committed during "normal" periods will involve such predictions, it becomes important to repeat a caution [of mine] on the application of psychoanalytic theory to law:

> "[T]he meaning of an actual experience [for example, being subjected to or imposing a specific sanction] in giving direction to a person's life rests . . . on countless internal and external variables. Not only may what appears to be a similar event

Joseph Goldstein

have different significance for the same person depending upon his stage of development at the time of its occurrence, but it may also have different implications for different people at similar stages of development. Implicit in this observation is an insight of substantial significance to anyone seeking to evaluate the consequences of decisions in law. It points to a limitation frequently obscured in assumptions in empirical studies about the impact or likely impact of a statute, judgment, or administrative ruling. Unless such decisions are perceived as external events in the lives of many people—events which have different meanings for different people—statistical evidence of success may include, without recognizing a distinction, a number of people upon whom the decision had no impact; and, even more significant, it may include in the failure column a number upon whom the decision had a direct impact contrary to that sought—not just no impact.

"For example, in evaluating a decision to impose a criminal sanction against a specific offender for purposes both of satisfying the punitive demands of the community and of deterring others from engaging in the offensive conduct, the student of law can or ought to assume that the decision may for some satisfy, for some exacerbate, and for some have nothing to do with punitive wishes, and may for some restrain, for some provoke, and for some have no impact on the urge to engage in the prohibited conduct. Recognition of the multiple consequences of every law-created event makes comprehensible both the never-ending search for multiple resolutions of what is perceived to be a single problem in law and the resultant need to find an ensemble of official and unofficial responses which on balance come closest to achieving the social control sought."[7]

A more significant and complex issue than retribution is whether more severe sanctions will on balance serve to reinforce or to undermine the criminal law's general deterrent impact. Additional pre- and postconviction sanctions, it is often reasoned, will deter "potential offenders," civilian and police, by making them weigh the risk of being treated more harshly if convicted or discovered *against* the reduced risk of getting caught or convicted because law enforcement facilities are overtaxed. In other words, it is assumed that because of more severe sanctions "potential civilian and official offenders" caught up in a crowd will choose either consciously or unconsciously not to commit a crime or choose more "normal periods" for their criminal activity, i.e., periods when a test of reality would reveal that the usual deterrent forces at work have not been weakened.

This assumption contains two concepts—"normal periods" and "choice"—which require examination. First, what is often forgotten in the righteous cries for a return "to law and order" which accompany official orders to "shoot to kill arsonists and shoot to maim looters"[8] is that during "normal periods" law enforcement is and has always been selective, not full or total enforcement. Society has generally been unwilling to provide, for financial and other reasons, enough police, prosecutors, defense counsel, and judges to fully enforce, even within constitutional limits, the substantive law of crimes. To the extent that the breakdown, by riot, of an already overtaxed system of criminal law administration is a consequence itself to be deterred, an increase not of sanctions but of law enforcement manpower available during such critical periods offers the most direct and promising deterrent capability. Greater numbers of men with specialized training in nonprovocative control should minimize consequences which otherwise would compound the progress of violence. By establishing emergency procedures for utilizing police, prosecutors, defense counsel, judges, supportive staff and facilities and by thus safeguarding the power of local and state authorities to determine priorities of enforcement, government can substantially reduce the possibility of paralyzing the administration of justice. It can, with due regard to constitutional safeguards, maintain an external reality which continues to function at the "normal" level of deterrence, whatever that may be.

Such contingency plans can also serve to reduce the likelihood of police panic and thus deter excesses of force. What Freud observed about the military would seem to apply as well to the police:

"[E]ach individual is bound by libidinal ties on the one hand to the leader . . . and on the other hand to the other mem-

Joseph Goldstein

bers of the group . . . the essence of a group lies in the libidinal ties existing in it. . . . A panic arises if a group of that kind becomes disintegrated. Its characteristics are that none of the orders given by superiors are any longer listened to, and that each individual is only solicitous on his own account, and without any consideration for the rest. The mutual ties have ceased to exist, and a gigantic and senseless fear is set free . . . it is of the very essence of panic that it bears no relation to the danger that threatens, and often breaks out on the most trivial occasions."[9]

Evidence of police brutality, such as that characterized by Walker as "police riot,"[10] may bear this out and should prompt the development of emergency plans and training designed to reinforce or at least keep intact the libidinal ties essential to a disciplined professional police department. Without such plans, or in failing to carry out such plans, the consequent weakening of mutual ties within the department releases each for membership in a new, possibly, leaderless group—a mob in which as Freud observed "individual inhibitions fall away and all the cruel, brutal and destructive instincts, which lie dormant in individuals . . . , are stirred up to find free gratification."[11]

Of course a "police riot" may be evidence not of panic but rather of strong libidinal ties between the members of a police department and their leaders whose orders they obediently follow. As Freud observed:

"[E]verything that the object [the leader] does and asks for is right and blameless. Conscience has no application to anything that is done for the sake of the object; in the blindness of love remorselessness is carried to the pitch of crime. . . . *The object has been put in the place of the ego ideal.*"[12]

Since both libidinal and aggressive forces are inherently neither "good" nor "bad" but underlie all behavior, the main question is how they are employed by the ego responding to external demands. Thus the very same strong libidinal ties between members of a police department and their leaders provide the greatest opportunity for restrained as well as excessive exercise of authority.

Law, particularly the administration of the criminal law in a democratic society, is, as both an ego and superego nutriment, to command respect for the dignity of each individual as a human being. It generally authorizes the use of lethal force only when life is endangered. Ramsey Clark, while Attorney General of the United States, reaffirmed the law's restriction on the exercise of police power: "An express mandate to the entire police complement to use the minimum force necessary to execute lawful orders, to refrain from use of excessive force must be understood by every officer."[13] Obscured then by the emotional freight carried by the cry for "law and order" in demands for increased sanctions against rioters is its real meaning which includes a mandate to the governors—the police, the judge, the prosecutors and legislators as well—for due process, for the orderly administration of justice at all times, whether normal or not.

The deterrence argument for increased sanctions rests on another concept, "choice." Generally the criminal law uses choice in terms of some undefined conscious exercise of free will which it calls voluntariness and *mens rea*. In so doing, it uses choice to mean control—self-control—which incorporates, in practice if not in theory, unconscious as well as conscious factors. While the following discussion responds primarily to an argument which seems to rest on choice, in a conscious sense, it will address itself to choice or control in terms of both the conscious and unconscious forces at work in each individual.

What little is known about crowd psychology seems to suggest that excessive sanctions, particularly preconviction sanctions involving physical force, will, on balance and in the long run, increase the frequency or duration of the violence which characterizes riots. Indeed, any such "violence count" must include this very exercise of official force which society, through the criminal law, seeks to keep at a minimum.[14]

Existing psychological theories of the riot phenomenon reinforce doubts about the view that more severe sanctions will serve a deterrent function, and cast doubt on voluntariness and *mens rea*—both being fundamental requisites of all major crimes for which a rioter might be held criminally responsible.

In his now classic *Psychology of the Herd* (1895), Le Bon's

Joseph Goldstein

major thesis about the crowds of the French Revolution was that once merged in a group, a law-abiding person seems temporarily to lose his critical and moral standards and thereby becomes prone to violence and capable of other unlawful activity. In his *group psychology*, Freud devotes much thought to the pioneering work of Le Bon and restates his observation in psychoanalytic terms: "For us it would be enough to say that in a group the individual is brought under conditions which allow him to throw off the repressions of his unconscious instinctual impulses."[15] Why some people in a group regress to become a mob and what releases the hostile and aggressive forces in some "reasonable men" and not in others and why and how such forces can sweep through a crowd is yet to be fully understood. It is as if the anonymity which an individual acquires in a crowd loosens, like alcohol, the ties between the inner checks which constitute conscience, and its many external nourishing forces (parents, friends, police, public opinion, etc.) which are a part of each man's reality—the "average expectable environment." More specifically, to the extent that a riot constitutes a breakdown of law and its enforcement, external nutriments essential to the work of both *ego* and *superego* are weakened in their efforts to control hostile and aggressive *id* forces. The effect of this withdrawal of external nutriment is found in the often uninhibited conduct of soldiers and travelers abroad. In a riot, however, there seems to be something more than withdrawal of the "usual" environment. There is the substitution of a new external nutriment—the crowd, which imposes new demands under rules of its own.†

Thus, for example, a civilian rioter facing a wide-open store full of goods can actually exclaim: "It would be a crime not to take something," or a police rioter can threaten news photog-

---

† "A group impresses the individual as being an unlimited power and an insurmountable peril. For the moment it replaces the whole of human society, which is the wielder of authority, whose punishments the individual fears, and for whose sake he has submitted to so many inhibitions. It is clearly perilous for him to put himself in opposition to it, and it will be safer to follow the example of those around him and perhaps even 'hunt with the pack.' In obedience to the new authority he may put his former 'conscience' out of action, and so surrender to the attraction of the increased pleasure that is certainly obtained from the removal of inhibitions." Freud, S., Group Psychology and the Analysis of the Ego, Standard Edition 18: 84 (London: Hogarth Press, 1955).

raphers with: "You take my picture tonight and I'm going to get you," or scream: "Get the fucking photographers and get the film."[16]

Related to the anonymity and breakdown of internal controls that may characterize membership in a crowd is what Bernard, Ottenberg, and Redl call "dehumanization—a composite psychological defense."† In its maladaptive form "dehumanization" allows a person to perceive others as if they lacked human attributes, to increase his emotional distance from them, and to experience conscious feelings of great fear and excessive hostility coupled with a blindness or denial of actual and generally foreseeable consequences of his conduct. A person stops identifying with other human beings, no longer seeing people outside his immediate group as essentially similar to himself. His relationships become stereotyped and rigid. His usual feelings of concern become anesthetized, replaced by powerfully destructive forces within himself. The Nazis' capacity to perceive Jews as swine and to slaughter them by the millions is a dramatic illustration of this mechanism. Today, in the cities and on the campus, whites, as members of a subgroup, or white policemen, as members of an even more tightly bound subgroup, may cry: "Get the niggers"; reverse the color and the cry may be: "Get whitey"; integrate and hear the Yippies or the Hippies scream: "Police are pigs, kill the pigs." Such manifestations of the dehumanization mechanism which indiscriminately lumps individuals into groups labeled "nigger," "whitey," or "pig" are more likely to lead to excesses of force—to the release of aggression—in both directions than to the release of libidinal energy in the form of assistance, cooperation, and sympathy which would characterize mechanisms of "rehumanization."

† Dehumanization also "serves important adaptive purposes in many life situations. . . . Certain occupations in particular require such selectively dehumanized behavior. These occupations . . . carry the extra risk of their requisite dehumanization becoming maladaptive if it is carried to an extreme or used inappropriately. Examples of these include law enforcement (police, judges, lawyers, prison officials); . . . Indeed, some degree of adaptive dehumanization seems to be a basic requirement for effective participation in any institutional process." Bernard V., Ottenberg, P., & Redl, F., Dehumanization: A Composite Psychological Defense in Relation to Modern War. In: *Behavioral Science and Human Survival*, ed. M. Schwebel. Palo Alto: Science Behavior Books, 1965, pp. 64–82.

Joseph Goldstein

Dehumanization is further reflected, more subtly and thus less visibly but no less insidiously, in the monumental indifference of city dwellers to their urban ghettoes and the widespread and long-standing violations of building safety and sanitation codes which inevitably take their toll in life, health, and human dignity. As Allen has observed:

> "The departments of city government charged with the inspection of dwellings and the enforcement of building regulations are typically understaffed, lackadaisical, inefficient, and devoid of ingenuity, even when (as is often true) they are not literally corrupt or amenable to political pressures. . . . But many members of that same community reveal anything but indifference to the noise, inconvenience, and incidental law violations associated with demonstrations organized to protest the conditions of life in the slum tenements."[17]

And that indifference, both private and official, reasserts itself when those communities deny, without investigation, that excesses in police force took place during such demonstrations and fail to take disciplinary action against those police who engaged in criminal activity.

. . .

An appreciation of the psychology of a riot mob and its sociological determinants, though more descriptive than explanatory, leads to the conclusion that additional or more severe sanctions would on balance, and in the long run, weaken the general deterrent function of the criminal law. Individual choice (control), essential to effective deterrence, is destroyed or substantially impaired when a person, police officer or civilian, loses his moral and critical faculties in or to a crowd or to its leader. Increased sentences, denial of an opportunity for government employment and, more particularly, authorization of lethal force or excessive force to apprehend looters or youthful protestors or anyone may be a temporary deterrent which affects some individuals but it can only serve, in the long run, to increase structural strain and undo libidinal ties, allegiance if you will, to society at large. To further alienate the alienated, to place the value of property over the value of human life, or the value of official feelings hurt by verbal taunts and obscenities over the value of an individual's physical integrity, can only make highly explosive situations more explosive. As the then Attorney General Clark observed:

> "Of all violence police violence in excess of authority is the most dangerous. For who will protect the public when the police violate the law? . . . It is the duty of leadership and law enforcement to control violence, not cause it. To seek ways of relieving tension, not to look for a fight."[18]

In addition to countering the deterrence argument for increased sanctions, our limited knowledge of the aberrant psychology of crowds would undercut, at least for some participants, the very basis of their criminal liability or pose an argument mitigating their postconviction sanctions. Briefly (to develop this point in detail would require another essay), the criminal law does not hold individuals responsible for involuntary conduct, coerced or automatized, or for offenses committed while insane, or for acts which are unintended, that is for acts unaccompanied by the appropriate degree of knowledge, purpose, intent (*mens rea*) on which the concept of "blameworthiness" is said to rest. Being caught up in a riot at the time of an offense might thus be perceived as evidence casting doubt on an individual offender's voluntariness or *mens rea*, requisites which are crucial to establishing guilt for all major offenses. Commission of an offense during the course of and as part of a riot might also be perceived as evidence constituting an insanity "defense" or a provocation depriving a "reasonable man" of his "capacity to conform his conduct to the requirements of the law." Le Bon's description of the behavior of the unorganized group—"like that of a wild beast, rather than like that of human beings"[19] recalls the early eighteenth-century test of insanity which allowed the accused to be relieved of criminal liability if he "does not know what he is doing, no more than a wild beast.[20] Whether the contagion of lawlessness that sweeps through a crowd and turns it into a riot is explained in terms of "regression," "anonymity," "dehumanization," "withdrawal of

Joseph Goldstein

external nutriments," or an exacerbating social setting,† an attorney for an "offender" might successfully develop a legal
defense based on such concepts with relevant evidence, particularly from psychoanalytic observations, about a specific defendant or group of defendants.

To sum up, recognition of the debilitating effect of the riot
environment on a participant's internal restraints and of the claim
of rioters that the rule of law has taken precedence over the rule
of justice, does lead to the realization that a repressive reaction by
lawmakers to riot-connected crimes, in the form of sanctions
more severe than usual, will more likely serve as an invitation to
regress and consequently more likely aggravate the problem
which the criminal law seeks to alleviate. In other words, an undue emphasis on the retributive function of the criminal law with
respect to riots would be counterproductive and would on balance defeat the more important function, deterrence.

On the other hand, proof of "commission during the course of
a riot" should not be given statutory recognition as a mitigating
circumstance and thereby automatically relieve an accused of
criminal liability. Understanding the effect of a riot on a partici-

---

† The observation is intended to forecast the use a defense attorney
might make of material from the social psychology of mobs in developing
an insanity defense or a direct challenge to *mens rea* or voluntariness. It
does not, however, constitute an acceptance of the conceptual relevance
of such concepts as insanity, *mens rea,* and voluntariness to the imposition
of criminal sanctions or to the multiple functions of the criminal law. Nor
does the observation mean that all group violence is the product of mob
psychology. Such conduct may be not only the most adaptive but even
the most just alternative to a repressive reality.

"Why not permit the defense of dwelling in a Negro ghetto? Such a
defense would not be morally indefensible. Adverse social and subcultural
background is statistically *more* criminogenic than is psychosis; like insanity, it also severely circumscribes the freedom of choice which a non-
deterministic criminal law (all present criminal law systems) attributes to
accused persons. True, a defense of social adversity would politically be
intolerable; but that does not vitiate the analogy for my purposes. You
argue that insanity destroys, undermines, diminishes man's capacity to reject
what is wrong and to adhere to what is right. So does the ghetto—more so.
But surely, you reply, I would not have us punish the sick. Indeed I would,
if you insist on punishing the grossly deprived. To the extent that criminal
sanctions serve punitive purposes, I fail to see the difference between these
two defenses. To the extent that they serve rehabilitative, treatment, and
curative purposes I fail to see the need for the difference." Morris, N.,
Psychiatry and the Dangerous Criminal, 41 *S. Cal. L. Rev.* 514, 520.

pant's internal controls does not justify his criminal conduct, nor should it lead legislators (who too are not immune from panic) to withdraw or weaken existing external controls by excusing such offenders. An expectation of reduced sanctions may be perceived, in advance, as a toleration of violence and serve as an invitation to riot. On balance, then, the argument that "riot" should generally (as opposed to individual cases in which, for example, a form of diminished responsibility is established) serve as a mitigating factor offsets the argument for treating it as an aggravating factor.

Thus, too, police who, under color of law, use excessive force, ought not to be subjected to more severe sanctions than would be authorized for such crimes committed by them during more "normal" periods. But at the same time neither should policemen be relieved of criminal liability as they are by the Civil Rights Act of 1968.[21] Moreover, because abuse by a professionally trained force, when coupled with an inadequate opportunity for the redress of community grievances, real or imagined, may cause or exacerbate riots, the usual restraints on the police must be strictly enforced if the danger of riots is not to be enlarged. Some procedure must be found for preventing police offenders from finding shelter not only in statutory exemptions but also in local lethargy, the apparent incapacity of the local authorities to police the police through the criminal law to which they, like other members of the community, are subject.

In the final paragraph of his paper on "The Theory of Ego Autonomy" Rapaport recalls the old adage that "freedom is the acceptance of the restraints of law.[22] That is true so long as those restraints are accepted in practice by the police as well as by the people, by the governors as well as by the governed. That is the meaning of law as a liberating force, that is the meaning of justice. To the extent then, that the criminal law has a role to play in riot control it is not to be found in a separate offense of "riot" or in treating "riot" as an aggravating or mitigating factor, but rather in holding police and civilians alike accountable for their violations of law

SANFORD H. KADISH

Some Observations on the Use of Criminal Sanctions in Enforcing Economic Regulations

Those who have had occasion to look for answers to the problems of the use of sanctions, taken to include the whole range of official modes of securing compliance with norms of conduct, have commonly agreed for some time now that there are few to be found. In view of the antiquity of the legal experience, which for the most part has always entailed the use of sanctions of one kind or another, this is a remarkable verdict. Indeed, works written at the turn of the eighteenth century by Jeremy Bentham are still the basic works in the area, a sobering observation which could scarcely be made of more than a handful of subjects of inquiry. In this state of affairs it is not surprising that we are largely ignorant of the impact of the penal sanction, which is only one aspect of the larger problem of sanctions; and still less

Reprinted with permission from *University of Chicago Law Review*, vol. 30, pp. 423–49 (1963).

Notes to this Selection will be found on pages 432–433.

Kadish is Professor of Law at the University of California at Berkeley. He is coauthor (with Paulsen) of Criminal Law and its Processes (1969).

Sanford H. Kadish

so that we know little about the use of the penal sanction in an area of relatively recent development, economic regulatory legislation. These are only sectors of a much larger unexplored terrain.

Moreover, unnecessary confusion has become an ally of ignorance in impeding understanding of these areas. Because strong ideological differences separate the proponents and opponents of economic regulation, judgments about the effect of penal sanctions in achieving compliance tend to turn upon judgments about the merits of the substantive regulation. Liberally oriented social scientists, otherwise critical of the case made for the deterrent and vindicatory uses of punishment of ordinary offenders, may be found supporting stern penal enforcement against economic violators. At the same time conservative groups, rarely foes of rigorous punishment for ordinary offenders, appear less sanguine for the criminal prosecution when punishment of business offenders is debated.

This statement of the undeveloped state of the art is by no means designed as an introduction to an ambitious effort to close the ancient gap in understanding. Quite the contrary, it is meant rather to excuse the modest ambit of these observations. What I would like to accomplish is to outline the special characteristics of economic regulatory legislation relevant to the use of the criminal sanction; to indicate what implications they have for effective use of the criminal law; and to suggest relevant concerns in the use of this sanction beyond the goal of enforcing the specific regulatory norm.

I

The kind of economic regulations whose enforcement through the criminal sanction is the subject of this inquiry may be briefly stated: those which impose restrictions upon the conduct of business as part of a considered economic policy. This includes such laws as price control and rationing laws, antitrust laws and other legislation designed to protect or promote competition or prevent unfair competition, export controls, small loan laws, securities regulations, and, perhaps, some tax laws. Put to one side, therefore, are regulations directly affecting business conduct which are founded on interests other than economic ones; for example, laws regulating the conduct of business in the interest of public safety and general physical welfare. Also to one side are laws indirectly affecting business conduct by their general applicability; for example, embezzlement, varieties of fraud and related white-collar offenses.

The class of regulations so defined possesses several characteristics that have a direct bearing upon the uses and limits of the criminal sanction as a means of achieving compliance. The first is the very feature suggested as the identifying characteristic of such legislation; that is, the nature of the interest protected. Certainly the use of criminal sanctions to protect interests of an economic character is not a contemporary departure. The extension of the classic larceny offense by courts and legislatures to embrace fraud, embezzlement and similar varieties of misappropriation that threatened newly developing ways of transacting business is a well documented chapter in the history of the criminal law. Indeed the process continues today. But there is an important difference between the traditional and expanded property offenses and the newer economic regulatory offenses—a difference reflecting the shift from an economic order that rested on maximum freedom for the private entrepreneur to one committed to restraints upon that freedom. The traditional property offenses protect private property interests against the acquisitive behavior of others in the furtherance of free private decision. The newer offenses, on the other hand, seek to protect the economic order of the community against harmful use by the individual of his property interest. The central purpose, therefore, is to control private choice, rather than to free it. But the control imposed (and this too has significance) is not total, as it would be in a socialistic system. Private economic self-determination has not been abandoned in favor of a wholly state regulated economy. Indeed, the ideal of free enterprise is maintained, the imposed regulations being regarded as necessary to prevent that ideal from consuming itself. Whether the criminal sanction may safely and effectively be used in the service of implementing the large-scale economic policies underlying regulatory legislation of this kind raises fundamental questions.

Sanford H. Kadish

A second relevant feature of these laws concerns the nature of the conduct restrained. Since it is not criminal under traditional categories of crime and, apart from the regulatory proscription, closely resembles acceptable aggressive business behavior, the stigma of moral reprehensibility does not naturally associate itself with the regulated conduct. Moreover, the conduct is engaged in by persons of relatively high social and economic status; since it is motivated by economic considerations, it is calculated and deliberate rather than reactive; it is usually part of a pattern of business conduct rather than episodic in character; and it often involves group action through the corporate form.

The third noteworthy attribute of this legislation is the role provided for the criminal sanction in the total scheme of enforcement. Typically the criminal penalty is only one of a variety of authorized sanctions which may include monetary settlements, private actions (compensatory or penal), injunctions, inspections, licensing, required reporting or others. Its role, therefore, is largely ancillary and takes either or both of two forms. On the one hand, the criminal penalty may serve as a means to insure the functioning of other sanctions, as, for example, penalties for operating without a license, or without prior registration or reporting. On the other hand, the criminal sanction may serve as a separate and supplementary mode of enforcement by directly prohibiting the conduct sought to be prevented, as in the Sherman Act. Furthermore, implicit in the legislative scheme is the conception of the criminal sanction as a last resort to be used selectively and discriminatingly when other sanctions fail. The array of alternative non-penal sanctions appears unmistakably to carry this message. That this is assumed by enforcement authorities is apparent from the relative infrequency of the use of the criminal as compared to other sanctions, and in the occasional appearance of published criteria of enforcement policy. And in some legislation, of course, the message of selective enforcement is explicit in the law. Finally, the responsibility for investigation, detection and initiating prosecution is often vested in a specialized agency or other body rather than left with the usual institutions for policing and prosecuting criminal violations. Moreover, these bodies, such as the Office of Price Administration during the war, or the Securities and Exchange Commission, commonly are not specialized organs of criminal enforcement, but are the agencies broadly charged with administering the legislative scheme.

This statement of the relevant features of the laws under inquiry, in terms of the interest protected, the behavior regulated and the contemplated role of the criminal penalty, is not meant to suggest that these laws are ultimately unique in the problems they raise for criminal enforcement. Apart from the nature of the interest protected, most, if not all, of these characteristics may be found in other areas of the criminal law: upper-class criminality in white-collar crime generally; selectivity in enforcement in the whole range of the criminal law, to a greater or lesser degree; deliberate, patterned conduct for gain engaged in by organizations in many other classes of offenses. And even though the nature of the interest protected is by definition unique, many of the problems it poses, such as making criminal morally neutral behavior, are common to other areas as well. All that is suggested is that if one asks, "What problems are raised for the effective use of the criminal sanction as a mode of achieving compliance in this area?" the beginnings of an answer are to be found in this congeries of characteristics. It remains now to suggest what bearing they have.

II

I propose to deal with the relevance of these characteristics in terms of three major problems: the problem of defining the proscribed conduct, the problem of corporate criminality and the problem of moral neutrality.

A. THE PROBLEM OF DEFINING THE PROSCRIBED CONDUCT

The fact that the protected interest is the preferred functioning of the economic system, and entails only partial restriction upon the operation of American business, bears directly upon the task of defining the proscribed behavior with sufficient specificity to meet the requirement of fair notice generally applicable to criminal legislation. Where the criminal sanction is used to police other enforcement devices, as for example, when it becomes criminal to market a security issue without registration or to do busi-

Sanford H. Kadish

ness without a license, the standard is met without difficulty. But the requirement of specificity is notably difficult of fulfillment where the crime itself purports to define the substantive economic behavior sought to be avoided. A notable example is the Sherman Act's prohibition of "restraint of trade or commerce" and "illegal monopolization." Only to a small degree, if at all, is the difficulty remediable by better draftsmanship. As Thurman Arnold observed, "antitrust policy touches fields and boundaries which recede as you approach them and disappear each time you try to stake them out." The reason for this arises from several sources. First, the economic policy is itself unclear, constituting largely a vague aspiration for a proper balance among competing economic goals. Second, illegality must turn on judgments that are essentially evaluative in character, rather than upon purely factual determinations. Third, the inevitable development of novel circumstances and arrangements in the dynamic areas under regulation would soon make precise formulations obsolete, even to the limited extent they proved feasible.

A key question is whether what would be an intolerable vagueness in conventional crime is less objectionable here in view of the preventive character of these laws. But deferring this question for the moment, are there alternatives for meeting the difficulty short of eschewing criminal sanctions where the conduct cannot be defined with acceptable specificity?

The requirement in an otherwise unconstitutionally vague definition of criminal conduct that the defendant must be shown to have acted willfully or knowingly has sometimes been held to remedy the defect of definition. Thus the Supreme Court found no unfairness in convicting a motor company for failing to reroute their explosive-laden truck "as far as practical, and where feasible" to avoid congested areas, where it was necessary to prove that this was done "knowingly";[1] or in convicting a taxpayer for attempting to evade taxes by making "unreasonable" deductions for commissions paid to stockholders as compensation for service, where the action was taken "willfully."[2] A requirement that the defendant have intentionally committed the act with a full and correct understanding of the factual circumstances is of no help to a defendant faced with an unclear definition of the conduct forbidden. On the other hand, however vague the line between what is permissible and what is criminal, where the actor is aware that his conduct falls squarely within the forbidden zone he is in no position to complain.[3] "A mind intent upon willful evasion is inconsistent with surprised innocence."[4] Apparently, therefore, it is scienter in this sense, that is, knowledge by the actor that he is violating the law, which is held in these cases to eliminate the vagueness problem. Yet this premise probably affords defenses to a larger group than intended, since a defendant who knew nothing of the existence of the law would be in as good a position.[5] If the prosecution must prove that the defendant knew his conduct fell within the terms of the law, it could hardly do so without proof as well that he knew of its existence. A legislature, however, could presumably resolve the semantic impasse by making it a defense that the defendant did not know his acts fell within its terms, or perhaps, more narrowly, that he could not reasonably know it, though not a defense simply that he did not know of the law's existence.

Another approach to mitigating the difficulties of a vague formulation is through administrative choice of cases to prosecute. If the enforcement agency initiates criminal prosecution solely where the meaning of the statute has become acceptably clear through judicial interpretation, the unfairness of the original unclarity may be thought adequately reduced. An example is the announced policy of the Department of Justice to institute criminal prosecutions for Sherman Act violations only where there is a per se violation, such as price fixing, a violation accompanied by a specific intent to restrain competition or monopolize, the use of predatory practices, or where the defendant has before been convicted of a Sherman Act violation. This approach, unlike the legislative requirement of scienter, is of no avail where the vagueness of the statutory formulation renders the law constitutionally unenforceable. It is also dependent upon the existence of means other than criminal prosecutions to develop clarifying interpretation. In the Sherman Act this is provided through the civil suit as a parallel means of enforcing the identical standard of conduct. This, in turn, however, may be a mixed blessing. One of the purposes of looseness and generality in the formulation of the standard is to create a flexibility that will allow judicial interpretation to keep pace with the changes in the character of the area under

Sanford H. Kadish

regulation. Courts may prove understandably reluctant to sustain expansive, although desirable, interpretations where the consequences will be to subject defendants to criminal as well as civil sanctions.

There are several alternatives to civil litigation as a means of producing clarifying interpretation. The most obvious is to delegate to the responsible administrative agency the authority to issue so-called "legislative regulations" in implementation of the statutory scheme. Providing criminal penalties for violations of these regulations then eliminates the vagueness problem to the extent of the clarity of the regulation. There is still, to be sure, a requirement of some specificity in the legislative standard from which the agency derives its authority. But this raises the different, though related, issue of delegation of powers, where requirements of specificity are considerably less than those applicable to criminal statutes. The declaratory order, in which the agency renders an advisory judgment on the legality of a contemplated course of action, is another possibility. This has utility both in providing further clarification of the applicability of regulations and in rendering interpretive guidance of the law when it, rather than a regulation, is the direct source of the prohibition. Section 5 of the Administrative Procedure Act provides a precedent for such an order, although the use authorized therein is considerably more limited than it might be.

Still another alternative is flatly to prohibit certain kinds of activity, except where an administrative agency, interpreting and applying general legislative standards, expressly allows it, as by issuing a license. The criminal penalty may then be imposed for the clearly defined offense of engaging in the activity without authorization. This, of course, is to use the criminal sanction, as previously suggested, as a means of enforcing another, non-criminal sanction. It is readily usable in such narrow areas as marketing securities, or engaging in other particular types of business. It is impractical where the thrust of the prohibition goes to ways of conducting any and all kinds of business, as in the Sherman Act.

B. THE PROBLEM OF CORPORATE CRIMINALITY

Conduct reached by economic regulatory legislation is typically group conduct often engaged in through the corporate form. This raises the formidable issue of corporate criminality.

From the legislative viewpoint, the principal questions are two-fold. First, what difficulties beset enforcement agencies in affixing criminal liability upon responsible actors where the principal violator is the corporation? Second, in any event, what are the possibilities of effective enforcement through the imposition of criminal penalties upon the corporation itself?

Fixing criminal liability upon the immediate actors within a corporate structure generally poses no special problem. But the immediate actors may be lower echelon officials or employees who are the tools rather than the responsible originators of the violative conduct. Where the corporation is managed by its owners, the task of identifying the policy formulators is not acute. But where the stock of the corporation is widely held, the organization complex and sprawling, and the responsibility spread over a maze of departments and divisions, then, as has recently been shown, there may be conspicuous difficulties in pin-pointing responsibility on the higher echelon policy-making officials. The source of the difficulty is the conventional requirement that to hold one person criminally liable for the acts of another he must have participated in the acts of the other in some meaningful way, as by directing or encouraging them, aiding in their commission or permitting them to be done by subordinates whom he has power to control. The difficulty is exemplified in the now famous antitrust prosecution of the electrical equipment manufacturers. Here the high policy makers of General Electric and other companies involved escaped personal accountability for a criminal conspiracy of lesser officials that extended over several years to the profit of the corporations, despite the belief of the trial judge and most observers that these higher officials either knew of and condoned these activities or were willfully ignorant of them.

It cannot be known to what extent this legal obstacle to convicting the policy initiators actually reduces the efficacy of the criminal sanction in achieving compliance. Certainly, it would prove more significant in those areas, like antitrust, where giant corporations are the principal targets of the law, than in areas where they are not. But other factors may be more influential in preventing widescale successful prosecution of individual corporate officials; under the antitrust laws, for example, there have been strikingly few convictions of corporate officials, even of

Sanford H. Kadish

officials of closely held corporations and the lesser officials of large, public corporations.

At all events, one means of reducing the difficulty would be to alter by statute the basis of accountability of corporate directors, officers or agents. An amendment, for example, of the antitrust law was recently proposed which would have changed the present basis of accountability (that such persons "shall have authorized, ordered or done" the acts) to make it suffice that the individual had knowledge or reason to know of the corporate violation and failed to exercise his authority to stop or prevent it. This falls short of outright vicarious liability since accountability is made to turn on fault in not knowing and acting rather than on a relationship simpliciter. Essentially it makes a negligent omission the basis of accountability. Still a standard of accountability resting on precisely how much of the far-flung operations of a nation-wide corporation an official should reasonably be aware of approaches vicarious liability in its indeterminateness, since neither the common experience of the jury nor even specialized experience affords substantial guidance. In effect, it introduces an element of uncertainty concerning accountability into laws that often, like the Sherman Act, are already marked by uncertainty concerning the conduct forbidden.

I defer to a later point the issue of whether such scruples are appropriate in business offenses. To the extent they are, a possible alternative is the legislative formulation of rules and standards of accountability. Where state regulatory laws are involved this might be accomplished through amendment of the corporation laws to fix the lines of accountability in intra-corporate relationships compatibly with the needs of an effective system of regulation. The problem, however, arises principally with national regulatory laws sought to be applied to officials of large interstate corporations. Professor Watkins has long suggested a federal incorporation law to restore responsibility in such corporate structures by eliminating the diverse and confusing lines of accountability under state corporation laws.[6] If, as he suggests, the problem of fixing accountability is due neither to the complexity of business nor to willful attempts to baffle outsiders, but rather to "the absence of uniform standards and rules for delegation of authority in these huge corporations in which nobody appears to know who is responsible for what," there may be no just means for meeting the problem short of his proposal. On the other hand, the complexity of the task and the further inroad into an area of traditional local jurisdiction might not be regarded as worth the cost, since the legal standards of accountability may prove to be only one of several factors, and not necessarily the most crucial, as we will see, militating against enforcement through conviction of corporate officials.

Fixing criminal liability upon the corporation itself has posed fewer legal obstacles in the enforcement of regulatory legislation. The earlier conceptual difficulties of ascribing criminal intent to a fictitious entity have been largely removed by the developing law. And whatever doubt may exist is readily met by expressly providing for corporate liability in the regulatory statute. But the problem of corporate accountability—that is, when the entity is liable for conduct of its agents at various levels of responsibility—is analogous to the problem of holding corporate officials accountable for the acts of lesser agents. It has been resolved more sweepingly in the case of the entity. For acts of its high managerial agents it is by definition accountable since a corporation cannot act by itself. For the acts of its lesser agents the tendency has been, at least in the regulatory offenses, to hold the corporation accountable for the acts of employees within the scope of their employment or while acting as employees. Whether the consequential imposition of vicarious responsibility upon the corporate entity, as well as upon shareholders, is justified raises the question of the deterrent efficacy of convicting and fining the corporate entity.

The case for corporate criminality rests presumably upon the inadequacy of the threat of personal conviction upon the individual actors. As said earlier, difficulties of proof under legal principles of accountability have interfered with effective prosecution of high corporate officials. And the commonly observed jury behavior of convicting the corporate defendant while acquitting the individual defendants, even where proof is apparently strong, further supports the case for the alternate sanction. Moreover, "there are probably cases in which the economic pressures within the corporate body are sufficiently potent to tempt individuals to hazard personal liability for the sake of company gain, espe-

Sanford H. Kadish

cially where the penalties threatened are moderate and where the offense does not involve behavior condemned as highly immoral by the individual's associates."[7] Yet the question remains of the effectiveness of corporate criminality as a supplementary deterrent.

The only two practically available modes of imposing criminal sanctions upon the corporate defendant are through the stigma of conviction and the exaction of a fine. The former, classified by Bentham as the "moral or popular" sanction, operates as he suggested through the adverse reactions to the conviction of persons in the community. Whether there is any substantial moral opprobrium attached to violation of economic regulatory legislation (even where individuals are convicted) I defer until later. Assuming there is, can it be said to have any appreciable significance when directed to a corporate entity? There is no substantial empirical basis for answering this question. It seems unlikely that whatever moral stigma may attach to a convicted corporation would be felt in any effectual way by the corporate individuals, especially in large corporations where responsibility is diffused. On the other hand, the point has been made (though denied as well) that the corporate stigma may operate as a deterrent by impairing the reputation of the corporation in its business operations and hence adversely affecting its economic position. Until there is more to go on one can only guess at the validity of this observation, though there is reason to expect that the impact of the conviction would operate differentially, depending on the size of the corporation, the extent of competition and the dominance of its market position, the degree to which its conviction attracted public notice, and the like.

The exaction of a corporate fine serves in part to give color to the moral stigma of conviction. Insofar as this is its role, its value depends upon the existence and power of the stigma to deter. On the other hand, the use of the corporate fine apart from the stigma of conviction raises no issue peculiar to the criminal sanction, since civil fines afford identical deterrent possibilities. Whether it would prove effective to increase the economic hazard of misconduct by authorizing higher fines than those now commonly authorized depends on such considerations as the general ability of the corporation to recoup its losses through its pricing policy and the likelihood that courts would impose the higher fines. An alternative recently proposed would substitute for the fine a governmental proceeding designed to compel the corporation to disgorge the profits attributable to its violation.[8] These alternatives raise substantial questions concerning sanctions, but not the criminal sanction, strictly speaking.

C. THE PROBLEM OF MORAL NEUTRALITY

Viewed in the large, the characteristic of the conduct typically proscribed by economic regulatory legislation most relevant for the purposes of criminal enforcement is that it is calculated and deliberative and directed to economic gain. It would appear, therefore, to constitute a classic case for the operation of the deterrent strategy. Nonetheless, it is a widely shared view that the strategy has not worked out in fact, that the criminal sanction has not proved a major weapon for achieving compliance. Part of the explanation may be attributable to the difficulties of enforcement suggested above, such as the resistance to vaguely defined standards of criminality, the difficulty of fixing culpability upon high corporate officials, and the muffled and absorbable impact of corporate criminal sanctions. But it is likely that the other factors play a more dominant role.

A common explanation of the failure of the criminal sanction is simply that the powerful business interests affected do not want these laws enforced and employ their power and position in American life to block vigorous enforcement. Influence is exercised over the legislatures to keep enforcement staffs impoverished and sanctions safely inefficacious. Enforcement officials, as prospective counsel for business interests, and judges as former counsel, identify with these interests and resist criminal enforcement. Moreover, news media, under the control of these same groups, work to create hostility to these laws and their vigorous enforcement and sympathy for the violators. In short, "those who are responsible for the system of criminal justice are afraid to antagonize businessmen. . . . The most powerful group in medieval society secured relative immunity from punishment by 'benefit of clergy,' and now our most powerful group secures relative immunity by 'benefit of business.' "

It would be dogmatic to assert that influences of this kind do

Sanford H. Kadish

not exist, but it may be doubted that they play a dispositive role. Business surely constitutes a powerful interest group in American life; but the profusion of regulatory legislation over the ardent protests of important economic interests in the past thirty years is some evidence that it is not all-powerful. Opposing forces have been able to marshal considerable public sentiment against a variety of business practices. Moreover, it is perhaps an over-simplification to identify all business as united in monolithic opposition. There is less a single business interest than a substantial variety of business interests. What then, in addition to business propaganda and influence, has accounted for the failure of the criminal sanction? Or, if we must have a villain, how has it been that business, which has not always gotten its way, has been this successful in devitalizing the use of that sanction?

It is a plausible surmise that the explanation is implicated in another feature of the behavior regulated by these laws; namely, that it is not generally regarded as morally reprehensible in the common view, that, indeed, in some measure it is the laws themselves that appear bad, or at least painful necessities, and that the violators by and large turn out to be respectable people in the respectable pursuit of profit. It is not likely that these popular attitudes are wholly products of a public-relations campaign by the affected business community. The springs of the public sentiment reach into the national ethos, producing the values that the man of business himself holds, as well as the attitude of the public toward him and his activities. Typically the conduct prohibited by economic regulatory laws is not immediately distinguishable from modes of business behavior that are not only socially acceptable, but affirmatively desirable in an economy founded upon an ideology (not denied by the regulatory regime itself) of free enterprise and the profit motive. Distinctions there are, of course, between salutary entrepreneurial practices and those which threaten the values of the very regime of economic freedom. And it is possible to reason convincingly that the harms done to the economic order by violations of many of these regulatory laws are of a magnitude that dwarf in significance the lower-class property offenses. But the point is that these perceptions require distinguishing and reasoning processes that are not the normal governors of the passion of moral disapproval, and are not dramatically obvious to a public long conditioned to responding approvingly to the production of profit through business shrewdness, especially in the absence of live and visible victims. Moreover, in some areas, notably the antitrust laws, it is far from clear that there is consensus even by the authors and enforcers of the regulation—the legislators, courts and administrators—on precisely what should be prohibited and what permitted, and the reasons therefor. And as Professor Freund observed, "if a law declares a practice to be criminal, and cannot apply its policy with consistency, its moral effect is necessarily weakened."[9]

The consequences of the absence of sustained public moral resentment for the effective use of the criminal sanction may be briefly stated. The central distinguishing aspect of the criminal sanction appears to be the stigmatization of the morally culpable. At least it tends so to be regarded in the community. Without moral culpability there is in a democratic community an explicable and justifiable reluctance to affix the stigma of blame. This perhaps is the basic explanation, rather than the selfish machinations of business interests, for the reluctance of administrators and prosecutors to invoke the criminal sanction, the reluctance of jurors to find guilt and the reluctance of judges to impose strong penalties. And beyond its effect on enforcement, the absence of moral opprobrium interferes in another more subtle way with achieving compliance. Fear of being caught and punished does not exhaust the deterrent mechanism of the criminal law. It is supplemented by the personal disinclination to act in violation of the law's commands, apart from immediate fear of being punished. One would suppose that especially in the case of those who normally regard themselves as respectable, proper and law-abiding the appeal to act in accordance with conscience is relatively great. But where the violation is not generally regarded as ethically reprehensible, either by the community at large or by the class of businessmen itself, the private appeal to conscience is at its minimum and being convicted and fined may have little more impact than a bad selling season.

Are there modes of dealing with these consequences of making morally neutral behavior criminal? A commonly suggested remedy for inadequate enforcement is a campaign of strict enforcement aided by strengthened prosecution staffs, and perhaps

Sanford H. Kadish

more severe penalties. But to the extent that the deficiency in enforcement is attributable to the moral inoffensiveness of the behavior, the major limitation of such a call to arms is that it is addressed to the symptom rather than the cause. How will legislatures be convinced to expend substantial sums for criminal enforcement, or prosecutors to go for the jugular, or courts or juries to cooperate in the face of a fundamental lack of sympathy for the criminal penalty in this area? Enlarged resources for prosecution may well afford staff enthusiasts an opportunity for more vigorous enforcement, but one may doubt that it can achieve more than a minor flurry of enforcement.

An attack on the cause, insofar as moral neutrality is the cause, would presumably require a two-pronged program: one directed at the obstacle of popular nullification; the other at inculcating the sentiment of moral disapproval in the community. Each, of course, would inevitably have an effect upon the other. The former might proceed, not simply by allocating greater enforcement resources, but by arrangements that would reduce the traditional discretionary authority of the various bodies involved in criminal law enforcement. For example, the decision to prosecute might be exclusively centered in the agency responsible for the whole regulatory program, conservative legal interpretation might be dealt with by authorizing agency interpretative regulations which are made relevant in criminal prosecutions; the temporizing of juries might be avoided by eliminating, where possible, jury trials; the judge's sentencing discretion might be curtailed by mandatory minimum penalties. There is, of course, the substantial task of persuading legislatures to abjure the traditional mediating institutions of the criminal law in an area where, the moral factor being largely absent, they might be thought to have their historic and most useful function to perform. But if enacted, one might reasonably suppose that such legal arrangements could result in a somewhat more frequent and rigorous use of the criminal sanction and a heightening of the deterrent effect of the law.

The other prong of the program, the cultivation of the sentiment of moral disapproval, is perhaps closer to the heart of the matter. To some extent the more frequent enforcement and the more stringent punishment of violators may tend to serve this objective as well as its more direct in terrorem purposes, especially where cases are selected for enforcement with this end in view. Whether a governmentally mounted campaign should be employed as well to give widespread publicity to successful convictions and to shape the public conscience in other ways may be questioned from various viewpoints, but it surely would be consistent with the basic strategy of using criminal sanctions in these areas.

How effective a campaign of selected prosecutions and attendant publicity would prove in creating a changed moral climate is problematical. Certainly one can not confidently deny that the spectacle of frequent conviction and severe punishment may play a role in molding the community's attitudes toward the conduct in question. Experience offers uncertain guidance. Tax evasion has a history that provides some support. We have come a considerable distance, though not all the way, from the day when an English judge could observe from the bench, "there is not behind taxing laws, as there is behind laws against crime, an independent moral obligation."[10] The change was accompanied in this country by a gradual tightening of the criminal sanction. In 1924 tax evasion was upgraded from a misdemeanor to a felony and maximum imprisonment raised from one to five years; reforms in 1952 converted the criminal prosecution from a tax recovery device and weapon against the professional racketeer to a means of general deterrence of tax evasion by widespread and selected enforcement against all levels of violators. While the tax evasion prosecution is still something of a special case, the record of successful prosecution has become genuinely impressive and the tax evasion conviction a sanction of some consequence. Experience such as this, however, gives little more than support for the plainly plausible assumption that criminal enforcement may play some part. One can not be sure of the extent to which other factors, not necessarily present in areas other than tax, created the conditions for optimum use of the criminal sanction as a moralizing weapon, or indeed, of the extent to which other influences rather than, or in addition to, the criminal sanction, produced the changed climate. The caution is further indicated (though, of course, not demonstrated) by less successful experiences in attempting to deal through the criminal law with behavior that did not attract any substantial degree of reprobatory unanimity,

Sanford H. Kadish

such as prohibition or gambling. At all events, Mannheim's caveat is a useful one: "It is only in a Soviet state and through a legal system on the lines of the Soviet penal code, which deliberately uses the political weapon of criminal prosecution to shape the economic system according to its ideology, that old traditions of such strength can be comparatively quickly destroyed."[11]

III

I have reserved for last those issues and concerns that arise out of goals other than the effectiveness of the criminal sanction in achieving compliance. Those which most prominently compete for consideration are: first, the sentiment of fundamental fairness—justice, in a word; and second, the retention of the vitality of the criminal law in its traditional sphere of application. They come into play in connection with two aspects of the use of the criminal law to enforce economic regulatory laws; namely, the loosening of minimum requirements for culpability in the cause of enforcement efficiency, and the criminalizing and punishing of behavior that does not generally attract the sentiment of moral reprobation.

A. REQUIREMENTS OF CULPABILITY

At several points attention has been called to the obstacles to effective prosecution created by certain conventional requirements of the criminal law; for example, the requirement of specificity in defining the prohibited conduct and the requirement of minimum conditions of accountability in holding persons responsible for the acts of others. Whatever basis these requirements have in the area of traditional crime, may they properly be diluted or dispensed with in the area of economic regulatory crime? The issue is fundamentally the same as that posed by the use of strict criminal liability, though, interestingly enough, this appears to have been much less commonly employed in economic regulation than in those controls on business directed to public health and safety.

The case for the irrelevance of these traditional requirements is reflected in the observation of a trust-buster of an earlier generation: "The rights of the accused which are of the utmost importance where liberty of an individual is in jeopardy, are irrelevant symbols when the real issue is the arrangement under which corporations in industry compete."[12] In essence the concept is that the purpose behind the criminal sanction in this area is not penalization, but regulation. Unlike the area of conventional crime against person and property where criminalization serves to reassure the community, to express condemnation and to set in motion a corrective or restraining regime, as well as to deter proscribed behavior, here the concern is solely with this last factor. "[T]he problem of responsibility is not the general social phenomenon of moral delinquency and guilt, but the practical problem of dealing with physical conditions and social or economic practices that are to be controlled."[13]

A countervailing consideration commonly adduced in discussions of strict liability is equally applicable where culpability requirements are otherwise withdrawn by statutes that do not adequately announce what is prohibited or that impose varieties of vicarious responsibility. Absent these requirements, it cannot be said, except in a strictly formal sense, that the actor made a choice to commit the acts prohibited. Hence, it is said that the law has no deterrent function to perform, offering no lesson to the actor or to other persons, beyond the Pickwickian instruction that even if he does the best he can, or anyone could, to comply with the law he may nonetheless be punished. Yet the argument does not quite persuade. For it may as plausibly be argued that the consequence of dispensing with the requirement of proof of culpability eases the task of the enforcing authorities, rendering successful prosecution more likely and, through discouraging insistence on trial and simplifying the issues when trials are held, enhances the efficiency of prosecution. In a word, certainty of conviction is increased. This may readily exert an added deterrent force upon the actor faced with a choice, since the chances of escaping punishment for a culpable choice, intentional or negligent, are decreased. And even where there is no immediate choice, the effect could sometimes be to influence persons to arrange their affairs to reduce to a minimum the possibilities of accidental violation; in short, to exercise extraordinary care. Further, the persistent use of such laws by legislatures and their strong support by persons charged with their enforcement makes it dogmatic to insist they can not deter in these ways.

Closer, perhaps, to the core of the opposition to dispensing with culpability is the principle that it is morally improper and ultimately unsound and self-defeating to employ penal sanctions with respect to conduct that does not warrant the moral condemnation that is implicit, or that should be implicit, in the concept of a crime. The issue is whether these considerations are adequately dealt with by the contention that laws dispensing with culpability are directed to regulation rather than penalization.

The contention plainly proves too much. If the sole concern is a non-reprobative deterrent threat, then it follows that the sanction should be drastic and certain enough to overcome the motive of economic gain, and not necessarily that the sanction should be criminal. Civil fines, punitive damages, injunctions, profit divestiture programs or other varieties of non-criminal sanctions would thus appear to offer equivalent possibilities of enforcing the regulatory scheme. Indeed, these alternatives might enhance the possibilities, since proof and evidentiary requirements are more onerous in criminal prosecutions than in civil suits. The conclusion appears difficult to resist that insistence on the criminal penalty is attributable to a desire to make use of the unique deterrent mode of the criminal sanction, the stigma of moral blame that it carries. If so, the argument of regulation rather than penalization turns out in the end to be only a temporary diversion that does not escape the need to confront the basic issue: the justice and wisdom of imposing a stigma of moral blame in the absence of blameworthiness in the actor.

So far as the issue of justice is concerned, once having put the moral question the footing becomes unsteady. Is the moral difficulty inconsequential, requiring simply the side-stepping of an otherwise useful symbol that happens to stand in the way of attaining immediately desirable goals? Does it yield to a pragmatic evaluation in terms of an estimate of the soundness of departing from principle to some degree in particular cases in order to attain goals of greater consequence?[14] Does it present an insuperable objection entailing commitment to values of such profundity that compromise is unthinkable? For present purposes it is perhaps enough to put the questions, though three points may be suggested. First, the starkness of the moral issue is to some degree assuaged by regarding laws dispensing with culpability as empowering enforcement officials to use their discretion to select for prosecution those who have in their judgment acted culpably. Plainly, however, the issue is not escaped since it remains to justify dispensing with the safeguards of trial on this single and crucial issue. Second, the recognition of the moral impasse does not necessarily require agreement that the criminal law *should* use its weapons for the purpose of fixing moral obloquy upon transgressors. It is sufficient that it is broadly characteristic of the way criminal conviction operates in our society. Third, and in consequence, the moral difficulty exists only so long as and to the extent that criminal conviction retains its aura of moral condemnation. The impasse lessens to the extent that the element of blame and punishment is replaced by a conception of the criminal process as a means of social improvement through a program of morally neutral rehabilitation and regulation. (Though such a development has important implications which I mean to return to shortly.)

Concerning the issue of ultimate wisdom, the point frequently made respecting strict liability is equally applicable to the dilution of these aspects of culpability typically at issue in economic regulatory legislation. The dilution is not readily confined within the narrow area for which it was designed, but tends to overflow into the main body of conventional crimes. The distinction between offenses that regulate and those that penalize in the traditional sense proves inadequate to divide the waters. For example, traditional concepts of liability in the main body of criminal law tend to receive a new and diluted form when construed as part of a regulatory statute. Moreover, the habituation of courts and legislatures to crimes dispensing with culpability in the regulatory area may readily dull legislative and judicial sensitivity to the departures from minimum culpability requirements already fixed in the main body of the criminal law. This expansion of criminality without culpability in statutory offenses and convictions, and its spread and solidification in the general criminal law heightens the moral difficulty. As the area expands and deepens it becomes necessary at some point to face the issue as entailing a judgment

Sanford H. Kadish

on the abandonment of principle rather than one on the wisdom of utilitarian compromise for a larger good. Moreover, the risks entailed in depreciating the impact of condemnation in a criminal conviction become greater to the extent that conviction without culpability becomes more common and pervasive. To the extent that the crucial distinguishing factor of the criminal sanction is "the judgment of community condemnation which accompanies and justifies its imposition,"[15] and to the extent that this characteristic contributes substantially to its effectiveness in influencing compliance with proscribed norms, the proliferation of convictions without grounds for condemnation tends in the long run to impair the identity of the criminal sanction and its ultimate effectiveness as a preventive sanction, both in the area of economic crimes and in the areas of its traditional application.

B. THE CRIMINALIZATION OF MORALLY NEUTRAL CONDUCT

But let it be assumed that the traditional grounds of culpability have been adhered to so that the defendant can fairly be held accountable for a choice to violate the economic prohibition. May there be costs, even so, in terms of principle and other goals, in employing the criminal sanction where the violative behavior does not attract in the community the moral disapprobation associated with a criminal conviction? How different and how similar are the considerations involved in dispensing with culpability? The question is the obverse of an aspect of the relation between criminal law and morals which has been much considered—the use of the criminal law to prohibit and condemn behavior that is widely (either actually or formally) viewed as morally reprehensible, where secular interests, in the sense of concerns beyond the immorality of individuals, do not exist.[16] Here the issue is the use of the criminal sanction to prohibit and condemn behavior that threatens secular interests, but that is not regarded as fundamentally and inherently wrong.

The central consequence of diluting or eliminating requirements of culpability is, as suggested, the criminalization and punishment of persons who cannot be said to warrant the condemnation thereby imported. It is this consequence that gives rise to the hard question of principle and practical consequences. In a sense a similar consequence follows from punishing conduct that is not itself blameworthy, even when culpably engaged in: Persons are stigmatized with conviction for conduct not regarded as deserving the moral stigma. The problem of principle, however, is of considerably smaller dimension, since the choice to act in defiance of the criminal prohibition may be regarded as in some measure furnishing an independently adequate ground for condemnation. (Yet it is necessary to add that the ground exists only in cases where the culpability requirements are extended to include knowledge or culpable disregard of the existence of the prohibition, an extension only occasionally made in regulatory legislation.)

The danger of debilitating the moral impact of the criminal conviction and hence decreasing the overall effectiveness of the criminal law can not as readily be put aside. As Professor Henry Hart has noted, "the criminal law always loses face if things are declared to be crimes which people believe they ought to be free to do, even wilfully."[17] It may be mitigated to a degree by maintaining a proper proportion in the punishment authorized for various offenses in accordance with the moral culpability of the behavior. The limitations of such a strategy are, first, that there is always a strong pressure to raise authorized penalties when violations become widespread or conspicuous, and second, that there is an irreducible minimum in the moral condemnation comported by conviction of crime. Such considerations have led one observer to "decry the trend toward an increasingly undiscriminating employment of this branch of the law, and to repudiate the suggestion that criminal law should be applied more extensively in the areas of ordinary economic relationships."[18]

It may of course be answereed that the conviction of violators of laws of this character serves as a means of moral instruction to the community; in short, that the onus of conviction is transferred to the behavior prohibited. That there will be a transference would appear quite likely. But that it should necessarily or generally be expected to involve imparting moral onus to the behavior rather than moral indifference to the conviction is considerably less so. The more widely the criminal conviction is used for this purpose, and the less clear the immorality of the behavior so sanctioned, the more likely would it appear that the criminal conviction will not only fail to attain the immediate purpose of its use but will degenerate in effectiveness for other purposes as well.

There is another cost not paralleled in the dilution of culpability requirements. The behavior under discussion involves restraints upon the free operation of business without at the same time denying commitment to a free enterprise system. The demarcation of the line between the legitimate, indeed the affirmatively desirable, and the illegitimate in business conduct is continually in flux and subject to wide controversy in the community. To say there is no complete consensus on what business decisions should be regulated and what left free of regulation is to say what is minimally true. It would not follow from this that a legislature should abstain from enacting such controls as command a majority. But the appropriateness of the criminal sanction as a means of enforcing the imposed control is another matter. I have already suggested that the criminal remedy in this situation tends to be ineffective and destructive of its overall utility as a sanctioning device. Here the point is different. To the extent it is effective in generating strong moral commitments to the regulatory regime it supports it has the dangerous potential of introducing a rigidification of values too soon, of cutting off the debate, or at least restricting the ease of movement to new positions and a new consensus. This seems to me the wisdom of Professor Allen's caveat that "the function of the criminal law in these areas is not to anticipate but to reflect and implement the consensus already achieved in the community."[19]

A word in conclusion on lines of legislative action. The widescale abandonment of the criminal sanction in those areas where its cost is excessive is as unlikely as it is desirable. Legislative habit and the simple logic of here and now expediency have a compulsion not to be denied by contemplation of long range consequences in areas removed from the immediate target of legislative concern. A more acceptable and hence more fruitful course is the development of means of reducing the costs of the use of the criminal sanction in economic regulations, which do not demand that it be abandoned altogether. If such means exist one would expect they would be found in ways of dealing with the central fact principally responsible for the predicament, the irreducible core of condemnation in a criminal conviction. One possible approach is to institutionalize a system of gradation of convictions, just as systems of grading punishment have long been a part of the law. There is no adequate basis for accomplishing this under present law. The distinction between offenses mala prohibita and mala in se carries something of the flavor, but it is an informal rather than an institutionalized distinction and lacks any clear meaning. The felony-misdemeanor distinction has an established statutory basis. However, the categories have largely lost significance in distinguishing degrees of blameworthiness, some misdemeanors embracing crimes of serious moral import, and some felonies embracing relatively minor transgressions. Moreover, there is need for a category of offense carrying considerably less weight than a misdemeanor. The petty offense category which appears in many statutes is essentially a petty misdemeanor, retaining its label as a crime and being punishable with imprisonment. In those cases in which the label has been removed, the substance (that is, provision for imprisonment) has not. The Model Penal Code has attempted to meet the inadequacies of existing law by adding to its three categories of crime (felonies, misdemeanors and petty misdemeanors) a separate noncriminal category designated a "violation" which is punishable only by a sentence of fine (under 500 dollars or any higher amount equal to double the pecuniary gain made by the offender)[20] or civil penalty,[21] and which does not "give rise to any disability or legal disadvantage based on conviction of a criminal offense."[22] The design of this proposal "reflects the purpose of the Code to employ penal sanctions only with respect to conduct warranting the moral condemnation implicit in the concept of a crime."[23] Since strict liability even for crimes properly so regarded presents the same problem, the same solution is applied by treating crimes committed without culpability as "violations."[24]

. . .

One can hardly say that this approach through a tertium quid is the clear answer to the problems of using criminal sanctions to enforce economic restrictions. There are many imponderables with respect to its effectiveness both as a preventive and as a

Sanford H. Kadish

means of reducing the costs of an indiscriminate use of the criminal sanction. On the side of preventive effectiveness, is the reprobative association of a genuine criminal conviction a needed weapon of enforcement? Would the semi-criminal category of offense convey enough of a sense of wrongness to perform its tasks? Can these laws be enforced efficiently enough without such associations? Is the loss of the power to imprison a substantial loss? Does what is left of the criminal process still provide efficiencies not available in the pure civil remedy? Will the regulatory offense prove politically acceptable to legislators and administrators as an alternative to outright criminalization? On the side of reducing costs, how much will it help that a new label has been created so long as the criminal process is used, or that imprisonment is not available as a sanction, when in fact it is rarely used anyway? And finally, is whatever is lost in effectiveness worth what is gained in other respects? One cannot be dogmatic in answering these questions. But one can, I think, insist that these are the kinds of questions which must be asked about this alternative as well as others if we are to escape the limited options inherited from different days in the use of the criminal sanction.

ABRAHAM S. GOLDSTEIN

M'Naghten: The Stereotype Challenged

The *M'Naghten* rule is the sole formula used by the courts of thirty states (and of Great Britain) to define insanity for the jury. In most of the remaining states, it is the first half of a two-part rule which includes the so-called "irresistible impulse" test.[1] The language of *M'Naghten* is fairly simple. It tells jurors

> "that every man is to be presumed to be sane, and . . . that to establish a defence on the ground of insanity, it must be clearly proved that, at the time of the committing of the act, the party accused was labouring under such a defect of reason, from disease of the mind, as not to know the nature and quality of the act he was doing; or if he did know it, that he did not know he was doing what was wrong."[2]

The general thrust seems clear. It emphasizes knowledge of the sanctions threatened by the criminal code while ignoring self-control. The tacit assumption is that powers of self-control are

Reprinted with permission of Yale University Press, copyright 1967, from Goldstein, *The Insanity Defense*, pp. 45–66 (1967).

Notes to this Selection will be found on pages 433–434.

Goldstein is Dean of the Law School and Cromwell Professor of Law at Yale University.

Abraham S. Goldstein

strengthened by knowledge of sanctions; and that any injustices which might result—to those who were nevertheless unable to control their conduct—are less important than exerting the maximum possible pressure toward conformity with law. The rule also seems to assume that the community at large, acting through the jury, would be willing to "exempt" offenders from the criminal law only if they obviously did not know what they were about. Nevertheless, important questions of interpretation arise. What illnesses are to qualify as "diseases" of the mind? Is "know" to include emotional appreciation of the impact of an act upon both offender and victim or is it to be limited to abstract awareness? Does "wrong" refer to legal or moral wrong? Given the age of *M'Naghten*, it would be reasonable to assume that every one of these questions, and countless others, had been construed again and again in judicial opinions or settled by statute. The fact is that there has been surprisingly little construction of the words in the hundred-odd years since they were first formulated.

Despite this lack of authoritiative interpretation, *M'Naghten* has long been a focal point of controversy. The rule has been condemned as retributive in nature, making scapegoats of offenders who could not possibly have done otherwise; and lauded as uniquely suited to serve the deterrent function of the criminal law. Until recently, the critics have been far more vocal than the defenders, at least in the learned journals, and it is the critics' *M'Naghten* which tends to dominate the debate. The picture they present is that of a restrictive rule which reflects an outmoded faculty psychology. It sees thought processes as separated into cognitive, emotional, and control components and classes a man as insane, as having a "defect of reason," only if he suffers from serious cognitive or intellectual impairment. This, the critics argue, is at odds with the "new psychology" which sees man's personality as dynamically integrated and his mental condition as necessarily unsound if any part of its functioning is disordered. The principal consequence of *M'Naghten* is said to be that it denies to the jury the "insights of modern psychology" because it restricts the flow of expert testimony. As a direct result, the insanity defense is said to be barred to the great majority of those who suffer from serious mental illness—because so few psychotics suffer from major cognitive impairment and most who do are so deteriorated that they will not be competent to stand trial. *M'Naghten* thus becomes an immoral instrument for condemning persons who may be psychotic and consigning them to prison where they will be punished, not treated; it keeps from the jury the "true" facts regarding the mental condition of the accused, so that the law can do its punitive worst.

I

This interpretation of *M'Naghten* has been dinned into the professional literature for so long that it is generally assumed there can be no other. As a result, the elimination of *M'Naghten* and willingness to adopt one of the newer rules, has been treated as a test of liberal faith. It is not at all certain, however, that this picture is an accurate one. If an adequate assessment is to be made, *M'Naghten* must be seen as it is presented to the jury and as the jury is likely to understand it. An examination must be made of its effect upon counsel contemplating whether to assert the insanity defense, upon the evidence admitted to prove and disprove the defense, and upon the expert testimony offered by the parties. But first, the words themselves must be examined as they have fared in the courts, to see what limits they set to the inquiry.

"DISEASE OF THE MIND"

There has been almost no judicial definition of mental disease in cases concerned with the *M'Naghten* rule. The reason commonly advanced is that the more detailed part of the rule—dealing with knowledge—makes it plain that only a limited number of psychoses and the most extreme forms of mental defect can qualify. In any event, the words are usually presented, without explanation, as part of the charge to the jury. What little law on the subject does exist is found in cases which reject efforts to assert insanity by persons whose mental conditions are clearly marginal. In this group are cases involving intoxication due to the use of alcohol, narcotics withdrawal, temporary insanity, and borderline mental defects.

The intoxication cases tell us that it is ordinarily not enough for the defendant to show that, at the time of the crime, his

Abraham S. Goldstein

thought processes were seriously distorted by alcohol or narcotics. And the "temporary insanity" cases tell us that it is not enough that the defendant acted during an "emotional frenzy." In others, the defense is said to be unavailable to "a person of weak intellect or one whose moral perceptions were blunted or ill developed."[3] In all these cases, the focus is not so much on whether the defendant entertained the requisite mental state at the time of the crime as it is upon whether he had, in addition, a disease—preferably one of "a fixed or prolonged nature." The cases are relatively silent, however, on which diseases would qualify. The question is not treated as one of law at all, but rather as if the necessary link can be provided by the testimony of expert witnesses. If they are willing to affirm that the frenzy, or the distortion, was attributable to a mental disease and are willing to name and describe the disease, then the issue will ordinarily be passed to the jury. The disease named most often is some form of psychosis, on the assumption that psychopathy and other nonpsychotic illnesses cannot qualify.

The only other cases touching directly on the definition of "mental disease" are those dealing with the question whether a mental "defect," such as a low I.Q. or some other form of mental retardation, can qualify. While discussions of the question are often unclear and while there are some cases to the contrary, the rule generally seems to be that such defects qualify as mental diseases. However, to exculpate the defendant, the defects must be so severe as to deprive him of the "knowledge" specified by *M'Naghten.*

"KNOW"

The word "know" has been at the center of the controversy surrounding *M'Naghten.* The bulk of the critics read it as referring to formal cognition or intellectual awareness alone. They distinguish this, the "law's" meaning, from what they describe as the "psychiatric" meaning—which they take to connote a fuller, deeper knowledge, involving emotional as well as intellectual awareness. This fuller knowledge can exist only when the accused is able to evaluate his conduct in terms of its actual impact upon himself and others and when he is able to appreciate the total setting in which he is acting. According to the critics, the law's type of knowledge is to be found even in the most serious psychoses. Indeed, to borrow from a well-known comment, it is absent only in the "totally deteriorated, drooling, hopeless psychotics of long-standing, and congenital idiots."[4] The consequence, the argument continues, is that *M'Naghten* directs jurors to hold responsible a great many persons who are seriously disturbed and makes successful assertion of the insanity defense virtually impossible. Moreover, since only a handful of psychotics can meet the requirements of "know," efforts to expand the concept of "disease" to include those who are not psychotic are doomed to fail. Indeed, there seems little point in trying—hence the lack of judicial definition of "mental disease."

The assertion that "know" is narrowly defined has been made so often and so insistently that it comes as a surprise to find that very few appellate courts have imposed the restrictive interpretation. Indeed, most of the courts which have addressed themselves to the question have favored a rather broad construction. In eleven states, the jury is told that an accused "knows" only if he "understands" enough to enable him to judge of "the nature, character and consequence of the act charged against him," or if he has the "capacity to appreciate the character and to comprehend the probable or possible consequences of his act." The California court noted recently, for example, that "our trial courts place a commendably broad interpretation upon the M'Naghten 'knowledge' test." Commenting on the Canadian practice which uses the broader wording, the Canadian Royal Commission on Insanity concluded that "the act must necessarily involve more than mere knowledge that the act is being committed; there must be an appreciation of the factors involved in the act and a mental capacity to measure and foresee the consequences of the violent conduct." In this view, the word "appreciate" draws most psychoses under the *M'Naghten* rules, because it addresses itself to the defendant's awareness of "the true significance of his conduct."[5] Even in the first *Durham* trial, the trial judge said it was necessary to determine whether the defendant "knew the difference between right and wrong in connection with governing his own actions," not as an abstract matter.[6]

In the remaining jurisdictions, some nineteen in number, the jury is simply given the words of the rule, without explanation,

Abraham S. Goldstein

and left to find the "common sense" meaning from their own backgrounds or from the materials presented to them at trial. Nowhere, however, are they told they must adopt a restrictive interpretation.

"NATURE AND QUALITY OF THE ACT"

The phrase "nature and quality of the act" is sometimes omitted completely from the charge to the jury. More often, it is either stated to the jury without explanation or treated as adding nothing to the requirement that the accused know his act was wrong. The underlying theory is that if the accused did not know the nature and quality of his act, he would have been incapable of knowing it was wrong. There have been a few efforts to treat the phrase as if it added something to the rule. In England, for example, it was suggested that "nature" meant the act's physical nature, while "quality" referred to its moral aspect. The court rejected the suggestion, holding that "nature and quality" refers solely to the physical character of the act.[7] In the United States, the rule seems to be similar, though the Wisconsin court has held that "nature and quality" gives "important emphasis" to the realization of the wrongfulness of an act. It marks the distinction between "vaguely . . . [realizing] that particular conduct is forbidden" and "real insight into the conduct."[8] This construction illustrates the close connection between the definition of "know" and that of "nature and quality." The broader reading of "nature and quality" carries with it the broader construction of "know" and vice versa. To know the quality of an act, with all its social and emotional implications, requires more than an abstract, purely intellectual knowledge. Likewise, to talk of appreciating the full significance of an act means that "nature and quality" must be understood as including more than the physical nature of the act.

"WRONG"

In those situations where the accused does not know the nature and quality of his act, in the broad sense, he will not know that it was wrong, no matter what construction "wrong" is given. But assuming both "know" and "nature and quality" are read narrowly and the defendant knows the physical nature of his act, does "wrong" mean moral or legal wrong? The *M'Naghten* judges said a person is punishable "if he knew at the time of committing such crime that he was acting contrary to law; by which expression we . . . mean the law of the land." The matter was somewhat confused by a second passage in the opinion:

> "If the question were to be put as to the knowledge of the accused solely and exclusively with reference to the law of the land, it might tend to confound the jury by inducing them to believe that an actual knowledge of the law of the land was essential in order to lead to a conviction; whereas the law is administered on the principle that every one must be taken conclusively to know it, without proof that he does know it. If the accused was conscious that the act was one which he ought not to do, and if that act was at the same time contrary to the law of the land, he is punishable."[9]

The English courts have sought to remove the ambiguity by holding that the accused must be aware that the act was legally wrong.

In the United States, the issue has seldom been raised. The word is generally given to the jury without explanation. Where it has been considered, the courts have split. One group holds that an offender is classed as sane if he knew the act was prohibited by law. A second group takes the position that "wrong" means moral wrong "according to generally accepted standards" and offers, as an illustration of insanity, the defendant who thought it morally right that he kill (e.g. because he was ordered to do so by God) but knew it was legally wrong. The opponents of *M'Naghten* have urged the adoption of this second view because of its seemingly liberalizing tendency. They are often unclear, however, whether "moral wrong" is to be judged by the personal standards of the accused or by his awareness that society views the act as wrong. The latter, which is probably the one meant by the courts, adds very little. This is because most cases involving the insanity defense will involve crimes sufficiently serious to make society's moral judgment identical with the legal standard. It might even be argued that in such cases society's moral condemna-

Abraham S. Goldstein

tion will be more apparent to the accused than the fact that he violated the law, so that the use of a standard of "moral" wrong would narrow the defense—

> "e.g. a man may think he has the defense of self-defense or superior order and yet feel it is immoral for him to kill. If the attempt to draw the distinction between moral and legal wrong adds little or nothing to the defense, the only reason for urging it must be that some writers see it as a way to broaden an otherwise narrow definition of 'know.' The apparent hope is to bring to the jury's attention the moral, and emotional, perspective of the defendant."

II

The most pressing questions about *M'Naghton* have as yet been left unanswered; the key words remain undefined or only partially defined. Portraying the rule as rigid and narrow and condemning it wholesale would seem, therefore, to be unjustified. It may be, however, that the rule's impact is felt not when the jury is instructed on the law, which is all we have considered thus far, but at other stages of the process—as when evidence of mental illness is offered, or when experts seek to explain the facts of mental disease. Certainly, the criticism most frequently made of *M'Naghten* is that it "keeps out evidence of the defendant's mental life," denying the jury "the true picture of the defendant's mental condition" and the "insights of modern psychology." This is presumably done by the trial judge who interprets the rule narrowly and admits only such evidence as satisfies its terms. But the critics seldom cite cases and leave unclear not only the kinds of evidence that will be barred but also the precise objections that would be leveled. For example, will the court exclude lay evidence of aberrational behavior by the accused at various times in his life? Will it exclude evidence of his teachers, or of psychiatrists, psychologists, or social workers who had contact with him in the past? Will it prevent a psychiatrist who examined him for purposes of trial from testifying in full regarding his examination? There is virtually no support in law for the view that

M'Naghten: The Stereotype Challenged

M'Naghten is responsible for inhibiting the flow of testimony on the insanity issue. Wigmore states the rule to be that when insanity is in issue, "any and all conduct of the person is admissible in evidence." And the cases support Wigmore's view. The almost unvarying policy of the courts has been to admit *any* evidence of aberrational behavior so long as it is probative of the defendant's mental condition, without regard to the supposed restrictions of the test used to define insanity for the jury.[10] For example, where the defendant's father testified "that defendant was a pale, delicate boy from birth and disposed to be melancholic," the court held the testimony to be relevant to the condition of the defendant's mind.[11] Indeed, virtually never does one see any attempt to restrict the sort of lay evidence which is a staple of the insanity defense—that the defendant wept, or that he was given to violent rages, or that he threatened to throw his child out the window.

Even when the evidence offered seems to fly in the very face of *M'Naghten*, it has been admitted. *State v. Carlson* is an excellent illustration because it involved evidence of lack of self-control, the principal area allegedly removed from consideration by *M'Naghten*. A medical witness was called to testify that an electroencephalograph test showed the defendant could not control his behavior. This testimony had been rejected by the trial judge because

"it appeared that . . . [the doctor] would attribute any misconduct to irresistible impulse, rather than lack of ability to distinguish between right and wrong, and only the latter is the test of insanity under Wisconsin law."

The Supreme Court of Wisconsin held that the trial court had erred:

"We are of the opinion . . . that if the offered testimony, together with other expert testimony, had sufficiently tended to prove that at the time of the offense, defendant was subject to a compulsion or irresistible impulse by reason of the abnormality of his brain, the testimony should have been admitted. *Even under the right-wrong test, no evidence should*

Abraham S. Goldstein

> *be excluded which reasonably tends to show the mental con-*
> *dition of the defendant at the time of the offense* [emphasis
> supplied]."

The reason, said the court in a later opinion, is that a defendant
who can show lack of the power to control his actions may generate a reasonable doubt in the minds even of jurors applying
the *M'Naghten* standard.[12] Another example of the breadth of
inquiry possible under *M'Naghten* is *State v. Wolak*.[13] There the
defendant had offered his criminal record into evidence as part of
an effort to prove he was a "constitutional psychopath." The trial
judge admitted the evidence but then charged the jury that such
evidence could be considered "for the sole purpose of determining his credibility as a witness." This was reversed on appeal
because a history of crime was an "essential link in the proof"
of psychopathy which was, in turn, probative of the insanity
defense. Yet another illustration is *State v. Foster*, in which a
psychiatrist testified that the defendant showed evidence of a
"psycho-neurotic reaction" and "some dissociative trends"; that
"even in minor disorders, one may have conditions that do render
the person incapable of discriminating right from wrong and
weighing a situation accurately and coming up with an accurate
judgment."[14] These cases are not exceptions to the rule. The
American Law Institute has reported that it found

> "no American case . . . where a trial court excluded evidence
> or refused to charge on a defense of insanity merely because
> the evidence in support of the defense related to neurosis or
> psychopathic personality or other mental disturbance rather
> than a psychosis."[15]

In fact, judicial statements on the matter are sometimes so sweeping as to suggest that there is no restriction on the admissibiliy of
evidence of a defendant's behavior when "insanity" is in issue,
and that "every act of the . . . [defendant's] life is relevant to
the issue and admissible in evidence."[16]

There is another facet to the argument of those who claim
that *M'Naghten* limits the evidence to be presented. This is the
complaint that the rule places the psychiatrist in a "straitjacket";

he is allegedly required to testify in terms of a definition of "know" which is limited to formal cognition and excludes any emotional appreciation of the act and its consequences. Here again there is no such general rule. Indeed, an analysis of numerous transcripts shows that the psychiatrist is regularly permitted to explain his interpretation of the words of the rule.

In *People v. Roche*, for example, Dr. Brody, a psychiatrist for the defense, testified that the dictionary defines "to know" as meaning "to perceive with full clarity." To a psychiatrist, he continued,

> "mere memory of details, or recitation of what has gone on, does not necessarily imply the knowledge, the full knowledge, the ethical consequences, or the moral consequences, or full understanding of what the man is doing. . . . A child, a reasonably bright child, or a schizophrenic, may say he hit someone with a club and bled from the scalp, or even that they die, and might go so far as to say that it is wrong to do so, but unless there is a certain amount of integration of the personality, and an ability to realize with full emotional clarity the consequences of his act, psychiatrists do not feel that such rote recitation of memory implies knowing, in the full sense."

He did not "see how a schizophrenic [like Roche] can perceive with full clarity." His conclusion, therefore, was that Roche did not know right from wrong at the time of the crime. For the prosecution, Dr. Herman defined "know" as referring to "an intellectual level," "a collection of information which is reasonably pertinent to . . . average individuals." In his view, Roche did know right from wrong at the time of the crime. The trial judge adopted neither construction of the critical word. Instead, he told the jury to use the "commonly accepted" meaning of "know," thereby passing to it the choice between the broad and the narrow views.[17]

Cases like *Roche* are quite common.[18] They present to the jury both testimony that the accused "verbalizes" that it is wrong to kidnap and also that he does not know right from wrong in the "broad sense"; that he was "intellectually aware of the nature and social consequences of his deed" and yet lacking in "a normal

Abraham S. Goldstein

emotional awareness of the impact this act might have on his own life or [that of his victim]"; that, in one sense, he knew what he was doing but, in another, he did not because of the "shallowness of [his] understanding . . . [and] insight"; or because "his judgment was blunted by the emotions and he would not bother about thinking about the effects of his acts on right or wrong." The choice among the conflicting interpretations is then made by the jury, which is aided in the matter by its common sense, by counsel in their closing arguments, and by its appraisal of the experts and of the entire case.

In short, *M'Naghten* does not preclude a presentation to the jury of "the true picture of the defendant's mental condition." The source of this line of criticism, and it is a recurring one, seems to be a misunderstanding of certain aspects of the trial process. Occurrences which should be passed off as rulings on procedure are seized upon as illustrations of the baleful influence of *M'Naghten*. This becomes quite evident if we look closely at the much-discussed case of *People v. Horton*. On direct examination, the defense presented several psychiatrists who were allowed to testify in the most detailed terms about the nature of defendant's mental illness—that he was schizophrenic, that his behavior was delusional, that he was "incapable of distinguishing a right from wrong." They were also permitted to explain fully their understanding of the meaning of the words of the *M'Naghten* rule. Among them was Dr. Brancale. He testified that the defendant could not be said to "know" what he was doing unless he was emotionally aware of the significance of his actions. On cross-examination the prosecutor tried to obtain affirmative answers to questions which would show the defendant to be following a "normal behavior pattern" and to be aware of the physical nature of his acts. Again and again, Brancale, anticipating the implications of his answers and assuming that they would point to the sanity of the defendant, tried to qualify his answer by referring back to his definition of the word "know." The trial judge informed him that he should confine himself to specific answers to the questions; and that any elaboration could be brought out by the defense on redirect examination. From then on, the trial judge struck portions of Brancale's answers as going beyond the scope of the questions asked. This action was affirmed by the New York Court of Appeals which pointed out that ample opportunity for exploring the full meaning of the word "know" had been provided on direct. They did not add, as they might well have done, that the defense made no effort to go into the matter once again on redirect examination.[19]

Horton illustrates not so much the failings of *M'Naghten* as it does the abrasive effect of the adversary process, particularly when its assumptions and procedures are not clearly understood. Certainly, it cannot be used to support the view that the meaning of "know" is the narrow one, or that psychiatrists will not be permitted to explain what they understand the word to mean. The case holds no more than that the evidence must be presented in the manner dictated by existing procedural rules, which would be applicable under any test of insanity.

III

This study of the effect of *M'Naghten* on various stages of the trial process has made it apparent that the case law is hardly well developed. Nevertheless, it can safely be said that existing rules of law do not force a narrow view upon the participants at trial. Generally, trial judges do not vary the *M'Naghten* formula and the trial judge imposes no restrictive interpretation when he charges the jury. But if all this is true, the question remains: what is it about *M'Naghten* which impedes the trial of the insanity defense? If the rule had not been the center of controversy for so long, it would be tempting to answer either with an emphatic "nothing at all" or "very little." However, the attacks on *M'Naghten* have been so persistent and have come from such substantial sources that a deeper explanation must be sought.

A first clue comes from the fact that there are forces in addition to the case law which define the scope of the insanity defense. The question of responsibility is, after all, presented through an adversary process which leaves the principal initiative to the parties. Judges will not ordinarily ask for evidence which is not presented to them. They will not rule on objections which are not made. They will not tell counsel and expert how to present their positions. However confident we may be that rules of law

Abraham S. Goldstein

do not deny the insanity defense to anyone suffering from serious mental illness, it hardly follows that the defense will be asserted by everyone who can qualify for it. The preconceptions of the participants may be as important as the rules of law in determining the effective scope of the defense.

The most important of these preconceptions is the operative assumption of psychiatrists and lawyers that the law regards insanity and psychosis as identical. Certainly, the trial of the insanity defense tends to revolve around the issue of psychosis. In their testimony, psychiatrists often define insanity as a "psychotic reaction" and psychosis as "the medical term for insanity." A man who does not have the symptoms of psychosis (e.g. "delusional beliefs" or "hallucinations") is "for that reason . . . considered to be sane." If he is "in contact with reality," then he is "sane in our sense."[20] Even as experienced a witness as Dr. Guttmacher testified that insanity required "delusions and hallucinations" or a "melancholic illness" or a suicidal "depression."[21] As the trial takes shape, the defense tries to bring its evidence within the framework of a psychosis, the prosecution outside it. For example, in *State v. Lucas*, defense psychiatrists characterized the defendant as suffering from "basic mental retardation which is congenital and a mental disease known as schizophrenia." The prosecution's experts described him as being of "low average mentality, . . . a psychopathic personality, . . . a sex deviate and a pyromaniac."[22] In *Mullin v. State*, the defense psychiatrist found the accused to be "schizophrenic, . . . psychotic, . . . suffering from delusions and hallucinations." The state's psychiatrist testified that the accused was a "psychopathic personality."[23]

Equating insanity with psychosis has two contradictory consequences. It confirms the earlier assertion that *M'Naghten* does not limit the defense to a small group of "totally deteriorated" psychotics. At the same time, it perpetuates the view that the "lesser" mental illnesses cannot qualify. The roots of the equation are to be found in the widespread assumption among lawyers that insanity describes medical entities, and among psychiatrists that psychosis is the only such entity which satisfies the law's requirements. The misunderstanding was facilitated by the tenets of pre-Freudian psychology which tended to see mental life as divided into discrete parts. And it reflected what is still the practice in civil commitment, which is the area of law most familiar to psychiatrists.

It would be misleading, however, to leave the impression that the continuing emphasis on psychosis is entirely a matter of drift. Underlying it is a more purposive element—the quite widespread feeling among psychiatrists that all psychotics *should* be regarded as insane and that *M'Naghten* restricts the defense to a small number of psychoses. Psychiatrists holding these views tend to regard the equation of insanity and psychosis as accomplishing ends which may be contrary to law but which are justified by a higher moral obligation. Adopting the equation as a private definition, they communicate the definition to no one and answer "no" to the *M'Naghten* questions even when they believe a "yes" is required. The dilemma, and the method of resolving it, is described by the Group for the Advancement of Psychiatry (GAP): The psychiatrist called upon to answer the *M'Naghten* questions finds himself compelled to sacrifice his "honesty" if "psychiatric truth" is to carry the day. He must, therefore, answer in accordance with a "tacitly understood convention" and aver that the mentally ill defendant did not know right from wrong, even when he did. The psychiatric witness, GAP continues, has little alternative:

> "For suppose he answers "no"—the defendant did not know the difference between "right and wrong." Now he has given the "legal" answer which conveys the psychiatric truth; the defendant is mentally ill. Next comes the cross-examination and the psychiatrist finds that he cannot relate any vital information about the defendant without contradicting himself . . . [T]he psychiatrist learns too late that the existence of psychosis as such at the time of the offense does not automatically exempt the offender from punishment. He knows that the psychosis about which he is testifying involves a very distinct appreciation of society's judgments of "right and wrong" but finds too late that in affirming this he has answered so as to convict the defendant."[24]

The most curious feature of the GAP statement is its assumption that the psychiatrist must testify falsely in order to provide "the psychiatric truth." The fact is, as we have seen, that there is nothing in the form of the *M'Naghten* questions, or in the directions of court or counsel, which prevents the psychiatrist from answering in accordance with *his* understanding of what the questions mean. If he is asked whether a psychotic "knows" right from wrong, he may properly construe "know" as he understands the word—as including emotional as well as intellectual components, deep as well as formal comprehension. Cross-examination would then not involve him in "contradicting himself" at all but only in explaining the assumptions underlying his testimony and in matching those assumptions with others presented by the cross-examiner in his questions.

The process described by GAP tends to perpetuate the *M'Naghten* stereotype in several ways: first, it gives seemingly authoritative support to the narrow view, while at the same time calling for its rejection; second, by adopting private definitions, psychiatrists deny the courts the opportunity to provide authoritative interpretations; third, those who feel they must manipulate the process in order to participate in it tend to come away with a feeling of distaste for the insanity issue and a reluctance to become involved with it, thus reducing the pool of psychiatrists likely to testify in ways which might produce broadening interpretations.

Another source of the misunderstanding about *M'Naghten*, perhaps the most important of all, is the tendency of psychiatrists to treat *jury* rejection of the insanity defense as if it represented "the law's" affirmation of the narrow interpretation. If, for example, the jury finds a defendant guilty when there was ample evidence that he was psychotic, even that his cognition was seriously impaired, the critics have held *M'Naghten* responsible. This overlooks, of course, the fact that the jury has the *power* to decide cases for reasons which have nothing to do with the instruction on the law. Indeed, the phenomenon of jury disregard of law, sometimes amounting to nullification, is well known. The risk of such disregard is particularly great when the crime charged is a serious one, exciting a full measure of retributive and deterrent feeling. Moreover, the criticism ignores the extent to which the jury decision may be based on appraisals of the credibility of witnesses, lay and expert, who testify on opposite sides of the same issue. Finally, it does not take adequately into account the inherent difficulty of recapturing, at the time of trial, the state of mind of the accused at the time of the crime.

Even if such considerations could be eliminated or held constant, the defense would probably be rejected quite often. Jurors find it difficult to accept the idea of serious mental disorder unless it is accompanied by visible and gross psychotic symptoms—either a breakdown in intellect or the loss of self-control. In this respect, they share the reluctance of most people to concede that persons who seem very much like themselves may be seriously ill. Under such circumstances, defense counsel is understandably reluctant to assert the defense unless his client is reasonably likely to be able to persuade the jury he is insane. The problem here is that public attitudes regarding crime and mental illness limit the practical utility of the insanity defense, in whatever form it may be cast and however freely evidence may be admitted.

Two additional reasons why the case law has not challenged the stereotype of *M'Naghten* are to be found in the hard facts of trial and appellate procedure. First, if a defendant does press for an expanded definition at trial and is acquitted, the prosecution will be unable to appeal because of established doctrines of double jeopardy. The expanded interpretation will not, therefore, be brought to the attention of an appellate court and will not be recorded in an appellate opinion. Second, if the trial judge does allow considerable freedom in presenting the defense and the accused is convicted, he will have no ground for appeal.

History, psychiatric convention, public attitudes, and procedure combine to sustain a narrow view of *M'Naghten* and, in a sense, to deny the legal process the opportunity to take a broader view. The stereotyped view is so firmly established in the popular culture of the insanity defense that it has been acted upon regularly by lawyers and psychiatrists. It has been said so often that "the law" refuses to accept the "insights of modern psychology"—that the only psychotic who can qualify is one so deteriorated that he could not muster the resources to commit a serious crime—that counsel rarely see any purpose in pursuing the issue. The result has been either premature abandonment of the defense or a token presentation, supported by little or no testimony describing in detail the life history of the accused, the parts of that history which demonstrate how his responses differ from the "normal," the extent to which he has developed control, etc.

The critics of *M'Naghten* may be correct in their allegation that many defendants who are seriously ill are arbitrarily excluded from the insanity defense. But the fault lies less with the formulation of the defense than with its presentation. The responsible parties are counsel and psychiatrist who have contributed to a failure of the adversary process, allowing an unwarranted assumption of what the rule "must" mean to govern their conception of the defense.

IV

The nagging questions about *M'Naghten* will be answered only if lawyers begin to play a more aggressive role than they have in the past. Only if evidence of insanity is offered whenever defense counsel thinks his client suffered from a mental illness at the time of the crime, and then forces prosecutors to object to such evidence and trial judges to rule it admissible or inadmissible, will we know whether the rule is restrictive at the trial level. Only if a convicted defendant urges on appeal that his evidence has been improperly excluded, or that his insanity defense should have been submitted to the jury, will we know whether appellate courts approve a narrow construction. Only if lawyers proffer constructions of "mental disease" or "know" or "nature and quality"—through requests for instructions, through their experts, or through their arguments to the jury—will we know authoritatively what courts intend these words to mean. It may be that when all these failures are repaired, *M'Naghten* will be a narrow rule. At present, the law does not make it one and defense counsel should make the most of the opportunities available to them to keep it from becoming one. They should present the defendant's life history in full biographical and clinical detail and have experts explain carefully not only their diagnoses but the relation of those diagnoses to the words of the rule, as they believe they should be construed. If this course is successful and is ultimately approved by the appellate courts, it would, of course, leave us a *M'Naghten* which is little more than a legal standard applied to "any" evidence of mental condition, monitored only by fairly liberal rules regarding burden of proof. But that is the *M'Naghten* we now have whenever defense counsel chooses to make it so.

On analysis, the heart of the criticism may well be *not* that the words need have a narrow construction, either as a matter of law or as a matter of psychiatry, but that they will be given such a construction; that laymen are so given to associating serious mental disease with cognitive impairment that unless they are told, explicitly and emphatically, that they are to treat the matter more broadly, they will vote their preconceptions. It would, of course, take but a word from the judge to bring home to the jury that they are required to construe "know" to include emotional as well as cognitive impairment. That word should be spoken. There is already ample authority for the courts to construe *M'Naghten* broadly—as requiring of the defendant that he have enough grasp of a total situation to appreciate the full consequences of action. Yet it would be a mistake to assume that the words of *M'Naghten* are infinitely expansible. Even the broadest of constructions is not likely to communicate sufficiently the idea that impaired control should lead to acquittal by reason of insanity.

JOSEPH GOLDSTEIN and JAY KATZ

Abolish the "Insanity Defense"— Why Not?

Prologue

The criminal law is one of many mechanisms for the control of human behavior. It defines conduct that is thought to undermine or destroy community values. It seeks to protect the life, liberty, dignity, and property of the community and its members by threatening to deprive those who contemplate such conduct and by inflicting sanctions upon those who engage in proscribed activity. The sanctions authorized, whether intended to punish, restrain, reform, or deter, constitute a deprivation of life, liberty, dignity and property. Because of the inherent conflict between the values ultimately to be preferred and their deprivation by the sanctions authorized, the criminal law has sought to minimize the consequences of this paradox

Reprinted by permission of The Yale Journal Company and Fred B. Rothman & Company from *Yale Law Journal*, Vol. 72, pp. 852–72 (1963).

Notes to this Selection will be found on pages 434–436.

Goldstein is Hamilton Professor of Law, Science and Social Policy at Yale University. Katz is Adjunct Professor of Law and Psychiatry at Yale University. He is coauthor with Goldstein, J. of Family and The Law *(1965).*

Joseph Goldstein and Jay Katz

through rules of law which restrict the state's authority to sanction. One of these rules, a fundamental restriction, is that before the state can inflict sanctions it must overcome the presumption of innocence which favors all of us—by establishing beyond a reasonable doubt each element of the offense charged.

By defining crimes in terms of such traditionally material elements as a *voluntary act purposely causing* a specific *result*, the law seeks to exclude from criminal liability those who are not "appropriate" subjects for a given sanction or indeed for any sanction. Thus, if the state fails to produce evidence which establishes each element of the crime or, put another way, if the accused introduces evidence which leaves in doubt any material element, no sanction can be imposed for the crime charged. To illustrate, the state cannot hold a person criminally responsible for murder if there was no causal relationship between the shot fired and the death of the victim; or if the shot was fired without the intent (*mens rea*) to kill, even though death was caused by the shot; or if the victim did not die even though the shot was fired with intent to kill. Recognizing that the elements of a given offense may not be sufficiently precise to exclude all those who ought to be free of criminal liability, the state, in order to maximize preferred values, has formulated exceptions which are called defenses. Thus, to prevent the state from actually encouraging criminal activity, the defense of police entrapment, for example, will relieve an offender of liability even if each element of the crime is established beyond doubt. The evaluation of any device for sorting out who is and who is not an appropriate subject for criminal sanction requires identifying the values in issue. No device haunts the criminal law and clouds the values it seeks to reinforce more than "insanity" as a basis for relieving persons of criminal responsibility.

Why Before What

Criminal responsibility results when each element of a crime charged against an accused has been established beyond a reasonable doubt. Only then is the state authorized to exercise its power to impose certain specified sanctions against the offender. "Insanity at the time of the offense," we are told, relieves the offending actor of criminal responsibility. This may mean either that "insanity" is to serve as *evidence* which precludes establishing a crime by leaving in doubt some material element of an offense, or that "insanity" is to serve as a *defense* to a crime, even though each of its elements can be established beyond doubt, in order to protect a preferred value threatened by the imposition of an authorized sanction.

"Insanity," however formulated, has been considered a defense. An evaluation of such a defense rests on first identifying a need for an exception to criminal liability. Unless a conflict can be discovered between some basic objective of the criminal law and its application to an "insane" person, there can be no purpose for "insanity" as a defense. Until a purpose is uncovered, debates about the appropriateness of any insanity-defense formula as well as efforts to evaluate various formulae with respect to the present state of psychiatric knowledge are destined to continue to be frustrating and fruitless.

To demonstrate the kind of analysis we think essential to a meaningful examination of insanity as a defense, we first analyze the concept of the defense of self-defense. If a person intentionally kills another human being, the criminal law, in support of a basic community objective—the protection of human life—defines such conduct as a crime and authorizes as the sanction life imprisonment of the offender.†

Few would disagree about the ultimate objective of protecting life and about the elements of the crime, but there may be little or no consensus about the sanction or its purposes. The imposition of life imprisonment rests on a variety of oft-conflicting and mutually inclusive assumptions shared by legislature, court and community about deprivation of liberty and its psychological significance. As *punishment*, life imprisonment is assumed to satisfy and channel the community's need to express feelings of vengeance or desires to effect rehabilitation of the offender. As *restraint*, it is assumed to remove from circulation a person who is believed likely to kill again, to provide a structure for satisfying community vengeance or to offer an institutional opportunity for care and rehabilitation. As *rehabilitation*, it is

† We exclude from our analysis . . . the death penalty which may accompany a finding of murder in the first degree, for feelings about that sanction are likely to distort the already complex issues to be unravelled.

Joseph Goldstein and Jay Katz

assumed to reduce the likelihood that he who has killed once will kill again, to increase the likelihood of returning a life to the community or to provide a basis for rationalizing community vengeance. As a *deterrent of others*, it is assumed to reinforce internal controls over the urge to kill through external threats of punishment, restraint, rehabilitation and the accompanying stigma. Thus, via a variety of assumptions which may or may not be related to an actual impact on any one offender or on other members of the community, life imprisonment becomes the sanction for one who kills another intentionally.

Intentional killing in defense of self, however, is an exception which denies the state authority to impose the sanction authorized for intentional killings. This exception "rests upon the necessity of allowing a person to protect himself from . . . [lethal] harm in cases where there is no time to resort to the law for protection."[1] Thus under circumstances where, by definition, one of two must die, the law seeks a solution least incompatible with its overall objective of protecting life by preferring the life of the "law-abiding" citizen. He is the man whose inner controls reinforced by the threat of external sanction hold in check his urge to kill except when his own life is jeopardized by someone not so deterred. The law thereby recognizes that the sanction for intentional killings is drained of any deterrent strength when external reality's system for protecting life fails and in turn releases internal reality's instinct for self-preservation. Conceptualized another way, authorizing the potential victim to kill his assailant constitutes a sanction which may be assumed to fulfill punitive, restraining, and deterrent functions in the service of the community's objective to safeguard human life. To generalize, when a situation is identified in which the application of the authorized sanction would conflict with basic criminal law objectives, a rational system of law would seek first to articulate why such an application is inappropriate and then to formulate the exception to accord with those objectives.

Having articulated the reasons for an exception to liability for intentional killings in defense of self, it becomes possible to evaluate such competing formulations as for example, (a) the actor's "right to stand his ground" and meet force with force, or (b) the actor's duty to "do everything reasonably possible to escape [without resorting] to the use of deadly force." Formulation (a) subordinates the value of safeguarding human life whenever possible to the values of safeguarding a threatened man's right to protect his interest in property as well as his right to be free from the stigma or uneasiness associated with cowardice. Formulation (b) prefers the value of safeguarding human life whenever possible. Conceptually, and probably in practice, the second formulation would best serve to protect both lives. Its application would restrict to a minimum the number of instances where reality leaves no choice and forces favoring one life over another. The sanction authorized for intentional killings, therefore, remains operative except in those situations where the choice is between one of two lives, not between, for example, life and an interest in property, pride or reputation.

With this framework for identifying a need for an exception to criminal liability and for evaluating formulations to meet such a need, we turn to an examination of the "insanity defense."

Like self-defense, the insanity defense applies, theoretically at least, only to persons against whom each of the elements of the offense charged could be established. Like defense of self, the defense of insanity, if successfully pleaded, results in "acquittal." But unlike the acquittal of self-defense which means liberty, the acquittal of the insanity defense means deprivation of liberty for an indefinite term in a "mental institution." And unlike the purpose of self-defense the purpose of the insanity defense either has been assumed to be so obvious as not to require articulation or has been expressed in such vague generalizations as to afford no basis for evaluating the multitude of formulae.

Neither legislative report, nor judicial opinion, nor scholarly comment criticizing or proposing formulations of the insanity defense has faced the crucial questions: "What is the purpose of the defense in the criminal process?" or "What need for an exception to criminal liabilty is being met and what objectives of the criminal law are being reinforced by the defense?"

The Royal Commission on Capital Punishment (1953) disposed of this issue with apodictic assurance by asserting:

"We make one fundamental assumption, which we should hardly have thought it necessary to state explicitly. . . . It has for centuries been recognized that, if a person was, at the time of his unlawful act, mentally so disordered that it would

Joseph Goldstein and Jay Katz

> be unreasonable to impute guilt to him, he ought not to be held liable to conviction and punishment under the criminal law. Views have changed and opinions have differed, as they differ now, about the standards to be applied in deciding whether an individual should be exempted from criminal responsibility for this reason; but the principle has been accepted without question. . . ."

Thus the Royal Commission reiterated the well-rounded proposition that "if a person was . . . mentally so disordered that it would be unreasonable to impute guilt to him, he ought not to be held [guilty, *i.e.*] liable to conviction and punishment." The Commission neither sought to identify the purposes of not imputing guilt to "individuals whose conduct would otherwise be criminal," nor did it ask why and when does the imputation of guilt for being "mentally so disordered" become "unreasonable." The Commission had no basis for evaluating the changing views and opinions "about the standards to be applied," and the principle "accepted without question" remained without meaning.

A century earlier the pattern had been firmly set of accepting an insanity defense without asking: "Why an insanity defense?" or more appropriately, "What objective of the criminal law suggests the need for an exception to the law's general application— an exception which would require taking into account the mental health of the offender?" In *M'Naghten's Case* (1843), the House of Lords, acting in their judicial, not legislative capacity, asked only what is the law respecting alleged crimes committed by persons afflicted with "insane delusions."[2] And the innovating court in *Durham* (1954), after promulgating a new formulation gave no guide to evaluating its adequacy beyond noting:

> "Our collective conscience does not allow punishment where it cannot impose blame. . . .
>
> "The legal and moral traditions of the western world require that those who, of their own free will and with evil intent (sometimes called *mens rea*), commit acts which violate the law, shall be criminally responsible for those acts. Our traditions also require that where such acts stem from and are the product of a mental disease or defect . . . moral blame

shall not attach, and hence there will not be criminal responsibility. . . ."[3]

The court leaves without definition and without identification of purpose such ambiguous words as "punishment," and "blame," and thus in effect only says "he who is punishable is blameworthy and he who is blameworthy is punishable." Never established is the relevance of these words to a defense which would compel supposedly different dispositions of persons involved in activity labeled "criminal." Moreover, the court, though not blinded by precedent, left unasked and therefore unanswered: "What underlies the 'legal and moral traditions' in 'our collective conscience' which prevents us from inquiring why a rule is required?"

Likewise, the American Law Institute (1956–1962) provides no basis for evaluating its formula for a defense of insanity.[4] With focus on consequences, it "explains," echoing the Royal Commission and *Durham*, that the purpose of the insanity defense is "to discriminate between the cases where a *punitive-correctional* disposition is appropriate and those in which a *medical-custodial* disposition is the only kind that the law should allow." Once "*punitive*" is substituted for "*custodial*" and "*correctional*" for "*medical*," or however the terms are juxtaposed in the ALI statement the "distinctions" seem to disappear.† Moreover, criteria for evaluating what constitutes an "appropriate" disposition for either category remain unarticulate. Thus those characteristics which

† Similar confusion in judicial reasoning is reflected in the following statement: Two policies underly [*sic*] the distinction in treatment between the responsible and the non-responsible: (1) It is both wrong and foolish to *punish* where there is no blame and where *punishment* cannot correct. (2) The community's security may be better protected by hospitalization . . . than by imprisonment. *Williams v. United States*, 250 F.2d 19, 25–26 (D.C. Cir. 1957). (Emphasis supplied.) "Punish" and "punishment" are used in policy statement "(1)" to suggest different underlying meanings or concepts. The word is first used as a symbol of the vengeance or retribution function of the criminal law and then used as a symbol of the rehabilitation function. *Query:* If "punishment," however defined, were an effective rehabilitative device would the court find its use objectionable even if blameworthiness could not be established? Is involuntary confinement for an indefinite period in a mental hospital any less a deprivation, as the court seems to imply in policy statement "(2)," than involuntary confinement for a limited period in prison? Goldstein, J., "Police Discretion Not to Invoke the Criminal Process: Low-Visibility Decisions in the Administration of Justice," *Yale Law Journal*, Vol. 69, pp. 543, 546 (1960).

determine who is to fit into which category remain unidentified. This may be because the distinctions between alternative responses are never clarified. Finally, a Committee of distinguished doctors, lawyers and religious leaders, appointed by the Governor of New York (1958) to improve the defense of insanity, pronounced before formulating their rule:

> "We are unanimously of the view that there are compelling practical, ethical and religious reasons for maintaining the insanity defense; . . . . We believe . . . that it is entirely feasible to cast a formulation which . . . will sufficiently improve the statute to meet working standards of *good morals, good science,* and *good law.*"[5]

Never identified are the reasons labeled "practical," "ethical," and "religious," or the standards labeled "good morals," "good science" and "good law."

In enunciating yet another formula for insanity, the Court of Appeals for the Third Circuit in *United States v. Currens* (1961) contaminates its thinking by confusing and merging the inherently incompatible concepts of "insanity" as a defense to a crime with "insanity" as evidence to cast doubt on a material element of an offense. It suggests, as did the court in *Durham,* that some relationship exists between the insanity defense and *mens rea,* a material element of every major crime. In *Currens, mens rea* (guilty mind) is used to mean that criminal liability rests

> ". . . on the assumption that a person has a capacity to control his behavior and to choose between alternative courses of conduct. . . . When a person possessing capacity for choice and control, nevertheless breaches a duty . . . he is subjected to . . . sanctions not because of the act alone, but because of his failure to exercise his capacity to control. . . . For example, an act of homicide will create no liability, only civil liability or varying criminal liability depending on the nature of the mental concomitant of the act. Generally the greater the defendant's capacity for control of his conduct and the more clearly it appears that he exercised his power of

choice in acting, the more severe is the penalty imposed by society."

And the court criticized the *Durham* and *M'Naghten* formulae because:

"They do not take account of the fact that an "insane" defendant commits the *crime* not because his mental illness causes him to do a certain prohibited act but because the totality of his personality is such, because of mental illness, that he has lost the capacity to control his acts in the way that the normal individual can and does control them. If this effect has taken place he must be found not to possess the guilty mind, the *mens rea*, necessary to constitute his prohibited act *a crime*."[6]

At this point the court by the force of its own reasoning *should* have been led to say:

"*Without the essential element of* mens rea, *there is no crime from which to relieve the defendant of liability and consequently, since no crime has been committed, there is no need for formulating an insanity defense.*"

But instead the court actually concludes:

"We are of the opinion that the following [insanity] formula most nearly fulfills the objectives just discussed. . . ."[7]

The court uses the word "crime" first to mean "dangerous conduct" and then, without alerting itself to the shift, to mean technically the establishment beyond doubt of each material element of an offense. With this sleight of thought the court shifts focus from "insanity" as a *defense* to conduct "otherwise criminal" to insanity as *evidence* to negate an element essential to categorizing the accused's conduct "criminal."

In announcing a new formula for the insanity defense, the court fails to recognize that there is no need for such a defense to remove criminal liability since it has concluded that no crime is

Joseph Goldstein and Jay Katz

established once mental illness (however defined) has cast doubt on *mens rea* (however defined). Conceptually, at least, outright acquittal would result and instructions to the jury would reflect a time, pre-*M'Naghten*, when evidence of mental condition, like any other relevant evidence, was used to cast doubt on a material element of the crime.[8]

In our efforts to understand the suggested relationship between "insanity" and "*mens rea*" there emerges a purpose for the "insanity defense" which, though there to be seen, has remained of extremely low visibility. That purpose seems to be obscured because thinking about such a relationship has generally been blocked by unquestioning and disarming references to our collective conscience and our religious and moral traditions. Assuming the existence of the suggested relationship between "insanity" and "mens rea," the defense is not to absolve of criminal responsibility "sick" persons who would otherwise be subject to criminal sanction. Rather, its real function is to authorize the state to hold those "who must be found not to possess the guilty mind, *mens rea*,"[9] even though the criminal law demands that no person be held criminally responsible if doubt is cast on any material element of the offense charged. This, in some jurisdictions, is found directly reflected in evidentiary rules making inadmissible testimony on mental health to disprove a state of mind necessary to constitute the crime charged. A more dramatic expression of abandoning the rule of proof of each element beyond a reasonable doubt has slipped into those instructions to the jury which advise the ordering of deliberations:

> "If you find the defendant not guilty by reason of insanity, you will render a verdict of not guilty by reason of insanity.
> *"If you do not so find, then you will proceed to determine whether he is guilty or innocent* of one or both of the offenses charged on the basis of the same act.
> "[T]here are two principal issues for you to determine. The *first* is his mental condition and the *second* is whether he committed the offenses charged or whether he is innocent of them. . . .
> "Now, on the issue of guilt or innocence of the offenses charged, the essential elements of the first count or the house-

breaking count, *if you do not find the defendant not guilty by reason of insanity*, are as follows:

First, that the defendant broke and entered or entered without breaking . . . the place described in the indictment;

Second, that the place entered was occupied or belonged to the complaining witness; and,

Third, that he *intended* to steal or commit the offense of larceny. . . ."

Yet, since a verdict of not guilty results in outright release and a verdict of not guilty by reason of insanity results in incarceration, jury instructions must require *first* a determination of innocence or guilt and *second* a consideration of the insanity issue *only* after a determination that guilt can be established.

What this discussion indicates, then, is that the insanity defense is not designed, as is the defense of self-defense, to define an exception to criminal liability, but rather to define for sanction an exception from among those who would be free of liability. It is as if the insanity defense were prompted by an affirmative answer to the silently posed question: "Does *mens rea* or any essential element of an offense exclude from liability a group of persons whom the community wishes to restrain?" If the suggested relationship between *mens rea* and "insanity" means that "insanity" precludes proof beyond doubt of *mens rea* then the "defense" is designed to authorize the holding of persons who have committed no crime. So conceived, the problem really facing the criminal process has been how to obtain authority to sanction the "insane" who would be excluded from liability by an overall application of the general principles of the criminal law.

Furthermore, even if the relationship between insanity and "*mens rea*" is rejected, this same purpose re-emerges when we try to understand why the consequence of this defense, unlike other defenses, is restraint, not release. Even though each of the elements of an offense may be established, release will follow acquittal or dismissal if, for example, entrapment, self-defense, or the statute of limitations are successfully pleaded. Assuming, then, that all elements of an offense are to be established before the insanity defense becomes operative, the question remains: "Why restrain rather than release?" Restraint cannot be attributed to

Joseph Goldstein and Jay Katz

potential "dangerousness" associated with the crime charged, no matter how serious, for that kind of "dangerousness" is characteristic of defendants whose defenses prevail. The crucial variable leading to restraint seems to be the "insanity at the time of the offense," *i.e.*, a fear of danger seen in the combination of "mental sickness" and "crime." This fear of freedom for those acquitted by reason of insanity comes sharply into focus at the close of the *Currens* decision. The court, uncertain of the consequences of such an acquittal for federal offenses outside of the District of Columbia, warns, in reversing the judgment of conviction: "[W]e are concerned with the disposition of Currens should he be found not guilty by reason of insanity. . . . In any event [in the light of doubt about the appropriate federal procedure for commitment] should Currens be acquitted at his new trial, the federal authorities should bring him and his condition to the attention of State authorities to the end that he may not remain in a position in which he may be a danger to himself or to the public." That mandatory commitment, not release, generally follows the insanity defense becomes then particularly striking since, to the extent "insanity at the time of offense" is related to "mental health at the time of acquittal," the state is authorized to select from the mentally ill those who require civil restraint for custody and care. Thus the insanity defense is not a defense, it is a device for triggering indeterminate restraint.

The real problem which continues to face legislators, judges, jurors, and commentators is how to restrain persons who are somehow feared as both crazed and criminal. This oft-unconscious fear has precluded thinking about "insanity" in terms of traditional principles of law, whether that "insanity" is conceptualized as doubt-casting evidence or as an independent defense. Though unpleasant to acknowledge, the insanity defense is an expression of uneasiness, conscious or unconscious, either about the adequacy of such material elements of an offense as "*mens rea*" and "voluntariness" as bases for singling out those who ought to be held criminally responsible, or it is an expression of concern about the adequacy of civil commitment procedures to single out from among the "not guilty by reason of insanity" those who are mentally ill and in need of restraint.

The problem of "whether there should be an insanity defense" or "how to formulate it" must continue unresolved as long as largely unconscious feelings of apprehension, awe, and anger toward the "sick," particularly if associated with "criminality," are hidden by the more acceptable conscious desire to protect the "sick from criminal liability." What must be recognized is the enormous ambivalence toward the "sick" reflected in conflicting wishes to exculpate and to blame; to sanction and not to sanction; to degrade and to elevate; to stigmatize and not to stigmatize; to care and reject; to treat and to mistreat; to protect and to destroy. Such ambivalence finds expression in legislative proposals that persons acquitted by reason of insanity be "committed to the custody of the commissioner of correction [not mental health] to be placed in an appropriate institution of the department of correction [not mental health] for custody, care, and treatment."[10] And such ambivalence has blinded lawmakers to their tampering, via the insanity defense, with fundamental principles on which their authority to impose criminal liability presently rests. By obfuscating the function of the defense in terms of the ethical and religious values of Western civilization to care for the "sick," lawmakers have not only misled themselves but psychiatrists as well who, confused by their own ambivalence, have willingly, defiantly, unquestioningly, or with misgivings, joined in these deliberations. Psychiatrists have participated in the process without identifying the role they must play and without forcing the process to clarify that role. The plea to care for the "sick" muffles the call to segregate the "dangerous" whom the criminal law can not hold. With the real problem so disguised, the fruitless and frequent searches for new formulae and the frustrating and fighting exchanges between law and psychiatry become somewhat understandable. Thus, another low visibility purpose of the insanity defense emerges. That purpose is to keep sufficiently ambiguous the consequences of the defense, whatever the formula, so as to prevent at least conscious recognition that the prerequisites of criminal liability have been abandoned.

Lawmakers could decide to implement any or all of these now visible purposes. Provisions could be drafted to restrain: (1) persons *charged* with a crime who are feared to be dangerous and/or felt to need care and destigmatization because of a suspicion of criminality coupled with a finding of mental sickness; (2) persons

Joseph Goldstein and Jay Katz

acquitted outright of a crime who are feared to be dangerous and/ or felt to need care and destigmatization because of criminality coupled with a finding of mental sickness; and (3) persons who have *committed* a crime and are feared to be dangerous and/or felt to need care and destigmatization because of criminality coupled with a finding of mental sickness. In promulgating such provisions, answers are required to a series of question which must be consciously posed about *restraint*—restraint in what kind of an institution and for how long; restraint for what crimes and for what mental illnesses; and restraint at whose initiative and at what stage in the process. In responding to these questions lawmakers will be pouring meaning into "the fear of dangerousness," "the need for care," and the "need for destigmatization." And if obfuscating developments are to be avoided, lawmakers not only must acknowledge wishes to neglect, stigmatize, punish and destroy, but they must also consider the extent to which these wishes are to be realized through *restraint*. Awareness that such wishes constantly press for satisfaction in conflict with preferred goals should stimulate the development of formulations and procedures designed to maximize consciously thought-through preferences and to deflect those conflicting and otherwise unconscious wishes which might gain satisfaction under cover of these preferences. The operational significance of key phrases in any formulation will thus be shaped and joined by the values to be preferred.

But such efforts by lawmakers to formulate an exception to criminal liability would be premature and may prove unnecessary. More appropriately they should consider abolition of the insanity defense, and examine "voluntariness" and "mens rea" as requisites of criminal liability. Enormous confusion about the meanings of these concepts in the definition of offenses and their construction by the courts suggests that there will be great difficulty in establishing the purposes of these material elements as devices for sorting out those to be or not to be subject to criminal sanction. The need for such concepts must be examined in terms of the overall objectives of a law of crimes. Furthermore, abolition of the "insanity defense" should force focus on the why and the adequacy of criteria for civil commitment and discharge of the "mentally ill." The question underlying each of these examinations must be: "Who are to remain free of state intervention; who ought to be restrained, and for what purposes?" Ultimately this requires coming to terms with such emotionally-freighted concepts as "blame," "choice," "free will," "capacity-to-control," and "determinism," all of which, in the criminal law, have remained slogans of exhortation beyond the reach of definition. Will such explorations lead to an insanity defense? If they do, we must know *why*. . . .

Notes[†]

NOTES TO *Cohen: Moral Aspects of the Criminal Law*

1. GAROFALO, *Criminology* (Tr. Millar, 1914) p. 4.
2. *Id.* p. 215.

NOTES TO *Nelson: Emerging Notions of Modern Criminal Law in the Revolutionary Era*

1. See, e.g., Law and Authority in Colonial America (G. A. Billias ed. 1965); J. Goebel & T. R. Naughton, Law Enforcement in Colonial New York (1944); A. P. Scott, Criminal Law in Colonial Virginia (1930); R. Semmes, Crime and Punishment in Early Maryland (1938).
2. See, e.g., G. L. Haskins, Law and Authority in Early Massachusetts (1960); E. Powers, Crime and Punishment in Early Massachusetts 1620–1692 (1966). Seven of the ten articles in Law and Authority in Colonial America (G. A. Billias ed. 1965) concern Massachusetts.
3. Haskins, supra note 2, p. 16.
4. Grand Jury Charge by Hutchinson, C. J., Suffolk Super. Ct., March 1768, in J. Quincy, Reports of Cases Argued and Adjudged in the Superior Court of Judicature of the Province of Massachusetts Bay, Between 1761 and 1772, pp. 258, 259 (S. Quincy ed. 1865).
5. Engel v. Vitale, 370 U.S. 421, 425 (1962).
6. Grand Jury Charge by Cushing J., Nantucket Super. Ct., Aug. 1742, William Cushing Papers (mss. at Massachusetts Historical Society, Boston, Mass.).
7. See Grand Jury Charge by Cushing, J., Nantucket Super. Ct., Aug. 1742, in William Cushing Papers.
8. M. Foster, A Report on Some Proceedings on the Commission of Oyer, Terminer and Gaol Delivery for the Trial of Rebels in the Year 1746 in the County of Surry, and of other Crown Cases, pp. v–vi (1767).

† The editors have retained a very limited number of the footnotes which appeared in the original version of each selection. For those footnotes the numbers have been changed so that they are consecutive within each piece.

9. Remarks on the Existing State of the Laws of Massachusetts Respecting Violations of the Sabbath, p. 3 (1816).

10. See P. Goodman, The Democratic-Republicans of Massachusetts 89 (1964).

11. T. Dwight, A Discourse on Some Events of the Last Century, delivered Jan. 7, 1801, quoted in V. Stauffer, New England and the Bavarian Illumin, Vol. 82, Columbia University Studies in History, Economics, and Pub. L., 25 (1918).

12. W. Cushing, Notes on Biennial Elections and Other Subjects Under Debate in Massachusetts Ratifying Convention, Jan. 1788, in William Cushing Papers.

13. V. Stauffer, supra note 11, p. 26.

14. V. Stauffer, supra note 11, p. 26.

15. O. Handlin & M. F. Handlin, Commonwealth; a Study of the Role of Government in the American Economy: Massachusetts, 1774–1861, p. 35–36, 59–64 (1947); S. E. Morison, The Maritime History of Massachusetts 1783–1860, pp. 30–32, 35–36 (Sentry ed. 1961); W. B. Weeden, 2 Economic & Social History, New England 1620-1789, p. 843 (1890).

16. J. Quincy, Remarks on Some of the Provisions of the Laws of Massachusetts Affecting Poverty, Vice and Crime (1822).

17. Speech by His Excellency Caleb Strong, Esq., Before the Senate and House of Representatives of the Commonwealth of Massachusetts, Jan. 15, 1802, in Patriotism and Piety: the Speeches of His Excellency Caleb Strong, Esq., pp. 48, 50 (1808).

18. Commonwealth v. Andrews, 2 Mass. 14, 31 (1806).

19. Address by Governor John Hancock to a Joint Session of the Massachusetts Legislature, Jan. 31, 1793, quoted in Powers, Crime and Punishment in Early Massachusetts, pp. 192–93 (1966).

20. G. Bradford, State Prisons and the Penitentiary System Vindicated, p. 5 (1821).

21. G. Bradford, Description and Historical Sketch of the Massachusetts State Prison, p. 15 (1816).

22. G. Bradford, supra note 20, p. 12.

23. T. B. Chandler, A Friendly Address to All Reasonable Americans on the Subject of Our Political Confusions, p. 5 (1774), quoted in 1 Pamphlets of the American Revolution, 1750–1776, pp. 198–99 (B. Bailyn ed. 1965).

24. Grand Jury Charge by Hutchinson, C. J., Suffolk Super. Ct., Aug. 1766, J. Quincy, Reports of Cases Argued and Adjudged in the Superior Court of Judicature of the Province of Massachusetts Bay, Between 1761 and 1772, pp. 218-220 (S. Quincy ed. 1865).

25. Grand Jury Charge by Hutchinson, C. J., Suffolk Super. Ct., March 1, in J. Quincy, supra note 24, p. 110.

26. 1 Diary and Autobiography of John Adams, p. 260 (Butterfield, Faber & Garrett eds. 1961).

27. Letter From Oliver Prescott, Town Clerk of Groton, Mass., to Town of Boston, Mass., 1774, quoted in 12 C. K. Shipton, Sibley's Harvard Graduates 1746–1750, p. 570 (1962).

28. Grand Jury Charge by Hutchinson, C. J., Suffolk Super. Ct., Aug. 1776, in J. Quincy, supra note 24, pp. 218, 219.

29. Proclamation of the General Court, Jan. 23, 1776, in O. Handlin & M. F. Handlin, The Popular Sources of Political Authority, p. 68 (1966).

30. Draft of Grand Jury Charge by Cushing, C. J., 1783, in William Cushing Papers 21.
31. Msex Gen. Sess., Sept. 1786, pp. 396–97.
32. Message from Governor Hancock to the General Court, 1793, quoted in Powers, supra note 19, p. 193.
33. P. Miller, From the Covenant to the Revival, in 1 Religion in American Life 322, 354 (Smith & Jamison eds. 1961).
34. Commonwealth v. Waite, 5 Mass. 261, 264 (1809).
35. G. Bradford, supra note 20, p. 51.

NOTES TO *Erikson: On the Sociology of Deviance*

1. Emile Durkheim, *The Rules of Sociological Method,* translated by S. A. Solovayn and J. H. Mueller (Glencoe, Ill.: The Free Press, 1958), p. 67.
2. Emile Durkheim, *The Division of Labor in Society,* trans. George Simpson (Glencoe, Ill.: The Free Press, 1960).

NOTES TO *Wheeler: Criminal Statistics: A Reformulation of the Problem*

1. Sellin, *The Basis of a Crime Index,* 22 J. Crim. L. & C. 346 (1931).
2. Sellin & Wolfgang, *The Measurement of Delinquency,* pp. 82–114 (1964).
3. VanVechren, *The Tolerance Quotient as a Device for Defining Certain Social Concepts,* Am. J. Sociol., Vol. 46, pp. 35–42 (1940).
4. Mercer, *Social System Perspective and Clinical Perspective: Frames of Reference for Understanding Career Patterns of Persons Labelled as Mentally Retarded,* Soc. Probs., Vol. 13, 18 (1965).
5. Sabagh, Eyman & Cogburn, *The Speed of Institutionalization: A Study of a Preadmission Waiting List Cohort in an Institution for the Retarded,* unpublished manuscript.
6. Teele & Levine, *The Acceptance of Emotionally Disturbed Children by Psychiatric Agencies,* in Wheeler, *Controlling Delinquents,* Ch. 5 (1967).
7. Bell, *The Myth of Crime Waves,* in *The End of Ideology,* pp. 137–158 (1960).
8. Wilson, *The Police and the Delinquent in Two Cities,* in Wheeler, *Controlling Delinquents,* Ch. 2 (1967).
9. Greenhaigh, *A Town's Rate of Serious Crime Against Property and Its Association with Some Broad Social Factors,* Home Office, Scientific Advisers Branch, February 1964.
10. Goldman, *The Differential Selection of Juvenile Offenders for Court Appearance,* National Council on Crime and Delinquency, 1963.
11. Maccoby, et al., *Community Integration and the Social Control of Juvenile Delinquency,* J. Soc. Issues, Vol. 3, p. 38 (1958).

NOTES TO *Goldstein, J.: Police Discretion not to Invoke the Criminal Process: Low-visibility Decisions in the Administration of Justice*

1. The low visibility of these decisions must in a sense be preserved because of the author's obligation not to identify informants or the police de-

partment involved by specific citations to American Bar Foundation, *Pilot Project Report—The Survey of the Administration of Criminal Justice* (1957), or to supporting field reports. To effectuate the Foundation's policy of maintaining the anonymity of the police department and its officers, no citations to statutes, case law, or legislative hearings of the state or local jurisdiction, as well as congressional hearings, will be given when such citations would compromise confidentiality.

2. *Mich. Stat. Ann.* § 5.1752 (1949).
3. *E.g., Atlanta, Ga., Police Dep't Rules & Regs.*, rules 23 (Police Chief), p. 44 (Super. of Detectives), p. 282 (Super. Traffic Div.), p. 297 (Traffic Capt.), p. 332 (Traffic Lt.), p. 372 (Traffic Patrolman), p. 400 (Super. Uniform Div.), p. 412 (Field Capt. Uniform Div.), p. 479 (Patrolman Uniform Div.) (1958).
4. Letter From W. W. Vernon to Joseph Goldstein, Sept. 24, 1958.
5. Police Academy, Oakland, Cal., Police Dep't, Instructors' Material, Vol. 6, Bull. No. 35, Aug. 26, 1957, p. 3:

Felony Assaults	Reported to Police	Arrests	Charged
(For year 1956)	618	350	67
(1st 6 mos. of 1957)	394	197	62
Misdemeanor Assaults			
(For year 1956)	2631	941	454
(1st 6 mos. of 1957)	1322	522	not available

(Note the difference between the number arrested and the number charged. *The difference is attributed to the fact that the type of people involved do not prosecute in physical assault cases.*) (Emphasis added.)
6. Ibid., "In 1956 86.5% of the reported Misdemeanor Assults were cleared, and 53.4% of these Clearances were on the basis of non-cooperation of complainants. In the first quarter of 1958 the Clearance Rate was up to 92.9% and only 15.9% of these cases were cleared as Complainant Refuses to Prosecute." Ibid.
7. Ibid.

NOTES TO *Goldstein, A. S.: The State and the Accused: Balance of Advantage in Criminal Procedure*

1. United States v. Garsson, 291 Fed., 646, 649 (S.D.N.Y. 1923) (motion to inspect grand jury minutes denied).
2. Ibid.
3. James, Accident Liability: Some Wartime Developments, *Yale Law Journal*, Vol. 55, pp. 365, 388 (1946). . . .
4. 227 Fed., 788, 792 (8th Cir. 1915). . . .
5. 160 F.2d 229, 232 (D.C. Cir.), *cert. denied*, 331 U.S. 837 (1947). . . .
6. The leading opinions are those of Judge Clark in United States v. Valenti, 134 F.2d 362, 364 (2d Cir.), *cert. denied*, 319 U.S. 761 (1943) ("The requirement of proof beyond a reasonable doubt is a direction to the jury, not a rule of evidence; . . . it cannot be accorded a quanti-

tative value other than as a general cautionary admonition. . . . It is the court's function to decide whether evidence is competent to justify certain inferences."), and of Judge Learned Hand in United States v. Feinberg, 140 F.2d 592, 594 (2d Cir.), *cert. denied*, 322 U.S. 728 (1944). . . .

7. 267 Fed. 174 (4th Cir. 1920).
8. 81 F.2d 741 (3d Cir. 1936).
9. 267 Fed. 175.
10. 81 F.2d 742.
11. 9 Wigmore, *Evidence* § 2511 (2) (3d ed. 1940); Thayer, *Evidence*, pp. 566–76 (1898).
12. Thayer, *Evidence*, p. 562 (1898); Allen, *Legal Duties*, p. 255 (1931). But see the penetrating comments of Professor Hall in Objectives of Federal Criminal Procedural Revision, *Yale Law Journal*, Vol. 51, pp. 723, 728–32 (1942).
13. *National Commission on Law Observance and Enforcement Report on Prosecution* 34–37, 124 (1931).
14. 350 U.S. 359 (1956).
15. *Id.* 365.
16. *Id.* 363. . . .
17. United States v. Garsson, 291 Fed. 646, 649 (S.D.N.Y. 1923).
18. In a system of "trial by interval," the discovery machinery proceeds apace with the actual trial. The need for comprehensive pretrial preparation is minimized because all participants are prepared to halt the proceedings when it seems useful to do so and to reconvene at a later date, meanwhile permitting the accumulation of additional evidence made necessary by the course of the earlier proceedings. See Kaplan, von Mehren & Schaefer, Phases of German Civil Procedure, *Harvard Law Review*, Vol. 71, pp. 1193, 1211–49 (1958); . . .

In our system, for him who comes unprepared, practical and legal obstacles stand in the way of reopening the proceedings at a later date. The doctrines which have developed in connection with motions for new trial, particularly on grounds of newly discovered evidence, have not been generously applied. See, *e.g.*, Annot., *Fed. R. Crim. P.* 33, 18 U.S.C.A. (1951); *cf.* 6 Moore, *Federal Practice* § 59.08 (1953). So far as continuances during trial are concerned, lawyers of experience will attest to their reluctance to keep a jury waiting while leads to evidence are followed up.
19. United States v. Garsson, 291 Fed. 646, 649 (S.D.N.Y. 1923).
20. Ibid.
21. *Ex parte* Bain, 121 U.S. 1 (1887).
22. 295 U.S. 78, 82–83 (1935).
23. 207 F.2d 134 (D.C.Cir.), *cert. denied* 346 U.S. 885 (1953).
24. See 353 U.S. 657 (1957); 18 U.S.C. § 3500 (1958).
25. [Ed. note: But compare Ross v. Sirica, 380 F. 2d 557 (D.C.Cir. 1967) with Sciortino v. Zampano, 385 F. 2d 132 (2 Cir. 1967).]
26. U.S. v. Garsson, 291 Fed. 646, 648 (S.D.N.Y. 1923).
27. [Ed. note: Since this article was written, the Supreme Court decided *Miranda* v. *Arizona*, 384 U.S. 436 (1966), which provides in detail for advice as to rights, counsel, etc. in order to assure that admissions obtained from a suspect during "custodial interrogation" are "voluntary." *Miranda* is a construction of the due process clause of the Four-

teenth Amendment and is, therefore, binding on the states. It should be noted, however, that *Miranda* does not prohibit police interrogation; it seeks to define the conditions under which its product may be used. If a suspect should waive its protections, as he frequently does, then most of what is said, in the two paragraphs of text which follow, remains applicable. See Comment, *Interrogations in New Haven: The Impact of Miranda, Yale Law Journal*, Vol. 76, p. 1519 (1967); and see *Massiah* v. *United States*, 377 U.S. 201 (1964) which restricts questioning following the return of an indictment.]

28. [Ed. note: For a recent case which holds there is a right to counsel in such a line-up situation in order to assure that it is fairly conducted, see *Wade* v. *United States*, 388 U.S. 218 (1967).]

NOTES TO *Packer: Two Models of the Criminal Process*

1. *Mapp v. Ohio,* 367 U.S., p. 643 (1961); *Ker v. California,* 374 U.S. 23 (1963).
2. See President's Commission on Law Enforcement and Administration of Justice, *The Challenge of Crime in a Free Society,* Ch. 2 (Washington, D.C., 1967).
3. *Griffin v. Illinois,* 351 U.S. 12, 19 (1956).
4. *Finality in Criminal Law and Federal Habeas Corpus for State Prisoners, Harvard Law Review,* Vol. 76, pp. 441, 442 (1963).

NOTES TO *Hall: The Basic Dilemma of Criminal Procedure*

1. *A General View of the Criminal Law of England,* p. 175 (1863).
2. Allen, *Legal Duties,* p. 269 (1931).
3. 52 Stat. 438 (1938), 18 U.S.C. §729 (1940).
4. See Goldman, *Economies Effected by Public Defender Plan,* 23 J. Am. Jud. Soc., 63 (1939), and recent reports from the office of the Public Defender of Cook County.
5. Compare Beccaria, *Essay on Crimes and Punishments* pp. 53, 55 (3d ed. 1770).

NOTES TO *Goffman: Characteristics of Total Institutions*

1. Richard McCleery, "The Strange Journey," *University of North Carolina Extension Bulletin,* Vol. xxxii (1953), p. 24.
2. Lloyd F. McCorkle and Richard Korn, "Resocialization Within Walls," *The Annals,* May, 1954, pp. 88, 95.

NOTES TO *Allen: Criminal Justice, Legal Values and the Rehabilitative Ideal*

1. Quoted in Dalzell, *Benefit of Clergy and Related Matters* (1955) 13.
2. Bentham, *The Theory of Legislation,* pp. 338–339 (Ogden, C. K., ed., 1931). (Italics in the original.) But Bentham added: "But when [the writers] come to speak about the means of preventing offenses, of rendering men better, of perfecting morals, their imagination grows

warm, their hopes excited; one would suppose they were about to produce the great secret, and that the human race was going to receive a new form. It is because we have a more magnificent idea of objects in proportion as they are less familiar, and because the imagination has a loftier flight amid vague projects which have never been subjected to the limits of analysis." Id. at 359.
3. "*Law and the Social Sciences—Especially Sociology*," *Harvard Law Review*, Vol. 62, pp. 1286, 1287 (1949).
4. Barnes and Teeters, *New Horizons in Criminology*, p. 337 (2nd ed. 1954).
5. Garofalo, *Criminology*, p. 256 (Millar Translation 1914).

NOTES TO *Dershowitz: On Preventive Detention*

1. *Maung Hla Gyaw v. Commissioner*, 1948 Burma Law Reps., pp. 764, 766.
2. See *Hirabayashi v. United States*, 320 U.S. 81 (1942).
3. S.O.U.S.C. § 647.
4. *Commonwealth v. Franklin*, 172 Pa. Super. 152, 92 A. 2d 272 (1952).
5. *In re Gault*, 387 U.S., 1, 76 (1966).
6. *Commissioner's Committee on Arrests for Investigation* (D.C. 1962).
7. Penal Code of California, § 647.
8. 383 U.S. 107 (1966).
9. See Rappeport, *The Clinical Evaluation of the Dangerousness of the Mentally Ill* (Thomas, 1967).
10. Perhaps the proposed criteria for confinement could first be tested on records of past cases before they are applied—even experimentally—to live defendants. This could be done by giving to judges the past records of defendants, some of whom did and some of whom did not commit crimes while out on bail; they would then be asked to "predict"—or more accurately, postdict—which defendants fall into which category.

NOTES TO *Andenaes: The General Preventive Effects of Punishment*

1. Feuerbach, *Lehrbuch des Gemeinen in Deutschland Peinlichen Rechts*, p. 117 (1812).
2. Zilboorg, *The Psychology of the Criminal Act and Punishment*, p. 78 (1954).
3. Ball, "The Deterrence Concept in Criminology and Law," *J. Crim. L., C. & P.S.*, Vol. 46, pp. 347, 352 (1955).
4. Wilkins, "*Criminology: An Operational Research Approach*," in *Society —Problems and Methods of Study*, 322 (Welford, ed. 1962).
5. Mannheim, *Social Aspects of Crime in England Between the Wars*, pp. 156–57 (1940).
6. 2 Stephen, *The History of the Criminal Law of England*, p. 81 (1883).
7. Beutel, *Experimental Jurisprudence*, p. 366 (1957).
8. A strong increase in policing activities may, at least temporarily, lead to an increase in the number of convictions and perhaps in the number of reports to the police as well.
9. Tarde, *Penal Philosophy* § 87 (1912).
10. Kinberg, *Basic Problems of Criminology*, pp. 127–38 (1935).
11. Radzinowicz, *History of English Criminal Law* (1957).

12. Moore and Callahan, *Law and Learning Theory: A Study in Legal Control* (1943).

13. Hart, *Prolegomenon to the Principles of Punishment*, pp. 21–22 (1960).

NOTES TO *Goldstein, J.: On the Function of Criminal Law in Riot Control*

1. See, generally, *Report of National Advisory Commission on Civil Disorders*, Washington, D.C.: U.S. Government Printing Office, 1968; and the work of, for example, Erikson, E. H., "Growth and Crisis of the Healthy Personality," in: *Identity and the Life Cycle* (*Psychological Issues*, Monogr. 1), New York: International University Press, 1959, pp. 50–100; Mitscherlich, A., *Society Without the Father*, New York: Harcourt, Brace & World, 1963; and, Wangh, M., "National Socialism and the Genocide of the Jews," *Int. J. Psa.* 45:386–395; which are directly relevent to the design of long-range programs for reaching some of the underlying causes of mob violence through, for example, legislation concerned with education, housing, employment, welfare, and technology.

   On the law's potential for creating group safety valves through official holidays designed to release pent-up repressed feelings, to take another example outside the ambit of this essay, see Freud, S., "Group Pychology and the Analysis of the Ego," *Standard Edition*, 18:105, London: Hogarth Press, 1955:

   > "In all renunciations and limitations imposed upon the ego a periodical infringement of the prohibition is the rule; this indeed is shown by the institution of festivals, which in origin are nothing less nor more than excesses provided by law and which owe their cheerful character to the release which they bring. The Saturnalia of the Romans and our modern carnival agree in this essential feature with the festivals of primitive people, which usually end in debaucheries of every kind and the transgression of what are at other times the most sacred commandments. But the ego ideal comprises the sum of all the limitations in which the ego has to acquiesce, and for that reason the abrogation of the ideal would necessarily be a magnificent festival for the ego, which might then once again feel satisfied with itself."

   Similarly, Spiegel, J. P., The Nature of the Riot Process, *Psychiat. Opin.*, 5 (3): 6–9, in his four-phase analysis of the riot process calls Phase 3 "The Roman Holiday."

2. Brandenburg v. Ohio, 395 U.S. 444, 447 (1969). For attempts to enunciate the limits which the requirement of public order sets for the exercise of free speech generally, see Terminiello v. City of Chicago, 337 U.S. 1 (1949); Feiner v. New York, 340 U.S. 315 (1951); Kunz v. New York, 340 U.S. 290 (1951); Nietmotko v. Maryland, 340 U.S. 268 (1951).

3. Laski, H., *Reflections on the Revolution of Our Time*, pp. 15 ff., London: George Allen & Unwin.

4. See, generally, Report of the National Advisory Committee on Civil Disorders, *supra*. Sauter, V. G., and Hines, B., *Nightmare in Detroit*, Chicago: Henry Regnery, 1968, highlight one of those frustrations:

   > " 'The cat on Twelfth Street can look a hundred yards away and see another black cat living in an eight-room house with a 1967

Pontiac and a motorboat on Lake Michigan,' a Negro school-teacher told a visitor to Detroit during the summer of 1967. 'For that matter, General Motors itself is only a few blocks away. I've seen kids from my school walk over to the showroom and sit down in a new model Cadillac, sort of snuggle their little rear ends into the soft leather, slide their hands over the slick plastic steering wheel, and say "Man, feel that." It's all so close, and yet it's all so far away, and the frustration just eats them up'" (p. 122). See also Dynes, R. & Quarantelli, E., What Looting in Civil Disturbances Really Means, *Trans-Action*, 1968, 5:9.

Freud, Group Psychology and the Analysis of the Ego, supra, noted: [T]here grows up in . . . children a . . . group feeling. . . . The first demand made by this reaction-formation is for justice, for equal treatment for all. . . . If one cannot be the favourite oneself, at all events nobody else shall be the favourite [p. 120].

5. "In the interpretation of [13 Hen. IV. c. 7] it has been held, that all persons, noblemen and others, except women, clergymen, persons decrepit, and infants under fifteen, are bound to attend the justices in suppressing a riot, upon pain of fine and imprisonment; and *that any battery, wounding, or killing the rioters, that may happen in suppressing the riot is justifiable* [p. 1 Hal. P.C. 495; 1 Hark. P.C. 161]. So that our ancient law, previous to the modern Riot Act, seems pretty well to have guarded against any violent breach of the public peace" Blackstone, W., *Of Public Wrongs*, p. 155, Boston: Beacon Press, 1962.

And see *Michigan Revised Criminal Code* § 5510, comment at p. 426 (Final Draft, 1967). Michigan law also assigns to riot participants the liability for the death of one killed in trying to repress the riot. Mich. C.L. § 750.527 (1948).

6. 18 USC 245 (c) (1968).

7. Goldstein, J., Psychoanalysis & Jurisprudence, *The Psychoanalytic Study of the Child*, 23:473 f. 1968.

8. Walker, D., *Rights in Conflict*, Washington, D.C., 1968.

9. Freud, S., Group Psychology and the Analysis of the Ego, *supra*, p. 95 f.

10. Walker, *Rights in Conflict*, *supra*.

11. Freud, S., Group Psychology and the Analysis of the Ego, *supra*, p. 79.

12. Freud, S., Group Psychology and the Analysis of the Ego, *supra*, p. 113.

13. *New York Times*, September 22, 1968, §4, at 7, col. 3.

14. "[I]t is a fact that many of the recent riots in our urban centers had as one of their principal sparks a hostile reaction in the community to the use of a gun by a policeman. I am not passing judgment on the fairness or the unfairness of those reactions, nor am I suggesting that where force is clearly necessary a policeman must hold back for fear of causing such a reaction. But I do say that those incidents are one more reason why the community must know that the police policies and practices concerning firearms are fair and reasonable" Leary, H. R., *Law, Social Order and the Use of Deadly Force* (Press Release, March 21, 1967). New York: Police Department, Bureau of Public Information.

15. Freud, S., Group Psychology and the Analysis of the Ego, *supra*, p. 74.

16. Walker, D., *Rights in Conflict, supra*.

17. Allen, F., Civil Disobedience and the Legal Order, 36 *U. Cin. Law Rev.*, 1 (1967).
18. *New York Times*, September 22, 1968, §4 at 7, col. 3.
19. Freud, S., Group Psychology and the Analysis of the Ego, *supra*, p. 85.
20. Earl Ferrer's Case, 19 How. St. Tr. 886 (1760), and see generally Durham v. United States, 214 F. 2d 862, 869 (D.C. Cir. 1954).
21. 18 U.S.C. 245 §c (1968).
22. Rapaport, D., The Theory of Ego Autonomy, 22 *Bull. Meninger Clinic*, 13–20 (1958).

NOTES TO *Kadish: Some Observations on the Use of Criminal Sanctions in Enforcing Economic Regulations*

1. *Boyce Motor Lines v. United States*, 342 U.S. 337 (1952).
2. *United States v. Ragen*, 314 U.S. 513 (1942).
3. See *Screws v. United States*, 325 U.S. 91, 103–04 (1945).
4. *United States v. Ragen*, 314 U.S. 513, 524 (1942).
5. Cf. *Boyce Motor Lines v. United States*, 342 U.S. 337, 345 (1952) (Jackson, J., dissenting).
6. Watkins, *Federal Incorporation, Michigan Law Review*, Vol. 17, pp. 64, 145, 238 (1918–19); Watkins, *Electrical Equipment Antitrust Laws, University of Chicago Law Review*, Vol. 29, pp. 97, 108–9 (1961).
7. MODEL PENAL CODE § 2.07, comment at 148–149 (Tent. Draft No. 4, 1955).
8. Note, Yale Law Journal, Vol. 71, pp. 280, 297 (1961).
9. Freund, *Legislative Regulation* 253 (1932).
10. Mannheim, *Criminal Justice and Social Reconstruction*, p. 146 (1946).
11. Id., p. 166.
12. Assistant Attorney General Berge, quoted in *Att'y Gen. Nat'l Comm. Antitrust Rep.*, 353 (1955).
13. Freund, *op. cit. supra* note 9, at 302.
14. Holmes believed that the objective standard of criminal liability which disregards the personal peculiarities of the actor demonstrates that the existence of moral wrong is not a condition of punishment. HOLMES, THE COMMON LAW 45 (1923). He found support for this in the proposition that, "no society has ever admitted that it could not sacrifice individual welfare to its own existence." *Id.* at 43. Cf. Wasserstrom, *Strict Liability in the Criminal Law, Stanford Law Review*, Vol. 12, pp. 731, 739 (1960).
15. Hart, *The Aims of the Criminal Law*, 23 Law and Contemp. Prob., pp. 401, 404 (1958).
16. See the debate between Lord Devlin and Professor H. L. A. Hart in DEVLIN, *The Enforcement of Morals* (1959) and Hart, *Law, Liberty and Morality* (1963).
17. *Supra* note 15, p. 418 n.42.
18. Tappan, *Crime, Justice and Correction*, pp. 15–16 (1960). For a suggestive discussion of alternative ways of achieving favorable business sentiment, see Lane, *The Regulation of Businessmen*, pp. 118–30 (1954).
19. Allen, *Offenses Against Property*, 339 Annals 57, 76 (1962).
20. *Model Penal Code* § 1.04, § 6.03(4), (5) (Proposed Official Draft, 1962).
21. *Model Penal Code* § 6.02(4), (5) (Proposed Official Draft, 1962).

22. *Model Penal Code* § 1.04(5) (Proposed Official Draft, 1962).
23. *Model Penal Code* § 1.04, comment at 8 (Proposed Official Draft, 1962).
24. *Model Penal Code* § 2.05 (Proposed Official Draft, 1962).

NOTES TO *Goldstein, A. S.: M'Naghten: The Stereotype Challenged*

1. The jurisdictions following some form of the so-called "irresistible impulse" (or "control") rule, in addition to *M'Naghten*, . . . include 17 states and the federal system. This last tabulation includes jurisdictions which have adopted the ALI rule, or a variant thereof. Jurisdictions following some other rule . . . include New Hampshire, the District of Columbia, Maine, and the Virgin Islands. The remaining states use some form of the *M'Naghten* rule.
2. M'Naghten's case, *Clark & Fin.*, Vol. 10, p. 200 (1843).
3. *State v. Andrews*, 357 P.2d 739, 744 (Kans. 1961), cert. den. 368 U.S. 868.
4. Zilboorg, *Mind, Medicine and Man*, p. 273 (1943).
5. Report of Royal Comm. on Law of Insanity as a Defense in Criminal Cases (Canada), pp. 12–13 (1955).
6. Judge Holtzoff, quoted in *Durham v. United States*, 214 F.2d 862, 868 (D.C. Cir. 1954).
7. R. v. Codere, 12 C.A.R. 21, 26–27 (Cr. Ct. App. 1916).
8. *State v. Essex*, 115 N.W.2d, 505, 521 (Wis. 1962).
9. M'Naghten's case, *Clark & Fin.*, Vol. 10, pp. 200, 210–11 (1843).
10. Wigmore, *Evidence*, § 228 (1940).
11. *Howard v. State*, 172 Ala., 402, 409 (1911).
12. The quotations are at 93 N.W. 2d 354, 360–61 (Wis. 1958). The more recent case is *State v. Shaffer*, 143 N.W. 2d 458, 463 (Wis. 1966).
13. 140 A. 2d 385, 393–4 (N.J. 1958).
14. 354 P. 2d 960, 973 (Hawaii, 1960).
15. ALI, *Model Penal Code*, Tent. Dr. 4, App. A to Commentary, § 401, p. 162 (1955).
16. *State v. Odell*, 277 P. 2d 710, 719 (Wash. 1951).
17. *People v. Roche*, Trial Tr. 382–83, 399, 422, 476, aff'd w/o opin., 128 N.E. 2d 323 (N.Y. 1955).
18. [Ed. note: The quotations are taken from *McKenzie v United States* Trial Tr. 200, rev'd 266 F.2d 524, 535 (10 Cir. 1959); *Comm. v. Chester*, 150 N.E. 2d 914, 917, Mass. 1958); *State v. Lucas*, Trial Tr. 532–33, *aff'd* 152 A.2d 50 (N.J. 1959).
19. 123 N.E. 2d 609, 615 (N.Y. 1954).
20. The quotations are from: Howard v. United States, Trial Tr. 98, aff'd 229 F.2d 602 (5 Cir. 1962); *State v. Goza*, 317 S.W. 2d 609, 612 (Mo. 1958); *People v. Roche*, Trial Tr. 497, 506, 508, aff'd w/o opin. 128 N.E. 2d 323 (N.Y. 1955); *State v. Lucas*, Trial Tr. 1349, aff'd 152 A.2d 50 (N.J. 1959); *Johnson v. State*, 76 So.2d 841, 843 (Miss. 1955); *Thomas v. State*, Trial Tr. 307, aff'd 112 A.2d 913 (Md. 1955); *Mitchell v. State*, Trial Tr. 119–20, 159–61, aff'd 104 So.2d 84 (Fla. 1958).
21. *Thomas v. State*, Trial Tr. 307, aff'd 112 A.2d 913 (Md. 1955).
22. Trial Tr. 1349, aff'd 152 A.2d 50, 64 (N.J. 1959).
23. 115 S.E.2d 547, 549–50 (Ga. 1960); see also *Early v. State*, 352 P.2d 112, 114 (Colo. 1960).
24. Group for the Advancement of Psychiatry, *Criminal Responsibility and Psychiatric Expert Testimony*, p. 5 (1954).

NOTES TO *Goldstein, J., and Katz: Abolish the "Insanity Defense"—Why Not?*

1. Wis. Legislative Council Judiciary Committee, *Report on the Criminal Code* 44 (1953).
2. [T]o establish a defense on the ground of insanity, it must be clearly proved that, at the time of the committing of the act, the party accused was labouring under such a defect of reason, from disease of the mind, as not to know the nature and quality of the act he was doing; or if he did know it, that he did not know he was doing what was wrong. *Daniel M'Naghten's Case*, 4 St. Tr. N.S. 847, 931, 8 Eng. Rep. 718, 722 (H.L. 1843).
3. *Durham v. United States*, 214 F.2d 862, 876 (D.C. Cir. 1954):
   [A]n accused is not criminally responsible if his unlawful act was the product of mental disease or mental defect.

   We use "disease" in the sense of a condition which is considered capable of either improving or deteriorating. We use "defect" in the sense of a condition which is not considered capable of either improving or deteriorating and which may be either congenital, or the result of injury or the residual effect of a physical or mental disease. *Id.*, 874–75.
4. MODEL PENAL CODE § 4.01 (Proposed Official Draft 1962) provides:
   (1) A person is not responsible for criminal conduct if at the time of such conduct as a result of mental disease or defect he lacks substantial capacity either to appreciate the criminality [wrongfulness] of his conduct or to conform his conduct to the requirements of law.

   (2) As used in this Article, the terms "mental disease or defect" do not include an abnormality manifested only by repeated criminal or otherwise anti-social conduct. In conflict with the exclusion in (2), the chief reporter of the Model Penal Code has said:
   [T]he category of the irresponsible must be defined in extreme terms. The problem is to differentiate between the wholly *non-deterrable* and persons who are more or less susceptible to influence by law. (Emphasis supplied.)
   Wechsler, "The Criteria of Criminal Responsibility," *University of Chicago Law Review*, Vol. 22, pp. 367, 374 (1955). How to select from the non-deterrables who have committed a crime those non-deterrables who are to be relieved of criminal responsibility is not clarified by the Model Penal Code's exclusion from the term "mental disease or defect . . . an abnormality manifested only by repeated criminal or otherwise anti-social conduct.". . .
5. "Report of the Governors Committee on the Defense of Insanity," *New York Law Journal*, Vol. 140, No. 88, p. 4 (Nov. 5, 1958), No. 89, p. 4 (Nov. 6, 1958) (emphasis supplied).
   The Committee proposed:
   (1) A person may not be convicted of a crime for which he is not responsible.

   (2) A person is not responsible for criminal conduct if at the time of such conduct as a result of mental disease or defect he lacks substantial capacity:
   (a) to know or appreciate the wrongfulness of his conduct; or

(b) to conform his conduct to the requirements of the law.
. . .
(3) The terms "mental disease or defect" do not include an abnormality manifested only by repeated criminal or otherwise antisocial conduct.

6. *United States v. Currens*, 290 F.2d, pp. 751, 773, 774 (3d Cir. 1961).
7. 290 F.2d at 774. For its test the court proposed:
The jury must be satisfied that at the time of committing the prohibited act the defendant, as a result of mental disease or defect, lacked substantial capacity to conform his conduct to the requirements of the law which he is alleged to have violated.
Ibid.
8. As early as 1724, Justice Tracy, instructing the jury on "guilty mind" as a requisite element of murder in the Trial of Edward Arnold, said:
[T]he shooting . . . for which prisoner is indicted, is proved beyond all manner of contradiction; but whether this shooting was malicious, that depends upon the sanity of the man. That he shot, and that wilfully [is proved]; but whether maliciously, that is the thing; that is the question; whether this man hath the use of his reason and sense? . . . [G]uilt arises from the mind, and the wicked will and intention of the man. If a man be deprived of his reason, and consequently of his intention, he cannot be guilty; and if that be the case, though he had actually killed . . . he is exempted from punishment: punishment is intended for example, and to deter other persons from wicked designs; but the punishment of a madman, a person that hath no design, can have no example.
16 State Trials 596, 764 (1724). The paragraph goes on to construe narrowly the kind of evidence which might negative "guilty mind."
On the other side, we must be very cautious; it is not every frantic and idle humour of a man, that will exempt him from justice, and the punishment of the law. When a man is guilty of a great offense, it must be very plain and clear, before a man is allowed such an exemption; therefore it is not every kind of frantic humour or something unaccountable in a man's actions, that points him out to be such a madman as is to be exempted from punishment: it must be a man that is totally deprived of his understanding and memory, and doth not know what he is doing, no more than an infant, than a brute, or a wild beast, such a one is never the object of punishment;
. . .
Id., 764–65.
9. The court comes close to acknowledging this in *United States v. Currens*, 290 F.2d 751, 767 (1961). "The throwing of the mentally ill individual from the jail back into the community, untreated and uncured, presents a great and immediate danger."
10. *Report of the Governor's Committee on the Defense of Insanity, New York Law Journal*, Vol. 140, p. 4 (Nov. 5, 6, 1958).

> In extreme cases, such as that of the homicidal offender, the security required must exceed that required for even the most dangerous convict. . . . [W]e recommend that the dangerous offender who has been acquitted by reason of mental disorder should be placed in the custody of the Department of Corrections at one of its medical facilities.

State of California Special Commission on Insanity and Criminal Offenders, First Report, p. 34 (July 7, 1962).

Index

A

ABORTION, 301–303
ADAMS, JOHN
  On lawlessness, 83
ADMINISTRATION OF
    CRIMINAL JUSTICE
  Administrative discretion, scope
    of, 117–118
  Behavioral sciences' contribu-
    tions to, 271ff
  Difficulties, 113ff
    scope of discretion, 117–118
    unreliability of evidence, 117
  Limits of, 11–12
  Political implications, 278–279
  Public vengeance as earliest
    form, 113
  Reform of offender as ideal, 273
  Variations among individuals
    and groups, 113
ADMINISTRATION OF
    JUSTICE
  By judicial discretion, 105ff
  Chief factors in Pound's view,
    101
  Compromise between rule and
    discretion, 106
  Difficulties, 104ff
    human element in administra-
      tion, 111
    impatience of restraint as
      cause, 110
    inapplicability of rules to-
      ward human conduct, 111
    intangibleness of moral du-
      ties, 111

of obtaining facts, 111
    subtlety of ways of inflicting
      wrong, 111
  Discretionary justice, agencies
    of, 105ff
  Dissatisfactions with, 104ff
    due to public ignorance of
      difficulties, 108–110
    impossibility of dealing with
      all matters, 111ff
  Limitations, 111
  Organizations concerned with,
    103
  Public unawareness of difficul-
    ties, 108–110
  Strict adherence to rules,
    105
ADMINISTRATIVE AGEN-
    CIES, 367ff
ADMINISTRATIVE DISCRE-
    TION, 117–119
ADMINISTRATIVE
    PROCESS, 1–2
ADULTERY
  Limitations on invocation of
    statutes, 150
  Massachusetts crimes, 75, 78
ALLEN, FRANCIS A.
  On "corrections," 11
  On criminal sanctions, 384
  On rehabilitation, 271–282
AMERICAN LAW
    INSTITUTE
  Model Penal Code, 2, 283
    on abortion, 302
    on insanity defense, 396, 413
    on vagrancy, 301
    "violations" under, 385

Printed in the United States
By Bookmasters